# Open Source .NET Development

# Open Source .NET Development

*Brian Nantz*

✦Addison-Wesley

**Boston • San Francisco • New York • Toronto • Montreal
London • Munich • Paris • Madrid
Capetown • Sydney • Tokyo • Singapore • Mexico City**

Publisher: *John Wait*
Executive editor: *Stephane Nakib*
Editorial assistant: *Ebony Haight*
Marketing manager: *Curt Johnson*
Marketing specialist: *Heather Mullane*
Publicity: *Joan Murray*
Managing editor: *Gina Kanouse*
Senior project editor: *Sarah Kearns*
Production editor: *Kerry Reardon*
Manufacturing buyer: *Dan Uhrig*
Cover design: *Chuti Prasertsith*

Many of the designations used by manufacturers and sellers to distinguish their products are claimed as trademarks. Where those designations appear in this book, and Addison-Wesley was aware of a trademark claim, the designations have been printed with initial capital letters or in all capitals.

The authors and publisher have taken care in the preparation of this book, but make no expressed or implied warranty of any kind and assume no responsibility for errors or omissions. No liability is assumed for incidental or consequential damages in connection with or arising out of the use of the information or programs contained herein.

The publisher offers discounts on this book when ordered in quantity for bulk purchases and special sales. For more information, please contact:

U.S. Corporate and Government Sales
(800) 382-3419
corpsales@pearsontechgroup.com

For sales outside of the U.S., please contact:

International Sales
(317) 581-3793
international@pearsontechgroup.com

Visit Addison-Wesley on the Web: www.awprofessional.com

*Library of Congress Cataloging-in-Publication Data*

A CIP catalog record for this book can be obtained from the Library of Congress

ISBN 0-321-122810-3
LOC 2004106569
Text printed on recycled paper
1 2 3 4 5 6 7 8 9 10—MA—0605040302
First printing, August 2004

*For Candice, I love you.*

# Contents

## PART II    .NET DEVELOPMENT WITH OPEN SOURCE TOOLS

**Chapter 5      XML Documentation** . . . . . . . . . . . . . . . . . . . . . . . . . .**125**

**Chapter 6      Unit Testing** . . . . . . . . . . . . . . . . . . . . . . . . . . . . . . . .**151**

## P A R T   I I I   INTEGRATING .NET OPEN SOURCE PROJECTS IN YOUR DEVELOPMENT

## P A R T   I V   REFERENCES

# Preface

## Why I Felt the Need to Write This Book

Open Source is such a hotly debated topic today; at the same time, .NET is seeing unbelievably rapid acceptance as the programming platform of choice. As Microsoft creates its first Open Source project and many prominent Open Source teams rush to implement standards created by Microsoft, I felt a great necessity for this book. Running code created by Microsoft development tools on a Linux machine or including an Open Source component in your proprietary product are indeed worth noting. Admittedly, this book focuses on a uniquely overlapping portion of the software industry that somewhat blurs the line between Open Source and Microsoft. Ignoring a small minority of advocates within these two camps (having worked with Microsoft employees as well as Mono guys—some of who reviewed this book), I really believe there is not as much adversity as the press would indicate. Both sides have learned from each other, just like true rivals scoping out the competition at a big tradeshow or those closed-door sessions where a competitor's product is examined under a microscope and torn apart. Many Open Source projects are created using Microsoft Visual Studio .NET, and some of the Open Source projects featured in this book are meant to be plug-ins to VS.NET! Do not confuse the features of the various development tools or components with the features of the .NET platform itself. The true power of .NET is found in the standards.

## Who Should Read This Book?

Coders—those who are banging out the code, day in and day out. There are some portions of this book, mainly Chapters 1 and 2, that can be useful for managers who are wondering how Open Source licensing could affect their proprietary product. But for the most part, this book assumes a fair amount of C# and .NET knowledge. It is not a book on how to learn the .NET platform or necessarily how to set up the different .NET environments. Rather, this book shows how to use the many different projects and products together. To me, it all comes down to getting the job done and using the right tool for the job. Sometimes that tool, component, or framework might be Open Source; sometimes it is not. This book will help you understand how to evaluate the tool that best fits your needs.

Have you ever felt like you just kept doing similar coding tasks over and over again on different projects? This is initially a fun, "I know exactly how to do this!" sort of a thing. But then it turns into something unexciting and mundane, like the difference between the excitement of the very first business trip you ever took and the last one you endured for the sake of your company. At first creating something as basic as a logging mechanism sounds fun and easy, but when you are done and show it to the people who will use it, you quickly find out the inadequacies: "It's too hard to use," "This doesn't support enough," or "It isn't extendable!" Many of the projects in this book address just this problem. These frameworks and components have seen a lot of runtime and have nice APIs from the many developers who use them. However, keep in mind that the greatest feature of Open Source is that the Source is Open! Not that it saves you time in not having to implement some feature, or that it is cheaper, faster, or more secure than its closed source counterparts, but that you can gain a relatively large amount of experience in a small amount of time by looking at many different code bases and designs.

## How This Book Is Organized

This book is meant to expose the best Open Source and "Free" tools, frameworks, components, and products for .NET. Therefore, you can read it in pretty much any order. Undoubtedly, by the time this book reaches the shelves, many of these products will have improved, and of course many more good projects will materialize. My intention is to introduce you to the world of .NET Open Source, which is much vaster than most developers realize. For more in-depth information, see the user groups associated with these projects. Also, I strive to keep my Web site (http://www.Nantz.org) as up-to-date with these changes as possible, so you may want to check there as well.

The first two chapters are background information about Open Source and its implementations of the .NET standards. If you feel you have a good handle on these topics, I would suggest starting with Part II. Look at the different tools; see which ones would be most useful and immediately help-ful in your situation. Part III is essential if you are planning on deploying a .NET application on Linux or using an Open Source database engine and wonder how much .NET support these platforms have.

The examples in this book are meant to display the most useful aspects of .NET Open Source coding. They, along with many of the projects, are made available in the companion CD-ROM. I would love to hear back from you—ideas on the examples, improvements, comments, etc. (See my email address below.)

# Acknowledgments

I would like to thank Addison-Wesley for giving me the opportunity to write this book. What a great team to work with. Special thanks to Stephane Nakib, Ebony Haight, Michael Mullen, and Curt Johnson, who have gra-ciously guided me along the whole process.

I would also like to thank my family for putting up with many late nights and a constant state of distraction. Thanks to Candi, Charlotte, John, and Thomas for always supporting me. Thanks to Mom and Dad for invest-ing in my education from whence all things begin. Thank you all for letting me follow my dreams.

A thank you does not seem adequate enough acknowledgment for all my reviewers and those who helped with this book. Francisco Figueiredo Jr., Nicko Cadell, Ian MacLean, Nick Varacalli, Arild Fines, Rhys Weather-ley, Bernard Vander Beken, Tom Jordan, Chad Wach, Dan Maharry, Christophe Nasarre, and Ben Maurer. These reviewers are responsible for making this book readable and concise. Thank you all for your suggestions and insight.

Finally, I would like to thank all the Open Source developers out there, without whom this book would never have been written. Thanks for your constant devotion and dedication to your projects. Thanks for letting us all learn from you and your ideas.

*Brian Nantz*
*brian@nantz.org*
*Menomonee Falls, WI*

# Part I

# Introduction to Open Source and .NET

# CHAPTER 1

# What Is Open Source?

*There ain't no such thing as a free lunch.*
*A Libertarian Movement slogan*

—*Robert A. Heinlein,* The Moon is a Harsh Mistress, *1907*

## Introduction

Before we jump in and start looking at all the Open Source tools and components that are useful to any .NET developer (Chapters 3-8 if you want to skip ahead), and before we write ASP.NET and ADO.NET code that works on both Windows and Linux (Chapters 10 and 11), it is important that you understand exactly what Open Source is. "Is it really OK to use this code in your product?" "Does using the tools violate your company's procedures?" What are you going to say to a manager or other team member who asks these kinds of questions? Well, first you must have a clear understanding of Open Source. The term Open Source has drawn a lot of attention lately. Open Source has been all over the press as both success stories and failures. I have found that this term stirs great emotion in a person and makes for a great conversation piece at a meeting. I have seen development teams divided and management up in arms over Open Source software. However, in my experience very few Microsoft developers fully understand what Open Source is and base arguments and important design decisions on hearsay and half-truths about Open Source. This chapter could have been titled "How To Use Open Source with Microsoft Products." I assume that since you are reading this book, you have some interest in Open Source, and this chapter will help you get started. Since this book is about Microsoft .NET and about Open Source, this chapter helps you understand how to use them together. .NET is unique for Microsoft. Previously, Microsoft development tools were proprietary, but the .NET Software

Development Kit (SDK) is free! Because of the availability, academic institutions and other Open Source proponents have started adapting to .NET. The same availability contributed to the extreme popularity of the Java Development Platform by Sun Microsystems. I believe .NET will become even more popular over the next few years due to its Common Language Infrastructure (CLI) and its standardization. Because of the C# and the .NET CLI ECMA standard, several .NET and C# implementations have been created, and many operating systems are now beginning to support .NET (more on this in Chapter 2). The Common Language Infrastructure allows for many programming platforms to work with the .NET framework, resulting in multiple programming language implementations. Table 1.1

**Table 1.1** .NET Programming Langauges

| Programming Language | Web Site |
| --- | --- |
| F# | http://research.microsoft.com/projects/ilx/ |
| Ada.NET | http://www.usafa.af.mil/dfcs/bios/mcc_html/a_sharp.html |
| Ruby.NET | http://www.geocities.co.jp/SiliconValley-PaloAlto/9251/ruby/nrb.html |
| Forth.NET | http://www.dataman.ro/dforth/ |
| Pascal.NET | http://www.citi.qut.edu.au/research/plas/projects/cp_files/cpnet.jsp |
| Perl.NET | http://www.activestate.com/Corporate/Initiatives/NET/Research.html?_x=1 |
| Python.NET | http://www.activestate.com/Corporate/Initiatives/NET/Research.html?_x=1 |
| Haskell.NET | http://www.mondrian-script.org/ |
| Eiffel.NET | http://www.eiffel.com/products/envsn10/ |
| Fortran.NET | http://www.lahey.com/netwtpr1.htm |
| Cobol.NET | http://www.fsw.fujitsu.com/ |
| J#, C#, C++.NET, VB.NET, Jscript.NET | NET Framework |

shows just a few language implementations, some experimental and some commercially supported.

As you can see, .NET is really catching on, both in framework implementations as well as language implementations. Keep in mind that any tool discussed in this book will work with any CLS-compliant language. Most of the examples will be in the C# language only because it is a standard.

## Microsoft and Open Source

Much of the press hype about Open Source is in relation to Microsoft. Many of Microsoft's competitors have failed and practically closed up shop due to Bill Gates and Microsoft's business prowess. I am sure that some people could come up with other terms to end the last sentence and describe Microsoft's business strategies, but I respect the results of our free market system. So by default, everyone seems to want to rival Open Source against Microsoft. It is true that Linux, a popular Open Source server platform, is quickly invading Microsoft's territory; however, Microsoft makes most of its money on desktop products like client Windows systems and Microsoft Office. So, I do not see Open Source truly threatening Microsoft's stronghold anytime soon, but I am no fortune-teller, and as we all know, anything can happen. I think that Microsoft does see that somewhere down the road Open Source will encroach on its market share. My stance on the issue is this: Why can't we all get along? This book will show you many Open Source products running on Windows and a few C# applications running on Linux. I have worked mostly for Microsoft-based software houses, and I have worked with some engineers who will not accept Open Source as a hard and fast rule. I have also worked with software in embedded systems, and many engineers in that field would not be caught dead using Microsoft products. I do not feel strongly one way or the other. I say, "Use the best tool for the job." I know this sounds cliché and is not a strong advocacy statement for either side, but frankly I am growing tired of having to take sides at all. Obviously this book attests to the fact that I believe Open Source development projects are now a more viable solution on the Windows platform because of .NET.

# Open Source, Free Software, and Shared Source. Oh MY!

### Free Software

Free means many different things to different people. Free is such a simple term that you may not think it needs any clarification. We use this term rather loosely; for example, a free world, free enterprise, and of course a free lunch. Well, all I can say is that you better be very sure what is meant when someone refers to "free" software. To clarify matters, the Free Software Foundation (http://www.gnu.org/philosophy/free-sw.html) has defined "Free Software":

"Free software is a matter of the users' freedom to run, copy, distribute, study, change, and improve the software. More precisely, it refers to four kinds of freedom, for the users of the software:

- The freedom to run the program, for any purpose (freedom 0).
- The freedom to study how the program works, and adapt it to your needs (freedom 1). Access to the source code is a precondition for this.
- The freedom to redistribute copies so you can help your neighbor (freedom 2).
- The freedom to improve the program, and release your improvements to the public, so that the whole community benefits (freedom 3). Access to the source code is a precondition for this."

In this context, free then refers to "not suppressing the use of" rather than "reducing the price of" something. Figure 1-1 shows the relationship

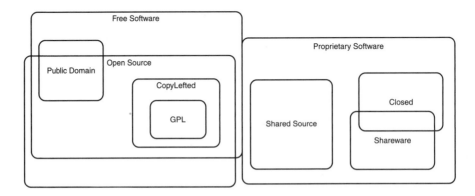

**Figure 1-1** Software Licensing Models.

between Open Source and Free Software. Note that these terms are not interchangeable but are overlapping somewhat.

## Shared Source

Shared Source is somewhat close to freedom level 1 but is not considered Free Software at all because you cannot adapt it to your needs. You can look at the source, and that is about it. Microsoft uses a modified version of Shared Source in their release of the System.Security.Cryptography Code (http://www.gotdotnet.com/team/clr/samples/eula_clr_cryptosrc.aspx). As the name implies, Microsoft's Shared Source Common Language Infrastructure (SSCLI) is also under this license. These are great learning tools, but you cannot use them or modified versions of these products in your product. For instance, you cannot use the SSCLI, which runs on Windows XP, FreeBSD, and Mac OS X to enable your clients to run your .NET applications on multiple platforms in a commercial setting.

## Open Source Software

The term "Open Source" was created by a group of people who thought that Free Software was too radical a concept to market to most corporations. Obviously, this book focuses on Open Source and freedom levels that allow you access to the source code. This is typically what is meant when referring to "Open Source." Bruce Perens has written a wonderful definition of Open Source on his Open Source Initiative (OSI) Web site (http://opensource.org/docs/def_print.php). In his definition, he outlines ten criteria for Open Source:

1. Free Redistribution
2. Source Code
3. Derived Works
4. Integrity of Author's Source Code
5. No Discrimination Against Persons or Groups
6. No Discrimination Against Fields of Endeavor
7. Distribution of License
8. License Must Not Be Specific to a Product
9. The License Must Not Restrict Other Software
10. The License Must Be Technology-Neutral

I will not elaborate on these criteria since Bruce puts it so succinctly on the OSI Web site. It is worth noting, however, that Open Source is a development philosophy or methodology. As such, it is not operating system- or programming language-specific.

### Open Source Licenses

The OSI Web site lists the accepted Open Source Licenses shown in Table 1.2. As listed in the definition of Open Source, the license must be distributed with the code. It is safest to only use code that uses one of these licenses.

**Table 1.2** Open Source Licenses

Academic Free License

Apache Software License

Apple Public Source License

Artistic License

Attribution Assurance Licenses

BSD License

Common Public License

Eiffel Forum License

Eiffel Forum License V2.0

Entessa Public License

GNU General Public License (GPL)

GNU Library or "Lesser" General Public License (LGPL)

Lucent Public License (Plan9)

IBM Public License

Intel Open Source License

Historical Permission Notice and Disclaimer

Jabber Open Source License

MIT License

MITRE Collaborative Virtual Workspace License (CVW License)

**Table 1.2** Open Source Licenses (cont.)

Motosoto License

Mozilla Public License 1.0 (MPL)

Mozilla Public License 1.1 (MPL)

Naumen Public License

Nethack General Public License

Nokia Open Source License

OCLC Research Public License 2.0

Open Group Test Suite License

Open Software License

Python License (CNRI Python License)

Python Software Foundation License

Qt Public License (QPL)

RealNetworks Public Source License V1.0

Reciprocal Public License

Ricoh Source Code Public License

Sleepycat License

Sun Industry Standards Source License (SISSL)

Sun Public License

Sybase Open Watcom Public License 1.0

University of Illinois/NCSA Open Source License

Vovida Software License v. 1.0

W3C License

wxWindows Library License

X.Net License

Zope Public License

zlib/libpng License

Mozilla Public License

You can obtain the licenses by visiting the OSI Web site. Using code that contains a license that someone has just made up is dangerous. A modification of one of the above licenses may be acceptable but would require in-depth inspection.

### Open Source "Free-ness"

The FSF has coined a term called Copyleft, which obviously is a play on the word "Copyright," to refer to software that fits their definition of Free Software – Freedom Level 3. This means that you are free to use, modify, and distribute code as you see fit, as long as you do not deny this same freedom to the code from someone else. In Figure 1-1 you can see that there is an overlap of Open Source and Free Software. That implies that the FSF does not view all Open Source as free. Of course Open Source software does imply Freedom Level 1 and 2. FSF's Web site categorizes the overlap (see http://www.fsf.org/licenses/license-list.html):

Copyleft Compatible Licenses

- GNU GPL
- GNU LGPL
- modified BSD License
- zlib
- W3C License
- Python License
- Zope Public License v2.0
- Eiffel Forum License v2.0

Non-Copyleft Compatible Licenses

- Apache
- origional BSD License
- Open Software License
- Zope Public License v1.0
- Nokia Open Source License
- Qt Public License (QPL)
- Jabber Open Source License

Keep in mind that it is fine to use an Open Source Licensed product that is not considered Free Software in your products. You just have to understand the license requirements as well as the goals of your product.

### Open Source Myths

I have found that there are a lot of unjustified claims about Open Source. As I have already mentioned, this topic leans somewhat toward advocacy. Open Source is a hotly debated topic with substantial firepower existing on both sides. Here I will do my best to take an objective look at Open Source so that you can make an informed decision in your Open Source policy, which all companies should have.

#### Open Source Code Is More Stable

More eyes do not equal better code. More educated and experienced eyes do mean better code. Cryptography best-practices suggest opening your code for public review. Most often, counterintuitively, this results in more secure code. On the other hand, I will say that with Open Source, most developers want to look good in the eyes of their peers and refine their code to the best of their abilities before releasing it to the public. Recently, Reasoning Inc. (http://www.reasoning.com) compared a few products to promote their Code Inspection Solutions for C and C++. While C and C++ code inspection tools are becoming more and more commonplace, the results of the study are interesting on two levels. First, most of the coding problems found were variable initialization and null pointer problems. These problems are all but eliminated in C#. Secondly, the results in a nutshell are that not all Open Source products are more stable; it just depends on the product. Sorry, no silver bullet here. The first study from Reasoning is comparing the Linux TCP/IP stack against five commercial equivalents. Their findings were that the Linux implementation's bug density is much smaller than even the best of the commercial products. So this proves that Open Source is more stable, right? Not so fast. The same company conducted a study of Apache 2.0 source code. It might shock you to find out that the density of defects in Apache was quite a bit higher than most commercial Web servers. But before you get too hard on Apache, realize that according to Netcraft (http://www.netcraft.com), the first version of their product pretty much runs the Internet (see Figure 1-2).

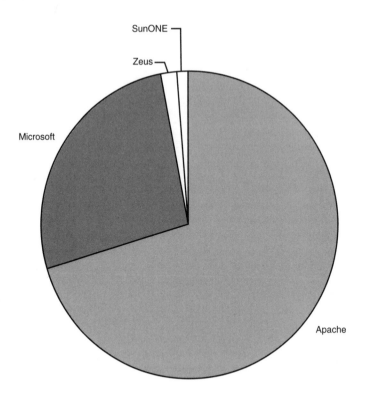

**Figure 1-2** Most Common Web Servers according to May 2003 Netcraft Survey.

*Open Source Code Is More Secure*

The CERT Coordination Center (http://www.cert.org) tracks computer security incidents and vulnerabilities and publishes security alerts based on this information to the general public. The rate of increase of security incidents is astounding (see Figure 1-3).

As you can see, to say that the security incidents have grown rapidly in the last few years is an understatement. For this reason, I have taken all the CERT incidents from 2000 to 2002 and categorized them based on whether they are proprietary products or Open Source. The results are found in Figure 1-4.

According to CERT Incidents, Open Source code is typically a little bit more secure than proprietary code. This categorization was a little difficult.

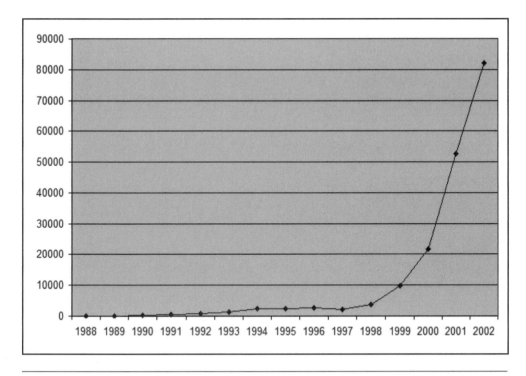

**Figure 1-3**  CERT Security Incident Reports.

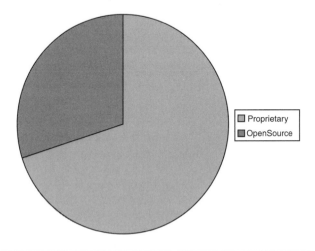

**Figure 1-4**  CERT Security Incidents from 2000-2002.

It was hard to determine whether some incidents applied to proprietary Unix distributions only or also to Linux-type Open Source projects. In this case, I assigned the incident to both proprietary and Open Source. The exact data can be found in Appendix E. This data is not conclusive and comprehensive by any means. There are many security incidents that are never reported to any organization, but CERT is definitely the authority in this area. My personal view on security is that the higher the reward, the more incentive for a hacker. In other words, a hacker may not have as much incentive to hack an Open Source product as a proprietary product because he will not get as much recognition. So there are subtle things to consider when interpreting security incidents.

*Open Source Code Is Cheaper*
Cost is the most controversial subject when it comes to Open Source. Even when you are given something, there are always costs associated with it. If given a free car, you must evaluate if the maintenance costs of that car are reasonable so that you can justify taking it. However, if given a house, you usually cannot go wrong in taking it unless it is in a bad location. These examples are decisions that are somehow easier for most people to make than when it comes down to software. Only time will tell if Open Source and its proponents will outperform proprietary software companies. Just as with cars and houses, Open Source software decisionmaking is going to be unique to every organization. For instance, I accepted cars in high school that I would be embarrassed to drive today. The same is true with software. A struggling startup company might find Mandrake Linux (http://www.mandrake.com) and Open Office (www.openofffice.org) wonderful solutions, whereas a middle-size or larger company may feel safer using a product that has commercial technical support such as Windows and Microsoft Office.

**NOTE:** This does not imply that Linux (and other Open Source products) do not have commercial technical support available because most of them do. Nor does this imply that Open Source products are only suitable for small companies, for there are several large companies that depend on Open Source.

# Tips on Selecting a License

Selecting an Open Source license is a very individualistic sort of thing, almost as personal as code itself. It reflects your views on software licensing and software in general. That is why there are so many different licenses to begin with. Some are subsets of others or based on others. Some are completely tailored by the author to meet his personal goals for his project. It is this author's opinion that when it comes to using an Open Source license in your product or choosing a license for your Open Source project, stick with the ones that are tried and true:

- GPL
- LGPL
- BSD
- Apache

These licenses are well respected and time-tested. Just about any company that has a TCP/IP stack started out by basing its code on the BSD implementation. In the case of Apache and GPL/LGPL licenses, entire companies have based their existence on the way these licenses work. IBM and Red Hat are good examples of such companies, respectively. Also notice that while these licenses are all Open Source, they span the whole definition of Free Software. GPL and LGPL are Copyleft and are therefore Free Software at its purest form. The BSD license is also considered Copyleft and Free Software but with fewer requirements about releasing improvements to the code back to the Open Source community. Apache is not considered Free Software by the Free Software Foundation (although it is Open Source), and there are several examples of proprietary Apache distributions and products.

**NOTE:** When I speak of the BSD license, I am technically referring to the modified BSD license. I consider the advertisement and various other requirements of the original BSD license to be incredibly annoying, and they render it pretty much useless. I believe the originators wisely realized this and therefore created the modified version.

# Using Open Source in Your Proprietary Product

I am definitely no Linus Torvalds, Bruce Perens, Bill Gates, or Don Box, but I have been working in the trenches developing software long enough to know something good when I see it. Here is what I am looking for when I look for a free or Open Source product:

*Source code I perceive to be well written that I can use without restriction in whatever project I am working on to save time by not having to implement the functionality myself while standardizing on something others can quickly pick up.*

This means that I want to be able to use the source without having to jump through many hoops or necessarily disclose any enhancements that may compromise the competitiveness of my product. I can use this software for other Open Source projects in a proprietary product or for academic use. Everyone perceives well-written code differently. It is humorous that most developers look at someone else's code and say, "That is horrible! What was he thinking?" We have all also experienced looking back at code we thought was good at the time, realizing that now we write much better code. This is why I say that you must perceive the code to be well written and useful to your project both in additional functionality and time saved.

Carefully read the license agreements and make sure the requirements meet your product's needs. If possible, it is only proper to release any fixes and enhancements back to the community. I am all for giving back to the community, and that can make for some rapid development. In fact, some of the projects I cover in this book have changed so quickly in the last few months that I am going to have to rework some of the chapters I already had completed! I am amazed at the dedication of some of these developers. However, in some cases you may develop a proprietary product based on an Open Source product or a proprietary feature for an Open Source product. For example, Covalent Technologies (http://www.covalent.com) has created a proprietary ISAPI extension for the Apache Web server that supports ASP.NET. This is wonderful if you are already using Apache and desire to use ASP.NET, but this is an important product for their company and would devastate them if they had to release the source. This is just one example of successfully using an Open Source product to develop a proprietary product. However, it is important to point out that this is all based on the Apache license. Be careful in examining licensing before using an Open Source product. Here are some things to watch out for:

- Advertisement clauses in the license that require you to advertise the original development project or their license.
- The requirement of releasing any changes in the code back to the originator.
- Requiring public availability of the Open Source code in your product.
- The requirement that any product you develop using an Open Source product must be Open Source itself.
- The originator or creator of the product retaining the copyright and intellectual property.

There is nothing wrong with these requirements if you are aware of them up front and plan for them, but these are typical things in Open Source licenses that you may not want in your end user's product.

## Summary

Open Source is a very controversial subject in the software industry. There is no one right answer that says Open Source is always better or that proprietary software is more advantageous. This decision is based upon your project goals and timeframe, the quality of the Open Source product, and your company and team's perception of Open Source. Now that Microsoft has released the .NET SDK to be freely available to anyone, the Open Source community has begun a rapid acceptance to developing Open Source in conjunction with Microsoft Products. Since Microsoft has standardized C# and the .NET CLI, I believe Microsoft has created a platform that will be more widely accepted than anything they previously have released and that is competitive with any other software platform available today.

# CHAPTER 2

# Open Source and the .NET Platform

*The nicest thing about standards is that there are so many of them to choose from.*

—Ken Olsen (1926–), founder of Digital Equipment Corp., 1977

## Introduction

This chapter can be summarized into something like this: Open Source meets .NET. There are more Open Source .NET projects than I can possibly list is this book.[1] But by far the projects listed in this chapter are the largest Open Source .NET initiatives because they focus on a specialized implementation of the .NET standard. The size and scope of some of these projects are comparable to even the largest of Open Source projects. The most unique aspect of the projects is that they are based on a Microsoft standard! In other words, they are Microsoft-related Open Source projects. In general, there is a lot of animosity between the Open Source Community and Microsoft, making .NET (and its associated standards) a true rarity. This chapter is a high-level overview of the projects. There are several books available today and many coming about the time of the release of this book that deal with just one of the projects listed here. I will try to do each of these projects justice. It is my not intention to compare and contrast each project critically in order to see who has done the best job, but rather

---

[1] For a list of .NET tools and projects, Open Source or proprietary, visit my .NET Tools WIKI at http://www.nantz.org/SushiWiki/wiki.aspx. If you know of a tool that is not listed there, then add it! That is what the WIKI is for.

to relish the fact "that there are so many of them to choose from," as the quote at the beginning of the chapter so well describes. Throughout the rest of the book, I will demonstrate some of these implementations on various platforms. Many of the tools listed in Part II work on most, if not all, of these platforms.

# .NET Standards

A programming language the size of C# has not been standardized since C++, and I cannot think of any programming platform as large as .NET that has been standardized. Unfortunately, Sun Microsystems retracted the Java programming platform and language from standardization on more than one occasion. .NET's standardization is one of the reasons I believe it will eventually become more popular than Java unless Sun takes action and standardizes Java as well. Academic institutions, large corporations, and governments take standardizations very seriously, and this is definitely weighing in favor of the .NET platform. This is probably most vividly illustrated by the forty-some international institutions that are receiving funds from Microsoft Research to research the SSCLI (http://research.microsoft.com/Collaboration/University/Europe/RFP/Rotor/rotorProjects.aspx).

Just as you must carefully and knowledgably pick a correct Open Source license or risk being surprised by your "free" software, you must be very careful and know exactly what parts of .NET are standardized. Also of great importance is the standardization organization by which .NET is declared a standard.

# Standardization

Microsoft worked hard to push the CLI and C# through standardization, and they did so with record results. I cannot think of a programming language or platform that made it from the Version 1 release to an international standard faster than C# and the Common Language Infrastructure (CLI). This is all due to Microsoft playing their cards correctly and not for aught.

## Standards Organizations

Microsoft originally submitted the CLI and the C# programming language to the European Computer Manufacturers Association (ECMA) for standardization. In December of 2002, the second edition of ECMA-335 Common Language Infrastructure (CLI) became a standard. The C# programming language became ECMA-334 simultaneously. Because of the close relationship of ECMA with the International Standards Organization (ISO), C# and the CLI finished their fast-track standardization in April of 2003. The CLI is now ISO 23271:2003, and C# has become ISO 23270:2003. So when working with the CLI and C#, you can be assured you are working with a real standard from a real standards body and not some unheard of organization. Microsoft's ISO standardization is an all-around win, especially in large organizations (such as governments) that may require the use of ISO programming languages. I do not believe that Microsoft would want to suffer the international humiliation of retracting a standard, even if ISO would allow them to. ISO standardization allows for other implementations of the CLI and C# standards to be created and used with great confidence and freedom. But this then begs the question, "What exactly is in the standards?"

## What Is in the Standards

Now that I am getting technical, it is time to start defining and using the technical terms associated with the standards. Figure 2-1 shows the different parts of the standards and how they interact.

All of the acronyms used in Figure 2-1 are definitely confusing. The CLI is the Common Language Infrastructure already discussed. To make things a bit more confusing, Microsoft called their implementation of the CLI a Common Language Runtime (CLR), which we will look at as one of the implementations later in the chapter. The CLI is meant to be a platform-independent virtual execution engine. Nothing in the standard would require a specific operating system or platform, but it intends to abstract your C# code from what lies beneath. The CLI uses a Common Intermediate Language (CIL) that is CPU-independent. CIL is an output from a compiler that is a step above native CPU-specific code. The CIL is typically fed to a just-in-time (JIT) compiler for transformation into native code. Perhaps the most critical component of the CLI is the garbage collector (GC) because if the garbage collector is not efficient, the whole platform

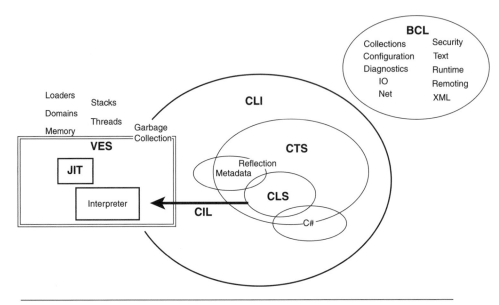

**Figure 2-1** The CLI Standard.

will not perform and must be discarded. Up to this point, the CLI sounds similar to a Java Virtual Machine (JVM). In fact, the CLI is similar to a JVM in allowing the "code-once-run-anywhere" dream that turned into the "code-once-test-everywhere" nightmare. But the best is yet to come. The Common Type System (CTS) sets the stage for the Common Language Specification (CLS).

**NOTE:** The Base Class Libraries (BCL) are not a part of the CLI standard. However, I included them in the graphics for this chapter to point out one of the biggest benefits of the CLI. This benefit is a collection of base classes that can be used from any language. This is great news for many languages like VB where you really could not do true threading, exception handling, and other critical functionality.

The CTS requires that all Types derive from the System.Object base Type and are broken down into two basic categories: Value Types and Reference Types. Figure 2-2 demonstrates the CTS Type Classification System.

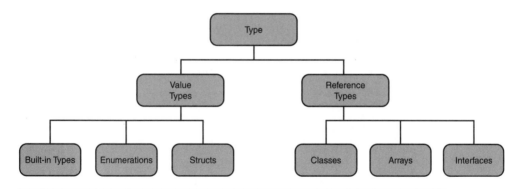

**Figure 2-2** Type Classification.

Because of the common types it is much simpler to produce a CLS. By requiring common types, the CTS eliminates cross language type incompatibilities. This is great news to anyone who used C++, MFC, and COM, where there are twenty-some definitions of a string. Trying to figure out which one to use became almost a status symbol in the Windows development community and made for a very mean interview question. The Common Language Specification (CLS) allows objects to operate with each other, regardless of the programming language in which they were implemented. If your assembly only publicly exposes CLS-compliant features, then it can be accessed from any programming language that supports the CLS. Table 1.1 in Chapter 1 lists just a few languages that support the CLS and are freely available for Open Source, but there are numerous other CLS languages available that are not listed in this table. CLS takes programming language integration a step further. Existing technology such as CORBA or COM allowed language interoperation to a point, but the CLS allows all languages access to the CLI base framework, easy language interoperation, and cross-language inheritance. Miguel de Icaza from Ximian's Mono project put it best:

> We [Ximian] were interested in the CLR because it solves problems that we face every day. The Java VM did not solve this problem.
>
> —*The .NET Framework: Using the ECMA Standards: An interview with Miguel de Icaza, MSDN*

My interest in .NET comes from the attempts that we have made before in the GNOME project to achieve some of the things .NET does:

- APIs that are exposed to multiple languages
- Cross-Language Integration
- Contract/Interfaced-based programming...

> —*Peeking under the Lid of Open Source .NET CLI Implementations, DevX*

This language agnostic approach truly sets the CLI apart from any other programming platform and provides a very rich set of APIs to all languages.

C# is the language of choice when using the CLI because it is a standard and shows off most (but not all) of the CLI functionality. For a good book on just the syntax and semantics of the C# language, see *A Programmer's Introduction to C#* (Second Edition) by Eric Gunnerson, Apress

I like Eric's book because he sticks to what the C# language can do without sidetracking into other parts of the .NET framework. When I want to know if a particular feature, such as defaulting optional function parameters, is supported by C#, I do not want a book that covers everything from ASP.NET in C# to XML in C#. While those parts of the framework are essential to understand, they are also broad and apply to all CLS-compliant languages.

I am not aware of a single CLS language that does push the CTS to the limits. Therefore, do not assume that because the CLI functionality is not exposed in the C# language (or any other language for that matter) that the capability does not exist in the CLI. Generics are a good example of a feature that the CLI's architecture could support with little modification but that was never built into any language. Microsoft is introducing Generics in the .NET 2.0 specifications. Generics in .NET and Java are on the surface a lot like C++ templates. To make things even more interesting, C++ will have both Templates and Generics! Visual Studio .NET 2005 and the .NET 2.0 SDK have many improvements for the Managed C++ language. Unfortunately, one example of the CLI not fully supporting a language is that multiple inheritance still will not be available. The good news is that the Managed C++ team is committed to pursuing the changes in the CLI necessary to support this critical functionality. For a good discussion on the differences between C# Generics and C++ Templates, see Bruce Eckel's Web log entry: http://www.mindview.net/WebLog/log-0050. Generics give us the ability to add "parameterized types" functionality to our classes, functions, collections, etc., so you can create a class that operates generically on a type, even though you do not know at design time what that type may be. Then the user of your class can at design time (or runtime for that matter) declare what type he wants your class to operate on. This is especially useful when using collections!

You cannot discuss C# for very long without the topic of Java similarities coming up. While the languages are similar, I think the competition in bringing new languages to the market is a good thing. Luke Hutteman, who created the wonderful C# Web log (blog) aggregator SharpReader (http://www.hutteman.com/weblog/2003/04/06-56.html), illustrates this perfectly as he observes on his blog, and I quote:

> It's interesting how C# and Java seem to be playing leapfrog. C# started out with many of Java's features and some useful improvements of its own, and now Java is taking a number of C# features like attributes, enums, foreach and autoboxing, and adds some more like generics, static imports, and extendable enums.
>
> Enums are something that are long overdue for Java, and their implementation in JDK 1.5 seems extremely powerful… .NET 2.0 will also add support for generics. From what I heard, they will leapfrog Java again on that one by allowing that type-information to be available at run-time as well. I seem to remember reading somewhere that Java's generics will be compile-time only. At run-time, a Collection<String> in Java will look like any other Collection…

Hopefully, in the near future, a language will support exceptions to my liking in a more robust way. In my opinion, no language does a good job of simplifying exception handling, but Java probably comes a little closer to this than other languages. A tool called CLRxLint (http://www.software4net.com/products/clrxlint.html) from software4net does provide Java-like checked exceptions for CLS-compliant languages, but it's still not an ideal solution. This awkward support for exceptions is why so many people punt and just catch the base Exception class and get themselves into trouble. It would be nice to be able to use reflection to find out what exceptions you should expect to be thrown. For more insight on this issue, see the interview (http://www.artima.com/intv/handcuffsP.html) with Anders Hejlsberg (the leader of the C# design team), Bruce Eckel, and Bill Venners, where Anders discusses his reasoning for not using checked exceptions.

## What Is Not in the Standards

If you peek ahead at Figure 2-3, you will see how Microsoft's implementation of the CLI is a lot more than just what they have chosen to standardize. Now that we know what is in the standards, we should look at what is not in the standards. Some of the most innovative parts of Microsoft's CLR (including ADO.NET, ASP.NET & Windows Forms) are not part of the CLI or C# standard. Windows Forms are a great advancement in rapid development and ease of use over traditional MFC

User Interface programming. I personally believe that Windows Forms and User Interfaces in general are probably the most difficult things to make platform-independent. Keeping a consistent look and feel is not adequately accomplished in Java's Swing, TCL/TK, GTK+, or any other toolkit I have seen. After just playing with a UI for a few seconds, I can tell what was used to create the UI. Although users do not explicitly understand the differences, it has been my experience that users subconsciously know when a UI does not quite fit with the paradigm of the operating system they prefer. ADO.NET is another non-standard that, once you have used it, is hard to live without. ADO.NET mixes XML and data access very well, making n-tier systems much easier to implement. Unfortunately, the non-standardization of ADO.NET truly hinders pure Web service development because datasets cannot be passed between .NET Web services and other Platforms (like Java's) Web service implementations. It is this author's opinion that Microsoft would benefit from standardizing ADO.NET because then it could be used more frequently to exchange data between programming platforms. ASP.NET is also a fairly large innovation that is not standardized. ASP.NET introduces the unique idea of using server-side controls, which gives the programmer a closer programming model to a thick client. This makes for faster Web UI coding and, with the help of vendor components, a richer UI for the client.

In addition to things that are not in the standard, there are a few things in the standard that are not very clearly defined. Platform Invoke (P/Invoke) is definitely a good example of that. Microsoft knew that .NET is not going to be able to replace all the existing functionality that other languages have. In addition, most users are going to want to use legacy code from .NET. To allow for this, Microsoft created P/Invoke. P/Invoke allows you to make calls into existing libraries or the system to gain additional functionality that .NET could not implement, such as serial port communication. The big question of course is, "How exactly is this supposed to work on other operating systems like Linux or Macintosh?"

# Implementations

The quick overview of the CLI and C# standards lays the foundation for exploring the various implementations of the standards. These are the well-known implementations. Who knows how many other implementations are out there that have not been announced or, like Palm 6, that have just been announced?

## Microsoft's .NET CLR

The most widely used and generally available implementation is of course Microsoft's. It only makes sense that the creators of the standard have the first implementation. Figure 2-3 shows Microsoft's CLR.

As you can see, Microsoft has added a whole slew of stuff to the CLI standard. Also in addition to the C# language, Microsoft provides Visual Basic.NET, C++.NET, Jscript.NET, and J#. .NET works on versions of Windows from Windows 98 to the latest Windows 2003 and beyond – the next version of Windows, codenamed Longhorn, will have new APIs available only to Managed code! Although a rather large distribution, .NET has

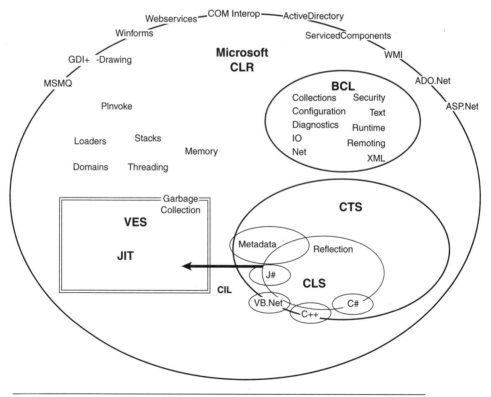

**Figure 2-3** Microsoft's Common Language Runtime.

more functionality than any other CLI implementation currently available at the time of this writing. There is too much functionality to properly address everything in one portion of a chapter. For a great in-depth look at the .NET runtime and its internals, see:

*Essential .NET Volume 1: The Common Language Runtime*
by Don Box and Chris Sells, Addison-Wesley

Microsoft has added the .NET runtime to the Windows Update site and to Windows 2000 and Windows XP service packs to aid in its distribution. It is the goal of Microsoft that in the near future, .NET can be assumed to be installed on all Windows client machines. In addition, the .NET runtime is installed by default on Windows 2003, and this indicates that it can be assumed to exist on any new operating systems from Microsoft. The .NET SDK is freely available from Microsoft and comes with some very good developer tools and probably the best graphical debugger available, as seen in Table 2.1.

**Table 2.1**  Common .NET Development Utilities

| Tool | Description |
| --- | --- |
| Al | Takes a resource file or IL file and adds an assembly manifest |
| Regasm | Exposes .NET assemblies to COM Objects |
| Fuslogvw | Displays details for failed assembly binds |
| Gacutil | Allows you to view and manipulate the contents of the global assembly cache and download cache |
| Installutil | Allows .NET assemblies to be installed and uninstalled as Windows services |
| Ngen | Creates native code from an assembly and caches it for faster execution |
| Regsvcs | Allows .NET assemblies to be installed and uninstalled as a COM+ component |
| Tlbexp | Generates a COM type library from an assembly |
| Tlbimp | Converts the type definitions found within a COM type library into equivalent definitions in managed metadata format for use with a .NET assembly |
| Cordbg | Provides command-line debugging services using the Common Language Runtime Debug API |

**Table 2.1** Common .NET Development Utilities (cont.)

| Tool | Description |
|------|-------------|
| DbgCLR | Provides a graphical debugger |
| Caspol | Allows you to manipulate machine, user, and enterprise-level code access security policies |
| Signcode | Digitally signs a portable executable (PE) file |
| Permview | Displays permission sets requested by the assembly |
| Peverify | Performs type safety verification and metadata validation checks on an assembly |
| Secutil | Extracts the strong name public key of an assembly |
| Sn | Enables strong naming of assemblies |
| Ilasm | Intermediate Language (IL) assembler |
| Ildasm | Intermediate Language (IL) disassembler |
| Resgen | Converts text files and .resx files to .resources files |
| Aximp | Allows an ActiveX control to work on a Windows Form |
| Winres | Simplifies localization by reading and displaying resource files |

By using the tools listed in this chapter, Chapter 3, and Part II of this book, you can create a full-featured and well-integrated product that targets the Windows platform, all without paying a single dime.

## Compact Framework

Not long after the .NET framework was released, Microsoft started beta testing the Compact Framework (CF) (see Figure 2-4 on p. 30). About a year after .NET's release, the Compact Framework was released. This framework is an implementation of the CLI target for Windows CE devices. Though only a subset of the CLI standard was implemented, the Compact Framework make mobile device programming easier than ever. The same programming model is available across devices, and both C# and VB.NET are available. However, each target device with different processors must be compiled for that target. Visual Studio.NET makes this programming much simpler via device emulators and integrated debugging on the devices through ActiveSync. Probably the nicest feature is the ability to

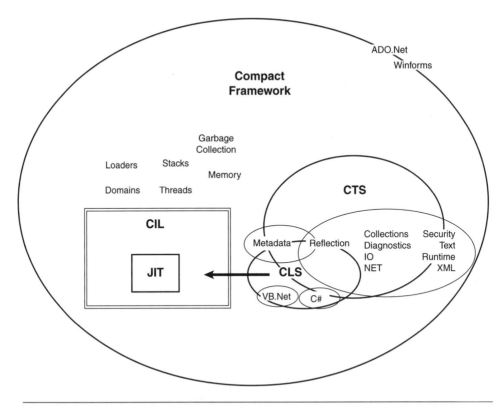

**Figure 2-4** Microsoft's Compact Framework.

consume Web services on a PDA; now that has potential! I also like the integration with SQL Server CE. However, you will notice that the CF has minimal XML support and is missing Remoting, Printing, and many other features available under the .NET CLR.

## SSCLI/Rotor

Microsoft teamed with Corel to create the Shared Source CLI (SSCLI), also know by its code name Rotor (see Figure 2-5). The SSCLI sticks pretty closely to the standards (except for the Jscript implementation) and is intended for academic and instructional study of how to implement a platform-independent CLI. Although useful for study, Rotor's Garbage Collection is not quite up to commercial quality. At the time of this writing, Rotor

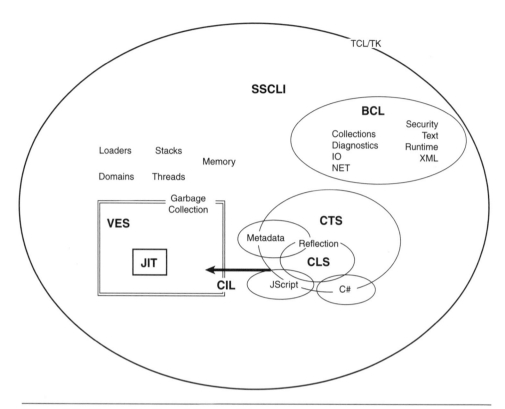

**Figure 2-5** Microsoft's Shared Source CLI.

can run on FreeBSD, Windows, and OS X. For a great book on the specifics of the SSCLI, see David Stutz, Ted Neward & Geoff Schilling. *Shared Source CLI Essentials,* O'Reilly, 2002

Rotor's low-level functionality is contained in the Platform Adaptation Layer (PAL). The PAL is written mostly in C++ and some C. Rotor's System runtime libraries are written using C#, which allows for great study of in-depth C# usage. This design simplifies the work of porting Rotor to another OS by allowing for a minimal amount of code change in the PAL. The SSCLI also goes beyond the CLI standard by implementing Jscript. (See Table 2.2 on p. 32).

The SSCLI also supports cross-platform UIs by using the TCL/TK toolkit. For more information on the Shared Source Common Language Infrastructure, see http://www.microsoft.com/downloads/details.aspx?FamilyId=3A1C93FA-7462-47D0-8E56-8DD34C6292F0&displaylang=en. To

**Table 2.2** Rotor Development Tools

| Tool | Description |
| --- | --- |
| Cordbg | Provides command-line debugging services using the Common Language Runtime Debug API |
| Peverify | Performs type safety verification and metadata validation checks on an assembly |
| Sn | Enables strong naming of assemblies |
| Ilasm | Intermediate Language (IL) assembler |
| Ildasm | Intermediate Language (IL) disassembler |
| Ildbdump | Dumps Debug information from an assembly |
| Metainfo | Dumps the metadata information about an assembly |

download and try Rotor, you can go directly to Microsoft's Research Web site at http://research.microsoft.com/collaboration/university/europe/rotor. Also, there is a Web site devoted to the SSCLI community at http://www.sscli.net.

## Portable.NET

Rhys Weatherley leads the Portable.NET (http://www.southern-storm.com.au/portable_net.html) Open Source implementation of the CLI (see Figure 2-6). Under the GNU project and the dotGNU steering committee, Portable.NET seems to be mainly focusing on the standards portion of the CLI similar to the SSCLI, but it is branching out into additional functionality by using TCL/TK for UIs and using some of Mono's implementations. Currently, Portable.NET runs on Linux, Windows, Solaris, and Mac OS X platforms. The Portable.NET lower-level libraries as well as the runtime and compiler are written in C. The Portable.NET team's approach is a little strange in that they developed an interpreter first. Some implementations do not even have an interpreter, just a JIT compiler. This interesting approach may prove to be a very fast implementation of a JIT compiler. This implementation is definitely the smallest and most portable, seeing that almost every processor and operating system has a C compiler, making it a good candidate for embedding. Portable.NET is under the Gnu GPL Open Source license. (See Table 2.3.)

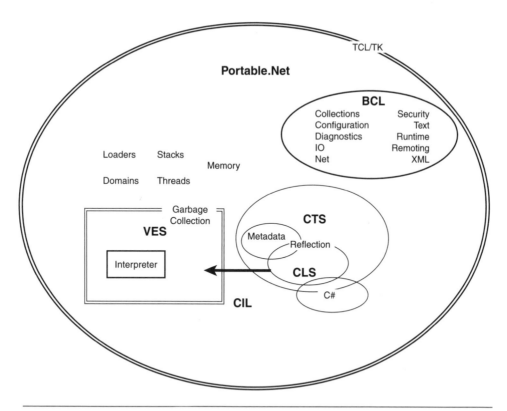

**Figure 2-6**  DOTGNU's Portable.NET.

**Table 2.3**  Portable.NET Development Tools

| Tool | Description |
| --- | --- |
| Ilasm | Intermediate Language (IL) assembler |
| Ildasm | Intermediate Language (IL) disassembler |
| Ilsize | Lists size information for each of the sections within the IL |
| Ilnative | Lists the native methods that are used within the IL |
| Ilfind | Searches for a pattern within the supplied IL input file |
| Resgen | Converts text files and .resx files to .resources files |

## Mono

Ximian, the creator of many Open Source projects including the popular Evolution email client, created the Mono project under Miguel de Icaza's leadership (see Figure 2-7). Mono's intent is to implement full functionality and keep pace with Microsoft's CLR implementation. So far, Mono is doing a remarkable job; they even have started an Apache (http://www.apache.org) module to support ASP.NET fittingly called mod_mono. The System.* namespaces are coming along, and they are adding additional functionality in the Mono.* namespace. Mono is the only implementation to have both a JIT compiler and an Interpreter, which they call Mint. Mono currently runs on Linux, Windows, and Solaris. Interestingly enough, the JIT engine and much of the low-lever workings are in C. The C# implementation is solid enough to allow the C# compiler to be written in C#. Uniquely, Mono ships a GTK+ binding for C# called Gtk#. How Mono decides to implement System.Windows.Forms is being watched with great anticipation. Mono's Compiler is under the GPL, the runtime is under LGPL, and the libraries use the MIT Open Source licensing. Mono also includes the useful tools described in Table 2.4.

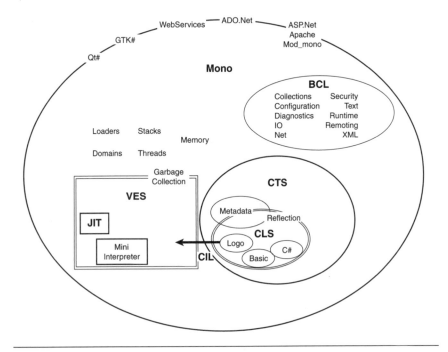

**Figure 2-7**  Mono.

**Table 2.4**  Mono Development Tools

| Tool | Description |
| --- | --- |
| Cilc | CIL-to-C binding generator exposing any CIL library to C and C++ |
| Ilasm | IL assembler |
| Monodies | IL disassembler |
| Monoresgen | Converts text files and .resx files to .resources files |
| Monosn | Enables strong naming of assemblies |
| PEDump | Portable Executable dump utility |
| Secutil | Extracts the strong name public key of an assembly |
| Monodoc | A tool for creating documentation from XML comments in C# code. |
| Sqlsharp | SQL command-line client |

Mono is available from http://www.go-mono.com and has a community site at http://www.gotmono.com.

**Implementation Quick Comparison**

Although all of these CLI implementations are rapidly changing and really hard to compare, a comparison will reveal where these implementations are going.

The following table on page 36 will help you pick the implementation that is right for you as well as help you understand the intent of the implementation. The SSCLI is academic and is not able to be used in a production environment. Mono and DOTGNU are good candidates for production implementation, but Mono is implementing everything, whereas DOTGNU is just sticking to implementing the standards. Of course, Microsoft is leading the pack since they had a head start on the whole thing. Again, this comparison is not set in stone. The Microsoft .NET and Compact Framework are changing fast, as are the Open Source implementations, so that this information will become dated soon, but hopefully you have found it useful.

Also, an interesting study to keep your eye on is Werner Vogels' performance comparison of the implementations (http://weblogs.cs.cornell.edu/AllThingsDistributed/archives/000052.html). This study is a part of the larger CLI-Grande effort (http://cli-grande.sscli.net/) and is a great idea if it can avoid advocacy issues and remain an objective study.

| | Microsoft .NET | Mono | DOTGNU | SSCLI | Compact Framework |
|---|---|---|---|---|---|
| Collections | X | X | X | X | X |
| Reflection | X | X | X | X | |
| Remoting | X | X | X | X | |
| Configuration | X | X | X | X | X |
| Diagnostics | X | X | X | X | X |
| IO | X | X | X | X | X |
| Net | X | X | X | X | |
| Security | X | X | X | X | X |
| Text | X | X | X | X | X |
| XML | X | X | X | X | |
| Threading | X | X | X | X | X |
| Drawing | X | X | X | X | X |
| Runtime | X | X | X | X | |
| Pinvoke | X | X | | X | |
| Component Model | X | X | X | X | X |
| CodeDom | X | X | X | X | X |
| Timers | X | X | X | X | X |
| Globalization | X | X | X | X | X |
| COM Interop | X | X | | | X |
| Windows Forms | X | X | | | X |
| Web–ASP.Net / Services | X | X | | | |
| Data–ADO.Net | X | X | | | X |
| WMI | X | | | | |
| Serviced Components | X | | | | |
| Queues/MSMQ | X | X | | | |
| LDAP/Active Directory | X | X | | | |
| Windows | | | | | |
| Windows CE | | | | | |
| MAC OSX | | | | | |
| Linux | | | | | |
| FreeBSD | | | | | |

# Summary

There is no perfect implementation of the CLI standard. Some implementations are further along than others. Some stick close to the specifications; others add some nice functionality above and beyond the standards. The Open Source projects could be embedded into a commercial product, but keep in mind the target OS platforms when choosing an implementation. Even though the implementations have minimized the amount of code porting required, porting an implementation is not a small task. If you decide you need to port an implementation, consider the language used in the lower-level workings of the framework (i.e., C versus C++) and try to match that language with one you are comfortable with. Review Chapter 1's discussion of Open Source licensing and research beyond the overview to see exactly what is expected from a specific license. MIT tends to lend itself a little better to proprietary extensions to the Open Source project than does the GNU GPL, but the GPL favors the product implementer. Make no mistake about it: Microsoft is in the business of making money. It will do whatever is in their best interest. Microsoft saw the advantages of standardizing the CLI and C# for acceptance in the community. The standards mutually benefited Microsoft, Open Source, and in the end, you the programmer. Recently, Microsoft has applied for patents for ASP.NET and ADO.NET. Implementers using these and other technologies that are not part of the standard should not be astonished if Microsoft decides to enforce the patents. While implementations that go beyond the specs offer greater compatibility with Microsoft's CLR and may be more attractive, they do run the risk of Microsoft changing the fundamentals of the non-standard technology or claiming it as intellectual property. Compared to many other companies, Microsoft has had a very good track record of keeping backwards compatibility in their APIs and functionality so as to not strand someone or force them to re-code their product. So far, Microsoft seems perfectly fine with the Open Source implementations of the CLI and even seems to encourage it somewhat through Rotor. Microsoft Research added the new functionality of Generics to the SSCLI as an experiment before putting it into .NET 2.0. From here on out, we are venturing into the unexplored territory of Microsoft .NET and Open Source.

# Part II

# .NET Development with Open Source Tools

# CHAPTER 3

# General Development

*Give us the tools and we will finish the job.*

—*Sir Winston Churchill (1874–1965), BBC radio broadcast, Feb 9, 1941*

## Introduction

This chapter is not about Open Source .NET projects or necessarily about .NET per se. This chapter is about using existing Open Source tools in your .NET development process. Not everyone is fortunate enough to have a Microsoft Developer Network (MSDN) license or Visual Studio.NET (VS.NET). Some people are just too impatient to endure the lengthy VS.NET install process. But I must admit that I do spend about as much time using VS.NET as Emacs. VS.NET's Integrated Development Environment (IDE) does an amazing job of truly integrating source code, database, and Web development, allowing you to use one tool for almost everything. The purpose of this chapter is to show how useful Open Source can be to you, the developer. Open Source is not something that only affects marketing decisions or business plans. The tools listed here have enabled companies to use .NET and still be just as competitive as a company that uses Microsoft's development tools. I would like to point out that you do not have to exclusively use Microsoft or Open Source. In most instances, you can play both sides. For instance, using Windows XP, IIS, and Web Matrix, you can create an ASP.NET page that runs on Mono. You can also use Mandrake Linux (http://www.mandrakelinux.com/en/), Emacs, nAnt, and Mono to create a database application that will eventually run on Windows and PostgreSQL. I should point out that some of these tools and products are not even Open Source but are free in the sense that there are no licensing fees or runtime royalties. Using products found in this chapter can greatly reduce the initial cost of starting a development project and allow smaller companies to see greater profits in the end, and yet some of these tools are scalable enough to handle larger projects and teams as well.

# .NET Editing Tools

As a developer, most of our time is spent using a glorified text editor. Therefore, choosing an editor is a very important task because you will be sitting in front of it for an awfully long time. There are literally hundreds of editors out there (proprietary and Open Source) that support various programming languages. You must weigh the goals of your project and your company to be able to choose the correct editor for your situation.

## Editor Features

Here are some features to look for in an editor. These are not the only methods you can use to compare editors but rather are a collection of useful features on which I have become dependent.

### Integrated Help

While the .NET SDK comes with great documentation, the way in which the editor integrates it (or the lack thereof) can almost determine the editor for you. However, switching back and forth between the editor and the documentation is not the end of the world. Each editor will have its little quirks. One annoying feature of VS.NET is when cutting and pasting from locations that use HTML (like MSDN or a Web page), VS.NET pastes the HTML markup, which is not exactly what is usually desired.

**TIP:** There is a wiiciwgp (What is in the clipboard is what gets pasted) plug-in for VS.NET available from http://www.codeproject.com/useritems/wiicwgp.asp that eliminates the HTML cut-and-paste problem.

I find myself using several of the editors later listed in this chapter, depending on the job at hand.

### Syntax Highlighting

We take this for granted in IDEs today, but syntax highlighting is a very important feature. Being able to easily distinguish language key words from built-in types just by the color of the word is extremely helpful. It is not possible to demonstrate this familiar feature in a black and white book, but all of the editors listed here do support syntax highlighting. However, with some of the editors, you may need to download a plug-in or specialized file that extends the editor for the desired language.

### Integrated Debugger

Another feature that is almost assumed in an editor today is an integrated debugger. This allows a developer to debug the application directly from the editor. Some IDEs support this better than others. Microsoft's freely available .NET SDK comes with a functional graphical debugger (Dbg-CLR) and a somewhat cryptic debugger (Cordg). Both tools can be found in the FrameworkSDK folder in the .NET SDK directory. The source for Cordg is also shipped with the SDK. The SDK documentation is very helpful in describing how to use the Cordg utility to print out variables and dump memory, so I will not rehash that information. Some editors wrap the functionality of the debugger of your choice into the IDE, allowing you to step line-by-line through the code. While this is much better than having to switch tools, probably the best debugger integration I have seen is in the Visual Basic 6 (VB6) IDE. VB6 allowed you to edit the code while debugging and continue on without having to break the debug session and recompile (which has been promised in the Visual Studio.NET 2005). Another nice feature is retrieving the value of a variable by just hovering the mouse over the text in the IDE. The integration and debugging with SQL also is very nice.

### Integrated Command Shell

Being able to issue various operating system commands from the IDE is often useful. I was surprised to find that many of the newer editors do not support this or support only a subset of commands. Many of the old-faithful editors that have been around forever have the best integration of issuing commands from the IDE.

**TIP:** Microsoft has finally released a command shell for VS.NET, which is available as part of the VS.NET Powertoys (http://www.gotdotnet.com).

### Intellisense Autocomplete

You may say that programmers have become lazy, but I think that the cleverest improvement in IDEs in a long time is Autocomplete. Later on, Figure 3-3 shows this feature in action. Intellisense saves a large amount of time in weeding out compiler syntax errors. I think one thing Microsoft has always done extremely well is put out development tools that are superior to any other tools available. Some of the more advanced tools available today rival Microsoft tools, but when attending conferences (and I do attend conferences not geared only to Microsoft), I have observed that usually a majority of developers use Microsoft development tools to get the job done. This is one of the sore spots with Java. Until the last few years, Java's IDEs were not as easy to use as other languages' IDEs. However, if you frequent MSDN TV (http://msdn.microsoft.com) as I do, you will note that many of the leading Microsoft developers use the very Open Source editors mentioned in this chapter and not Visual Studio.NET.

### Key Bindings and Shortcuts

By far the most powerful feature of an editor is key bindings and shortcuts. While these features are often overlooked, they provide greater time savings than any other feature. Editors provide these features in many different ways. VI is probably the most powerful at straight text editing. You can turn a file upside down and backwards with just a few keystrokes. (This can also be dangerous if not used properly!) But some editors have gone the extra mile and have specialized their shortcuts to .NET languages. For instance, a few editors support C# XML commenting much better than others. Of course the most specialized is Visual Studio.NET, and a list of facts and bindings can be found at http://www.sellsbrothers.com/spout/default.aspx?content=archive.htm#vs.net-funfacts.

**NOTE:** For visual studio .NET 2003 users there is a plugin at http://microsoft.com/downloads/detail.aspx?FamilyID=3FF96915-30E5-430E-95B3-621DCCD25150 that lists all key bindings in VS.NET.

### Source Code Management Integration

Most editors today have some sort of integration with Source Control Management (SCM). I am not a big fan of version control that is integrated into IDEs. This is probably because Microsoft's tools have never done a very good job of integration. Because of the level of integration (or lack thereof) in Microsoft's tools, I have developed a preference of just using a separate tool for SCM.

### Multiple Operating System Support

One feature you may not have thought of but should keep in mind when selecting an editor is the operating systems that it supports. As .NET matures on operating systems other than Windows, this editor feature becomes more important. Since many programmers memorize their key bindings and shortcuts, choosing an editor that works the same way on different operating systems eliminates having to learn a new editor and is a big timesaver. Of course this is not a key factor if you know you will always be using a specific OS.

## Emacs

Emacs is a GNU project in and of itself, which means it is free. Emacs also supports many operating systems and languages. I find Emacs easy to use and a very quick editor that is much more powerful than Notepad. Figure 3-1 shows Emacs with the C# plug-in.

Because Emacs did not originate on Windows, some of the common shortcuts (like Ctrl-X for cut and Ctrl-C for copy) are not supported. Ctrl-X is reserved to tell Emacs there is an upcoming command. For instance, Ctrl-X S saves a file. Many of the drop-down menus are consistent with Microsoft programs though. Emacs can integrate with just about any program, from CVS SCM to email.

**TIP:** For a list of Emacs commands, see
http://www.refcards.com/about/emacs.html.

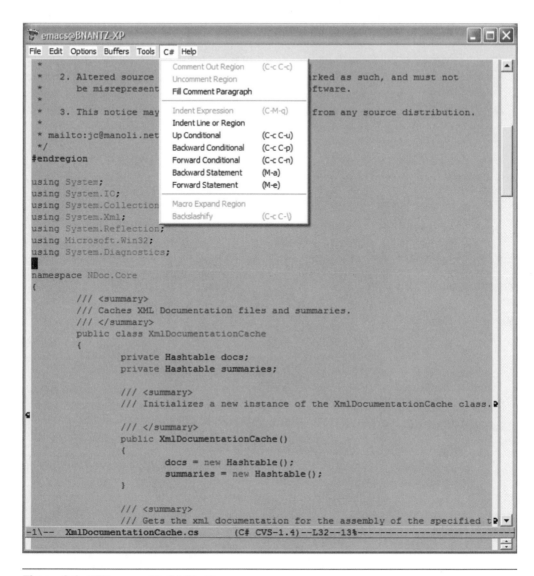

**Figure 3-1** NTEmacs with C# Plug-in.

### Setting Up Emacs

Since Emacs is already installed on most versions of Linux and Unix, I will focus this section on using Emacs on the Windows platform. First you must visit http://www.gnu.org/software/emacs/windows/ntemacs.html and download NTEmacs, which is the Windows port of the GNU project. Installing it is very simple. Then download the C# plug-in from http://www.cybercom.net/~zbrad/DotNet/Emacs/ and unzip it to the [emacsInsallDirectory]\site-lisp. Then copy the zbrad.emacs file to c:\.emacs from the command line. For Linux and other OSs that contain Emacs, you can just use the C# plug-in instructions and skip the Emacs installation steps.

## VIM

VI iMproved (VIM) is a very popular distribution of the powerful VI editor. Available under the GNU GPL license, VIM is downloadable from http://vim.sourceforge.net. VIM is easily installed on either Windows or Linux, and the latest version I downloaded has the C# syntax module already installed. Figure 3-2 shows VIM in action.

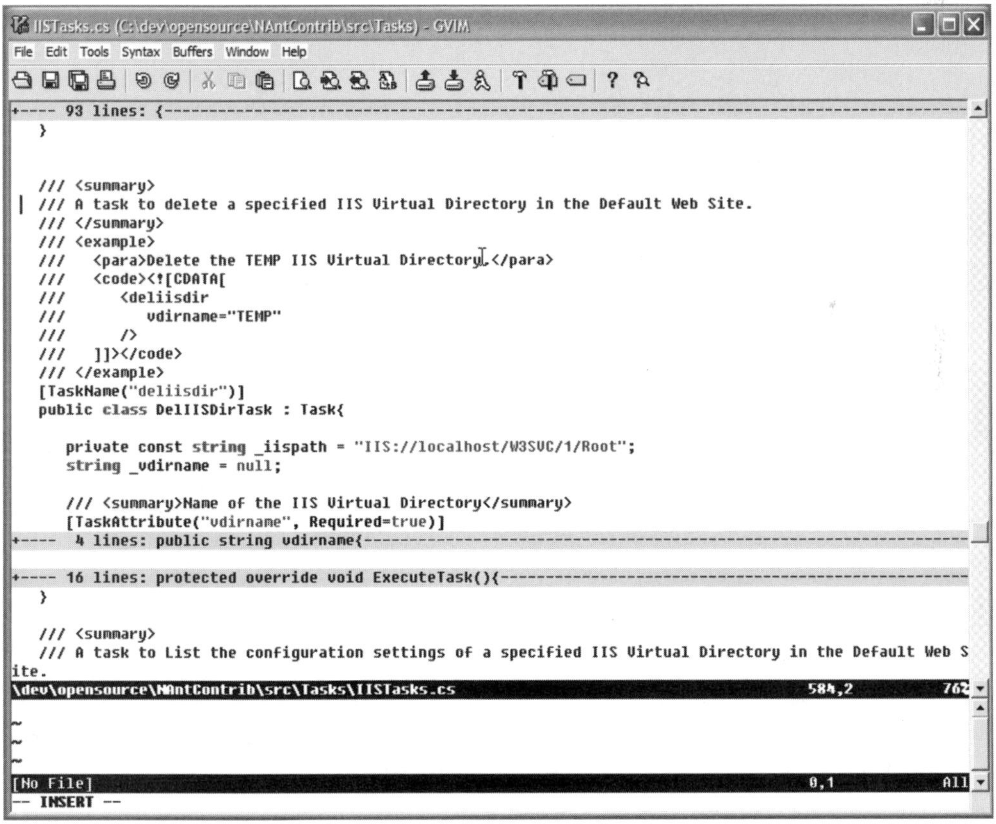

```
+---- 93 lines: {----------------------------------------------------
    }

    /// <summary>
    /// A task to delete a specified IIS Virtual Directory in the Default Web Site.
    /// </summary>
    /// <example>
    ///     <para>Delete the TEMP IIS Virtual Directory.</para>
    ///     <code><![CDATA[
    ///         <deliisdir
    ///             vdirname="TEMP"
    ///         />
    ///     ]]></code>
    /// </example>
    [TaskName("deliisdir")]
    public class DelIISDirTask : Task{

        private const string _iispath = "IIS://localhost/W3SVC/1/Root";
        string _vdirname = null;

        /// <summary>Name of the IIS Virtual Directory</summary>
        [TaskAttribute("vdirname", Required=true)]
+----   4 lines: public string vdirname{-----------------------------------

+---- 16 lines: protected override void ExecuteTask(){-----------------------
    }

    /// <summary>
    /// A task to List the configuration settings of a specified IIS Virtual Directory in the Default Web S
ite.
\dev\opensource\NAntContrib\src\Tasks\IISTasks.cs                    584,2          76%
~
~
~
[No File]                                                            0,1            All
-- INSERT --
```

**Figure 3-2** VIM's C# Editing Capabilities.

VI has two modes of editing a file: Command Mode and Insert Mode. Command mode allows commands such as file saves, file opens, etc. to be executed on the file. Insert mode allows text to be inserted in the file. VIM also has the same wide integration with other programs that Emacs has.

### Command Mode

VIM defaults to command mode. To issue a command, the colon (:) is used. Entering Insert Mode is just one of many commands available in VIM. VIM comes with great documentation, and almost any Unix book has a chapter on VI.

### Insert Mode

Once in Insert Mode, text can be inserted to the currently active buffer. Traditional VI cursor navigation is a little different than most Windows applications. However, VIM has graciously allowed the arrow keys to be used to navigate throughout the buffer.

## Sharp Develop

Sharp Develop (#develop) is an Open Source IDE for developing .NET applications, which itself is written in C# using Windows Forms (see Figure 3-3). #develop is available from http://www.icsharpcode.net/OpenSource/SD along with the GPL licensed code.

#develop uses other Open Source projects in a very interesting way. Internally, #develop uses nAnt (which we will look at in Chapter 4, "Build Automation") for its builds. Sharp Develop goes farther than most other editors by also supporting VB.NET, Resource Files, and Web services. Most editors listed here support XML, Java, C++ and a smattering of other languages, but #develop is the only one I have found so far that supports VB.NET- and .NET-based Webservices so well.

#develop uses other Open Source projects from icsharpcode.com including the CVS C# Module for Software Configuration Management (SCM) integration and #ziplib to zip all the files together into a solution file. Both #CVS and #ziplib are also used by the nAnt project, which goes to show how reusable Open Source is. Sharp Develop uses nAnt, and nAnt uses components of #develop. I am sure that neither team had each other in mind when creating the projects. This is the amazing power of Open Source. Sharp

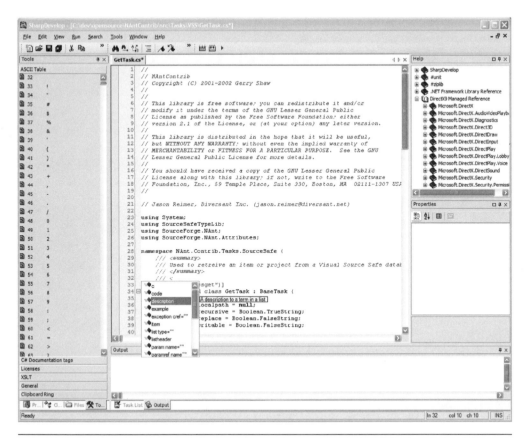

**Figure 3-3** Sharp Develop IDE.

Develop's beautiful user interface uses another Open Source project called Magic (http://www.dotnetmagic.com). Unfortunately, the Magic UI makes a lot of direct Win32 calls and thus prohibits #develop from working on any other platform than Windows, but the Sharp Develop team is working hard to remedy this and has replaced much, if not all, of the Magic Library with Lutz Roeder's CommandBar (http://www.aisto.com/roeder/dotnet/).

## Web Matrix

Although not an Open Source product, Web Matrix does qualify as free software per the FSF's freedom level 0 definition. Web Matrix is freely available (http://www.asp.net/webmatrix) and is the most powerful editor available for

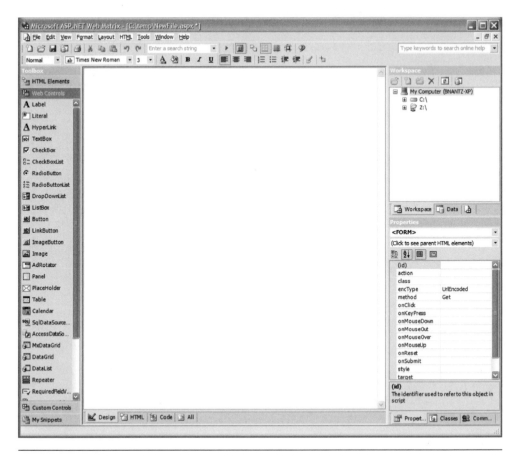

**Figure 3-4** Microsoft Web Matrix.

ASP.NET Webform Applications. This IDE is very similar to the Visual Studio.NET user interface but without the cost. Figure 3-4 demonstrates Microsoft's Web Matrix contribution to the development community.

## Eclipse

Eclipse (http://www.eclipse.org) started out as an IBM project and has become very popular after it became Open Source. Eclipse is by far the most advanced Open Source editor that supports C#. Eclipse integrates well with SCM and is very conducive to a team environment. Eclipse has a very flexible and extensible plug-in infrastructure. Improve Technologies

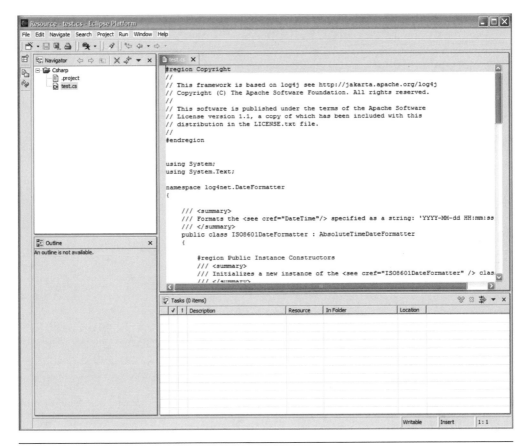

**Figure 3-5** Eclipse IDE.

(http://www.improve-technologies.com) has created one such plug-in that supports C#. Figure 3-5 shows the Eclipse User Interface (UI). Installing and updating the plug-ins as well as the IDE is very easy and straightforward. One advantage to Eclipse is that it runs on all platforms that .Net currently runs on (Windows, Linux, FreeBSD, and Mac OS X, as mentioned in Chapter 2, "Open Source and the .NET Platform").

Although I am rather new to Eclipse, I had no problem adjusting once I understood an overview of the editor. The Eclipse project is made up of basically two aspects: workspaces and workbenches.

### Workspaces

A workspace deals with projects. Projects contain files, folders, and other resources such as SCM. A workspace is a team-focused feature. The workspace is a container for workbenches, the project history (used almost like a mini-SCM to prevent data loss), and markers (used for status of things like error messages and to-do lists). Resources are so well managed that a user can open a workspace and receive the exact same views, plug-ins, tools, and overall project status.

### Workbenches

Workspaces are not really reflected in the user interface and are more of a conceptual thing. Workbenches are what you see when you fire up the UI. Workbenches consist of editors, views, and perspectives.

#### Editor

An editor (top-left portion of Figure 3-5) allows a user to create or modify an object. Most often, an object is a file type like C#, XML, or Java. Editors can be generic text editors or more specific and complex editors supplied by other plug-in tools.

#### View

Views provide information about an object. In Figure 3-5, Navigator, Outline, and Task are all views giving information about the test.cs object. Changes to a view are usually applied immediately, whereas changes to an editor are buffered until the user explicitly saves them. Additional views are supplied by other plug-ins.

#### Perspective

Perspectives are a collection of editor and view configurations. Only one perspective can be viewed in the workbench at a time. Eclipse comes with built-in perspectives (CVS, Install/Update, Java, Java-Browsing, and Resource). Figure 3-5 is in the Resource perspective. The icons on the top left of Eclipse allow you to change perspectives.

**TIP:** After installing Eclipse, you must switch to Install/Update Perspective to install the Improve Technologies C# Plug-in.

## One Last Word on Editors

In presenting and talking about Open Source .NET development, it has become increasingly apparent that developers confuse the features of Visual Studio .NET with the features of .NET in general. I have heard many coders protest that they cannot use Open Source because Visual Studio .NET is their favorite tool and that Edit and Continue is a cool Microsoft .NET feature. This is an example of a feature of the IDE and has nothing to do with .NET development in general. Do not make this mistake! When looking at Open Source projects, you will usually find that some of the developers use Visual Studio .NET. The dead give-away is the solution and project files, but sometimes things are a little more subtle, like the Visual Studio .NET autogenerated source (i.e., IntializeComponents). In addition, many Open Source projects are meant to be used with Visual Studio .NET, and you do not have to choose one way or the other. Visual Studio .NET is an impressive tool, but so is Sharp Develop. In fact, many of the C# refactoring tools featured in Visual Studio .NET 2005 are also found in Sharp Develop, and then some. (Also keep an eye on resharper from Jetbrains for some cool refactoring tools). One of the strengths of Open Source .NET development is that you can use Visual Studio .NET to develop and deploy your application using an Open Source CLI. If you want to see this in action, skip over to Chapter 11, "Web Development," and look at Listing 11.4: the HTML head meta tags give away that this ASP.NET Web page was developed using Visual Studio .NET 2003 and deployed on Linux using Mono! I did this to specifically prove this point. One of the unique features of Open Source .NET is the mixture of Microsoft and Open Source together. Generally, Microsoft is viewed as the biggest opponent to Open Source, and vice-versa. (Recently, though, I think SCO has taken the front seat in this area!) However, Microsoft is opening to the idea of Open Source. In communicating with Microsoft developers and watching some of their demonstrations, I have seen them use projects such as NUnit and SVG#. Obviously, Microsoft is aware of Open Source most evidently by the new MSBuild tool they released and its relation to another Open Source Tool called NAnt (more on this in Chapter 4). Unbelievable history was made with a recent Slashdot.org posting pointing out that Microsoft has released some of their code to Open Source (WTL— http://sourceforge.net/projects/wtl/ and WIX—http://sourceforge.net/projects/wix/). Having somewhat of an unconventional view of both Microsoft and Open Source, this does not surprise me at all.

Microsoft is taking advantage of the most powerful force of Open Source; not the great free tools and reusable components and the money they can save you or the access to the code that many proprietary companies charge extra for if they even allow you to have it. What Microsoft is taking advantage of is learning from other people's ideas and implementations. Behold the power of Open Source: even the largest software company in the world finds it irresistible!

# Documentation Tools

As a rule, I know that all developers love documentation. That is, they love it when they are taking over a project and want to quickly understand the concepts of the design. Unfortunately, most developers and development teams push off documentation until the very last minute. During the frenzy of a software release, most often the documentation is neglected and never completed. In my experience, projects go much more smoothly when the documentation is kept up-to-date incrementally with the code. While I am a firm believer in comments in the code, the most helpful documentation I have seen is usually a document describing the overall intent of the developers' design. Are you using Web services or remoting? Is the project using Single Call or Singleton design patterns? Of course, this can all be determined by looking at the code, but that is not as useful as a design document. The final and perhaps most important use of documentation is to communicate the author's intent. I sometimes find that a design document is very solid while the implementation is not. Documentation helps convey the intent, even if the code does not match the design.

## Open Office

Open Office (Figure 3-6) is an Open Source project available at http://www.openoffice.org. Open Office contains a word processor called Writer, a spreadsheet program called Calc, and a presentation tool called Impress.

Sun Microsystems also repackages a version of Open Office called Star Office in which they add a database to round off the office suite. These tools can read and write to Microsoft Office files and contain very similar functionality. Figure 3-6 shows Open Office on Mandrake Linux (http://www.mandrake-linux.com), but the project also has a Windows port available. Open Office's Writer application is great for creating first-class documentation.

## ArgoUML

Not long after starting in software and documentation, I began to think, "Wouldn't it be great if all the diagrams that are drawn in documentation were standardized!" Then I ran into UML. For a good book on UML, see:

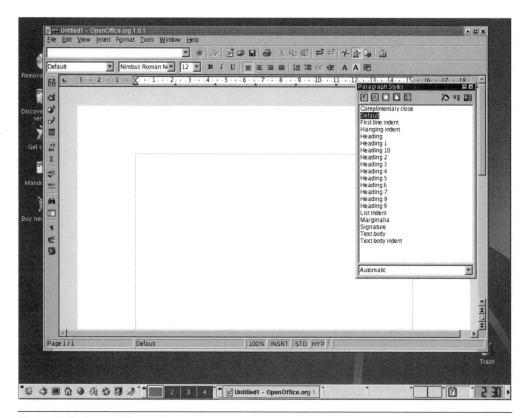

**Figure 3-6** Open Office Writer Application.

*UML Distilled,* Second Edition by Martin Fowler and Kendall Scott, Addison-Wesley

UML is not the only way to go, but I do find it helpful if followed loosely with a little improvising here and there. One thing I dislike about most UML editors is that they restrict what I want to do in my diagram. I am not a supporter of following UML to the tee and then allowing the tool to create my code. I just want to use UML to display my intent in a design document. For this, I like the ArgoUml Open Source project from http://argouml.tigris.com. This Java program, shown in Figure 3-7, runs on both Windows and Linux.

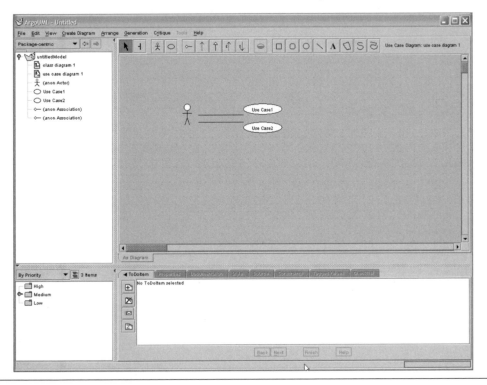

**Figure 3-7** ArgoUml UML Use Case Diagram.

# Source Control Management

Anyone who has done software development for any amount of time has been saved by Source Control Management (SCM), which is sometimes referred to as Source Control or Version Control. There are two predominating SCM systems that are used in Open Source development and are Open Source developments in and of themselves. Both of these systems are widely used and well documented. For more information on SCM and how to use it, see http://www.perforce.com/perforce/bestpractices.html.

## Concurrent Versioning System

Concurrent Versioning System (CVS) is used on most Open Source projects today. CVS is a client-server based application. Setting up the CVS server is very straightforward, and one feature I like best about the CVS is that its repository is file system-based. By that I mean text files and directories are the primary method of versioning used by the repository. This makes the repository very easily transported from machine to machine. CVS runs natively on Unix and Linux but also has a Windows port. The CVS server for Windows is fully functional and feature-rich. The only downfall is the attempted integration with NTLM authentication. But if you use CVS in tandem with Cygwin (http://www.cygwin.com), which brings a Unix-like environment to Windows, many other authentication methods are available. The CVS command-line client is functional but cryptic. Fortunately, there are other client programs available. The two most popular Windows-based CVS clients are WinCVS (http://www.wincvs.org) and TortoiseCVS. WinCVS is a familiar Windows Explorer-type user interface and is easily navigable.

TortoiseCVS takes a different approach, as seen in Figure 3-8. Instead of mimicking Windows Explorer, the TortoiseCVS project (http://www.tortoisecvs.org) developed a Windows shell extension for Explorer.

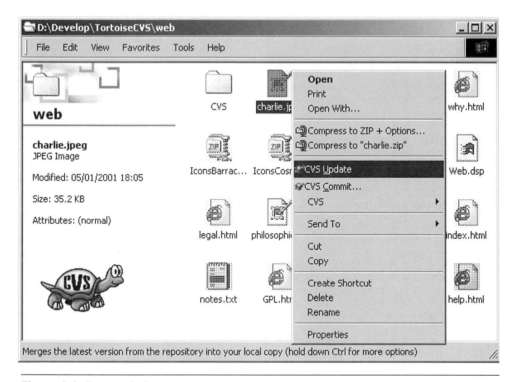

**Figure 3-8** TortoiseCVS.

CVSWeb (http://people.freebsd.org/~fenner/cvsweb/) and ViewCVS (http://viewcvs.sourceforge.net) are two Open Source products that allow your CVS repository to be browsable over the Internet. This can be useful for development teams that are far apart or for Open Source projects where you might just want to take a quick peek at the code.

### Using WinCVS with Sourceforge

If you are truly interested in Open Source, once you start, you will find yourself hooked and will shortly find it necessary to use CVS to commit a change or get the "bleeding edge" stuff. Figure 3-9 shows how to set up WinCVS to check out a project from Sourceforge. Most people who set up a CVS repository also give you the information to check out the Open Source code anonymously.

On each Sourceforge.net project's page is a CVS link that gives you the information on how to access their repository. You can also browse the repository thanks to ViewCVS.

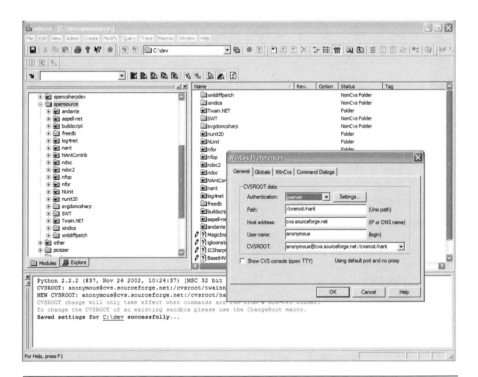

**Figure 3-9**  WinCVS Setting Up to Check Out nAnt from Sourceforge.net.

## Subversion

The creators of CVS got the opportunity that many developers never get. Many development projects I have worked on start out as a prototype and evolve into a product. In the end, I have looked back and said, "I could do that so much better now!" Subversion is the CVS creator's opportunity to start all over and do it better. Subversion adds many new features that the architecture of CVS does not allow, like versioning of the entire repository! Subversion also has a Windows client based on the TortoiseCVS idea called TortoiseSVN (http://tortoisesvn.tigris.org/). Figure 3-10 shows Tortoise CVS in action.

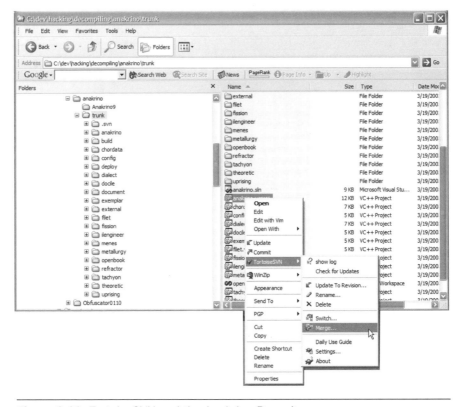

**Figure 3-10** TortoiseSVN and the Anakrino Repository.

### Using Subversion

Anakrino is a very useful tool in .NET development. For more information on the project and what it does, see the description under "Other Development Tools for .NET" at the end of the chapter. Anakrino's author has made the source available to the public via a Subversion repository. Subversion can also be viewed over the Web using the WEBDAV standard.

# Databases

Most applications boil down to one thing: data. Where to store that data is the big question. While XML is becoming more widely accepted, most applications still use a relational database. Large companies invest a lot of time and money into enterprise-level database systems. Despite the large price tags that accompany such database products, more expensive does not always mean better. The Open Source community (and ironically some proprietary companies) have released free database systems that can be used for small and large systems alike.

## MSDE

Microsoft released a version of its expensive SQL Server product called Microsoft Desktop Engine (MSDE); see http://www.microsoft.com/sql/msde/default.asp. MSDE is limited compared to SQL Server in three ways. First, MSDE only allows databases of a size less than 2GB. Second, only 10 concurrent connections are allowed in MSDE. Finally, Microsoft removed the nice administrative and development tools from the MSDE distribution. However, MSDE does integrate very well with Web Matrix's tools. Many companies design product lines based on MSDE with the ability to upgrade the customer to a full version of SQL Server on down the line. Several Open Source administration tools have surfaced for MSDE. SQL-Buddy (http://sqlbuddy.sourceforge.net) is a very similar tool to Query Analyzer and is much more useable (see Figure 3-11) than the OSQL command-line tool shipped with MSDE.

For administering over the Web, ASP Enterprise Manager (http://www.aspenterprisemanager.com) is a very useful tool, as you can see in Figure 3-12.

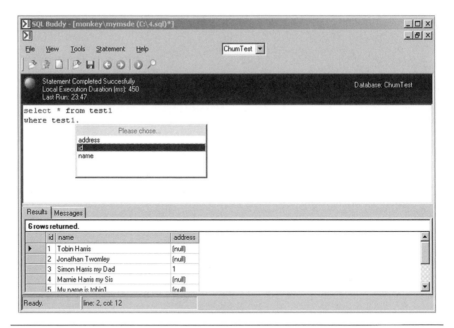

**Figure 3-11** SQLBuddy Administration Tool.

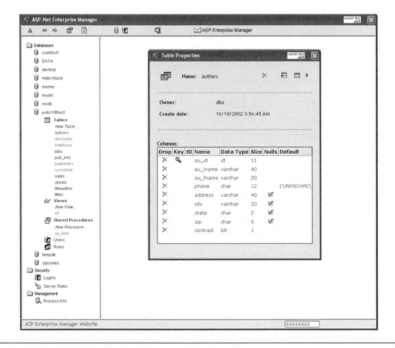

**Figure 3-12** ASP Enterprise Manager Tool.

While MSDE is a free tool (freedom level 0), it is very limited for enterprise-level and other large-scale applications.

**TIP:** Microsoft has just released the beta for SQL Best Practices Analyzer available at http://www.microsoft.com/downloads/details.aspx?familyid= B352EB1F-D3CA-44EE-893E-9E07339C1F22&displaylang=en. This tool is very valuable if you use MSDE or SQL Server 2000 in development.

## MySQL

MySQL (http://www.mysql.com) is an Open Source database that is widely accepted and well supported. MySQL has possibly seen more runtime than any other Open Source database. According to the license (http://www.mysql.com/products/licensing.html), MySQL is great if the product you are developing is also Open Source. To quote their Web site:

> This is our licensing policy in brief: Our software is 100% GPL, and if yours is also 100% GPL (or OSI compliant), then you never have to pay us for the licences. In all other instances, you are better served by our commercial licence. Read the details below!

This is the way the GPL license works. This is one of the reasons that the GNU organization created the LGPL license to allow reuse in a more commercial-friendly way. There are a few projects such as (http://source-forge.net/projects/mysqlnet) that have brought an ADO.NET-managed provider to MySQL. MySQL probably has more administrative tools and utilities than just about any other Open Source database. Figures 3-13 through 3-16 show just a few management tools with their screen shots.

The Java SQL Admin tool has the nice feature of working on all platforms and with almost any database, eliminating the need of learning different tools.

**Figure 3-13**  PHPMyAdmin
http://www.phpmyadmin.net/.

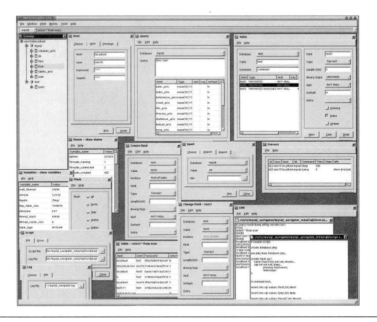

**Figure 3-14**  MySQL Navigator
http://freshmeat.net/projects/mysqlnavigator/?topic_id=68.

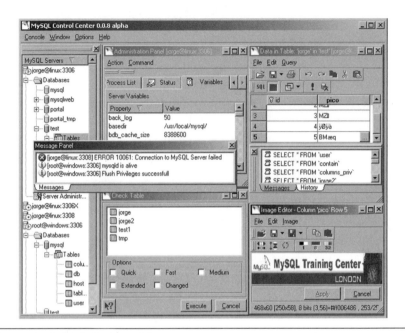

**Figure 3-15** MySQL Control Center
http://www.mysql.com/downloads/mysqlcc.html.

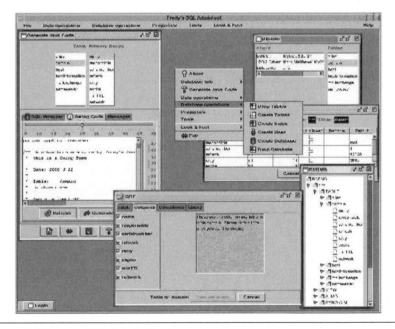

**Figure 3-16** Java SQL Admin Tool
http://freshmeat.net/projects/sql-admin.

## PostgreSQL

One of the ways to choose an Open Source product is based upon the excitement the project creates. I cannot think of a more excited and motivated Open Source project than PostgreSQL (http://www.postgresql.org, . PostgreSQL not only powers the Sourceforge Open Source Web site, but also the .org Internet namespace! The nicest feature of PostgreSQL is its freedom in the licensing. Because the BSD license is used, PostgreSQL is available to Open Source developers and proprietary products. Many ADO.NET drivers have surfaced, but by far the best one is npgSQL (http://gborg.postgresql.org/project/npgsql/projdisplay.php), which we will explore in Chapter 10, "Database Development." PostgreSQL also has many administrative tools available. (See Figures 3-17 through 3-19.)

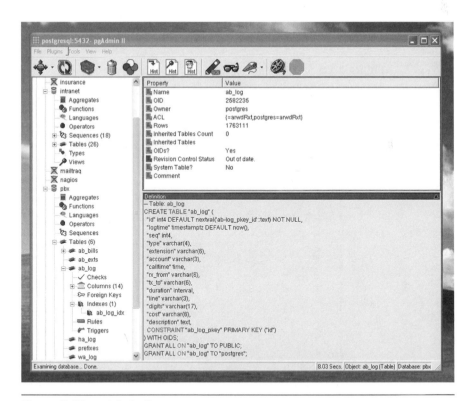

**Figure 3-17** pgAdmin II
http://pgadmin.postgresql.org.

**Figure 3-18** PHPPgAdmin
http://phppgadmin.sourceforge.net.

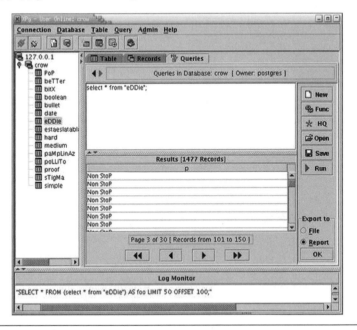

**Figure 3-19** XPg: PostgreSQL Java Admin Tool
http://www.icewalkers.com/Linux/Software/516870/XPg.html.

# Web Servers

Webservers are used quite a bit in .NET development, whether it is for ASP.NET Web applications or Web services. Choosing a Web server that is right for a project is a large task. Remember from Figure 1-2 in Chapter 1 that there are basically two mainstream Web servers, IIS and Apache, and the good news is that they both work with ASP.NET.

## IIS

IIS is Microsoft's Web server that comes free with every Microsoft Professional and Server Windows version. The new version of IIS 6 that comes with Windows 2003 has some significant architectural changes that will increase its speed and robustness considerably.

## Apache

Apache is the Open Source Web server that currently dominates the Internet Web serving space. Apache has a very flexible modular extension architecture (mod) that supports just about any language available. Covalent (http://www.covalent.com) has created a commercial mod that allows ASP.NET to run using Apache. The Mono project also has an ASP.NET Apache mod that is Open Source.

## Cassini

Cassini is Microsoft's Shared Source Web server written entirely in C# using the ASP.NET Hosting API (System.Web.Hosting). Although not robust enough or appropriately licensed to run a production application, Cassini does illustrate the point that you really do not need a monstrous Web server application to host ASP.NET, only a way to simply service client requests.

## XSP

XSP is Mono's Open Source Web server, which, like Cassini, is written entirely in C#. Unlike Cassini, XSP is completely Open Source, so it is licensed to run production applications, but the load balancing is still not robust enough to use in a real application. For this reason, most people using ASP.NET on Linux use Mono's Module for Apache. We will use XSP in Chapter 11 to show ASP.NET and ADO.NET running on Linux.

# Other Development Tools for .NET

These tools really did not fit anywhere else, but they are essential enough to create a sort of catch-all group. Some of these tools are written in .NET; some are not. Some of these tools are Open Source, and some are not. But all are useful for developing .NET applications.

## BugZilla

Occasionally when developing software, you may perhaps run across a bug. All joking aside, we all know that there are so many bugs, feature requests, and third-party bugs in our software that there has to be a system for keeping track of bugs. BugZilla (http://www.bugzilla.org) is the tracking system that the Open Source developers use, most notably the Mozilla team responsible for Netscape 6.x. BugZilla will also send emails to the team members responsible for the bug fixes. BugZilla can also integrate with CVS so that when checking the fixes into CVS, BugZilla will automatically set the bug to be resolved and send an email to the testing team. BugZilla saves its information to a MySQL database and has a convenient Web browser interface.

## Merge and Diff Utilities

A good merge and diff utility is an absolute must in software development. Winmerge (http://winmerge.sourceforge.net) is a good graphical merge and diff utility that can be plugged into most SCM applications for easier differentiation through the versions in SCM. Normal merge and diff utilities usually do not work well with XML. This is because of XML Canocialization, which means that XML files can be structurally different but syntactically identical. For this reason, Microsoft (http://www.gotdotnet.com/team/xml-tools/) and IBM (http://www.alphaworks.ibm.com/tech/xmldiffmerge) have both created a tool that can accurately compare XML files.

### Decompilers and Disassembler

A disassembler is also very useful in low-level development and in creating System class libraries. The .NET framework, Rotor (SSCLI), and Portable.NET all ship with a disassembler.

### Anakrino

Anakrino was the first available .NET decompiler. Available at http://www.saurik.com/net/exemplar/, Jay Freemans' project turned into a widely used tool. Why do you need a decompiler? Well, primarily to look at Runtime Managed code in IL, C#, or VB.Net, to debug low-level problems, and to interpret the code's implementation. I have also found a decompiler greatly helpful when using embedded resources to find the correct path to the resource.

### Reflector

Lutz Roeder's Reflector (http://www.aisto.com/roeder/dotnet/) started out its life as an object browser. Reflector was then expanded into a full-fledged decompiler, and a good one at that (see Figure 3-20).

Reflector's most impressive feature is that it is almost entirely written in .NET code (unlike Anakrino). Users quickly added to Reflector's usefulness by

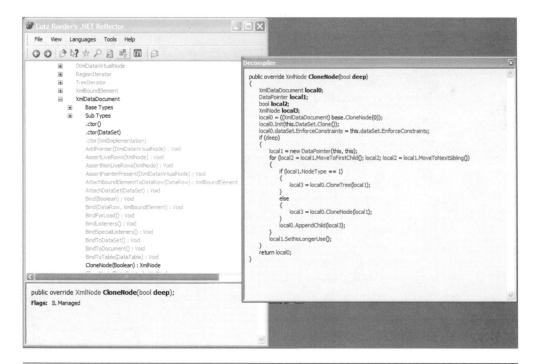

**Figure 3-20** Reflector Decompiler.

adding it to the right-click context menu (http://www.managedcomponents.com/ Weblog/permalink.aspx/0c16e449-ad8b-4f3f-b52b-49c64fb3e3ab) and writing a Visual Studio.NET plug-in for it (http://www.codeproject.com/csharp/ReflectorAddin.asp). The most impressive addins to Reflector are File disassembler (http://www.denisbauer.com) and IL Graph (http://blog.dotnetwiki.orglarchive/ 0001/01/01/287.dspx.

## Obfuscator

After seeing how easily .NET assemblies are decompiled, you may want to consider using an obfuscator. For a more in-depth exploration of how decompilers and obfuscators work, see my book:

*WebService Security in the .NET Platform*
by Apress

Of course obfuscating Open Source would be an exercise in futility. However, if you are using an Open Source product in your proprietary application, or if you are interested in the internal workings of an obfuscator, there is an Open Source obfuscator called QNDObfuscator (http://www.desaware.com/downloadsqndl2.htm).

## Web Service Utilities

.NET Web services are powerful, fairly easy to develop, and somewhat simple to debug on a local machine. Visual Studio.NET does a great job of abstracting you from the ugly facts about Web services. Be careful when developing Web services because they require a different mindset. In DCOM or Remoting, you can use singleton design patterns, where one instance of a service object exists and knows all about the client. Setting attributes on the server object and having the server object maintain the state of the client is pretty common. This is a horrible design for Web services. Web services are mostly stateless (although you can keep sessions) and very costly to do round trips with. Also because XML Serialization is costly and because the structure of the message or data passed is essential, most Web service experts suggest starting with the design of the XML passed over the wire and working back though the layers of Web services to the Object Model. There really are not many tools available today that do this; however, there are numerous articles on how to get this accomplished.

When debugging and hacking a Web service, I have found the following tools to be priceless. Web service Studio is a general application to consume Web services, and it provides a quick way to test your Web methods. For this and other Microsoft Web service tools, visit the gotdotnet Web site at http://www.gotdotnet.com/team/tools/Web_svc/default.aspx.    ProxyTrace, TcpTrace, PcapTrace, YATT, and WSDL Tools (http://www.pocketsoap.com) are all useful in looking at the various layers that go across the wire (i.e., WSDL, SOAP, TCP, etc). Ethereal (http://www.ethereal.com) removes all doubt about who or what is to blame when there is a network problem. This Open Source project is top-notch when it comes to a network sniffer.

Web Service Enhancements allow for security and other Web service standards to be added to a .NET Web service. With the addition of these and some upcoming Web service standards, Web services will be a more stable and more secure inter-platform system.

Newtelligence has released some Open Source Web Service Extensions (http://www.newtelligence.net/wsextensions/index.aspx) to show how easily the asmx Web service architecture can be extended and customized.

## Regular Expressions

Regular expressions (regex) are a powerful and wonderful thing. Sometimes. Figuring out a language's regex idiosyncrasies can be a nightmare, but you cannot search or parse text any better than regex. Whether it is for searching the registry or creating a Regular Expression Validator for ASP.NET, the Regular Expressions Workbench (http://www.gotdotnet.com/Community/UserSamples/Details.aspx?SampleGuid=c712f2df-b026-4d58-8961-4ee2729d7322) or RegexDesigner.NET (http://www.sellsbrothers.com/tools/) will save you time.

## CLRSpy

CLRSpy (http://www.gotdotnet.com/Community/UserSamples/Details.aspx?SampleGuid=C7B955C7-231A-406C-9FA5-AD09EF3BB37F) is a great tool to help understand the inner workings of the .NET runtime, especially when you are working with Platform Invoke (P/Invoke) or Com Interop. Allocation Profiler (http://www.gotdotnet.com/Community/UserSamples/Details.aspx?SampleGuid=36a3e666-6877-4c26-b62d-bfd7cb3154ac) is very useful in learning how Garbage Collection works. And Dependency Walker (http://www.gotdotnet.com/Community/UserSamples/Details.aspx?SampleGuid=d5e6ae32-0ed3-41d7-b731-8bdf34c13833) helps to track down missing dependencies.

## Vil

Vil is a very interesting tool that graphically tells you about your coding tendencies. You can download it from http://www.1bot.com. This command-line tool analyzes .NET assemblies, provides metrics, and allows for queries regarding the Object Oriented design. This tool can point out code that needs to be refactored and help you better execute the coding of your architectural design. Vil can tell you how many try/catch blocks you use, class/struct/enumeration counts, local variable counts, events params, and much more!

# Summary

Just as when choosing an Open Source project to use, choosing a programming platform can be a daunting task. The momentum surrounding an Open Source project or programming platform can be used as a thermometer to help your decision. Because of all the tools that are available (this chapter is a small subset of the most valuable tools in the .NET tool chest), all the .NET language bindings to choose from, the Open Source communities' reception of .NET, and the number of CLI implementations, I believe .NET is here to stay and on pace to be the most popular programming platform available today.

# CHAPTER 4

# Build Automation

*An important part of any software development process is getting reliable builds of the software. Despite its importance, we are often surprised when this isn't done."*

*—Continuous Integration (http://www.martinfowler.com/articles/ continuousIntegration.html)*

*By Matthew Foemmel and Martin Fowler*

## Introduction

I have seen some of the most bizarre things when it comes to automating builds. I have used many different tools to try to automate a build. The result is usually a frail build that is not easily extendable and only works on a few machines. This is why most companies I have worked with have resorted to always using a single machine for the build. This machine usually has a defined set of service packs and development tools installed, which becomes a maintenance nightmare. This is a disaster because now you (and if you are lucky, one other guy) are the only people that can build the product and on only one machine. If that machine goes down, or if you want to go on vacation, you are out of luck! Tons of time could be wasted on creating a build infrastructure that is portable and extendable. Luckily, NAnt, a .NET port of a Java tool Ant, is freely available to use.

This chapter is meant to get you up and running in one day. Many of the examples can be used as templates for any build. For instance, you can take the Master Build example tied together and build both the Windows Application example and the Web Services example to create quite an application. For advanced applications that have hundreds of projects, you can see the need for a tool like NAnt.

## What NAnt Is

NAnt is a fast, extensible, easily readable, automated build tool. NAnt makes a large-scale .NET project possible and manageable using only the freely available .NET SDK or any other CLI Implementation discussed in Chapter 2, "Open Source and the .NET Platform." Because a NAnt build file is XML, your build is platform-independent and easily editable with any text editor. Microsoft also saw the advantage of using XML and modeled the structure of Visual Studio.NET's Solution and Project files using XML. The use of XML in builds allows tools to interact in a more advanced and dynamic way using XSL to change the build on-the-fly. NAnt is compatible with Mono, .NET, and the SSCLI and therefore works with Windows, Linux, FreeBSD, and Mac OS X.

## What NAnt Is Not

NAnt is not a magical solution. If proper software engineering techniques are not applied, NAnt can actually complicate a project. However, this could be said of any software engineering tool (such as Software Configuration Management). Even though NAnt is a powerful tool, it still requires good communication and organization of the development team. Everyone on the team should know NAnt, but at least one person on the team should specialize in NAnt and be the coordinator for the automated build.

NAnt is not an XML version of MAKE (http://www.gnu.org/software/make/make.html). NAnt and MAKE have similar goals and even some similar nomenclature; however, they really are more different than alike. A NAnt target is closest to a MAKE ghost target. A MAKE target is assumed to reside in a separate file. A NAnt target (see Figure 4-1) is assumed to exist in the same file as the project. NAnt creates target dependencies and allows the tasks (Figure 4-1) to determine the file dependencies. This is much different in MAKE.

NAnt is not meant to replace an Integrated Development Environment (IDE). IDEs are a definite time-saver. A strong point of Microsoft development has always been high quality IDEs. However recently even Microsoft's Consulting Division and an internal division in Redmond announced an automated build technology called BuildIt, which is covered later in this chapter, becuase Microsoft now realizes the advantage of an IDE as well as scriptable builds. GNU also saw the importance of a scriptable build, and

Portable.NET created csAnt. NAnt is meant to free you from a specific IDE. In Chapter 2, I showed several IDEs for C#. NAnt allows everyone on the team to use his or her favorite IDE. This actually saves time in that everyone does not have to abandon the editor they are familiar with and waste time learning a new one.

NAnt is not a scripting language, although at first you may be tempted to think of it as such. It is easy in the first few projects to create builds that are very script-like. I hope the best practices shown here that result from my experience will help you along faster.

NAnt is not Ant. NAnt is the .NET port of the Apache Java project Ant (see http://ant.apache.org). Some of the Ant documentation can be helpful, but a lot of Ant was designed to compile Java code. The Java compiler puts strict restrictions on the class naming matching the directory structure of your code. This is not true with C#, and NAnt builds are simpler because of it. NAnt has a lot of .NET-specific tasks that require an in-depth knowledge of the .NET runtime.

## Standard Build Goals

Before I get too deep into NAnt and building, I thought I should take the time to clarify some terminology and define some of the philosophy I use in build projects. First, terminology. A build is an automated way of retrieving source code from a repository (normally Source Control Management or SCM), versioning both the code and SCM, compiling the code into product, and creating a redistributable package. The need for this to be automated and repeatable is paramount. If a feature is added or a bug fixed, the entire build process has to be restarted. In order to create a reliable product, the redistributable package must be created in the exact same way each time for the functionality to remain the same, except for the intentionally changed functionality for the feature or bug fix. To the users of a build, there are configurations and targets. Configurations could include a Release build optimized for execution speed, a Release build optimized for package size, a Release build with checked debugging information, or possibly a Debug build for developmental testing. Each of these build configurations is useful to achieve a specific goal. For instance, if a bug is very reproducible in a Release build and a developer can not reproduce it in a Debug build, then a Checked Release build with some debugging information could be helpful in tracking down the cause of the error. Switching between configurations should be simple and intuitive. Targets give the build user callable functionality, allowing the user to operate upon the

> build. A "build" target, for example, will allow the user to build the project in the specified configuration. Another useful target is "clean," which removes any output from the build. Some builds may even have an "install" target to create redistributables for the product. Second, the philosophy I use when creating a build is to make the build useful to the developer. For instance, I do not require the developer to build the entire product just to build his specific project. On a large product, a build could take hours. If a developer is working on a simple fix or a small project, do not require him to build for the entire project. Just let him build only what he needs by using the proper configuration and targets.

## Using NAnt

Now that you are convinced that you need to use NAnt, how do you use the thing, anyway? Well, it is easy to get started with a few projects, but as your project gets larger, the build will get more complicated. A little design time up front will save you a lot of time in the end. There are basically only three important concepts to understanding NAnt build projects:

- Task – A single predefined build action.
- Target – A user-defined collection of tasks.
- Dependency – Relationships or requirements between targets.

Figure 4-1 illustrates how these concepts interact with one another.

**NOTE:** Appendixes A and B list the built-in tasks available in NAnt and NAntContrib.

The following snippet is a simple Hello World program in C# that we will build using NAnt:

```
using System;
namespace Simple
{
    class HelloWorld
    {
```

```
        [STAThread]
        static void Main(string[] args)
        {
            Console.WriteLine("Hello World.");
        }
    }
}
```

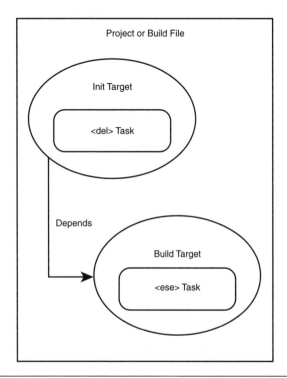

**Figure 4-1** Conceptual View of a NAnt Build File.

Here is the NAnt build file for compiling the obligatory Hello World application:

```
<project name="Simple" default="build">
   <target name="build" description="compiles the source code">
       <csc target="exe" output="helloworld.exe">
           <sources>
               <includes name="HelloWorld.cs"/>
           </sources>
       </csc>
```

```
    </target>
</project>
```

While this may seem like overkill compared to a simple compiler command line (below), as the builds get more complex and add multiple references to dependent assemblies, you will quickly see the usefulness of a NAnt build over a command-line compile.

```
csc /target:exe helloworld.cs
```

In order to build the Hello World C# file using the NAnt build here, you must know how to execute NAnt.

## Executing NAnt

Listing 4.1 shows the output if you were to run nAnt.exe –help.

**Listing 4.1** NAnt Command-Line Parameters

```
usage: nant [options] [target [target2 [target3] ... ]]
options:
  -help                       print this message
  -projecthelp                print project help information
  -buildfile:<file>           use given buildfile
  -find                       search parent directories for
buildfile
  -D:<property>=<value>    use value for given property
  -k                               defaultframework.
  -verbose                    displays more information during build
process
  -logger:                    use given class name as logger
  -logfile:, -l:              use value as name of log output file
A file ending in .build will be used if no buildfile is specified.
```

By default, NAnt looks for a .build file in the current directory to build. If one does not exist or if more than one .build file exists, then the –buildfile option must be used to specify the exact location of the intended build file.

The –D options allow users to set properties that are used in the build. This allows the user to override the default values of properties in the build.

A NAnt project allows for setting a default target to be run if no target is specified. By using inter-target dependencies, a number of targets could automatically be executed. Alternatively, the NAnt tool allows a sequential list of targets to be specified at execution.

## Why Use NAnt?

NAnt is not the only option for scriptable building of .NET projects. Some other XML-based build tools are Ant, csAnt, and BuildIt. The correct tool completely depends upon your situation and your team's goals. Each of these tools is completely free and comes with source. As always, take the time to review the license to ensure it fits with your intended usage.

### Ant

Ant is the original Java-built tool on which NAnt is based. Created by the Apache team, Ant was originated merely as a way to effectively build the Apache Tomcat project. The popularity of an XML-encoded build file took off from there, and today, practically every Java IDE uses Ant. Ant does have a few .NET compiler tasks built in that can be used to build .NET projects. However, according to active members of the Ant development team, this is mainly to support building .NET applications to test .NET and Java interoperation. Therefore, Ant is mainly focused on Java and probably will not expand its support of .NET to the extent of other .NET build tools.

### csAnt

Southern Storm Software, Pty Ltd. in accordance with GNU created Portable.NET. In order to build the project, csAnt was created. It has limited functionality but is very similar to Ant functionality. csAnt does not have nearly the functionality and community support that NAnt has but is another perhaps more portable build tool that is written in the C language and therefore does not rely on an existing .NET CLI implementation.

### BuildIt

Microsoft teamed with Sapient Corporation (http://www.sapient.com/) to create an automated Visual Studio.NET build tool. This, of course, requires that you use Visual Studio.NET. Using VS.NET can be a slight drawback, in that it requires the user to set all dependencies, targets, and configurations in the Visual Studio.NET (VS.NET) solution file. For large projects, this can be cumbersome. If your team is using VS.NET, you should know that the same functionality of building from the solution or project file is available using NAnt's slingshot or solution task. However, if the team is not committed to learning a new tool (this author has found NAnt much more intuitive than VS.NET's build configuration), then BuildIt can be a good compromise. BuildIt has good integration with Visual Source Safe and allows build logging and emailing of results.

### MSBuild

Microsoft unveiled at their last Professional Developers Conference (PDC) their new build tool called MSBuild. MSBuild is an XML-based build file similar to NAnt and Ant. However, the format of the XML file and the fundamentals of the new build system are not as similar as they first look. MSBuild does use tasks, targets, and properties in a way similar to NAnt, but it adds the concept of items. The way MSBuild handles dependencies and various other things is also quite different from NAnt. Visual Studio.NET will use MSBuild as the project file format for both C# and VB.NET projects, and MSBuild will be freely available in the .NET SDK. While these are advantages for MSBuild over NAnt, NAnt has many advantages over MSBuild. First, it is Open Source and therefore useable in a proprietary build product. Second, NAnt currently has more tasks available for use in your targets. Third, it is unclear if MSBuild will support earlier versions of .NET and Visual Studio.NET.

## Other Build Tools

There are miscellaneous build tools, both free and commercial, that will also build .NET projects, including FinalBuilder (http://www.atozedsoftware.com/finalbuilder/), Visual Build Professional (http://www.kinook.com/VisBuildPro/), and MegaBuild (http://mywebpages.comcast.net/bmenees/index.html). While these build tools are more graphically oriented, they offer no more functionality and in most cases far less functionality than NAnt. Chapter 7, "Continuous Integration," will offer much of the graphical functionality of these miscellaneous build tools.

Overall, NAnt is the best tool for building .NET projects. Even for developers who are familiar with MAKE, I would suggest switching to NAnt. MAKE is not transformable, easily parsable, or extensible. MAKE also does not have .NET-specific tasks built in. If you are used to using an IDE to do your build, NAnt is going to make your life much easier. Although IDEs are time-savers, to change something advanced like building a release build with debugging information to get line numbers is very difficult to explain to someone. It is much easier to just design it into a NAnt build using properties and make it configurable. A NAnt build then should be able to be run on any machine repeatedly. I have found that even the most resistant developers fall in love with NAnt because it is just so cool. Who can resist an XML-based build file that is easy to use and amazingly fast?

# Data Types

In addition to the syntax of the build files, there are several useful datatypes in NAnt. These datatypes can change the way a task functions and can simplify complex actions.

### Fileset

Frequently, a build operates on a file: it compiles a file, copies a file, deletes a file, and so forth. A fileset is a set or collection of files to apply an operation to. For example, look at the copy task's use of filesets:

```
<copy todir="release">
    <fileset basedir="bin">
        <includes name="*.*"/>
        <excludes name="*.pdb"/>
        <excludes name="*.obj"/>
    </fileset>
</copy>
```

This code will copy all files except .pdb and .obj from the bin directory to the release directory.

## Patternset

Patternsets allow modification to a fileset based on a pattern (see Table 4.1).

**Table 4.1**  Patternsets

| Pattern | Description |
| --- | --- |
| * | Wildcard, matches 1 or more characters |
| ? | Wildcard, matches 1 character |
| ** | When used for a directory, this includes all subdirectories. |
| Trailing / or \ | Implies a trailing ** |

Applying a patternset to the csc's (C# compiler task) sources fileset is demonstrated in Listing 4.2:

**Listing 4.2**  Patternsets with the csc Task

```
    <csc target="library" debug="${debug}"
output="${releasedir}\LogKit.Net.dll" doc="${docdir}\LogKit.Net.xml">
        <sources basedir="..\src\org\apache\log">
            <includes name="**/*.cs" />
        </sources>
        <references>
            <includes name="System.dll" />
            <includes name="System.Collections.dll" />
            <includes name="System.Data.dll" />
        </references>
                    <arg value="/nowarn:1591" />
    </csc>
```

This compiles all C# files under the ..\src\org\apache\log directory.

## Optionsets

An optionset is an alternative way for a task to receive input. Typically, tasks use XML attributes to receive input, but this doesn't always make sense. Consider the SlingshotTask's use of an optionset:

```
<slingshot solution="MySolution.sln" format="nant"
output="MySolution.build">
    <parameters>
        <option name="build.basedir" value="..\bin"/>
    </parameters>
</slingshot>
```

## Environment Variables

By using the <sysinfo> task, you can access any environment variables in the build. Listing 4.3 is an example of using system environment variables:

**Listing 4.3**  The sysinfo Task

```
<sysinfo verbose="true"/>
<copy todir="${sys.env.BASEDIR}">   _ Copy to a directory set in
    <fileset basedir="bin">              the environment.
        <includes name="*.dll"/>
        <includes name="*.exe"/>
    </fileset>
</copy>
```

## Properties

Properties allow for changing the behavior of a build, just as properties on a component alter that component's behavior (see Table 4.2). In NAnt, properties can also be used as variables to store information that can be read or set by the build at runtime or by the user when running the NAnt utility (see the section "Executing NAnt" in this chapter).

**Table 4.2** Built-in NAnt Properties

| Property Name | Explanation |
| --- | --- |
| ${nant.version} | The version of NAnt. |
| ${nant.filename} | The full path to the NAnt assembly. |
| ${nant.location} | The location of the nant.exe file. |
| ${nant.onsuccess} | Properties to target names that you want executed when the build file is done. |
| ${nant.onfail} | Properties to target names that you want executed when the build file is done. |
| ${nant.project.basedir} | The absolute path of the project's basedir. |
| ${nant.project.buildfile} | The absolute path of the buildfile. |
| ${nant.project.name} | The name of the project. |
| ${nant.project.default} | The name of the project's default target. |
| ${nant.task.°} | Each task available to nant has a "true" value, e.g., nant.task.copy. |
| ${nant.settings.currentframework.frameworkassemblydirectory} | The fully qualified path to the current .NET framework global aasembly cache. |
| ${nant.settings.currentframework.name} | The name of the current .NET framework. |
| ${nant.settings.currentframework.version} | The current .NET framework version. |
| ${nant.settings.currentframework.description} | The description of the current .NET framework. |
| ${nant.settings.currentframework.csharpcompilername} | The C# compiler for the current CLI framework. |
| ${nant.settings.currentframework.resgentoolname} | The resgen tool for the current CLI framework. |

**Table 4.2** Built-in NAnt Properties (cont.)

| Property Name | Explanation |
|---|---|
| ${nant.settings.currentframeworkframeworkdirectory} | The fully qualified path to the current .NET framework directory. |
| ${nant.settings.currentframework.runtimeengine} | The runtime engine for the current CLI framework. |
| ${nant.settings.currentframework.sdkdirectory} | The fully qualified path to the current .NET sdk directory. |

### Handling Multiple Versions of .NET

Through the use of the nant.settings.currentframework.version property, you can safeguard your builds against a user who has the wrong version of the .NET runtime.

### References

The version of .NET used to compile mainly affects what .NET framework assemblies are used as references in the compiler task. Listing 4.4 shows a common use of reference filesets.

**Listing 4.4** Filesets

```
<csc target="library" output="${output}" debug="${debug}"
define="${define}" doc="${doc}">
    <sources>
      <includes name=" *.cs" />
    </sources>
    <references>
      <includes name="System.dll" />
      <includes name="System.Data.dll" />
      <includes name="System.Drawing.dll" />
      <includes name="System.Windows.Forms.dll" />
      <includes name="System.Xml.dll" />
      <includes name="Accessibility.dll" frompath="true" />
```

```
        <includes name="System.Web.dll" />
        <includes name="System.Web.Services.dll" />
    </references>
</csc>
```

For a second, I want to take a brief sidetrack and talk about how NAnt knows to compile C# code. Currently, the NAnt csc task wraps the command-line compiler, but how does it know where to find that compiler, you might ask? That is a great question. The csc task in Listing 4.5 will compile using the default framework version of .NET (or other CLI implementation) that is specified in the nant.exe.config. The first frameworkinfo element is complete, and the following ones are abbreviated just to show you the CLI frameworks supported by NAnt.

**Listing 4.5**  Configuration File Showing NAnt CLI Framework Support

```
    <nantsettings
        defaultframework="net-1.0">
        <frameworks>
            <frameworkinfo
                name = "net-1.0"
                description = "Microsoft .NET Framework 1.0"
                version = "1.0.3705"
                runtimeengine=""
                csharpcompilername = "csc"
                basiccompilername = "vbc"
                jsharpcompilername = "vjc"
                jscriptcompilername = "jsc"
                resgenname = "resgen">
                <sdkdirectory useregistry="true"
regkey="Software\Microsoft\.NetFramework" regvalue="sdkInstallRoot" />
                <frameworkdirectory useregistry="true"
regkey="Software\Microsoft\.NetFramework" regvalue="InstallRoot" />
                <frameworkassemblydirectory useregistry="true"
regkey="Software\Microsoft\.NetFramework" regvalue="InstallRoot"/>
            </frameworkinfo>
            <frameworkinfo
                name = "net-1.1"
                description = "Microsoft .Net Framework 1.1"
                ...
            </frameworkinfo>
```

```
    <frameworkinfo
        name = "netcf-1.0"
        description = "Microsoft .Net Compact Framework Framework
1.0"
        ...
    </frameworkinfo>
    <frameworkinfo
        name = "mono-1.0"
        description = "gnome projects port of the .Net Framework"
        ...
    </frameworkinfo>
</frameworks>
```

**NOTE:** Regarding the nant.exe.config in Listing 4.5, if you get an error from NAnt saying that it cannot find the DefaultFramework, then you know right where to go: the config file.

OK, back to the references discussion. The references in Listing 4.4 would be the same as using the asis parameter and setting it to true, as seen here:

```
<includes name="System.dll" asis="true" />
```

Unfortunately, filesets do not handle relative paths very well, so if you are using a third-party assembly like Log4Net, then you have to do something different. The following relative path will NOT always work, depending upon what the basepath is.

```
<includes name="..\..\log4net.dll" />
```

In order to include this assembly reference, you can either use the basedir property on the references fileset:

```
<references basedir="${build.dir}/bin">
    <includes name=" log4net.dll" />.
</references>
```

use the frompath property on the include node:

```
<includes name=" log4net.dll" frompath="true" />
```

or read the path from the environment variables:

```
<includes name=" ${sys.env.AssemblyDirectory}\log4net.dll" />
```

### Handling Multiple Versions of NAnt

Similarly to multiple versions of .NET, you may run into a problem with a user who has an outdated version of NAnt. Depending on the tasks used in your build, this could either produce the wrong result or cause a NAnt build exception for a missing task. If this is a concern, check the nant.version property and ensure it is at least the version you require.

### Embedded Scripting

Although not technically a property, the example of Embedded Scripting fits well under this section of the chapter. For the truly advanced user who wants functionality that NAnt just does not support, there is an answer: Embedded Scripting. NAnt allows for embedded C# and VB.NET scripts to be executed within a target. Most often the base tasks within NAnt are sufficient enough, and embedded scripts are not needed. The danger of embedded scripts is that the code is obviously unique and has the potential for bugs. In contrast, the tasks that are intrinsic to NAnt have a considerable runtime and testing user base. Listing 4.6 is from the NAnt WIKI site (http://nant.sourceforge.net/wiki/) and lists all available properties.

**Listing 4.6**  NAnt Scripting

```
<script language="C#">
   <code><![CDATA[
     public static void ScriptMain(Project project)
     {
         Log.WriteLine("Properties:");
         foreach(DictionaryEntry entry in project.Properties)
         {
             Log.WriteLine(string.Format("{0}={1}", entry.Key,
entry.Value));
         }
     }
```

```
    ]]></code>
</script>
```

### Error Handling

When an error occurs in a NAnt build, the build automatically fails and does not continue. The output to the command window will indicate what line the build failed on. If the failure is a compiler error, the offending code's line number is given. NAnt provides two special properties for handling error conditions in a build project: nant.onsuccess and nant.onfailure. Listing 4.7 shows the use of nant.onfailure to email a failure report.

**Lisitng 4.7**  Emailing Failures

```
<property name='nant.onfailure' value='emailfailure'>
<target name="email failure">
        <mail
                    from="buildmaster "
                    tolist="devgroup@yourdomain.com"
                    cclist=""
                    subject="Build Failed"
                    message=" Build Failed "
                    mailhost="mail.yourdomain.com" />
</target>
```

The value of the onfailure task is the name of task in the existing project that you want to execute on a failure.

### Logging

NAnt uses Log4Net (see Chapter 8, "Application Logging") to log to an output file. This will log the messages that are put to the screen. Some tasks may include more logging information than others, but you can always use the <echo> task to indicate milestones in the build. Used together with error handling, Listing 4.7 can be extended to include emailing the results of the build, as in Listing 4.8.

**Listing 4.8**  Emailing Build Results

```
<property name='nant.onfailure' value='failure'>
<property name='nant.onfailure' value='success>
<target name="success">
    <property name='emailsubjet' value='Build Success'>
    <property name=' emailmessage' value='Build Succeeded.'>
    <call target="email">
</ target>
<target name="failure">
    <property name='emailsubjet' value='Build Failed'>
    <property name=' emailmessage' value='Build Failure See attached
log.'>
    <call target="email">
</ target>
<target name="email ">
    <mail
                from="buildmaster "
                tolist="devgroup@yourdomain.com"
                cclist=""
                subject="${emailsubjet}"
                message=" ${emailmessage}"
                file="build.log"
                mailhost="mail.yourdomain.com" />
</target>
```

To set the location of the build file's log, look back to the section "Executing NAnt."

# SCM Integration

NAntContrib supports Microsoft Visual Source Safe (http://msdn. microsoft.com/ssafe/), CVS (http://www.cvshome.org/), VAULT (http://www. sourcegear.com/vault/index.asp), Star Team (http://www.borland.com/ starteam/), and Perforce (http://www.perforce.com). In extending NAnt later in this chapter, we will add subversion (http://subversion.tigris.org/) support. This integration allows your build to check files in and out of source control and label the repository. This is useful for automatically checking in and labeling a successful build. Depending on your SCM structure, NAnt can be useful in checking out only the specific code needed. If there are large, time-consuming projects in SCM that are not needed, it is worthwhile to have the build check out specific paths in SCM rather than checking out a base project recursively. Listing 4.9 is an example of checking out projects from Visual Source Safe (VSS):

**Listing 4.9** Using Visual Source Safe Integration

```
<target name='get'>
<vssget localpath="${3rdparty}\Genghis"
        recursive="true"
        dbpath="${ssdir}"
        user="${ssuser}"
        password="${sspassword}"
        replace="true"
        path="$/3rd_party/Genghis"
        writable="true"/>
<vssget localpath="${3rdparty}\Logkit_net"
        recursive="true"
        dbpath="${ssdir}"
        user="${ssuser}"
        password="${sspassword}"
        replace="true"
        path="$/3rd_party/Logkit_net"
        writable="true"/>
    <vssget localpath="${software}"
            recursive="true"
            dbpath="${ssdir}"
            user="${ssuser}"
            password="${sspassword}"
            replace="true"
            path="$/clarity"
            writable="true"/>
</target>
```

Listing 4.9 shows the NAnt get task recursively getting everything under the software directory but only what it needs (Genghis and LogKit.NET) from the many available projects under 3rdparty. This greatly shortens the amount of time required to retrieve the code from SCM and therefore shortens the entire build time.

## NAnt Best Practices

Here are a few helpful hints I have compiled from my experience with NAnt:

- Isolate destructive clean targets and constructive setup tasks.
- Use single quotes around XML attributes to allow double quotes to be embedded for command-line parameters.
- Everything hinges on your directory structure. Depending on your SCM system, changing this in the future might be painful, so put some thought into it now.
- Although NAnt can integrate with most SCMs (such as Visual Source Safe, CVS, and others), use a script to check out the build scripts. This allows the build scripts to reside in a convenient repository and more importantly to be under Source Control themselves. Use the SCM for checking in and labeling.
- Standardize on a version of NAnt. The easiest way is to store the build tools also in Source Control. This would allow the entire team to use the same version of the build, and all will upgrade at the same time. Nothing is worse than trying to debug a build problem only to find out a person was using the wrong tools or an old version of the build. Use the nant.version properties.
- Separate the deployment version of NAnt from any development versions of NAnt.
- Use the nant.settings.currentframework property to ensure that the proper version of the .NET runtime exits on the target machine. If the proper version of the .NET runtime is not there, fail the build, but have this functionality as a configurable command-line property.
- For large projects with multiple sub-projects, use a standard set of targets.
- Use a properties file.
- Run your build and upgrade NAnt often. This allows the maintenance work for Unit Tests and makes keeping synchronized with NAnt changes a small task.
- Use the replace task to increment build numbers.
- Use the SMTP task to email build results.

## Migrating to NAnt

Here are some tips to help you implement a NAnt build for existing projects.

1. Check everything into SCM.
2. Make sure everything builds.
3. Label SCM.
4. Refactor directories.
5. Create the NAnt build.
   If you are currently using Visual Studio.NET, try out the slingshot or solution task. This can give you a starting point but is not as good as designing your own build because this still relies too heavily on the IDE to set build properties.
6. Use verbose mode and logging properties until the build is stable.

## Examples

Using NAnt can be intimidating. That is why I would like to include several examples of building different types of .NET projects. I will try to show off as many of the built-in NAnt tasks as possible. My goal is to give many practical build scripts that can be used in building real life applications.

### Simple Exe

Listing 4.10 demonstrates the simplest of NAnt build projects to create an exe file. This simple build is an example included in the NAnt distribution:

**Listing 4.10**  Simple Build

```
<project name="Simple" default="build">
    <property name="debug" value="true"/>
    <target name="clean" description="remove all generated files">
        <delete file="Simple.exe" failonerror="false"/>
        <delete file="Simple.pdb" failonerror="false"/>
    </target>
    <target name="build" description="compiles the source code">
```

```
        <csc target="exe" output="Simple.exe" debug="${debug}">
            <sources>
                <includes name="Simple.cs"/>
            </sources>
        </csc>
    </target>
</project>
```

Starting from the top, the project name is very fitting: Simple. The default target that will be executed is "build." The next line is an example of a property that will be used later in the project. The next target, "clean," will never be executed unless specified from the command line. The build target executes the csc task using the debug property set previously and outputs a file called simple.exe, which is an exe file. Notice the use of filesets for specifying the source files. However, there are a few issues that I have with this simplistic project. First, I would change the "includes" line of the source's fileset to use patternsets. Changing the line to <includes name="*.cs"/> would allow you to add files to the directory and project without affecting the build. This is very useful when adding a component, especially because each Windows Form in an executable typically has its own .cs file. Usually, a file only contains a single class and any related functionality. I would also add a few more properties to make the project much more reusable (Listing 4.11).

**Listing 4.11** Simple EXE Build with Properties

```
<project name="Simple" default="build">
    <sysinfo verbose='true'/>
    <tstamp/>
    <property name="project.name" value="simple"/>
    <property name="target.type" value="exe"/>
    <property name="output.type" value="exe"/>
    <property name="define" value="DEBUG;TRACE" />
    <property name="debug" value="true" />
    <property name="build.dir" value="${nant.project.basedir}\Release"
/>
    <if propertytrue="debug">
        <property name="build.dir" value="${nant.project.basedir}\Debug"
/>
    </if>
```

```
    <property name="output"
value="${build.dir}\${project.name}.${output.type}" />
    <property name="doc" value="${build.dir}\${project.name}.xml" />
    <target name="clean" description="remove all generated files">
        <delete file="${project.name}.${ output.type }"
failonerror="false"/>
        <delete file="${project.name}.pdb" failonerror="false"/>
    </target>
    <target name="build" description="compiles the source code">
      <mkdir dir="${build.dir}" />
      <csc target="${target.type}" output="${output}" debug="${debug}"
define="${define}" doc="${doc}">
            <sources>
                <includes name="*.cs"/>
            </sources>
      </csc>
    </target>
</project>
```

While this build may look more complicated, it really is not once the concept of properties is understood. By using properties in this manner, this build file can be used as a template for many other types of builds.

### Simple DLL

Listing 4.12 shows just how simple it is to change a build template to compile a different type of project.

**Listing 4.12** Simple DLL Build with Properties

```
<project name="Simple" default="build">
    <sysinfo verbose='true'/>
    <tstamp/>
    <property name="project.name" value="simple"/>
    <property name="target.type" value="library"/>
    <property name="output.type" value="dll"/>
    <property name="define" value="DEBUG;TRACE" />
    <property name="debug" value="true" />
    <property name="build.dir" value="${nant.project.basedir}\Release"
/>
```

```
    <if propertytrue="debug">
        <property name="build.dir" value="${nant.project.basedir}\Debug"
/>
    </if>
    <property name="output"
value="${build.dir}\${project.name}.${output.type}" />
    <property name="doc" value="${build.dir}\${project.name}.xml" />
    <target name="clean" description="remove all generated files">
        <delete file="${project.name}.${ output.type }"
failonerror="false"/>
        <delete file="${project.name}.pdb" failonerror="false"/>
    </target>
    <target name="build" description="compiles the source code">
      <mkdir dir="${build.dir}" />
      <csc target="${target.type}" output="${output}" debug="${debug}"
define="${define}" doc="${doc}">
            <sources>
                <includes name="*.cs"/>
            </sources>
        </csc>
    </target>
</project>
```

This builds all the cs files in the current directory into a dll. Notice the only difference between Listing 4.11 and 4.12 is that target.type and output.type are changed to output a dll.

## ASP.NET and Web Services

Building an ASP.NET or Web Service project is essentially just the same as building a simple dll. ASP.NET assumes the dll to be in a bin subdirectory. The biggest difference is that with Web-based products, NAnt can also be useful in deploying the redistributables. While NAnt certainly could be used in installing traditional thick clients, NAnt's ease of use really is displayed best in the Web development environment.

Listing 4.13 is just the same as the dll build project in Listing 4.12 except for the addition of the deploy target. I would not suggest actually deploying a product without testing, but that topic is for Chapter 6, "Unit Testing."

**Listing 4.13**  WebService Build

```
<project name="Webservice" default="build">
   <sysinfo verbose='true'/>
   <tstamp/>
   <property name="project.name" value=" Webservice1"/>
   <property name="target.type" value="library"/>
   <property name="output.type" value="dll"/>
   <property name="define" value="DEBUG;TRACE" />
   <property name="debug" value="true" />
   <property name="build.dir" value="${nant.project.basedir}\bin" />
   <property name="output"
value="${build.dir}\${project.name}.${output.type}" />
   <property name="doc" value="${build.dir}\${project.name}.xml" />
   <property name="localpath"
value="C:\inetpub\wwwroot\${project.name}" />
   <target name="clean" description="remove all generated files">
       <delete file="${project.name}..${ output.type }"
failonerror="false"/>
        <delete file="${project.name}..pdb" failonerror="false"/>
   </target>
   <target name="deploy" description="Create Virtual Directory and copy
redistributables">
       <mkdir dir="${localpath}" />
<mkdir dir="${localpath}\bin" />
       <mkiisdir dirpath="${localpath}" vdirname="${project.name}"
authntlm="true"/>
       <copy todir="${localpath}">
            <fileset>
               <includes name="**\*.aspx"/>
               <includes name="**\*.asax"/>
               <includes name="**\*.asmx"/>
               <includes name="**\*.ashx"/>
               <includes name="**\*.config"/>
            </fileset>
       </copy>
       <copy todir="${localpath}\bin" file="${output}" />
   </target>
   <target name="build" description="compiles the source code">
     <mkdir dir="${build.dir}" />
     <csc target="${target.type}" output="${output}" debug="${debug}"
define="${define}" doc="${doc}">
```

```
            <sources>
                <includes name="*.cs"/>
            </sources>
        </csc>
    </target>
</project>
```

After building this project, the Webservice can be tested in Internet Explorer using the auto-generated test page.

## Windows Service

Windows Services are the same as a simple exe, but to install the service into Windows, Service Control Manager (SCM) requires the use of the NAntContrib <installutil> task in Listing 4.14.

**Listing 4.14** Building and Installing a Windows Service with NAnt

```
<project name="Simple" default="build">
    <sysinfo verbose='true'/>
    <tstamp/>
    <property name="project.name" value="simpleservice"/>
    <property name="target.type" value="exe"/>
    <property name="output.type" value="exe"/>
    <property name="define" value="DEBUG;TRACE" />
    <property name="debug" value="true" />
    <property name="build.dir" value="${nant.project.basedir}\Release"
/>
    <if propertytrue="debug">
        <property name="build.dir" value="${nant.project.basedir}\Debug"
/>
    </if>
    <property name="output"
value="${build.dir}\${project.name}.${output.type}" />
    <property name="doc" value="${build.dir}\${project.name}.xml" />
    <target name="clean" description="remove all generated files">
        <delete file="${project.name}.${ output.type }"
failonerror="false"/>
        <delete file="${project.name}.pdb" failonerror="false"/>
    </target>
```

```
  <target name="build" description="compiles the source code">
    <mkdir dir="${build.dir}" />
    <csc target="${target.type}" output="${output}" debug="${debug}"
define="${define}" doc="${doc}">
          <sources>
              <includes name="*.cs"/>
          </sources>
    </csc>
  </target>
  <target name="install" description="installs the exe as a windows
service">
      <servicecontrol
            machinename="."
            servicename="${project.name}"
            command="stop"
            failonerror="false" />
      <installutil assembly="${output}" />
      <servicecontrol
            machinename="."
            servicename="${project.name}"
            command="start"
            failonerror="false" />
  </target>
  <target name="uninstall" description="uninstalls the exe as a windows
service ">
      <servicecontrol
            machinename="."
            servicename="${project.name}"
            command="stop"
            failonerror="false" />
      <installutil assembly="${output}" uninstall="true" />
  </target>
</project>
```

## Windows Form

A Windows form project is again very similar to a simple exe project, except for the use of license files and resource files. Resource files can also be used in ASP.NET projects, as seen in Listing 4.15.

**Listing 4.15**  Windows Form Build

```
<project name="Simple" default="build">
   <sysinfo verbose='true'/>
   <tstamp/>
   <property name="project.name" value="simplewinform"/>
   <property name="target.type" value="winexe"/>
   <property name="output.type" value="exe"/>
   <property name="define" value="DEBUG;TRACE" />
   <property name="debug" value="true" />
   <property name="build.dir" value="${nant.project.basedir}\Release"
/>
   <if propertytrue="debug">
       <property name="build.dir" value="${nant.project.basedir}\Debug"
/>
   </if>
   <property name="output"
value="${build.dir}\${project.name}.${output.type}" />
   <property name="doc" value="${build.dir}\${project.name}.xml" />
   <target name="clean" description="remove all generated files">
       <delete file="${project.name}.${ output.type }"
failonerror="false"/>
       <delete file="${project.name}.pdb" failonerror="false"/>
   </target>
   <target name="build" description="compiles the source code">
     <mkdir dir="${build.dir}" />
     <license input="licenses.licx" output="${output}.licenses"
licensetarget="}\${project.name}.${output.type}">
           <assemblies>
              <includes name="${build.dir}\bin\${licenses.dotnetbar}"/>
              <includes
name="${build.dir}\bin\${licenses.ultrawingrid}"/>
           </assemblies>
     </license>
     <resgen input="${project.name}.resx" output="${build.dir}\
${project.name}.resources" />
     <comregister unregister="false">
         <fileset>
            <includes name="treegrid.OCX"/>
         </fileset>
     </comregister>
```

```
    <aximp ocx="treegrid.ocx" keyfile="strongname.key"/>
    <csc target="${target.type}" output="${output}" debug="${debug}"
define="${define}" doc="${doc}">
        <sources>
            <includes name="*.cs"/>
        </sources>
        <references>
            <includes asis="true" name="System.dll"/>
            <includes asis="true" name="System.Data.dll"/>
            <includes asis="true" name="System.Drawing.dll"/>
            <includes asis="true" name="System.Windows.Forms.dll"/>
            <includes asis="true" name="System.XML.dll"/>
            <includes name="treegrid.dll"/>
        </references>
<arg value="/resource:${build.dir}\${project.name}.resources" />
    </csc>
  </target>
</project>
```

Listing 4.15 shows the use of a few references, resource files, and an ActiveX OCX control. The use of a license file is simply for illustration in case a third-party assembly requires it; a license file is not very useful here in my opinion.

### Unsafe, Interop, and Other

There are so many tasks and so much functionality to apply that I devote an entire chapter to a case study of NAnt and other tools that we will cover in the next few chapters.

### Handling Large Products

Remember, architecting a build is much more than just understanding NAnt. Architecting a successful build of a large product containing many projects can be a full-time job. The build, being code, should also have documentation and well thought-out structure. Figure 4-2 is a UML Use Case Diagram showing a simple build. Each of the UML Use Cases actually is a build target.

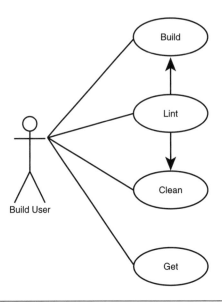

**Figure 4-2** UML Use Case Diagram of the Build.

This is a simplistic build, and this documentation may seem to be overkill, but Chapter 9, "ASpell.NET Case Study," will demonstrate a very complex build in which this forethought is greatly needed. There are a lot of features that could be implemented in a build such as this. For instance, we could use NAntContrib's asminfo task to change the version numbers of the assemblies or other assembly information to all be the same. We could also use the NAnt <touch> task to mark all the files with the exact same date and time. Either of these could be useful in quickly determining what version of a product a customer has.

The biggest challenge in a large product is to create a build that is easily updatable with new NAnt projects. Typically, when checking out the latest version from SCM, the source should be ordered under a single directory on the file system. This may be easy if the source is already ordered that way in SCM but could require some work if the source is in various paths in SCM. There are a few approaches to use when attempting this, but you must keep in mind that the NAnt projects could be interdependent (i.e., referencing each other). One approach could be to use NAnt's <foreach> task to iterate the subdirectories, as in Listing 4.16.

**Listing 4.16** Using Foreach to Get All Files in a Directory

```
<foreach item="Folder" property="foldername">
    <in>
      <items>
        <includes name="*"/>
        <excludes name="CVS"/>
      </items>
    </in>
    <do>
      <nant buildfile="${foldername}/default.build"
target="${project.config} ${target}"/>
    </do>
  </foreach>
```

This goes through each subdirectory and executes the <nant> task on the default.build file. This also passes in the configuration and target to the subproject. So in this design, there is a Master project that has the "get" task and that knows where everything is in SCM and where it is going on the file system. Then all other tasks are just dummy tasks that are passed on down to the subprojects. Therefore, the subprojects have knowledge about how to build, clean, and lint themselves, but not how to get themselves because you would have already had to get the project out of SCM before running the NAnt build anyway. This fulfills the general build principle that the Master build can conveniently get everything out and structure it for you, but because all other knowledge is self-contained in the subproject, you could also just run the get task of a specific subproject to wherever working directory you want to and build it using its NAnt project. The problem with this approach is that it does not handle inter-project dependencies. This design will happily recurse the subdirectories and build each project, but what if one project depends upon another? Unless the directory structure was such that the projects were built in the correct order, this build will fail.

Another similar approach is the one used by NAnt itself. Yes, NAnt is built using NAnt! This approach is to use the foreach task again but to put the list of projects into an XML file. This file could contain the dependency information and be transformed to the appropriate text file since <foreach> currently only works on text files. Listing 4.18 shows the Master build's XML list of projects to build, complete with dependency information. Listing 4.17 is the Helper Application to transform Listing 4.18 to a projects.txt file, and Listing 4.19 is the actual NAnt Master build project.

**Listing 4.17**  Helper Application to Order the Master Build in the Correct Order

```
using System;
using System.Collections;
using System.Diagnostics;
using System.IO;
using System.Xml;
using System.Xml.XPath;
using System.Xml.Xsl;
namespace NAnt
{
    class DependancyChecker
    {
        private static ArrayList al;
private static XmlDocument xdoc;
        [STAThread]
        static void Main(string[] args)
        {
    try
    {
        if(args.Length>0)
        {
            al = new ArrayList();
            StreamReader sr = new StreamReader(args[0]);
            xdoc = new XmlDocument();
            xdoc.Load(sr);
            XmlNodeList projectNodes =
xdoc.SelectNodes("/projects/project");
            foreach(XmlNode projectNode in projectNodes)
            {
                ProcessProjectNode(projectNode);
            }

            sr.Close();
            StreamWriter sw = new StreamWriter("projects.txt");
            for(int i=0; i<al.Count; i++)
            {
                sw.WriteLine(al[i]);
            }
            sw.Close();
        }
        else
        {
```

```
                    Console.WriteLine("A path to the dependency file is
required!");
            }
        }
        catch(Exception ex)
        {
            Console.WriteLine(ex.ToString());
        }
    }
    private static void ProcessProjectNode(XmlNode projectNode)
    {
        if(projectNode.SelectNodes("dependencies").Count > 0 )
        {
            XmlNodeList dependencyNodes =
projectNode.SelectNodes("dependencies/dependency");
            foreach(XmlNode dependencyNode in dependencyNodes)
            {
                ProcessDependencyNode(dependencyNode);
            }
            if(!al.Contains(projectNode ["name"].InnerText))
                al.Add(projectNode ["name"].InnerText);
        }
        else
        {
            if(!al.Contains(projectNode["name"].InnerText))
                al.Add(projectNode ["name"].InnerText);
        }
    }
    private static void ProcessDependencyNode(XmlNode dependencyNode)
    {
        XmlNodeList projectNodes = xdoc.SelectNodes("/projects/project
[name='" + dependencyNode.InnerXml + "']");
        if(projectNodes.Count > 0 )
        {
            XmlNodeList dependencyNodes = projectNodes
[0].SelectNodes("dependencies");
            if(dependencyNodes.Count > 0 )
            {
                ProcessProjectNode(projectNodes [0]);
            }
            else
            {
                if(!al.Contains(dependencyNode.InnerText))
```

```
                    al.Add(dependencyNode.InnerText);
                }
            }
        }
        }
}
```

**Listing 4.18**  The XML List of Projects to Build

```xml
<?xml version="1.0"?>
<projects>
    <project>
        <name>middletier\ws</name>
        <dependencies>
            <dependency>middletier\datalib</dependency>
        </dependencies>
    </project>
<!--
    <project>
        <name>presentation\testapp</name>
        <dependencies>
            <dependency>middletier\ws</dependency>
        </dependencies>
    </project>
-->
    <project>
        <name>presentation\widgetapp</name>
        <dependencies>
            <dependency>middletier\ws</dependency>
        </dependencies>
    </project>
    <project>
        <name>middletier\datalib</name>
    </project>
</projects>
```

**Listing 4.19**  Master Build File

```xml
<project name="Master Build" basedir="." default="build">
   <sysinfo verbose='true'/>

   <property name="debug" value="true" />
   <property name="define" value="DEBUG;TRACE" />
   <property name="build.dir" value="C:\dev" />
   <property name="refassemblies" value="${build.dir}\refassemblies " />
   <property name="ssdir" value="\\server\SourceSafe\vss\srcsafe.ini" />
   <property name="ssuser" value="User1" />
   <property name="sspassword" value="" />
   <target name='get'>
    <delete dir="${build.dir}" failonerror="false"/>
    <mkdir dir="${build.dir}" />
    <vssget localpath="${build.dir}\Genghis"
                recursive="true"
                dbpath="${ssdir}"
                user="${ssuser}"
                password="${sspassword}"
                replace="true"
                path="$/3rd_party/Genghis"
                writable="true"/>
    <vssget localpath="${build.dir}"
                recursive="true"
                dbpath="${ssdir}"
                user="${ssuser}"
                password="${sspassword}"
                replace="true"
                path="$/software"
                writable="true"/>
   </target>
   <exec program="NantHelper.exe" commandline="projects.xml"
output="projects.txt" basedir="." />
   <!-- After applying transform pass the target to the subprojects -->
   <target name='clean' depends='transform'>
      <foreach item='Line' property='filename' in='projects.txt'>
         <nant buildfile='${build.dir}\${filename}.build' target='build'
/>
      </foreach>
   </target>
</project>
```

The output of the NAnt exec task (that runs the Helper Application) is a text file that is properly ordered for dependencies. The advantage of using XML to store the list of projects is that it is transformable and you can easily temporarily comment out projects you do not want to build. Target dependencies are handled in the subprojects. Chapter 9 will elaborate on this design in detail.

# Extending NAnt

When extending NAnt, be sure to use the latest NAnt build. Use the development lists to ensure that someone has not already created the functionality you desire. Also, consider if the task is platform-independent; if it is not, the task is probably more appropriate in NAntContrib.

## NAnt Base Classes

Table 4.3 lists the available base classes to inherit from when extending NAnt. If you were building a compiler task (i.e., a jsharp or csc task), then you would inherit from TaskCompilerBase. Most tasks, however, just inherit from the Task base class.

**Table 4.3**  NAnt Base Classes

| Class | Description |
| --- | --- |
| SourceForge.Nant.Task | The base class that all custom tasks must derive from in order to plug into the NAnt architecture. |
| SourceForge.Nant.Task.ExternalProgramBase | Executes an external application from the path. |
| SourceForge.Nant.Task.CompilerBase | Compiler tasks that use the path. |

### NAnt Tasks' Error Handling

If an error in your custom task occurs, you should throw a BuildException so that the error will automatically be sent to the builds log using Log4Net (see Chapter 7, "Continuous Integration," for more information). Since your task inherits from Task, the failonerror task will function as expected. If the flag is true, the build will fail. The more descriptive the error message, the better:

```
BuildException(String message, Location location, Exception e)
```

This gives a very verbose error including the message, the location in the build file, and exception information.

### Enabling Your Task to Handle Multiple Versions of .NET

If you are using functionality that is only available in a specific .NET runtime version, check the .NET runtime to ensure the .NET version your task requires is being used.

```
if(this.Properties["nant.settings.currentframework.version"] != "1.1")
{
    BuildException("Wrong .Net runtime");
}
```

### Extending NAnt Example

Before we extend NAnt with an example task, Listing 4.20 shows a simple task for inserting an assembly into the Global Assembly Cache (GAC). Most tasks expect input through XML attributes, but a task can also use optionsets or built-in properties as input as well, as in Listing 4.20. Since our task is going to wrap an existing command-line tool, it's a good idea to look at how similar tasks are structured, so let's take a quick look at the Gac-Task (from NAntContrib), which also happens to wrap an executable, gacutil.exe, and several of its features.

**Listing 4.20** NAntContrib's GAC Task

```
[TaskName("gac")]
public class GacTask : ExternalProgramBase {
```

```
    string _assemblyName = null;
    bool _uninstall = false;
    int _timeout = Int32.MaxValue;
    [TaskAttribute("assembly", Required=true)]
    public string AssemblyName {
        get { return _assemblyName; }
        set { _assemblyName = value; }
    }
    [TaskAttribute("uninstall")]
    [BooleanValidator()]
    public bool Uninstall {
        get { return _uninstall; }
        set { _uninstall = value; }
    }
    [TaskAttribute("timeout")]
    [Int32Validator()]
    public override int TimeOut {
        get { return _timeout; }
        set { _timeout = value; }
    }
    public override string ProgramFileName {
        get { return "gacutil"; }
    }
    public override string ProgramArguments {
        get {
            string assemblyName = AssemblyName;
            if (Uninstall) {
                int dllExtension =
assemblyName.ToUpper().IndexOf(".DLL");
                if (dllExtension > -1) {
                    assemblyName = assemblyName.Substring(0,
dllExtension);
                }
                return "/u " + assemblyName;
            } else {
                return "/i " + assemblyName;
            }
        }
    }
    protected override void ExecuteTask() {
        Log.WriteLine(LogPrefix + "{0} {1}", Uninstall ?
"Uninstalling" : "Installing", AssemblyName);
```

```
        base.ExecuteTask();
    }
  }
}
Usage:
<gac
assembly='hello,Version=1.0.0.1,Culture="de",PublicKeyToken=45e343aae32
233ca' uninstall="true"/>
```

[TaskName("gac")] defines the name of the task. The best practice is to always use lowercase.

[TaskAttribute("assembly", Required=true)] is a required attribute. It is senseless to call gacutil without an assembly to gac.

Also notice the validators. These tell NAnt to validate that the attribute is a valid Boolean or Integer input. The task's Execute method is called after all attributes are validated. This is where the actual task code exists. Let's use this as a template for our tasks.

### Subversion Tasks

Subversion (SVN) is an Open Source Control Management (SCM) system available at http://subversion.tigris.org. It is similar to CVS (created by many of the same people) but with additional features not available under CVS's architecture. Since CVS tasks are located in NAnt proper, that is probably where the SVN tasks should go as well. Other SCM tasks probably should go in NAntContrib for two reasons. First, Visual Source Safe and some of the other SCMs are not platform-independent. Second, CVS and SVN are the only freely available SCMs. IGLOO (http://www.jalindi.com/igloo/) and AnkhSVN (http://ankhsvn.tigris.org/) are promising Open Source projects that are add-ins to Visual Studio.NET to better integrate with CVS and Subversion directly from the IDE. Arild Fines from the AnkhSVN project started a Subversion NAnt task, and that is what this example is based on.

Figure 4-3 is a simple design where an abstract base class holds all the common information like username, password, and derived classes for checking out of Subversion and updating it. The code for the Abstract class is in Listing 4.21, and the code for checking out of Subversion is in Listing 4.22.

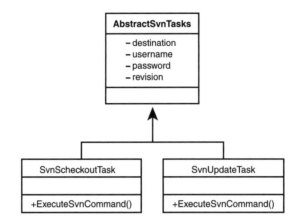

**Figure 4-3**  UML Class Diagram of the Design of the SVN NAnt Tasks.

**Listing 4.21**  Common SVN Base Class

```
namespace NAnt.SourceControl.Tasks
{
      /// <summary>
      /// A Nant task to check out from a SVN repository.
      /// </summary>
      public abstract class AbstractSvnTask : Task
      {
      private string username = null;
      private string password = null;
      private string localDir = null;
      private string url = null;
      private int revision = -1;
      private static readonly log4net.ILog Logger =
log4net.LogManager.GetLogger(System.Reflection.MethodBase.GetCurrentMet
hod().DeclaringType);
          /// <summary>
          /// Initializes a new instance of the <see
cref="AbstractCvsTask" />
          /// class.
          /// </summary>
          protected AbstractSvnTask ()
          {
          }
```

```
/// <summary>
/// The local path to check out to.
/// </summary>
[TaskAttribute("destination", Required = true )]
public string LocalDir
{
    get { return this.localDir; }
    set { this.localDir = value; }
}
/// <summary>
/// The username to authenticate with.
/// </summary>
[TaskAttribute("username", Required=false)]
public string Username
{
    get { return this.username; }
    set { this.username = value; }
}
/// <summary>
/// The password to authenticate with.
/// </summary>
[TaskAttribute("password", Required=false)]
public string Password
{
    get { return this.password; }
    set { this.password = value; }
}
/// <summary>
/// The URL to check out from.
/// </summary>
[TaskAttribute("url", Required=true)]
public string Url
{
    get { return this.url; }
    set { this.url = value; }
}
/// <summary>
/// The revision to check out - defaults to HEAD.
/// </summary>
[TaskAttribute("revision", Required=false)]
public int Revision
{
    get { return this.revision; }
```

```
        set { this.revision = value; }
    }
    protected abstract void ExecuteSVNCommand();
     protected override void ExecuteTask ()
     {
     }


    #region class Context
    protected class Context : NSvnContext
    {
        public Context( string logPrefix )
        {
            this.logPrefix = logPrefix;
        }
        protected override void
NotifyCallback(NSvn.Core.Notification notification)
        {
            Log.WriteLine( "{0}Checked out {1}", this.logPrefix,
notification.Path + Environment.NewLine);
        }
        private string logPrefix;
    }
    #endregion
  }
}
```

**Listing 4.22**  SVN Checkout Class

```
namespace NAnt.SourceControl.Tasks
{
    /// <summary>
    /// A Nant task to check out from a SVN repository.
    /// </summary>
    [TaskName( "svn-checkout" )]
    public class SvnCheckoutTask : AbstractSvnTask
    {
    /// <summary>
    /// The funky stuff happens here.
    /// </summary>
    protected override void ExecuteSVNCommand()
    {
```

```
            try
            {
                Revision revision = NSvn.Core.Revision.Head;
                if ( this.Revision != -1 )
                    revision = NSvn.Core.Revision.FromNumber(
this.Revision );
                RepositoryDirectory dir = new RepositoryDirectory(
this.Url, revision );
                if( this.Verbose )
                    dir.Context = new Context( this.LogPrefix );
                if ( this.Username != null && this.Password != null )
                {
                    dir.Context.AddAuthenticationProvider(
                        new SimpleProvider( new
SimpleCredential(this.Username, this.Password) ) );
                }
                dir.Checkout( this.LocalDir, true );
            }
            catch( AuthorizationFailedException )
            {
                throw new BuildException( "Unable to authorize against
the repository." );
            }
            catch( SvnException ex )
            {
                throw new BuildException( "Unable to check out: " +
ex.Message );
            }
            catch( Exception ex )
            {
                throw new BuildException( "Unexpected error: " +
ex.Message );
            }
        }
    }
}
```

As you can see, NAnt is extremely extensible. The ease of creating tasks has been the key to NAnt's success. The Open Source community has contributed tasks that have elevated NAnt above any other build tool available.

# Extending NAntContrib

If a task is not platform-independent and instead is specific to one operating system or CLI implementation, then the task should be added to NAntContrib. Extending NAntContrib is very similar to extending NAnt, and many of the same principles apply. In fact, many tasks in NAntContrib started out as NAnt tasks.

## Enabling Your Task to Handle Multiple Versions of NAnt

If your task in NAntContrib task depends on functionality introduced in a specific version of NAnt, then it may be useful to check the NAnt version in the code of the NAntContrib task.

```
if(Convert.ToDouble(this.Properties ["nant.version"].ToString()) < 1.1)
{
      BuildException("Wrong NAnt Version");
}
```

## MakeIsoFs Task

Cygwin (http://www.cygwin.com) is an Open Source UNIX environment for Windows platforms. Part of the distribution includes mkisofs. This tool allows you to create an ISO CDROM image file. Let's make a <mkisofs> task for NAntContrib. For a full description of mkisofs, see Appendix C, "Mkisofs Man Page." A common use of mkisofs is to create CDs that are readable on multiple operating systems.

To create an HFS hybrid CD with Rock Ridge extensions of the source directory cd_dir, use the following:

```
mkisofs -o cd.iso -R cd_dir
```

So, as you can see in Listing 4.23, the required inputs are the output file name and input directory.

**Listing 4.23**  The NAnt mkisofs Task Code

```
[TaskName("mkisofs ")]
public class MkIsoFsTask : ExternalProgramBase {
    int _timeout = Int32.MaxValue;
```

```
string _isofilename;
string _inputdir;
bool _rockridge=true;
[TaskAttribute("rockridge")]
[BooleanValidator()]
public bool rockridge {
    get { return _rockridge; }
    set { _rockridge = value; }
}
[TaskAttribute("isofilename", Required=true)]
public string isofilename {
    get { return _isofilename; }
    set { _isofilename = value; }
}
[TaskAttribute("inputdir", Required=true)]
public string inputdir {
    get { return _inputdir; }
    set { _inputdir = value; }
}
[TaskAttribute("timeout")]
[Int32Validator()]
public override int timeout {
    get { return _timeout; }
    set { _timeout = value; }
}
// The base class calls this to build the command-line string.
public override string ProgramFileName {
    get { return " mkisofs "; }
}
// The base class calls this to build the command-line string.
public override string ProgramArguments {
    get {
    if(!rockridge)
        {
            return "-o " + isofilename + " " + inputdir ;
        }
        else
        {
            return "-o " + isofilename + "-R " + inputdir ;
        }
    }
protected override void ExecuteTask() {
    if(this.Verbose)
```

```
{
Log.WriteLine("Creating {0} from directory {1}",  isofilename ,
inputdir);
}
        // we'll let the base task do all the work.
        base.ExecuteTask();
    }
  }
}
```

If I had picked a task that was not a wrapper around an exe, I would have inherited from just Task (like the NAnt task did), and the ExecuteTask would be much more interesting. Take a look at the <mkdir> task code in Listing 4.24 for an example of a task that inherits from Task.

**Listing 4.24**  NAnt's mkdir Task Code

```
[TaskName("mkdir")]
 public class MkDirTask : Task {
     string _dir = null; // the directory to create

     [TaskAttribute("dir", Required=true)]
     public string Dir { get { return _dir; } set { _dir = value; } }
     protected override void ExecuteTask() {
         try {
             string directory = Project.GetFullPath(_dir);
             if (!Directory.Exists(directory)) {
                 Log.WriteLine(LogPrefix + "Creating directory {0}",
directory);
                 DirectoryInfo result =
Directory.CreateDirectory(directory);
                 if (result == null) {
                     string msg = String.Format("Unknown error
creating directory '{0}'", directory);
                     throw new BuildException(msg, Location);
                 }
             }
         } catch (Exception e) {
             throw new BuildException(e.Message, Location, e);
         }
     }
```

```
        }
}
```

After building all the projects into a product and using the MSI tasks to create an install, this task can be useful for creating an ISO CDROM image for release to Quality Assurance for testing and eventually to manufacturing for distribution.

## Useful Tools for Use with NAnt

A scriptable build gives greater opportunity to uniformly automate tasks across all projects of a product. Several tools are very useful for catching common coding mistakes and flagging potential bugs.

### FxCop

FxCop (Figure 4-4) is a Microsoft tool that can check managed assemblies for common design and implementation problems. It checks for security, versioning, language interoperability, and naming guideline problems,

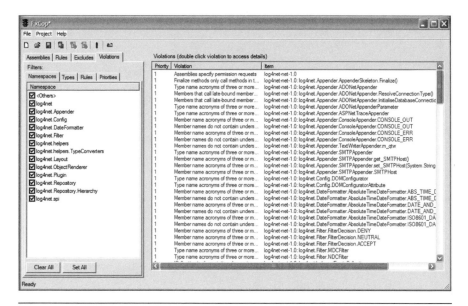

**Figure 4-4** FxCop GUI.

most of which are described in the .NET Framework Design Guidelines. This tool is available for download from http://www.gotdotnet.com/team/fxcop/. The tool comes with over one hundred predefined rules. The output file is in XML (Listing 4.25), and the tool is extensible. It allows third parties to write new rules that execute during FxCop analysis. For information on developing your own rules, download and install FxCop and read the docs/FxCopSdk.htm file.

**Listing 4.25** FxCop XML Output File

```
<?xml version="1.0"?>
<FxCopReport Version="1.072">
    <Violation Kind="AssemblyRule" Name="AssembliesHaveStrongNames"
Priority="1"
FullName="Microsoft.Tools.FxCop.Rules.Standard.AssembliesHaveStrongName
s, DesignRules, Version=1.0.7.2, Culture=neutral,
PublicKeyToken=31bf3856ad364e35">
        <Assembly Name="log4net" FullName="log4net,
Version=1.2.0.23661, Culture=neutral, PublicKeyToken=null"/>
        <Suggestion>Sign 'log4net' with a strong name
key.</Suggestion>
    </Violation>
    <Violation Kind="AssemblyRule"
Name="AssembliesHavePermissionRequests" Priority="1"
FullName="Microsoft.Tools.FxCop.Rules.Standard.AssembliesHavePermission
Requests, UsageRules, Version=1.0.7.2, Culture=neutral,
PublicKeyToken=31bf3856ad364e35">
        <Assembly Name="log4net" FullName="log4net,
Version=1.2.0.23661, Culture=neutral, PublicKeyToken=null"/>
        <Suggestion>Add permission requests to the assembly
'log4net'.</Suggestion>
    </Violation>
....
</FxCopReport>
```

FxCop could be called using the exec task, or FxCop could be wrapped as a NAnt task similar to the GacTask we just looked at. This tool is invaluable at pointing out code problems, almost like a lint program that can be easily integrated into your build using NAnt's exec task. There have been a lot of requests for the creation of an FxCop task. There may even be one by the time this book reaches the shelves, but I would suggest that this task belongs in NAntContrib because FxCop is currently only available on Windows platforms.

## Artistic Style

AStyle (astyle.sourceforge.net) is a free, fast auto-indention tool for C/C++/C# and Java source. This is the only resolution to the age-old tab versus spaces debate, or exactly how many spaces should be used. If your editor does not handle the automatic transformation between tabs and spaces, then this tool is for you. No matter how everyone else formats his or her code, you can reformat the code for the entire product by integrating AStyle into NAnt. But be forewarned that when you check the code back into SCM, you may upset many team members. If you are going to use this little trick, then everyone on the team should also use it and let everyone format away, to each their own.

## HTML Tools

For ASP.NET projects, there are a number of helpful tools that can be automated simply using NAnt. Many of these tools are free, and some are even Open Source. The W3C has many of these tools, including:

- HTMLTidy - http://www.w3.org/People/Raggett/tidy/
- Links checker - http://validator.w3.org/docs/checklink.html
- CSS Validator - http://jigsaw.w3.org/css-validator

These tools can help find countless HTML syntax errors and cut down on many problems before they reach the production Web server machine.

## NAntPad

Figure 4-5 shows a graphical tool to aid in the creation of NAnt projects. NAntPad (http://www.nantpad.com) is a great way to start building NAnt .build files. Without having to look through the NAnt documentation all the time, NAntPad has a list of available tasks. This functionality allows users to quickly see the options available for each task and build targets and projects that are syntactically correct.

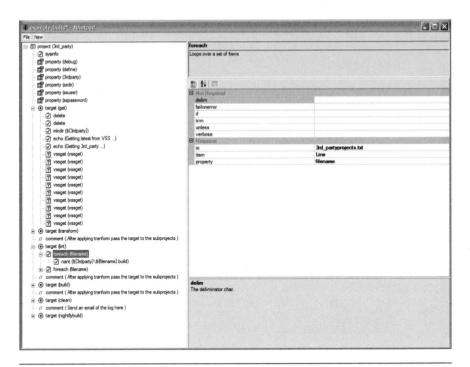

**Figure 4-5**  NAntPad.

## NAntMenu Shell Extension

If you spend a majority of your time creating NAnt build files, you may want to use this Windows Explorer Shell extension (Figure 4-6). NAnt-Menu (http://taschenorakel.de/mathias/nantmenu.en.html) will give you quick actions to perform on a .build NAnt file. The extension automatically queries the build file for available targets and lists them for you to run. By following the instructions in the Readme file, you can go into the Folder Options and File Types of Windows Explorer for build files and add an edit action. This action will launch any application you browse to on your file system. A good suggestion would be a favorite text editor or NAntPad.

## Visual Studio.NET 2003

Visual Studio.NET 2003 is unfortunately not Open Source but is incredibly extensible. One of the extensibility features of VS.NET is that you can define new schemas and use them in an editor with complete intellisense. If you place an XSD file in the C:\Program Files\Microsoft Visual Studio

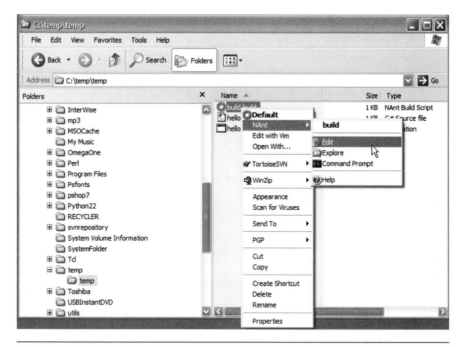

**Figure 4-6** NAntMenu.

.NET 2003\Common7\Packages\schemas\xml directory, then you can use it in an XML file, and Visual Studio.NET will not only validate it but also will give you nice intellisense for that file. First, though, you have to add the namespace to the XML file so that Visual Studio knows which XSD Schema file to use. You do this by adding the xmlns="" in the root of node of the XML file. In Figure 4-7, you can see this in action; the root node of the XML file being edited looks like this:

```
<project name="GetOpenSourceProjects" default="dotnetprojects"
xmlns="http://nant.sourceforge.net/schema/ ">
```

If you want to be sure you are always in sync with the latest NAnt offerings, then you can download the schema at http://nant.sf.net/schema, or you can use the <nantschema> task:

```
<nantschema output="c:\Program Files\Microsoft Visual Studio. NET
2003\Common7\Packages\schemas\xml\nant-current.xsd" target-
ns="http://nant.sourceforge.net/schema/"/>
```

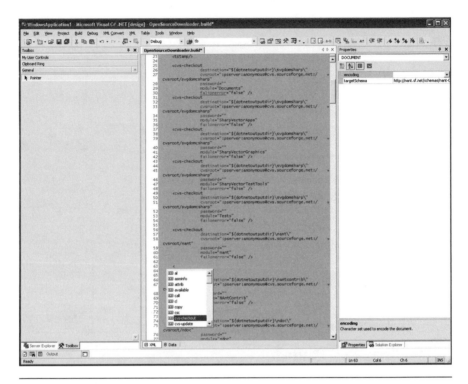

**Figure 4-7**   Visual Studio.NET NAnt Schema.

This will create the file correctly for you. Be sure to change the path if you are using a version other than Visual Studio.NET 2003. I hope soon that NAntContrib tasks will also be supported!

## Summary

NAnt and NAntContrib are incredibly useful for building .NET projects, whether you have Visual Studio.NET or not. NAnt gives some functionality that VS.NET does not have. NAntContrib makes some tasks, such as creating Virtual Directories in IIS for ASP.NET and Webservices, much easier. NAnt allows Open Source developers and VS.NET users alike to easily build large projects with complicated inter-dependencies. In the next few chapters, the most powerful functionality of NAnt will be introduced, so the best is yet to come.

# CHAPTER 5

# XML Documentation

*Be careful about reading health books. You may die of a misprint.*

—Mark Twain

## Introduction

Have you ever received a component either from a vendor or another programmer in your organization, only to find out that the API documentation is out of date? If not, count yourself lucky, but it is just a matter of time. It is a fact of life that programmers do not like to write documentation, and as a result, sometimes the documentation does not match the functionality of a product. As I mentioned in Chapter 2, "Open Source and the .NET Platform," design documentation should be done in the design phase, not during the release. At the very least, the code should be well documented. Some argue that the best place for this documentation is inline with the code. Others say this unnecessarily clutters the code. This will be argued to the end of software development time almost as vehemently as use of tabs vs. spaces in code. The team should decide the best way to keep the documentation in sync with the code and enforce strict coherence. But no matter what the documentation, one thing everyone can agree on is that an XML format should be used in the documentation.

The Magical Documentation Tool in Figure 5-1 does in fact exist and it is called NDoc. There are many tools to create this nicely formatted user documentation, but NDoc offers the most functionality. But before going straight into what NDoc can do, some knowledge about the workings of the C# XML documentation and compiler is necessary. In addition, other documentation tools will be evaluated to help you determine which one is right for you.

**125**

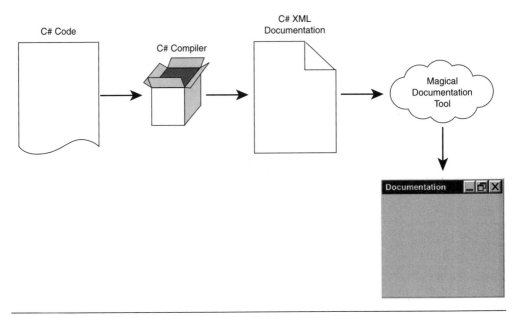

**Figure 5-1** Developer Documentation Dream.

# C# XML Documentation

Deep within the C# compiler is a parser with the great built-in feature of XML documentation. Using the combination of a specialized comment construct of three slashes (///) and built-in documentation tags, XML documentation can be created. The compiler ignores the comments because of the first two slashes, which are standard single-line commenting, and the C# parser looks for the third slash to signify documentation. While the tags used in XML documentation are configurable, the C# standard has predefined a set of tags. The standard tag set has special meanings for the C# compiler, but you can create your own tags to enforce standard documentation and consistent formatting options for your project. The C# compiler only requires that XML comments be well formed. The predefined documentation tags can be subdivided in a couple of different ways. First, I will categorize the tags into two categories: Validated and Nonvalidated.

## Validated Tags

The C# compiler validates the syntax of these tags. This is to ensure that the documentation matches the code. Table 5.1 shows the documentation tags that are verified by the C# compiler.

**Table 5.1** Verified C# XML Documentation Tags

| Documentation Tag | Description |
|---|---|
| <exception> | Apply this tag to a method definition to indicate which exceptions can be thrown. |
| <include> | This tag allows you to specify an XML file that contains the documentation as an alternative to placing the documentation in the code. |
| <param> | Use this tag to describe a parameter of a method. The object browser and intellisense both use this tag to give better information at design time. |
| <paramref> | Used in documentation to indicate that you are talking about a parameter. This is not used by intellisense or the object browser but can be used in building documentation to give indication to the reader that you are talking about a parameter to the method. |
| <permission> | Use this tag to describe the accessibility of your method. |
| <see> | This tag lets you specify a link from within documentation text. |
| <seealso> | Documentation that uses this tag appears in the See Also section to direct readers to other related documentation. |

If the syntax of these tags is not correct, then you will receive a compiler level 1 warning. Table 5.2 lists the XML documentation compiler warnings.

**Table 5.2** C# XML Documentation Compiler Warnings and Errors

| Warning Number | Description |
| --- | --- |
| CS1570 | XML comment on *"construct"* has badly formed XML |
| CS1571 | XML comment on *"construct"* has a duplicate param tag for *"parameter"* |
| CS1572 | XML comment on *"construct"* has a param tag for *"parameter"*, but there is no parameter by that name |
| CS1573 | Parameter *"parameter"* has no matching param tag in XML comment (but other parameters do) |
| CS1574 | XML comment on *"construct"* has cref attribute *"item"* that could not be found |
| CS1580 | Invalid type for parameter *"parameter number"* in XML comment cref attribute |
| CS1581 | Invalid return type in XML comment cref attribute |
| CS1584 | XML comment on *"member"* has syntactically incorrect cref attribute *"invalid_syntax"* |
| CS1587 | XML comment is not placed on a valid language element |
| CS1589 | Unable to include XML fragment *"fragment"* of file *"file"*—reason |
| CS1590 | Invalid XML include element – Missing file attribute |
| CS1591 | Missing XML comment for publicly visible type or member *"Type_or_Member"* |
| CS1592 | Badly formed XML in included comments file – *"reason"* |
| CS1596 | XML documentation not updated during this incremental rebuild; use /incremental- to update XML documentation |
| CS1598 | XML parser could be not be loaded for the following reason: *"reason"*. The XML documentation file *"file"* will not be generated |

These warnings can be ignored by setting a high threshold for warnings or by ignoring a specific error number. The main reason that these tags are validated is that the resulting XML file is used for VS.NET's and Sharpdevelop's intellisense autocomplete. When an assembly reference is added to a project, both the DLL and the XML file are copied to the output directory of the application. IntelliSense will now parse the XML file and give the appropriate ToolTips.

**NOTE:** The XML Documentation files for Microsoft's .NET CLR Implementation can be found in [WindowsDir]\Microsoft.NET\Framework\ vx.x.xxxx\*.xml for each version of the framework SDK that is installed.

### Nonvalidated Tags

The documentation tags listed in Table 5.3 are not validated by the compiler. Mostly, these tags are for documentation purposes only.

**Table 5.3** Nonvalidated C# XML Documentation Tags

| Documentation Tag | Description |
| --- | --- |
| <example> | This tag creates an example of how to use a method to insert into the documentation. |
| <c> | Wrap code in a description within this tag. |
| <code> | This tag indicates multiple lines of code in documentation. |
| <list> | This tag allows you to add lists and tables to your documentation. The listheader tag will add headers to your list, and the item tag enables you to add items to your list. |
| <para> | This tag allows you to structure your documentation into paragraph like groups. |
| <remarks> | The object browser uses this tag to allow you to specify additional information about a class that is additional to the summary section. |
| <returns> | This tag describes what will be returned from a method. |
| <summary> | Use this tag to describe your class. This description will be used by intellisense and the code browser. |
| <value> | This tag allwos you to describe the value of the property. |

These nonvalidated tags are simply passed through the compiler just as a custom tag would be. Therefore, these tags will not cause a warning but are meant mostly for formatting the output to make it more readable.

## C# XML Documentation Tag Reference

Another way of categorizing the tags is to group them again into two groups. Each of these tags will be accompanied with a short code example and brief description. The first group is major tags, which always start an XML comment and are never embedded within another set of tags. There are eleven major documentation tags.

### Major Documentation Tags

*<example>*

The example tag is probably the most-used piece of documentation by users. This is the wonderful piece of code that can be cut and pasted from your documentation into the end users' code. Listing 5.1 shows the XML documentation required to create this example code in your documentation.

**Listing 5.1** Example XML Documentation Tag

```
///<example>
/// <code>
///    int result = Add(1, 2);
// </code>
///</example>
public static int Add(int a, int b)
{
  //...

}
```

*<exception>*

The exception tag is very important to include with your documentation. Because C# (and most .NET languages, for that matter) does not have a throws keyword like Java, the exception documentation becomes very important. Short of using a decompiler or reflection, there is no easy way of finding out what exceptions a method throws other than the exception documentation tag, as shown in Listing 5.2.

**Listing 5.2**  Exception XML Documentation Tag

```
public class DataLib
{
  /// <exception cref="System.Data.DataException"></exception>
  public static DataSet getCustomers()
  {
     throw new System.Data.DataException();
     // ...
  }
}
```

### <include>

In the beginning of the chapter, I mentioned that some developers like to have the documentation with the code to ensure synchronization, but some developers consider well-documented code to be cluttered with XML and find it hard to decipher the code from the comments. This is where the include tag (see Listing 5.3) can help. The include tag allows the C# XML documentation to be in a separate XML file and still be included in the automatic generation of the documentation.

**Listing 5.3**  Include XML Documentation Tag

```
/// <include file='xml_documentation_file.xml' path='dev/src/docs' />
public void Test()
{
  // ...
}
```

### <param>

The param tag allows you to give the user a little insight into the parameters of a method. Although the code alone should be very readable, this tag can be very useful to a user who may not be thinking along the same lines as the implementer. A good illustration of this is Listing 5.4.

**Listing 5.4** Param XML Documentation Tag

```
/// <param><c>x</c> is a given point</param>
/// <param><c>y</c> is the point to subtract from <c>x</c>.</param>
public void Subtract(Point x, Point y)
{
    // ,,,
}
```

### <permission>

Like the exception tag, the permission tag allows you to communicate information to your user that will save him or her valuable time. Again the only way to find out the permissions that a method requires is to use reflection on the Permission Attribute Metadata or to read it in the documentation. Listing 5.5 shows a normal, public method that does not have any special requirements.

**Listing 5.5** Permission XML Documentation Tag

```
/// <permission cref="System.Security.PermissionSet">Anyone can
/// call this method.</permission>
public string HelloWorld()
{
    // ...
}
```

### <remarks>

Other than the example tag which gives a user some quick code to cut and paste, the remarks tag will probably be the most read part of your documentation. This is the tag that allows you to describe to your user the purpose of your class, as seen in Listing 5.6.

**Listing 5.6** Remarks XML Documentation Tag

```
/// <remarks>Class <c>Rectangle</c> enables drawing of a
/// rectangle.</remarks>
public class Rectangle
{
  // ...
}
```

### *<returns>*

For publicly available methods, a simple object browser can reveal the return type of the function. However, it is nice for complete documentation to include everything an end user would want, and more importantly, it is very useful when coding with intellisense-enabled IDEs. Listing 5.7 shows the common use of the returns tag.

**Listing 5.7** Returns XML Documentation Tag

```
/// <returns>This method overrides the Equals method of
/// Object and could do a special comparison.  It returns if the
/// Objects are Equal or not.</returns>
public override bool Equals(object o)
{
  return base.Equals(o);
}
```

### *<seealso>*

Listing 5.8 demonstrates the seealso tag to direct users to other useful documentation.

**Listing 5.8** Seealso XML Documentation Tag

```
/// <summary>This method determines whether two Rectangles
/// are the same.</summary>
/// <seealso cref="operator=="/>
/// <seealso cref="operator!="/>
public override bool Equals(object o)
```

```
{
  // ...
}
```

*<summary>*

Similar to the remarks tag, a summary (shown in Listing 5.9) gives useful information to the user about the author's intended functionality. Whereas remarks are used at a class level, the summary tag is used on methods and properties of a class.

**Listing 5.9**  Summary XML Documentation Tag

```
/// <summary>Logger is a general class to Log information.</summary>
public Logger()
{
    ///...
}
```

### Minor Documentation Tag

The second grouping of tags is minor tags. In contrast to the major tags, which stand alone, these tags are descriptive tags that are usually embedded within a major tag. There are eleven minor tags.

*<c>*

The c tag is used to mark code within a textual description. As you can see in Listing 5.10, the c tag is for simple, single line code. For more verbose code examples, use the code tag.

**Listing 5.10**  C XML Documentation Tag

```
/// <param><c>x</c> is a given point</param>
/// <param><c>y</c> is the point to subtract from <c>x</c>.</param>
public void subtract(Point x, Point y)
{
    // ,,,
}
```

*<code>*

The code tag is usually embedded within an example tag for multiple lines of code. As was already mentioned, most users heavily depend upon this. The major difference between an example and code is that code is a subset of an example, which may contain more information than just code. Listing 5.11 illustrates the code tag.

**Listing 5.11** Code XML Documentation Tag

```
///<example>
/// <code>
///    int result = add(1, 2);
// </code>
///</example>
public static int add(int a, int b)
{
  //...
}
```

*<list>*

A list can really improve the look of your documentation. Listing 5.12 shows how to use, in this case, a numbered list.

**Listing 5.12** List XML Documentation Tag

```
/// <list type="number">
/// <item>
/// <description>Never call this function.</description>
/// </item>
/// <item>
/// <description>There is no guarantee of what it will
do.</description>
/// </item>
/// </list>
/// </remarks>
public void Test()
{
  // ...
}
```

*<para>*

Without formatting, documentation would be much harder to read. Imagine this book without chapters or paragraphs. If documentation is hard to read, then users will not use it and in turn will perceive your product as hard to use. The para tag (Listing 5.13) is used to format your documentation by creating paragraph breaks.

**Listing 5.13**  Para XML Documentation Tag

```
/// <summary>Log is a general class to Log information.
///  <para> I find general functions like this one to be very
useful.</para>
///</summary>
public static void Log()
{
  // ...
}
```

*<paramref>*

The paramref tag in Listing 5.14 is meant as a compliment to the param tag. While the parm tag is used for intellisense and required for robust documentation, the paramref tag is usually found within a summary or remarks tag. This links the user to the parameter, as defined by the param tag.

**Listing 5.14**  Paramref XML Documentation Tag

```
/// <summary>This constructor initializes the new Line to
///(<paramref name="a"/>,
/// <paramref name="b"/>).</summary>
public Line(Point a, Point b)
{
 // ...
}
```

*<see>*

Similar to the seealso tag, the see tag points the readers to more useful documentation. The see tag, however, can be embedded within other tags, as shown in Listing 5.15. Typically, a hyperlink or other method of link is used to allow the users to quickly look at something else; in this case, it's the documentation for the Point class.

**Listing 5.15** See XML Documentation Tag

```
/// <value>Property <c>X</c> represents the Rectangles
/// top left <see cref="Point"/>.</value>
public Point X
{
 // …
}
```

### <value>

The value tag is used to describe a property. The summary tag is typically used to describe a property, but the value tag is used to convey the actual value the property represents.

**Listing 5.16** Value XML Documentation Tag

```
/// <value>Property <c> TopLeftPoint</c> represents the Rectangles
/// top left <see cref="Point"/>.</value>
public Point TopLeftPoint
{
 // …
}
```

These are the ISO standard tags for XML documentation in C#. Most modern languages support some type of documentation that can be converted into an XML file. For VB.NET users, Microsoft has released a tool as a part of the Visual Studio.NET Powertoys called VB Commenter (http://www.gotdotnet.com/community/workspaces/viewuploads.aspx?id= 112b5449-f702-46e2-87fa-86bdf39a17dd). This tool allows VB.NET users to add similar style comments into their code using the triple comment ('") and to use the standard C# tags. Although this is currently a plug-in to Visual Studio.NET, the code is available on the gotdotnet Web site and could be converted into a standalone tool for use with something like Mono's Basic.NET or Sharpdevelop. In addition, it's likely to become a standard part of the language in the next release of .NET.

## Configuring the C# Compiler to Create the XML File

There are many different ways to tell various C# tools to create the XML documentation file. For Microsoft's .NET csc and Mono's mcs compiler, use the doc option of the compiler. Portable.NET isolates their parsing tool called csDoc (http://www.southern-storm.com.au/docs/pnettools_3.html) that, similar to Javadoc, parses the source file for comments, constructing the XML documentation as output. Interestingly enough, Portable.NET has added a number of tags to their standard set of supported tags (`<overload>`, `<devdoc>`, `<altcompliant cref="CREF"/>`, `<altmember cref="CREF"/>`, `<internalonly/>`, `<nodoc/>`, `<platnote platform="PLATFORM">` ... `</platnote>`, and `<threadsafe>` ... `</threadsafe>`). See the csDoc documentation for more details.

Invoking the parser validates the appropriate tags. Listing 5.17 is example source code documentation (from LogKit.Net see http://logkit-net.source-forge.net) that uses raw HTML to further format the see major validated tag.

**Listing 5.17**  Example of C# Comments

```
/// <summary>
/// Class to write to an EventLog Target.
/// </summary>
/// <remarks>
/// <table><tr><td>Logging Priority  <see
cref="Priority"/></td><td>Event Log Entry  <see
cref="EventLogEntryType"/></td></tr><tr><td>DEBUG</td><td>Information</
td></tr><tr><td>INFO</td><td>Information</td></tr><tr><td>WARN</td><td>
Warning</td></tr><tr><td>ERROR</td><td>Error</td></tr><tr><td>FATAL_ERR
OR</td><td>Error</td></tr></table>
/// </remarks>
public class EventLogTarget : AbstractOutputTarget{
….. // Class contents left out.
}
```

Listing 5.17's C# XML documentation, when run through a C# compiler, results in the XML output in Listing 5.18.

**Listing 5.18** XML Output from C# Comments

```
<?xml version="1.0"?>
<doc>
    <assembly>
        <name>LogKit.Net</name>
    </assembly>
    <members>
            <member name="T:org.apache.log.EventLogTarget">
            <summary>
            Class to write to an EventLog Target.
            </summary>
            <remarks>
            <table><tr><td>Logging Priority  <see
cref="T:org.apache.log.Priority"/></td><td>Event Log Entry  <see
cref="T:System.Diagnostics.EventLogEntryType"/></td></tr><tr><td>DEBUG<
/td><td>Information</td></tr><tr><td>INFO</td><td>Information</td></tr>
<tr><td>WARN</td><td>Warning</td></tr><tr><td>ERROR</td><td>Error</td><
/tr><tr><td>FATAL_ERROR</td><td>Error</td></tr></table>
            </remarks>
        </member>
        … <!-- other members omitted />
    </members>
</doc>
```

The documentation is now in a form that can be transformed into virtually any output desired. But before you run and get your XSLT book, take a look at some of the readily available tools from the Open Source community.

# Documentation Tools

Because of the versatility of the XML output, many developers in the Open Source community began to see the usefulness of a project that could centralize a collection of programs to transform C# XML documentation to other more distributable documentation formats (see Figure 5-2 on p. 140).

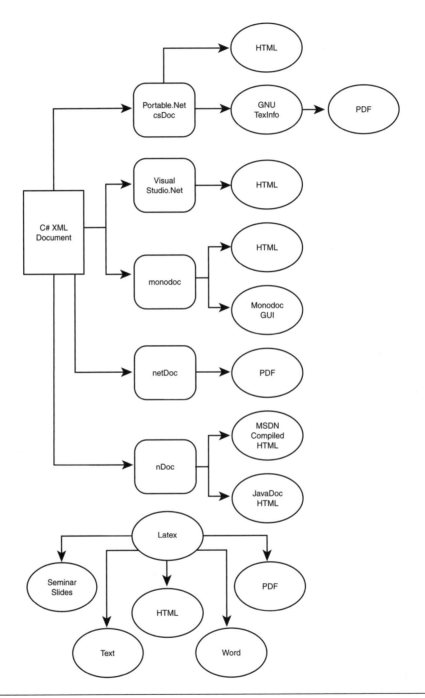

**Figure 5-2** Available Documentation Outputs.

Each of the following documentation tools has a unique advantage. The most advanced tool is NDoc. NDoc can convert the C# XML documentation to more output types than any other tool, so I will save the discussion of NDoc for last. Some of these tools work on multiple CLI implementations and therefore on multiple operating systems. Other tools support unique documentation output formats that you may desire.

**NOTE**: Most IDEs like Visual Studio.NET and #Develop have document generation tools as well that can be found under their Tools menu dropdown.

## MonoDoc

MonoDoc (http://www.go-mono.com) can create HTML pages (Figure 5-3) and has a GUI (Figure 5-4 on p. 142) to read from the C# XML file.

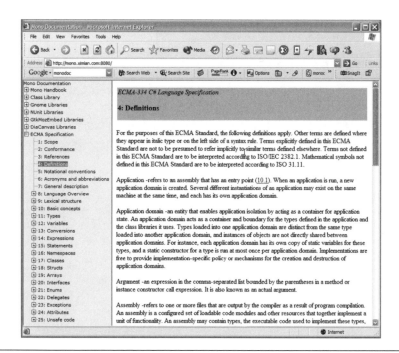

**Figure 5-3**  MonoDoc HTML Output.

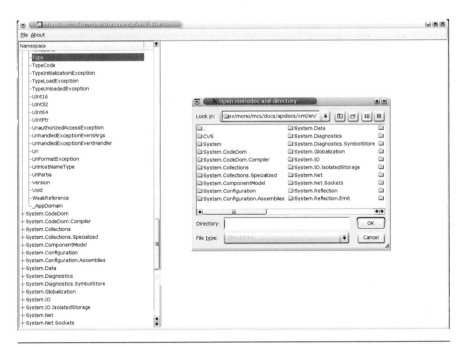

**Figure 5-4**  MonoDoc's GUI.

## Portable.NET csDoc

csDoc (http://www.southern-storm.com.au) can transform the C# XML output to two output targets: HTML and TexInfo. CsDoc2HTML outputs standard W3C HTML. TexInfo, (http://www.gnu.org/software/texinfo/) the GNU standard for project documentation, is created by the csDoc2Texi utility.

## NetDoc

NetDoc (http://www.sydlow.com/) is a freely available tool from SYDLOW, LLC that can format the C# XML file to Portable Document Format (PDF).

## Documentor for .NET

Although not a tool for converting C# XML documentation files, Lutz Roeder's Documentor for .NET (http://www.aisto.com/roeder/dotnet/) can be helpful in creating the comments. The tool, shown in Figure 5-5, shows HTML output in real time, along with syntax and format validation.

**Figure 5-5** Documentor.NET.

# NDoc

NDoc (ndoc.sourceforge.net) is by far the most sophisticated and well-supported documentation tool for C# XML documentation. There is even contributed code to convert between other formats like monodoc and ndoc. NDoc is a little more sophisticated than the other tools in that NDoc does not rely on the C# XML documentation alone but uses reflection to look at the assemblies' metadata tables and extracts all the types. If the types are built into the .NET SDK, NDoc will automatically link to the MSDN documentation. NDoc can even be configured to support multiple .NET runtimes or link to MSDN online documentation. When the types are not found in the .NET SDK, NDoc queries a user-specified XML file. Figure 5-6 shows the easy-to-use NDoc GUI.

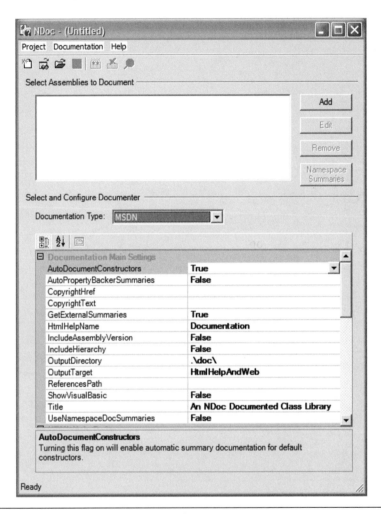

**Figure 5-6** NDoc Graphical User Interface.

NDoc integrates well with Visual Studio.NET and can even understand Visual Studio.NET's file structures. Remember that I pointed out that Microsoft also saw the advantage of using XML-based solution and project files. In the NDoc GUI, if you select "New from Visual Studio Solution" from the Project menu item and select a Visual Studio .NET Solution (.sln) file, then NDoc automatically finds all the assemblies in the solution for you.

## NDoc Functionality

Like Portable.NET's csDoc, NDoc extends the set of Microsoft-defined tags by defining new <overloads> and <events> tags. This allows for documenting overloaded functions and events raised by a member function. NDoc also extends the grammar of the <see> and <seealso> tags to allow linking to arbitrary URLs (not just other code items). Listing 5.19 shows an example of using embedded HTML to achieve the same linking to a Web site, and Listing 5.20 shows how to use this functionality to link two unrelated MSDN output files together.

**Listing 5.19** LogKit.Net's Summary

```
/// <summary>
/// A Simple logging toolkit. Built on <a target="_blank"
href="http://www.pinetree-
tech.com/projects/fog0000000007.html">LogKit.Net</a> which was ported
from <a target="_blank"
href="http://jakarta.apache.org/avalon/logkit/index.html">LogKit</a>.
/// </summary>
```

Some documentation for these extended tags exists in the tags.html file, which is included in the NDoc distribution. NDoc currently runs on Microsoft's .NET CLR and Mono.

## NDoc Documentors' Formats

NDoc also has more supported output formats, called documentors, than any other C# XML documentation tool.

### MSDN

This output creates a .chm (Compiled HTML) file, which is a nicely packaged help file, as seen in Figure 5-7 on p. 146. This task creates all the HTML files as well, so these files could be posted to a Web page. The MSDN documenter even automatically creates the C# and VB.NET signature for the publicly available methods and properties, allowing the users to practically cut and paste functionality. The NDoc team is already talking about supporting a Microsoft Help version 2 output target, but it seems Microsoft is not going to support this help format for much longer. The benefit would be that it would be easier to integrate into VS.NET's help system.

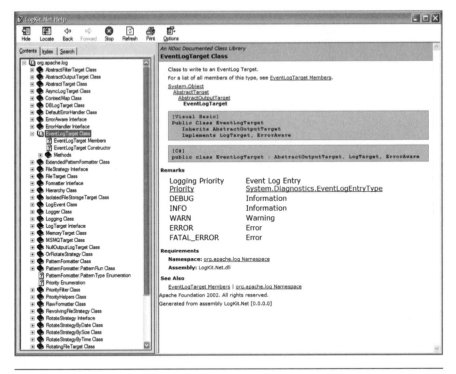

**Figure 5-7** MSDN NDoc Output.

In case you did not notice, Figure 5-7 is the formatted output from Listings 5.17 and 5.18. As I mentioned, the links to the .NET SDK documentation were generated automatically. If, however, you want to link to a CHM file yourself, ensure that the CHM file is in the same directory and use the code in Listing 5.20.

**Listing 5.20** Linking CHM files with NDoc

```
<A HREF="ms-its:Log4net.chm::/log4net.htm">
```

### JavaDoc

JavaDoc (java.sun.com/j2se/javadoc) is probably the most familiar format for the Web, complete with frames similar to Figure 5-8.

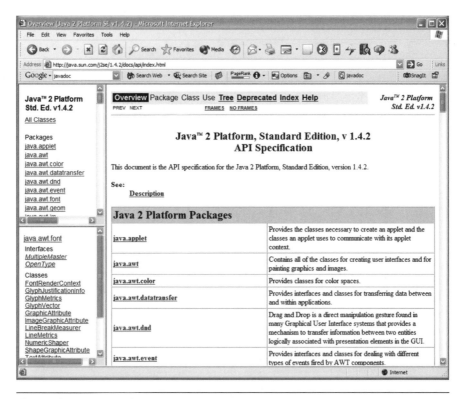

**Figure 5-8**  Javadoc Ouput Format.

### XML

XML output is the most configurable. You can write an XSL Transformation to format it however you want.

### LaTeX

LaTeX (www.latex-project.org) is a long time standard for technical documentation. From LaTeX, you can target many outputs, including HTML, PDF, and DocBook (www.docbook.org).

### Linear HTML

Similar to Javadoc, Linear HTML outputs an HTML file, but this HTML output does not use frames and contains all documentation in one file.

# NAnt Integration

Probably the best selling feature of NDoc is that it is already built into NAnt. That means it is very easy to integrate into the build process. Because of the complexity of the <ndoc> task in NAnt, I delayed the discussion until now. Listing 5.21 shows the NAnt <ndoc> task.

**Listing 5.21**  The NDoc NAnt task used to document the NAnt product

```
<ndoc failonerror="false">
    <assemblies basedir="${build.dir}/bin">
        <includes name="NAnt.Core.dll" />
        <includes name="NAnt.*Tasks.dll" />
        <includes name="NAnt.NUnit.dll" />
    </assemblies>
    <documenters>
        <documenter name="MSDN">
            <property name="OutputDirectory"
value="${build.dir}/doc/sdk" />
            <property name="HtmlHelpName" value="NAnt-SDK" />
            <property name="HtmlHelpCompilerFilename"
value="${project.html-help.dir}\hhc.exe" />
            <property name="IncludeFavorites" value="False" />
            <property name="Title" value="NAnt SDK Documentation -
v.${project.version}" />
            <property name="ShowVisualBasic" value="True" />
            <property name="ShowMissingSummaries" value="${build.debug}"
/>
            <property name="ShowMissingRemarks" value="${build.debug}"
/>
            <property name="ShowMissingParams" value="${build.debug}" />
            <property name="ShowMissingReturns" value="${build.debug}"
/>
            <property name="ShowMissingValues" value="${build.debug}" />
            <property name="DocumentInternals" value="False" />
            <property name="DocumentPrivates" value="False" />
            <property name="DocumentProtected" value="True" />
            <property name="DocumentEmptyNamespaces" value="False" />
            <property name="IncludeAssemblyVersion" value="False" />
            <property name="CopyrightText" value="Copyright (C) 2001-
2003 Gerry Shaw" />
```

```
            <property name="CopyrightHref"
value="http://nant.sourceforge.net" />
          </documenter>
      </documenters>
  </ndoc>
```

As I mentioned, I held off discussion of the NDoc task because it is one of the more complex tasks in NAnt, but with the information covered in Chapter 4, the NDoc task now is much simpler to understand. Remember that a fileset is a grouping of files. NDoc's Assemblies fileset lists the assemblies you want to include in your documentation. NDoc does not completely rely on just the C# XML documentation output of the compiler but also uses some reflection on its own to make the documentation more complete. Also notice in the second assembly in the fileset the clever usage of a patternset. Remember that a patternset is a pattern to match (in this case a wildcard character) that specifies all the different NAnt task dll files, and there are a lot. This saves you from having to list a number of dlls and decreases the chances of typos. In Listing 5.21, the NAnt team chose to use just one documentor, the MSDN documentor type. This documentor type produces a nice CHM file and, from the many Open Source projects I have seen, seems to be the most popular documentor type.

The many properties can be overwhelming, but in most situations, you can just cut and paste the example NDoc task from NAnt's documentation. Listing 5.21 only uses one documentor as its output, the aforementioned MSDN documenter, but the task does allow for many different documenter outputs. The example could output to Linear HTML or Javadoc as well, but that would have made the listing even more confusing. The outputdir element is where the output of the documentor will reside. The HtmlHelpName is the name of the CHM file. The include favorites tag allows you to include the favorites from Internet Explorer. Title controls the title of the CHM's window. The ShowVisualBasic element controls whether the function declarations are shown in the Visual Basic.NET language as well as C#. The ShowMissing* elements determine whether the items (Summary, Results, etc.) are shown even if they are empty because they are not in the original C# XML documentation. The Document* elements allow you to control what will be in the documentation. For example, do you want to include the private stuff in you documentation? IncludeAssemblyVersion is pretty self-explanatory. This is a great example of NDoc using reflection. The Copyright elements determine the copyright statement and URL at the bottom of each documentation page in the CHM file.

In Listing 5.21, the NAnt team used pretty much the standard NDoc property settings except for the ShowMissing properties. For those properties, they have tied the Boolean value to the build.debug property. Therefore, if you are building NAnt in Debug mode, the documentation will be more verbose (including missing things in the documentation) than a release build. This is a great idea to show the team where the missing documentation is when debugging, but it allows the release builds to be clean for the users of NAnt.

**TIP:** The process of creating the documentation via reflection and transforming the XML to the desired output can be expensive, although it is getting faster. This means you may want to add a new conditional target to your build specifically for documentation. This is a target you probably will not want to run with every build, but certainly with any builds that leave the engineering department.

## Summary

Everyone seems to want documentation in a different format. Tech Support wants it one way, while Marketing wants it yet another way. Quality Assurance needs it in PDF format, while Engineering wants it in XML. Because of the forethought to use XML-based documentation files in C#, and due to the hard work of many Open Source developers, this is not only possible but also relatively simple using NDoc.

# CHAPTER 6

# Unit Testing

*Software development is full of best practices which are often talked about but seem to be rarely done.*

*—Martin Fowler*

## Introduction

When building a house, the best three tips you will receive are: location, location, location. When building a software application, the best three tips you will receive are: testing, testing, testing. In software development, there are so many different kinds of testing that even the developers can get confused. "What do you mean by white box testing?" is something I have heard in many an interview. There is Unit testing, Integration testing, Validation, Verification, Performance testing, Usability testing, and then Regression testing, which means we have to be able to do all these types of tests in a reproducible way over time and code changes. As you can see, testing is the most time-consuming part of software and ironically, in my experience, the least automated and most haphazardly organized. Validation and Integration are testing how the whole product works together and are not very useful in the beginning stages of development. Perhaps worse is that these types of tests are dependent on others in the team, which takes the control for meeting your deadlines out of your hands and into the hands of the developer that is the furthest behind. Verification testing should definitely not be done by developers because they cannot objectively verify that the requirements were met. Of course the developers believed they met the requirements or else they would have created the solution differently. Usability testing should be conducted by people not even familiar with the project. That leaves two kinds of testing that can be done by the developers themselves at any time during the development process: Unit testing and Performance testing.

# Unit Testing

I am going to state the obvious here. Are you ready? If the developer finds the bug, it is easier and cheaper to fix. Obviously, it's cheaper to fix because the code has not shipped, and there is no install base to upgrade. It's easier to fix than if a non-developer finds the bug and proceeds to explain his or her perception of what stars aligned to cause the erroneous situation.

Some developers may argue that simply stepping through the debugger is testing enough. This has little value because it is not reuseable and available for Regression testing. (Not to mention the fact that many issues, such as timing issues and race conditions, are not always reproducible in the debugger.) This may prove the code is OK for now, but what about a year from now? What about running the code on computers other than the developer's machine that do not have development tools and special configurations? Tests must be useable and interpretable by other programmers. In three years, when the original implementer is long gone, the tests should still live on. In fact, even if the module is completely refactored, the tests should still be valuable. Every time someone changes the code to fix a bug, the potential of introducing a new bug or reintroducing a past bug arises. If these tests are run with every build, it guarantees a bug will not appear or, worse, reappear down the road. If the test fails, the build should also fail. Therefore, this testing must be tightly integrated with the build process. The overall problem is that testing is too far removed from development. The goal is to closely integrate testing with development. For this to be achieved, writing a test must be easy, lightweight, and quick. Martin Fowler puts it this way:

> Whenever you are tempted to type something into a print statement or debugger expression, write it as a test instead.

The testing framework should be extensible and flexible and should generate standard output for reporting. Sound like a huge task? Are you ready to say, "We don't have time to test?" Well, extensive testing frameworks and tools already exist for .NET, and the best part is that they are free!

# Unit Testing Platforms

There are a number of Unit Testing platforms that are useful in .NET development, including .NETUnit (http://sourceforge.net/projects/dotnet unit), csunit (http://www.csunit.org), and HarnessIt (http://www.unittesting.com/), but by far the most well-supported and feature-rich Unit testing platform is NUnit (http://NUnit.sourceforge.net).

> **A Word About Extreme Programming**
>
> It may seem as if I am pushing Extreme Programming, and this is typically met with one of two Extreme Reactions. Let me assure you that I am not blindly endorsing Extreme Programming. Having said that, I do believe that .NET does seem to lend itself to many of the Extreme Programming (XP) fundamentals. There are three aspects of XP that are somewhat alluded to in this part of the book. First is Test-First development. Test-First development is more of a necessity than a best practice. Testing does take time, and just like many other things in life, you only get better at it with experience. With the time-crunched schedules of most developers, if you do not write the tests first, the tests will never get written, just as when you are committed to jogging to get more exercise. If you are pressed for time, the best time to jog is first thing in the morning to ensure it gets done. It's the same with testing software: test first thing in the development process to ensure it gets done. The second XP aspect is small coding teams, which Microsoft's own Solution Framework Model (http://www.microsoft.com/msf), in line with XP, recommends. Third is continuous integration, which is covered in the next chapter. Continuous integration, when used where it makes sense, can automate many of the tasks of building and testing in a nice graphical display.

# NUnit Architecture

The secret to NUnit's success is its simple architecture. Figure 6-1 on p. 154 shows a conceptual view of NUnit tests. Using NUnit is very easy.

Figure 6-1 shows that a full NUnit Test Suite is made up of one or more Test Fixtures. Test Fixtures, in turn, are made up of one or more Tests. A test can have a setup and teardown method for preparing for and cleaning up after a test.

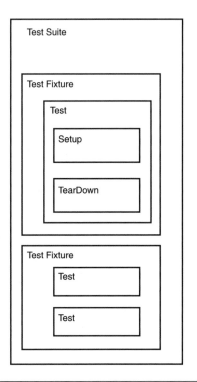

**Figure 6-1** NUnit Conceptual View

Setting up your first test and integrating it into your NAnt build should not take very long. Once the unit testing dll is created, adding new tests into it is very simple. As you create more unit testing dlls, the process gets faster and faster.

**TIP:** If you tried NUnit early on when it was pretty much a port of jUnit, you need to take another look. In version 2.0, NUnit was pretty much rewritten to use the features of .NET that do not exist in Java.

## NUnit Example

We will revisit Unit Testing in the ASpell.NET case study in Chapter 9. But to demonstrate the usefulness of NUnit, let's write a test to test the custom <mkisofs> NAntContrib task we wrote in Chapter 4's "Extending NAntContrib."

**NOTE:** NUnit 2.0 was used for this chapter. There have been some changes to NUnit 2.1, which was recently released. Most of the concepts discussed here are applicable to any NUnit 2.x version.

## NUnit Attributes

To begin the test, we have to understand how to create a TestFixture or Test. One of the features of NUnit 2.0 is the use of C# Custom Attributes. Table 6.1 shows the available NUnit attributes first introduced in Figure 6-1 that can be applied to your testing component.

**Table 6.1** Unit Testing Pseudo-Code

| Attribute | Description |
| --- | --- |
| TestFixture | A collection of tests. |
| Test | A unit test. |
| Ignore | Ignore this test. |
| Setup | NUnit calls this method before running the test. |
| TearDown | NUnit calls this method after running the test. |
| ExpectedException | Tell NUnit to Expect an Exception. |
| Suite | A depreciated attribute supported for backward compatibility. |

TestFixture usually equates to a class attribute. All other attributes are associated with a method. The Ignore, Setup, and TearDown attributes are not required. Note that the method marked with TearDown will be run even in the case that the test fails. Listing 6.1 shows some pseudo-code for a unit test.

**Listing 6.1** Unit Testing Pseudo-Code

```
[TestFixture]
public class TestAClass
{
    [Setup]
    public void ThisMethodIsCalledBeforeAnyTests() {…}
```

```
   [Test]
   public void FirstTestOfTheClass() {…}
   …
   [Test]
   public void LastTestOfTheClass() {…}

   [Teardown]
   public void ThisMethodIsCalledAfterAllTheTests() {…}
}
```

Listing 6.1 shows how easily NUnit uses reflection to enumerate any class decorated with the TestFixture custom attribute. Once a class with TestFixture is found, NUnit looks for a method marked with the Setup attribute and executes it first. Then each method with a Test attribute is executed. Finally, the TearDown method is run.

### Example

To properly test mkIsoFs, we need to create a test directory structure with several files from which to create an iso file. After the test is done, we want to delete the directory structure and corresponding iso file. This is a perfect opportunity to use the TearDown and Setup methods.

**Listing 6.2** NUnit Test for the mkisofs NAntContrib Task

```
using System;
using System.IO;

using NUnit.Framework;

namespace  Tests.NAnt.Core.Tasks
{
   /// <summary>Some simple Tests.</summary>
   ///
   [TestFixture]
   public class MkIsoFsTest : BuildTestBase
   {
      private string DIR = Path.Combine(Path.GetTempPath(),
"\\isotest");
```

```
      private  string ISOFILE = Path.Combine(Path.GetTempPath(),
"\\mkfsiso.iso");
      private const string SUBDIRNAME = "Directory";
      private const string FILENAME = "File";
      private const string FILEEXTENSION = ".txt";
      private const string FILECONTENT = "This will be written to each
file.";
      private const int NUMSUBDIR = 10;
      private const int NUMFILEPERDIR = 10;


   [SetUp]
   public void Init()
   {
      // lets create a temp directory with same bogus files
      Directory.CreateDirectory(DIR);

      for(int i=0; i<NUMSUBDIR; i++)
      {
          Directory.CreateDirectory(Path.Combine(DIR, "\\" +
SUBDIRNAME + i));

          for(int j=0; j<NUMFILEPERDIR; j++)
          {
              FileStream fs = File.Create(Path.Combine(DIR, "\\" +
SUBDIRNAME + i) + "\\" + FILENAME + j + FILEEXTENSION);

              StreamWriter sw = new StreamWriter(fs);
              sw.Write(FILECONTENT);
              sw.Flush();
              sw.Close();

              fs.Flush();
              fs.Close();
          }
      }
   }


   [TearDown]
   public void Clean()
   {
      //Lets delete the iso file and bogus directory.
      if(Directory.Exists(DIR))
```

```
        Directory.Delete(DIR);

    if(File.Exists(ISOFILE))
        File.Delete(ISOFILE);
}


[Test]
public void MakeISO()
{
    string _xml = "<project>" +
                "<mkisofs inputdir='\"" + DIR + "\"'" +
                    " isofilename ='\"" + ISOFILE + "\"'" +
"/>" +
                "</project>";

    string result = RunBuild(_xml);

    Assertion.Assert("ISO File: " + result + " should have been
created.", File.Exists(ISOFILE));
}


[Test]
[Ignore("ignored test")]
public void FutureOptions()
{
}
    }
}
```

The first thing you may notice is how nice the attribute-based design is. You can call your methods any name that makes sense to you, and by using the NUnit attributes, everybody is happy. Also notice the simplicity of the test. This obviously encourages a Test-First approach because it is so easily developed. If you are thinking that I actually developed this test after the code (instead of before it), then move to the head of the class! I will remedy this in the case study of Chapter 9. Thinking what tests your component should pass before writing the code can even make you think of use cases you may have initially overlooked for the component you are designing. Finding these cases in development instead of testing or worse in the field is a big time and money saver.

**NOTE:** The unit test for mkIsoFs is using the infrastructure of NAnt's NUnit tests (thus the BuildTestBase parent class), even though this task exists in NAntContrib. This means that the test would actually have to be integrated into the NAnt task's tests to work properly. This of course is not an issue for the svn unit test since the svn task already is a part of NAnt proper. "Why did I cheat like this?" you may ask. Mostly because NAntContrib does not have an infrastructure for testing. This is somewhat of a sore spot between the projects that will surely be resolved soon.

After compiling the test, running it is simple. Figure 6-2 is a common test run from NUnit.

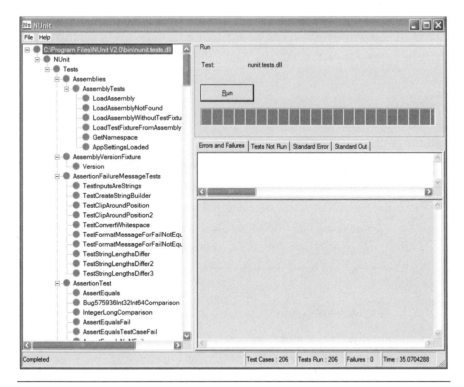

**Figure 6-2** NUnit Graphical Interface.

**NOTE:** NUnit 2.1 is now working on Mono and has a very useable graphical interface called NUnit-Gtk. NUnit-gtk is a gtk# port of the NUnit tool shown in Figure 6-2 and is therefore useable on multiple operating systems. You can get NUnit-gtk from the Mono distribution.

If a test were to fail, it would appear in red with the failure text. The example tests in this chapter do not need any information from a configuration file. Normally, this is not the case. Since .NET configuration files are only used by applications, NUnit uses reflection to allow your test to have a [testname].dll.config file. This configuration information can be accessed as normal, even though your application is really being hosted, or tested, by NUnit.

## NUnit Assertions

In Listing 6.2, you can see the use of Assertions. The example checks to see if the ISO file was created. If the mkisofs task somehow completes without error but doesn't create the iso file, then I want to fail the test. NUnit allows this by implementing Assertions. Table 6.2 shows the Assertions available in NUnit.

**Table 6.2** NUnit Assertions

| Assertion Type | Description |
| --- | --- |
| Assert | Always Asserts |
| AssertNull | Assert if parameter is null |
| AssertNotNull | Assert if parameter is not null |
| AssertEquals | Assert if given values are equal |

## ExpectedException

In some situations, you may want to test the error handling of the code you are testing. In other words, the test may intentionally do something illegal and check to see that the proper exception is raised from the tested code. This functionality is available by using ExpectedException.

**Listing 6.3**  Testing Exceptions and Error code paths

```
[Test]
[ExpectedException(typeof(DivideByZeroException))]
public void DivideByZeroTest()
{
        Decimal.Divide(1, 0);
}
```

Listing 6.3 shows a simple test of the Decimal Division static method to ensure that you cannot divide by zero.

## NUnit Exceptions

Table 6.3 shows the exceptions used by NUnit.

**Table 6.3**  NUnit Exceptions

| Attribute | Description |
|---|---|
| AssertionException | Indicates that an Assertion has failed. Replaces the AssertionFailedError in NUnit 1.x. |
| InvalidSuiteException | Depreciated exception for the Depreciated Suite Attribute. Indicates an Invalid Test Suite. |
| InvalidTestFixtureException | Indicates an Invalid TestFixture. |
| NoTestFixtureException | Missing TestFixture attribute, which is equivalent to nothing to test. |
| NUnitException | General NUnit exception. |
| TargetInvocationException | An error occurred when invoking a target. |

This is not an exhaustive list of exceptions. NUnit does use some of the exceptions from the .NET framework, but Table 6.3 is the explanation of the exceptions that NUnit defines.

# Integration with NAnt

Running tests in a graphic display is nice, but it is time-consuming for large projects. Adding tests to a test fixture is as quick as adding the functionality it is supposed to check. But now it would be nice if the tests were automated, right? Right. This is where the integration of NUnit and NAnt comes into play. Integrating a little knowledge about the tests into the build is a marvelous thing because it does not make much sense to allow a build to leave Engineering that does not even pass the unit tests!

## NUnit Task

Looking back at the NAnt Build File Template in Listing 4.11, the output property was the fully qualified path name to the built assembly. Listing 6.4 shows a simple NUnit task making use of the output property.

**Listing 6.4**   NUnit NAnt Task

```
<target name="test" depends="build">
    <nunit2>
        <test assemblyname="${output}"/>
    </nunit2>
</target>
```

Listing 6.4 shows the dependency on the build target so that the latest code is always tested. It would make sense to have the test target run automatically in the master build file. However, you should design the build in such a way that the developers can directly call just the build target for faster compilation at design time.

The code in Listing 6.4 is the simplest use of the NUnit2 task. There are other attributes that allow further customization of the task.

### NUnit2 Attributes

There are two main attributes for the NUnit2 task beyond the common attributes that all NAnt tasks have. Those NUnit2-specific attributes are formatter and test. Formatter allows customization of the default formatter output for the task. The test attribute allows you to specify a specific test or tests to run. If no tests are specified, all tests are executed.

### Test Attributes

The test child node of the NUnit2 task in Listing 6.4 also has additional properties that are not exhibited in the example. Having a test be a child node of NUnit2 allows tests to be run from multiple assemblies. Three additional attributes for test are appconfig, transformfile, and testname. The functionality of these attributes is almost self-describing. Appconfig allows you to specify the name and location of the .NET XML config file to use in testing. The transformfile allows you to specify an XSL transform to run on the formatter output when using XML. Testname allows you to specify a specific test to run. Again, if no tests are specified, all tests are run.

## NUnit Report Task

The problem with automating the tests is that you lose the nice graphic display of passed and failed tests. In the design of the build, you want to fail the build if a test fails, but you do not want to abort the build on a single failure. If code early in the build fails its unit tests, continue the build to allow other code to be tested. This is possible by using a global property, possibly as an environment variable. Then at the end of a large build, how do you tell which test passed and which failed? By using the NUnit2Report task (http://NUnit2report.sourceforge.net/index.html), you can capture the results of the tests in the easy-to-read graphical format shown in Figure 6-3.

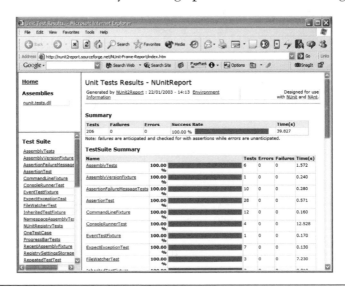

**Figure 6-3** NUnit2Report for NUnit Tests from the NUnit2Report Web Site.

The results in Figure 6-3 are the same results and tests displayed in Figure 6-2, but run in an automated fashion and with a little nicer output format.

The NUnit2report task is a NAnt task that is simple to use and install. Listing 6.5 shows the simplicity of the task.

**Listing 6.5**  NUnit2report NAnt Task

```
<nunit2report format="frames" opendesc="yes" todir="HTMLResults">
  <fileset>
    <includes name="result.xml" />
  </fileset>
  <summaries>
    <includes name="result.summary.xml" />
  </summaries>
</nunit2report>
```

Table 6.4 gives a full listing of the available attributes for the NUnit2report task.

**Table 6.4**  NUnit2report Attributes

| Attribute | Description | Required |
|-----------|-------------|----------|
| Out | The name of the HTML file that will result in the transformation. Default to "index.htm". | False |
| Lang | The language ouput. Default to "english." | False |
| Format | The format of the generated report. Must be "noframes" or "frames." Default to "noframes." | False |
| Todir | The directory to where the files resulting from the transformation should be written. | False |
| Opendesc | Open all description method. Default to false. | False |

By designing the tests first and with proper use of this task, you can almost track the status of your code. This, in conjunction with Continuous Integration discussed in the next chapter, can help you schedule more accurately.

# NUnitASP

Once you start religiously using unit tests, you will find that user interfaces are really hard to unit test. Yes, of course you can use reflection to call all the control's Event Handlers but this is not adequate because most UIs have some sort of progression to their functionality. For instance, it is common for UIs to disable a button until some other dependent action is performed. There is screen-recording software available to "record" your clicks and play them back in an automated fashion, but if you are using an ASP.NET Webform for your application, there is an easier way—NUnit ASP. As an extension to NUnit, NUnitASP's functionality will already be somewhat familiar. Running the tests from the NUnit UI or within NAnt is exactly the same, and so is the results report. NUnitASP currently supports the following ASP.NET controls:

- Button
- CheckBox
- DataGrid
- DropDownList
- Label
- LinkButton
- Panel
- RadioButton
- TextBox
- UserControl
- ValidationSummary

Listing 6.6 shows how easy it is to link test code to a control on your page.

**Listing 6.6**  NUnitASP Test

```
[Test]
public TestASP()
{
    LinkButtonTester linktester = new LinkButtonTester("linkButton1",
CurrentWebForm);

    Browser.GetPage("http://localhost/examples/link.aspx");

    linktester.Click();
```

```
    AssertEquals("Clicked once.", linktester.Text);
    linktester.Click();
    AssertEquals("Clicked twice.", linktester.Text);
}
```

This tests that a LinkButton was clicked twice. By using this model, you can test the progressions of your user interfaces. The functionality of the button on the tested page is only to change its text to the amount of times it was clicked. The Assert ensures that the button truly was clicked twice.

NUnitASP is not only a great study in extending NUnit but also a very useful tool in ASP.NET testing and development.

# Other Tools Useful with NUnit

One paragraph on each of these tools is barely adequate to describe their functionality, but the chapter would not be complete without mentioning these tools that can help with the testing of your code.

## NCover

The one useful outcome of testing by stepping through a debugger is that you can ensure that every line of code is tested, including the most obscure and remote error handling that may never see the light of day in normal operating conditions. Unfortunately, stepping through a debugger is very time-consuming and not very repeatable because of human error. NCover is a coverage tool (available from http://www.gotdotnet.com/community/workspaces/workspace.aspx?ID=3122EE1A-46E7-48A5-857E-AAD6739EF6B9) to keep track of what code was executed. Combined with NUnit, NCover can tell you exactly what lines of code were executed and can provide full statistics on how often lines were executed. There is also an NCover project (completely unrelated) on Sourceforge that is meant to be a NAnt task. Take a look at it on http://www.sourceforge.net/projects/ncover.

## Object Mocking

Mock Objects can be very useful in conjunction with unit testing. A Mock class can replace a real class that your code depends on. This allows quick identification of where the bug resides. Is the bug in your code? In dependent code? Or is the bug in the framework? The real power of Mocking comes in real-world simulation like network and database transient connectivity. POCMock (http://www.prettyobjects.com/) and nMock (http://nmock.truemesh.com/) are Mock Object Platforms for .NET development.

### HttpUnit

NUnitASP mostly focuses on unit testing the server-side portion of your code. As a complement, HttpUnit (httpunit.sourceforge.net) is available and can provide the missing functionality. HttpUnit can test client-side JavaScript, authentication, and cookies. HttpUnit heavily relies on Java and easily integrates with Ant.

### DbUnit

NAntContrib does include a handy SQL task, but if your application needs more functionality than this, there is DbUnit (dbunit.sourceforge.net). DbUnit is an extension of jUnit and does require knowledge of Java. Teamed with Ant, DbUnit allows unit testing of stored procedures and other very useful database functionality.

# Performance and Other Testing Tools

### Windows Application Verifier

Windows Application Verifier (AppVerifier) is a great tool if you are targeting the Windows platform. AppVerifier comes with the freely available Application Compatibility Toolkit (http://www.microsoft.com/windows/app-compatibility/toolkit.mspx) from Microsoft. If you are creating shrink-wrapped applications and desire to have Windows Logo Certification, this tool will save you countless time and money. Even if you are just creating an application that is distributed in a highly controlled environment, AppVerifier can check your program for common coding mistakes including memory and security problems.

Table 6.5 shows the eleven AppVerifier tests that can be run on your application.

**Table 6.5** Application Verifier Tests

| Test Name | Test Description |
|---|---|
| PageHeap | This test inserts pages around all of the memory your application allocates on the heap. This allows the tool to catch buffer overruns and misuses of memory. |
| Locks | This tests for proper handling in the critical sections of your code. |
| Handles | If your application tries to access a null handle (one you have possibly already freed, for example), this test will catch your mistakes. |
| FilePaths | This test ensures that your program is obtaining path information by using the proper APIs and not hard-coding path strings. |
| HighVersionLie | This bizarrely named test shims itself between any calls to determine the version of Windows running and returns a very large version number. |
| RegistryChecks | Proper use of registry is tested by this test. |
| KernelModeDriverInstall | This tests the proper installation of drivers into Windows and that the driver is signed. |
| SecurityChecks | If your program does not have the permissions necessary to access resources or create process, this test will fail. |
| DFWChecksAll | This tests for Windows Logo Certification. |
| DFWChecksSetup | This tests for Windows Logo Certification of Setup programs. |
| DFWChecksNonSetup | This tests for Windows Logo Certification for non-Setup programs. |

Figure 6-4 shows AppVerifier running on a simple picture resizing program I wrote.

Even this simple C# program has a number of issues to resolve, although it runs flawlessly on every machine on which it is installed. Imagine what a more complex large application would look like!

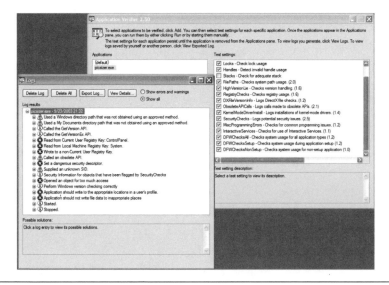

**Figure 6-4**  Windows Application Verifier Verifying a Simple Program.

## nProf and nProfiler

nProf (http://nprof.sf.net) is an Open Source .NET profiler that can be helpful in exposing the bottlenecks in your code. Figure 6-5 shows the tool's user interface.

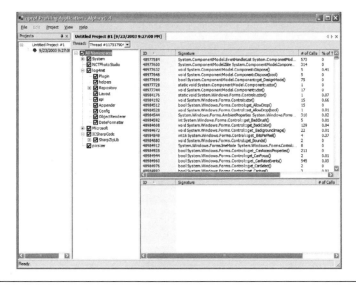

**Figure 6-5**  nProf of a Simple Picture Resizing Program.

nProfiler (http://nprofiler.sf.net) is another Open Source .NET profiler that, as you can see from Figure 6-6, is not as feature-rich as nProf but that is still very useful because it profiles slightly differently than nProf.

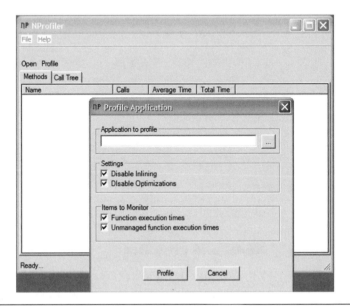

**Figure 6-6**  nProfiler User Interface.

## FxCop

Chapter 4 explored integrating FxCop with the build process using NAnt. FxCop checks the .NET assembly for correctness, CLS compliance, and a number of other common design mistakes.

## HTML Tools

HTML and browsers are evil in that they may hide your coding mistake, and you will not catch it until an end user browses your site with an old or obscure Web browser. The HTML tools that Chapter 4 suggested using with NAnt can also save a lot of time and money in Web development.

# Summary

There are many tools and methodologies for testing your code. The most important thing is not some "silver bullet" or magical tool. The tools can sometimes be wrong (FxCop often reports problems in assemblies that are not necessarily errors). The most important thing is that testing, and especially a test-first philosophy, makes you think before you code. This often improves your design and shortens the overall development and testing time for your application by helping prevent costly mistakes.

# CHAPTER 7

# Continuous Integration

*Success is more a function of consistent common sense than it is of genius.*

*—An Wang*

## Introduction

After spending all the time required to create a repeatable, portable build that includes automated tests, you obviously want to use all that work to its fullest potential. Continuous integration helps elevate the all-too-common "It compiles on my machine" problem. It is meant to help in team development environments. The larger the team and the larger the project, the more useful this type of automated integration becomes. If you have ever wasted a weekend trying to "get ahead," only to find that the project state in source control is not even useable, then you unknowingly have longed for Continuous Integration.

### What Is Continuous Integration?

Continuous Integration (CI) is a term coined by the Extreme Programming portion of the Agile Development movement. Every developer is all too familiar with the pains of integrating his or her code or portion of the system together with everyone else's. This is usually not a pleasant experience because so much time has elapsed since the last integration process. Software, like many other things in life, is high maintenance, and if you do not keep up on the maintenance, the costs in the end could be much higher than the maintenance would have been all along the way. Continuous Integration is meant to give instant feedback upon committing code to source control. This allows integration problems to be seen and corrected early in the coding process. Many times this may mean a redesign of the architecture. It's better to catch any problems now and not after much time has been invested in the code.

Continuous Integration also provides a complete and automated build system. Once a developer checks in the changes to the code, the build is automatically started, and the results are distributed to the development team. Alternatively, you can schedule a build on a recurring basis. Using a proven automated building system not only saves on the time required to roll your own, but oftentimes also provides greater flexibility and extendibility and a larger feature set than a homegrown system. Most Continuous Integration systems have been in use for a while and have the kinks worked out. Because most of the systems are Open Source, many different developers work on the projects. This ensures that a system works in multiple environments and provides a large enough feature set to please many different developers and companies.

## What Are the Benefits of Continuous Integration?

We have already seen the following advantages of Continuous Integration:

- Ensures a buildable project state in source control
- Exposes integration issues immediately
- Enables automatic backups of each build
- Enables automatic installation of every build for testing purposes
- Equips you with a complete automated build system

Beyond these surface benefits, Continuous Integration has a lot to offer. It allows for faster development by giving instant feedback. This alleviates a developer's fear of getting the latest code from source control, which might be in a useless state and might not even compile. Having spent the time creating automated and unit tests now pays off big by preventing a bug from entering or reappearing in the code base.

While initially hesitant about spending time on something that does not generate revenue, management generally loves Continuous Integration. This is due to the fact that the status of the project is pretty visible. A manager can easily scan an email message output from the Continuous Integration system and see the progress of the team and the status of the project. While some developers may view this as a downside, it is really an all-around win because management will now see how many projects and how much code the product really requires. Most of the code of a large system exists below the presentation layer of the user interface and is often never even seen. Continuous Integration can be a great communication channel between management and engineering.

The best ideas always are the simple ones, and Continuous Integration is a simple idea.. However, the power of Continuous Integration is in the many different features it provides taken together as a whole. Taking one feature of Continuous Integration alone often justifies using the system, but this is really missing the point. For instance, whether you subscribe to the Extreme Programming/Agile Development mindset, every development team sees the need for an automated and repeatable build process. NAnt alone can provide this, but comparing Continuous Integration to just an automated build process is like comparing Instant Messaging to email; similar technologies with completely different usages. At the end of the day, Continuous Integration is even better than the proverbial "break the build and bring in the doughnuts" rule.

## How Does Continuous Integration Fit with .NET?

Continuous Integration can certainly be useful with any programming language or platform, but .NET and Continuous Integration go very well together. This is in part due to the fact that .NET development is rapid (not necessarily "Rapid Development" but just plain rapid). It's also partly because of the other Open Source .NET Tools like NAnt and NUnit that use the reflection and attributed programming features of .NET heavily.

There are a few systems (Hippo.NET, Draco.NET, and CruiseControl.NET) that not only support .NET but also were built with .NET specifically in mind. These systems were themselves implemented using .NET. Before looking at each of these systems in detail, first we must set up some criteria for evaluating them.

## How to Evaluate a Build System

Many Open Source and commercial products address the issue of a complete build system: FinalBuilder (http://www.atozedsoftware.com/finalbuilder), Visual Build Professional (http://www.kinook.com/VisBuildPro/index.html), X-Unity (http://x-unity.miik.com.ua/Default.aspx), and the SourceForge front end from VA Software (http://www.vasoftware.com). However, most of these systems fall short of true Continuous Integration. Many features of a system could be looked at, but the ones we focus on in this part of the chapter are meant to help determine which Continuous Integration system is best for your environment.

### Build System Support

The biggest concern with a Continuous Integration system is which build systems it supports. Of all the features of a Continuous Integration system, this one is premier because it would be the biggest thing for you to change. If you are already using a build system that Continuous Integration does not support, it may be worth your while to look at a different system. Any of the build tools discussed in Chapter 4, "Build Automation," would be a good choice, but NAnt is definitely the predominant one. Ideally, a Continuous Integration system would work with multiple build systems, but because of the tight integration between the systems, this is rarely the case.

### Source Control Support

Another highly visible feature of a Continuous Integration system is the Source Code Management (SCM) system that it supports. It would be a large undertaking to change the SCM once a company is already used to a specific system. However, this is not as difficult as changing the build system because most SCM vendors realize the fiscal importance of being able to automatically import a competitor's SCM repository, with complete history, into their system. Still, this directly affects the developer's everyday task and the overall development cycle and should be carefully considered.

### Unit Testing Support

This is almost an assumed feature of Continuous Integration because without Unit testing, it is not really Continuous Integration. Chapter 6 discusses Unit Testing in .NET and of course features NUnit. Many times, the Unit testing platform is closely linked to the build system used. For example, if the Continuous Integration system supports NAnt, it gets NUnit support for free. If it used csAnt, then csUnit would be an obvious Unit Testing choice.

### User Interface and Output Formats

The useability of the system is definitely a big factor in selecting the system, although once the system is configured and working, it rarely needs to be reconfigured. What are used day in and out are the build output formats. If the output is well laid out and easy to read, then the system will work well for communication. The delivery of the output is also important, whether it is a Web page, email, or XML file. Figure 7-1 shows a design overview of the Continuous Integration systems.

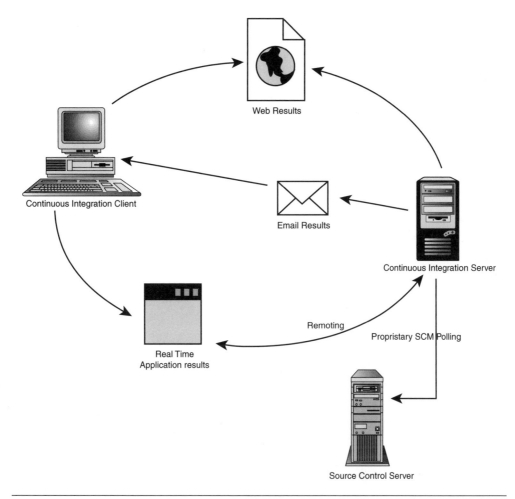

**Figure 7-1** Design Overview of the Continuous Integration Systems.

As you can see, the client Windows applications usually use .NET remoting for displaying real-time results. However, depending upon the product, some results can be reported via email or over the Web. This does not require any installation of software and is very popular with management teams.

### Community Support

Here is the resounding theme throughout Open Source and this book. Choosing between two Continuous Integration systems, if all else is equal (code quality, products supported, etc.), should come down to which one is better supported and has a more enthusiastically development community surrounding it.

## Conceptual Design Overview

You will notice that all of the systems listed in this chapter are very similar in their design (see ".NET Continuous Integration Quick Comparison Chart" at the end of the chapter). The basic design is that a person on the development team sets up a Continuous Integration server. This usually is not the same machine that contains the source control repository because depending upon your configuration the Continuous Integration can be intensive and can even install and test the results of the build. Normally this is not desirable on the machine that contains you source code repository. Once the Continuous Integration server is set up and configured with a build schedule and a watch on the source control management system, then anyone can check or receive the results.

# Hippo.NET

Hippo.NET (http://hipponet.sourceforge.net) integrates Draco.NET Continuous Integration, Microsoft BuildIt, and Microsoft Visual SourceSafe (VSS). This product obviously targets the Visual Studio.NET users. A clear advantage of using BuildIt is the automatic understanding of Visual Studio.NET project and solution files. The biggest drawback is the support of the single VSS SCM.

## Installing

The installation is fairly easy and well documented. Download a zip file distribution and install the Hippo.Server by using the SDK's InstallUtil.exe tool.

**NOTE:** This is based upon Hippo.NET version 1.2.0.

## Configuring

Before running Hippo.NET, you have to configure the projects.xml file included in the Server directory of the zip file distribution. Listing 7.1 shows an example projects.xml file.

**Listing 7.1** Hippo.NET's Project File

```xml
<?xml version="1.0" encoding="utf-8"?>
<ArrayOfProjectConfiguration
xmlns:xsd="http://www.w3.org/2001/XMLSchema"
xmlns:xsi="http://www.w3.org/2001/XMLSchema-instance">
  <ProjectConfiguration>
    <ProjectName>TestProject</ProjectName>
    <SourceSafeINI>C:\Program Files\Microsoft Visual
Studio\Common\VSS\srcsafe.ini</SourceSafeINI>
    <SourceSafeProject>$/TestApp2.root</SourceSafeProject>
    <SourceSafeUsername>Admin</SourceSafeUsername>
    <SourceSafePassword></SourceSafePassword>
    <WorkingFolder>C:\Temp\VSS\TestApp2.root\</WorkingFolder>
    <BuildCommand>nant.exe</BuildCommand>
    <BuildCommandArguments>-
buildfile:TestApp2\project.build</BuildCommandArguments>
  </ProjectConfiguration>
</ArrayOfProjectConfiguration>
```

The SourceSafeIni file node is the path to the SCM repository. The SCM project, username, and password are also required nodes. Working-Folder is the path to get and build the code. BuildCommand nodes are for the path and arguments to the build tool used (in this case, NAnt).

## Running

The client (shown in Figure 7-2) and server service communicate using .NET. Remoting the .NET configuration files should be using the same host and TCP port.

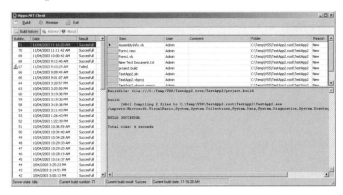

**Figure 7-2** Hippo.NET Client User Interface.

While the UI is very nice, checking a Hippo.NET build would require using the client application. This is not very conducive to large development teams.

# Draco.NET

Draco.NET (http://draconet.sourceforge.net), inspired by the Java CruiseControl Continuous Integration system, was the first .NET Continuous Integration system to appear (although under a different name). Because of this, Draco.NET is the most mature and easy to implement Integration system currently available.

**NOTE:** This is based on Draco.NET 1.5

Draco.NET supports the following SCM products:

- CVS
- Subversion
- Visual Source Safe
- Perforce
- PVCS

Draco.NET supports building using NAnt or Visual Studio.NET and has a very intuitive and easily extendable pluggable architecture.

## Installing

Installing Draco.NET is incredibly easy. The distribution contains a client and server MSI (Microsoft Installer) setup package that runs flawlessly.

## Configuring

Listing 7.2 should look familiar since the Hippo.NET project was based upon this Draco.NET implementation.

**Listing 7.2**  Draco Server Configuration File

```
<draco xmlns="http://www.chive.com/draco">
        <pollperiod>60</pollperiod>
        <quietperiod>60</quietperiod>
        <mailserver>mail.yourdomain.com</mailserver>
        <fromaddress>you@yourdomain.com </fromaddress>
        <builds>
                <build>
                        <name>aspell-net</name>
                        <pollperiod>10</pollperiod>
                        <quietperiod>30</quietperiod>
                        <notification>
                                <email>
                                    <recipient>you@yourdomain.com</recipient>
                                </email>
                                <file>
                                    <dir>C:\book\BuildOutput</dir>
                                </file>
                        </notification>
                        <nant>
                                <buildfile>build\master.build</buildfile>
                        </nant>
                        <svn>
                                <url>file:///C:/book/svnrepository</url>
                        </svn>
                        <ignorechanges>
                                <ignore comment="autobuild"/>
                        </ignorechanges>
                </build>
        </builds>
</draco>
```

Listing 7.2 has the comments removed for sake of space, but the file is so well structured and commented that it is almost self-explanatory. The omitted comments are so good that you can literally cut and paste them into the configuration file and change the settings for your specific scenario. Note that this example uses Subversion (SVN) SCM. This build name (bolded in Listing 7.2) is very important because it will be in the notifications (like emails) and is used by the client to manually start a build.

**TIP:** James Geurts has recently released a Web-based log viewer for Draco.NET (http://blogs.biasecurities.com/jim).

A nice feature here is that you can use multiple notifications. This logs to an XML file (Listing 7.3) on the server and sends out an email (shown in Figure 7-3).

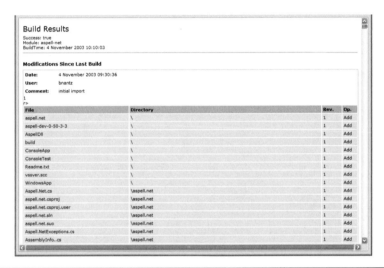

**Figure 7-3**  Draco.NET Email Notification.

**Listing 7.3** XML File Notification

```
<BuildResult xmlns:xsd="http://www.w3.org/2001/XMLSchema"
xmlns:xsi="http://www.w3.org/2001/XMLSchema-instance">
  <Success>true</Success>
<BuildOutput>
...
</BuildOutput>
  <Module>aspell-net</Module>
  <BuildTime>2003-11-04T10:10:03.0391010-06:00</BuildTime>
  <Modifications>
    <Modification>
      <Date>2003-11-04T09:30:36.1214920-06:00</Date>
      <User>bnantz</User>
      <Comment>initial import</Comment>
      <Files>
```

```
    <File>
      <Type>Add</Type>
      <Directory>\</Directory>
      <File>aspell.net</File>
      <Revision>1</Revision>
    </File>
    <File>
      <Type>Add</Type>
      <Directory>\</Directory>
      <File>aspell-dev-0-50-3-3</File>
      <Revision>1</Revision>
    </File>
...
    </Files>
  </Modification>
 </Modifications>
</BuildResult>
```

## Running

Once the system is set up, any check-in like the one shown in Figure 7-4 will trigger a build.

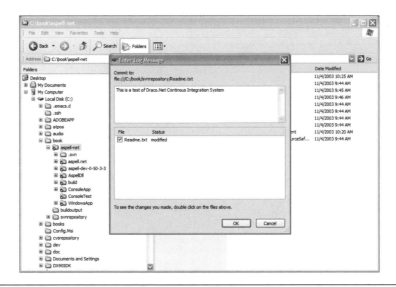

**Figure 7-4** Checking in to SVN Using Tortoise.

Draco.NET builds can also be arbitrarily started or scheduled using the Draco.NET Command-Line Client (Figure 7-5).

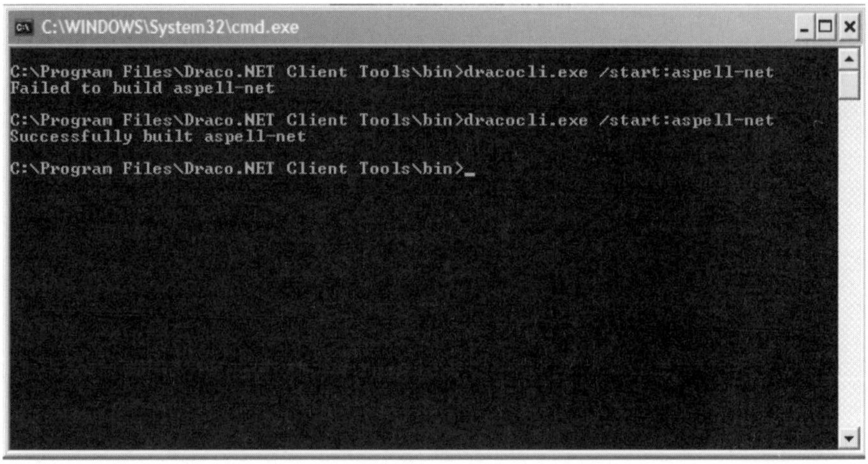

**Figure 7-5**  Draco.NET Command-Line Client.

Draco.NET server requires that the build tool (nant.exe) and the SCM tool (svn.exe) be in the path unless you change the build/nant/program config setting. If anything goes wrong, Draco.NET will either write to the Windows Event Log or to the Logfile in the C:\Program Files\Draco.NET Service folder.

**TIP:** Remember that .NET configuration files are only read upon starting the .NET executable, so when editing the configuration files, remember to restart the Draco.NET service.

## Build System

Draco.NET now supports building without using NAnt. You can use the <solution> tag in the config file to point to the path of the solution you want to build. I am not sure, but I suspect this is based on the NAnt <solution> task. I think this because neither implementation supports Enterprise Template Projects.

# CruiseControl.NET

Draco.NET was inspired by the Java CruiseControl project created by Thoughtworks (http://www.thoughtworks.com). Recently, Thoughtworks has created a .NET version of CruiseControl. Each of the two systems has its strengths and weaknesses. CruiseControl.NET (CC.NET) uses NAnt for its build system and NUnit for its Unit testing. CC.NET supports the following version control systems:

- CVS
- Visual Source Safe
- Perforce
- Star Team
- Subversion
- PVCS

## Installing

Installing CruiseControl.NET is a little more challenging than Draco.NET, but is worth it for all the additional functionality! To run the server, you must use the StartCCNet.bat file. If you want CC.NET to run as a service (like Draco.NET), then you have to install the service exe by using the installutil.exe shipped with the .NET SDK Framework.

**NOTE:** This is based on CruiseControl.NET version 0.4-Pre1.

You have to create the configuration file (ccnet.config), which is not a .NET configuration file but is very simple to create, and the documentation includes plenty of examples.

**NOTE:** To get the ASP.NET build output, you have to configure your Web server to serve up the Web directory from the distribution zip file as documented at http://ccnet.thoughtworks.com/docs/webapp/index.html.

## Configuring

Configuring CC.NET is very intuitive and well documented.

**Listing 7.4**   Configuring CruiseControl.NET

```
<cruisecontrol>
  <project name="aspell-net">
    <webURL>http://buildserver/myproject</webURL>
    <schedule type="schedule" timeout="60000"/>
    <modificationDelay>10000</modificationDelay>
    <sourcecontrol type="cvs">
      <executable>c:\temp\cvs.exe</executable>
      <workingDirectory>c:\fromcvs\myrepo</workingDirectory>
      <cvsroot>/cvsrepository</cvsroot>
    </sourcecontrol>
    <build type="nant">
      <executable>c:\temp\nant.exe</executable>
      <baseDirectory>c:\book\aspell-net</baseDirectory>
      <buildFile>master.build</buildFile>
      <targetList>
        <target>build</target>
      </targetList>
      <buildTimeout>300000</buildTimeout>
    </build>
    <publishers>
      <email from="buildmaster@mycompany.com"
mailhost="smtp.mycompany.com" includeDetails="TRUE">
        <users>
          <user name="BuildGuru" group="buildmaster"
address="buildguru@mycompany.com"/>
          <user name="JoeDeveloper" group="developers"
address="joedeveloper@thoughtworks.com"/>
        </users>
        <groups>
          <group name="developers" notification="change"/>
          <group name="buildmaster" notification="always"/>
        </groups>
      </email>
      <xmllogger>
        <logDir>..\..\website\log</logDir>
      </xmllogger>
    </publishers>
  </project>
</cruisecontrol>
```

**NOTE:** To create a daily build rather than building with each check-in, change the <schedule> element to <schedule type="daily" integrationTime="19:00" />.

The name element once again is very important for specifying a manual build and for build notifications like emails and the Web dashboard. The <webURL> is the path to the virtual directory that hosts the Web dashboard which is described in the installation notes in the online documentation at http://ccnet.thoughtworks.com. The URL link specified by <webUrl> is embedded into the email notification if the recipient wants more detail on the build. Also is the URL used by the cctray client to directly launch Internet Explorer (or your browser of choice) to the Web dashboard.

## Running

One of the biggest advantages to CC.NET is the many different ways to monitor the build and capture the output right out of the box. Because of its XML output, Draco.NET can also perform many of these actions, but they would require a little extra work. Figure 7-6 shows the ASP.NET output on the build server.

**Figure 7-6**  CruiseControl.NET ASP.NET Output.

Figure 7-7 shows CruiseControl.NET automatically kicking off a build when a CVS check-in occurs.

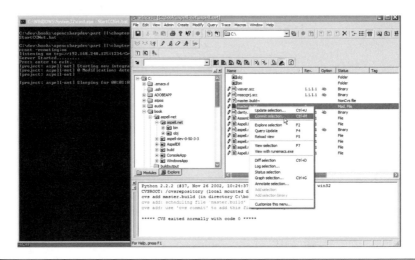

**Figure 7-7** WinCVS and CruiseControl Command-Line Client.

Figure 7-8 is the resulting email notification from the build, and Listing 7.5 is the XML log on the server.

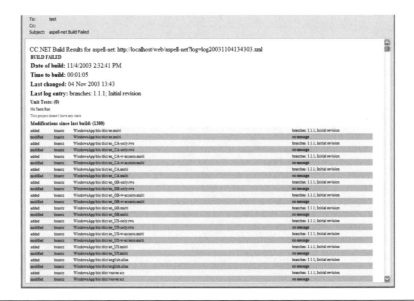

**Figure 7-8** CruiseControl.NET Email Notifications.

**Listing 7.5** Cruise Control XML Report

```
<cruisecontrol>
    <modifications>
        <modification type="added">
            <filename>Readme.txt</filename>
            <project></project>
            <date>04 Nov 2003 13:42</date>
            <user>bnantz</user>
            <comment>branches:  1.1.1;Initial revision</comment>
        </modification>
...
    </modifications>
</cruisecontrol>
```

The final way to monitor the CC.NET server build is the tray icon shown in Figure 7-9 that can be run on any Windows client, which is much cooler than the command-line client Draco.NET uses. This uses the standard balloon to tell you the status of your build in real time. You can also configure it to play an mp3 file to tell you the status of the build. You can manually start a build by right-clicking on the tray icon and telling the build to start. Alternatively, there is a Web service for starting builds or checking status.

**Figure 7-9** CruiseControl.NET Tray Icon.

## FXCop Integration

CruiseControl.NET has a nice optional <fxcop> element in the config file that offers an integrated way to run FxCop on all assemblies if you have not already done so in the NAnt build.

**.NET Continuous Integration Quick Comparison Chart**

Because all of the systems discussed in this chapter are very similar in design, a decision on which system to use will probably come down to a matter of feature sets. Therefore, this quick comparison chart should ease your decisionmaking.

|  | Draco.NET | CC.NET | Hippo.NET |
|---|---|---|---|
| **Output Types** | | | |
| XML | X | X | X |
| Remoting Application | X | X | X |
| ASP.NET | | X | |
| Mail | X | X | |
| | | | |
| **SCM Support** | | | |
| Source Safe | X | X | X |
| CVS | X | X | |
| Subversion | X | X | |
| Perforce | X | X | |
| PVCS | X | X | |
| Star Team | | X | |
| | | | |
| **OS SUPPORT** | | | |
| Windows | X | X | X |
| Linux | | ? | |

# Summary

All of the Open Source Continuous Integration projects explored here are very similar. All use .NET Remoting in a client-server application. Hopefully, these systems soon will be platform-independent as the different forms of CLI implementation support for remoting and other technologies expand. Which CI is right for you depends heavily upon your environment and mostly upon your build tool. Setting up a Continuous Integration sever is relatively quick and painless. The results from the system will have a positive effect on your development process, as will be seen in Chapter 9, "ASpell.NET Case Study."

# CHAPTER 8

# Application Logging

*Sometimes I lie awake at night, and I ask, "Where have I gone wrong?" Then a voice says to me, "This is going to take more than one night."*

—Charles M. Schulz, Charlie Brown in "Peanuts"

## Introduction

It is five o'clock on a Friday evening, and you are looking forward to a great weekend. As you turn off your computer and put on your coat, you turn around, and standing directly in front of you is your boss, and by the look on his face, he is not there to wish you a happy weekend. "Our largest customer is having major problems, and I'm going to have to ask you to help me figure them out," he says. After some research, you find that the problem is only on certain machines and is not even in the part of the application that is your code. Does this sound familiar? Where do you start? How do you figure out the problem?

One of the best ways to quickly diagnose a problem is to have good application logging. By "good," I mean logging that is configurable and robust, something that can log more than just the standard application error messages that users are accustomed to seeing but will also log information useful to a developer. To avoid spending your weekend diagnosing and solving someone else's mistake, you need to be able to capture information about the state of the application that is more detailed than just error messages.

# Application Logging

There are many logging components available today, both Open Source and proprietary. Microsoft and others working on the CLI specification had the foresight to build logging into System.Diagnostics.Trace. By using the Trace class in conjunction with System.Diagnostics.TraceListner, System.Diagnostics.Switch, and their child classes, you can do rudimentary logging using only the CLI. Most developers find that the built-in CLI framework's functionality is better than that of previous languages but still lacking in that they cannot log to the targets they want or log in a specific, configurable way.

**TIP:** As shown later in Table 8.3, Log4NET has a TraceAppender output that can output just like a regular TraceListener but of course with a lot more configurable outputs.

Several other logging frameworks have been created for .NET. Microsoft's Patterns & Practices group created an Exception Management Block (http://msdn.microsoft.com/library/default.asp?url=/library/en-us/dnbda/html/emab-rm.asp) that is a little better than the CLI logging at being exception-aware, and they recently announced the Logging Application tion Block (http://msdn.microsoft.com/library/default.asp?url=/library/en-us/dnpag/html/Logging.asp?frame=true) that goes even further into application logging under some sort of end user license agreement. Justin Rudd originally ported LogKit (http://avalon.apache.org/logkit/), another Apache project, and I added a lot of functionality to it. You can find it at http://www.sourceforge.net/projects/logkit-net.

**NOTE:** Watch for the C# version of the Apache group's Avalon framework (http://www.apache.org/~hammett/avalondotnet/index.html). This project will provide a standard way to handle exceptions, logging, advanced serialization, and more! Similar projects are available under shared source from Microsoft's Pattern & Practices group (see the Application Blocks available from http://msdn.microsoft.com/library/default.asp?url=/library/en-us/dnbda/html/emab-rm.asp).

By far, the best logging kit available on the market happens to be Log4Net (http://log4net.sourceforge.net), and it also happens to be Open Source. Log4Net is a .NET port of a popular Java tool, Log4J. Log4J is a stable tool that has seen a lot of runtime and has been ported to many languages with great success. It's based on the research of the SEMPER (http://www.semper.org) group who, commissioned by the European Union to create a secure framework for e-commerce, decided to create their own logging API.

Some developers, especially with a C++ background, do not initially see the advantages of runtime logging over compile-time tracing. While allowing the compiler to map out all trace statements is the most popular type of logging available, it is not at all flexible. Runtime logging offers the advantage of setting and changing level thresholds at runtime for the code or even turning the logging off altogether. The advantages of this type of flexibility outweigh the proportionately small performance loss in most developers' minds.

## Architecture

Log4Net (http://log4net.sourceforge.net) is a cross-platform, exception-aware application logging framework that has a very simple API for ease of use, but it is complex enough to work in even the largest enterprise applications. A great amount of functionality is available in Log4Net, but to get the system up and logging, there are only five objects needed from Log4Net: Loggers, Appenders, Layouts, Levels, and Filters. Figure 8-1 on p. 194 is a very simplistic flowchart of Log4Net.

Though admittedly a simplistic diagram, Figure 8-1 gives an overview of how the main classes interact with each other. In fact, the Filter and Layout stages of the flowchart are not even required, making it even simpler. A log message is sent from your code using a Logger. The message then is checked against the current logging Level. If the message Level is such that it needs to be logged, the message is sent to any configured Appenders. If Filters are set up, the Appender asks the Filter if the message should be logged. If the message passes through all this, it is then sent to the Layout object to correctly format the message, and the Appender then writes out the message to the log.

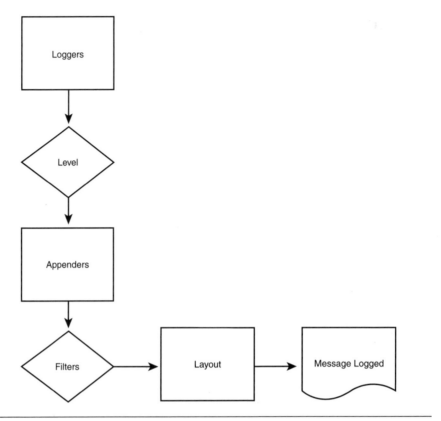

**Figure 8-1** Flowchart of Log4Net.

**NOTE:** This chapter is based on Log4NET version 1.2.0 beta 8.

Log4Net is compatible with almost all of the CLI implementations available. The one caveat with this is that some Appenders only work on specific platforms. This will be addressed in detail in the "Appenders" section later in this chapter.

**TIP:** One of the most powerful features of Log4NET that will be covered later in the chapter is its ability to be configured using an XML configuration file as the program is executing.

# Loggers

A log message in your code using Log4Net all begins with the Logger class. The Logger is the portal into your code. While all of the five main objects can be configured from code, most often you will only need to use the Logger class. Because the LogManager class implements the ILog interface, there is a well-defined strong contract between Log4Net and your code. The ILog interface simply implements the following methods: Debug, Info, Warn, Error, and Fatal. The first set of methods corresponds to the available Levels covered in the next portion of the chapter. All of this makes logging in your program very simple, as shown in Listing 8.1.

**Listing 8.1** A Simple Log4NET Log Message

```
_logger.Error("This is an error message.", exception);
```

Well, if using a Logger to log is so easy, then how is a Logger instantiated? A Logger is created one of two different ways. The first way to obtain a Logger is by passing in a string to associate with the Logger (see Listing 8.2).

**Listing 8.2** Creating a Logger

```
Logger _logger = LogManager.GetLogger("MyLogger");
```

The second way to obtain a Logger is to associate the Logger to the type of the class, as in Listing 8.3. This way, once a Logger is instantiated, you are essentially linking that instance of the Logger with that class.

**Listing 8.3** The Recommended Way of Getting a Logger

```
Logger _logger = LogManager.GetLogger(typeof(namespace.class));
```

Whatever messages are logged will be flagged as coming from this class. The reason for the functionality differences in Listing 8.2 and Listing 8.3 is found in Logger Hierarchy and inheritance.

## Hierarchy

Loggers are by default hierarchical and based on a named hierarchy. This allows for powerful inheritance of Loggers and ease of use from multiple assemblies. Named hierarchy should be familiar to .NET developers because it is used in namespaces and fully qualified class names in .NET development. Listing 8.4 is an example of Loggers that are related in a parent-child relationship.

**Listing 8.4**  Hierarchical Loggers

```
Parent Logger - LogManager.GetLogger(typeof(foo));
Child Logger - LogManager.GetLogger(typeof(foo.bar));
```

If foo.bar is not assigned a Logging Level, it will inherit it from the parent Logger foo. Also, any log messages for foo.bar will be forwarded to any Appenders in foo.bar as well as up the hierarchy to foo's Appenders. Consequently, there is a Logger that exists as the base or root for all Loggers. This Logger always exists and cannot be retrieved by name. Therefore, you must use the getRootLogger static method of the Logger class to retrieve it. This functionality is due to the fact that every child Logger has a reference to its parent, but the parent Logger knows nothing about the child. Fortunately, this allows for child Loggers to be created before parent Logger, and the hierarchy will all work out in the end.

This inheritance and hierarchy functionality can be turned off via the additivity method on the Logger:

**_logger.setAdditivity(false);**

Alternatively, this functionality can be achieved by using the following code under the Logger section of the Log4Net config file:

**<additivity value="false" />**

Looking at this hierarchy from a different angle, Listing 8.5 shows two Loggers that refer to the exact same instance of a Logger object.

**Listing 8.5** Identical Logger References

```
Logger a = LogManager.GetLogger(typeof(foo));
Logger b = LogManager.GetLogger(typeof(foo));
```

This greatly reduces the amount of code needed to use Log4Net by eliminating the need to pass around a reference to a particular instance of the object throughout all the code. This can be useful when using multiple assemblies and should be very useful for Partial Types in .NET 2.0.

## LogManager

The LogManager class works with the Hierarchy class to manage all the Loggers for a given instance of Log4Net. LogManager allows for greater runtime control, as seen in Table 8.1.

**Table 8.1** Helpful LogManager Methods

| Method | Description |
| --- | --- |
| ILog [] GetCurrentLoggers() | Gets all the currently available Loggers |
| ILog [] GetCurrentLoggers(Assembly assembly) | Gets all the currently available Loggers for a given assembly |
| ILog GetLogger(string name) | Gets a Logger by name |
| ILog GetLogger(string domain, string name) | Gets a Logger by domain and name |
| ILog GetLogger(Assembly assembly, string name) | Gets a Logger by assembly and name |
| ILog GetLogger(Type type) | Gets a Logger by type |
| ILog GetLogger(string domain, Type type) | Gets a Logger by type for a given domain |
| ILog GetLogger(Assembly assembly, Type type) | Gets a Logger by type for a given assembly |
| ILog Exists(string name) | Checks if a Logger exists by name |
| ILog Exists(string domain, string name) | Checks if a Logger exists by name for a given domain |

**Table 8.1**  Helpful LogManager Methods (cont.)

| Method | Description |
|---|---|
| ResetConfiguration() | Defaults the configuration of all Loggers including the Appenders, Levels, and additivity flags |
| ResetConfiguration(string domain) | Resets the configuration based on domain |
| ResetConfiguration(Assembly assembly) | Resets the configuration based on the assembly |
| Shutdown() | Safely shuts down Log4Net |

Using the static methods in Table 8.1 can allow your logging code to be very dynamic at runtime as well as give a great deal of information on the current status of your logging system.

## Levels

After obtaining a Logger and writing a log message, the first check on the message is whether it is loggable based on the Level of the message and the threshold of the logging in your application. Not including the generic log method, there are five logging Levels that correspond to the five methods required by ILog to exist in all Loggers (see Table 8.2). In addition, there are two special log Levels to turn logging off or to turn it on full-blast.

The default Level inherited from the root Logger if no Level is specified is the DEBUG Level. New levels can be added to the map on the Hierarchy. Unfortunately, these new levels cannot be used through the ILog interface. A new interface would need to be written to utilize the new levels.

**TIP:** See the TraceLog extension for an example of defining new levels and using them in a new interface.

**Table 8.2**  Logging Levels

| Level | Description |
|---|---|
| OFF | Log no messages. |
| DEBUG | Developer-oriented messages, usually used during development of the product. |
| INFO | Useful information messages such as state changes, client connection, user login, etc. |
| WARN | A problem or conflict has occurred, but it may be recoverable; then again, it could be the start of the system failing. |
| ERROR | A problem has occurred, but it is not fatal. The system will still function. |
| FATAL | Something caused the whole system to fail. This indicates that an administrator should restart the system and try to fix the problem that caused the failure. |
| ALL | Log all messages. |

The Levels are cumulative in that they allow all messages at their Level and at any Level less strict than themselves. Figure 8-2 demonstrates which messages will be logged in a given Level.

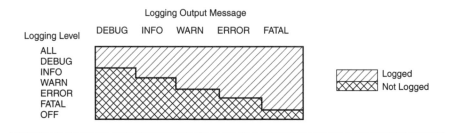

**Figure 8-2**  Logging Levels.

For example, if your application's logging Level is set to WARN (left axis of the graph) and your logging code is

```
_logger.Info("Informational message");
```

then the message will not be logged because the top axis of the graph shows that in WARN, only WARN, ERROR, and FATAL messages are logged. This is the first Filter of the message. Additional, more powerful Filters can be set using the Filter class. If the message passes through the Level check, it is then passed to any configured Appenders.

# Appenders

The nicest feature of Log4Net is that you do not have to consider at design time how your log messages will be persisted. Log4Net abstracts that functionality by allowing you to log to a variety of destinations via an Appender. Because a Logger logs to an Appender interface, adding an Appender or changing an Appender at runtime is very easy! More importantly, logging code does not have to change to log to a different destination. Also, you do not have to implement the code to actually write the log to its destination. Table 8.3 is a list of available Appenders in Log4Net:

**Table 8.3** Log4Net Appenders

| Type | Description |
| --- | --- |
| ADONetAppender | Writes logging events to a database using either prepared statements or stored procedures. |
| ASPNetTraceAppender | Writes logging events to the ASP trace context. These can then be rendered at the end of the ASP page or on the ASP trace page. |
| BufferingForwardingAppender | Buffers logging events before forwarding them to child Appenders. |
| ConsoleAppender | Writes logging events to the application's Console. The events may go to either the standard output stream or the standard error stream. |
| EventLogAppender | Writes logging events to the Windows Event Log. |
| FileAppender | Writes logging events to a file on the file system. |
| ForwardingAppender | Forwards logging events to child Appenders. |
| MemoryAppender | Stores logging events in a memory buffer. |

**Table 8.3** Log4Net Appenders (cont.)

| Type | Description |
| --- | --- |
| NetSendAppender | Writes logging events to the Windows Messenger service. These messages are displayed in a dialog on a user's terminal. |
| OutputDebugStringAppender | Writes logging events to the debugger. If the application has no debugger, the system debugger displays the string. If the application has no debugger and the system debugger is not active, the message is ignored. |
| RemotingAppender | Writes logging events to a remoting sink using .NET Remoting. |
| RollingFileAppender | Writes logging events to a file in the file system. The RollingFileAppender can be configured to log to multiple files based upon date or file size constraints. |
| SMTPAppender | Sends logging events to an email address. |
| TraceAppender | Writes logging events to the .NET trace system. |
| UdpAppender | Sends logging events as connectionless UDP datagrams to a remote host or a multicast group using a UdpClient. |

**TIP:** You can use a TraceAppender to write to the DebugWindow of Visual Studio.NET. OutputDebugStringAppender also writes to most IDE Debug Windows; alternatively, you can use the DebugView tool from http://www.sysinternals.com to view these messages.

Having your application log to multiple Appenders is also a prominent feature of Log4Net. You do not have to choose just one Appender. You may want to use the ADONetAppender and the EventLogAppender so that a client application has the log locally and so that the message is also centrally located in a database.

**NOTE:** Just about every database, Open Source or not, has a Data Provider for ADO.NET. Chapter 10, "Database Development," explores the ADO.NET provider for PostgreSQL, which would make an excellent log target.

Unfortunately, Log4Net does not yet support a Fallback Appender, but I know it is on the to-do list. A fallback Appender allows you to specify a preferred Appender but also another Appender in case the preferred Appender fails.

To add an Appender to a Logger, use the Logger method addAppender(Appender appender). As Figure 8-3 depicts, all Appenders inherit from AppenderSkeleton.

Therefore, all Appenders must have the following properties:

- Layout—Tells the Appender how to format the message before writing it to the destination target.
- Threshold—A Level that tells the Appender which Levels are acceptable to log. This can be used to direct log output to different Appenders based on their Levels.
- Filter—Allows an Appender to filter out messages in a more configurable way than by just using the Threshold Level.

By using multiple Appenders and the threshold of the Appenders, you can direct log messages to different targets. So, as Listing 8.18 shows later in this chapter, you can configure Log4Net to log all messages to the eventlog and all FATAL messages to send email to a pager system.

You may have noticed that Figure 8-3 alludes to BufferingAppenders. Some of the Appenders, like the SMTPAppender, may need to buffer up a specified number of messages before sending them.

As was mentioned, Log4Net is platform-independent. Log4Net does support different CLI implementations in some capacity. This is not a flaw in Log4Net but is basically due to the lack of support in either the CLI implementation or the operating system platform itself. For instance, Log4Net does work on Windows CE, but the current version of the CLI implementation (.NET Compact Framework) does not support Remoting,

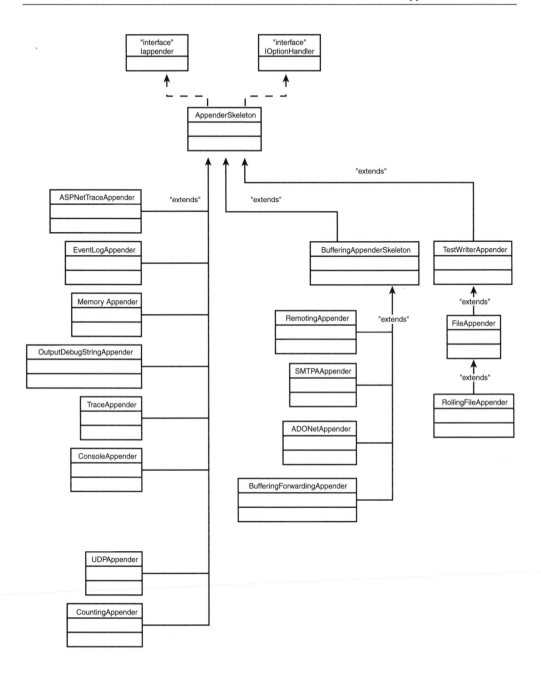

**Figure 8-3**  Logger Inheritance.

so the Remoting Appender will not work on that platform. Table 8.4 lists the platforms currently supported by Log4Net.

The Appender is responsible for actually writing out the log messages. While you already have the ability to "Filter" messages based on the Logger's Level, you may want to "Filter" in a more configurable, larger capacity. Of course, Log4Net provides this functionality in the Filter class.

**Table 8.4** Appender Platform Support

| Appender | .NET Framework 1.0 | .NET Framework 1.1 | .NET Compact Framework 1.0 | Mono 0.25 or Higher | Shared Source CL 1.0 |
|---|---|---|---|---|---|
| ADONetAppender | X | X | X | X | |
| ASPNetTraceAppender | X | X | | X | |
| BufferingForwardingAppender | X | X | X | X | X |
| ColoredConsoleAppender | X | X | | | |
| ConsoleAppender | X | X | X | X | X |
| CountingAppender | X | X | X | X | X |
| EventLogAppender | X | X | | | |
| FileAppender | X | X | X | X | X |
| ForwardingAppender | X | X | X | X | X |
| MemoryAppender | X | X | X | X | X |
| NetSendAppender | X | X | | | |
| OutputDebugStringAppender | X | X | X | | |
| RemotingAppender | X | X | | X | X |
| RollingFileAppender | X | X | X | X | X |
| SMTPAppender | X | X | | X | |
| SmtpPickupDirAppender | X | X | X | X | X |
| TraceAppender | X | X | X | X | X |
| UdpAppender | X | X | X | X | X |

# Filters

Filters are associated with an Appender. A Filter allows you to set even stricter requirements on your LoggingEvent message. A number of predefined Filters are available in Log4Net. The DenyAll Filter allows you to deny all LoggingEvents unless specifically granted access. This is the exact opposite of the default behavior, but obviously it can be useful. The LevelMatch and LevelRange Filters are pretty self-explanatory for Filtering based on a Level. The StringMatch Filter allows you to filter a Logging Event based on a regular expression query. The NDC and MDC Filters are also similar string-based Filters. All of these Filters inherit from FilterSkeleton, which in turn implements IFilter. This makes creating your own custom Filter fairly straightforward, as shown later in the chapter under "Custom Filters."

When a LoggingEvent is passed through a Filter, one of three values is returned: ACCEPT, DENY, or NEUTRAL.

The real power of filtering comes when you link several Filters together. This is referred to as Filter Chaining. If DENY is returned from a Filter, the LoggingEvent is "dropped" for that Appender, and there is no need for the message to be passed on down the chain. If ACCEPT is returned, the LoggingEvent is logged, and the chain is broken. If NEUTRAL is returned from the Filter, the LoggingEvent is passed on to the next Filter in the chain, so forth and so on, down through all the Filters. If the LoggingEvent passes through the Filter Chain without an explicit ACCEPT or DENY, then it is implicitly accepted. The DenyAll Filter can be placed at the end of the Filter chain to reverse this implicit acceptance behavior.

While Filters allow flexibility in what to log to the Appender, Layouts tell the Appender how the logged message should look.

# Layouts

Once it has been determined that the LoggingEvent should be written using the Appender, the message is passed to the Layout object. Table 8.5 on p. 206 lists the currently available Layout classes.

**Table 8.5** Log4Net Layouts

| Type | Description |
|------|-------------|
| log4net.Layout.SimpleLayout | Formats the logging event very simply: [Level] - [message] |
| log4net.Layout.XMLLayout | Formats the logging event as an XML element. |
| log4net.Layout.PatternLayout | Formats the logging event according to a flexible set of formatting flags. |

If an Appender utilizes a layout, the Simple Layout will be the default Layout for an Appender. The XMLLayout is a very useful Layout, as seen in Listing 8.6.

**Listing 8.6** Sample Output Using XMLLayout

```
<log4net:event logger="IPWindowsApp.Form1" timestamp="2003-10-
26T23:34:01.4237872-06:00" level="DEBUG" thread="3348"
domain="ProcWindowsApp.exe" username="BNANTZ-XP\bnantz">
   <log4net:message>This is just a test of using WMI with
Log4Net.</log4net:message>
   <log4net:mdc>
      <log4net:data name="clock" value="1993 MHz" />
      <log4net:data name="mem" value="536199168 bytes" />
   </log4net:mdc>
</log4net:event>
```

Probably the most flexible Layout is the Pattern Layout. The Pattern Layout allows you to specify a ConversionPattern string to transform the LoggingEvent into a more useful message. Table 8.6 shows the variables you can use to form a ConversionString.

**Table 8.6** Pattern Layout Format Strings

| Variable | Description |
|---|---|
| %m | Outputs your message. |
| %p | Outputs the priority of the logging event. |
| %r | Outputs the number of milliseconds elapsed since the start of the application until the creation of the logging event. |
| %c | Outputs the category of the logging event. Example: For the category name "a.b.c," the pattern %c{2} will output "b.c." {2} means "output last two components of the dot-separated category name." If no {n} is there, the full category name is output by default. |
| %t | Outputs the name of the thread that generated the logging event. |
| %x | Outputs the nested diagnostic context (NDC) associated with the thread that generated the logging event. Useful when multiple clients are handled by separate threads at a server process. |
| %X{} | Outputs the message diagnostic context (MDC) associated with the thread that generated the logging event. Useful when multiple clients are handled by separate threads at a server process. |
| %n | Outputs the platform-dependent newline character(s). Preferable to specifying "\n" or "\r\n" etc. |
| %% | Outputs a single percent sign. |
| %d | Outputs the date of the logging event. The date conversion specifier may be followed by a date format specifier enclosed between braces. Example: %d{HH:mm:ss,SSS} or %d{dd MMM yyyy HH:mm:ss,SSS}. If no date format specifier is given, then ISO8601 format is assumed. The date format specifier admits the same syntax as the time pattern string of Java's SimpleDateFormat, which is slow. For faster performance, use %d{ISO8601}, %d{ABSOLUTE}, %d{RELATIVE} (millisecs since program start, fastest) or %d{DATE}, which use log4j's ISO8601DateFormat, AbsoluteTimeDateFormat, RelativeTimeDateFormat, and DateTimeDateFormat date formatters, respectively. |

**Table 8.6** Pattern Layout Format Strings (cont.)

| Variable | Description |
| --- | --- |
| %C | Outputs the fully qualified class name of the caller issuing the logging request. Example: For the class name "org.apache.xyz.SomeClass," the pattern %C{1} will output "SomeClass." {1} means "output last one component of the fully-qualified class name." If no {n} is there, the full class name is output by default. |
| %M | Outputs the method name where the logging request was issued. |
| %F | Outputs the file name where the logging request was issued. |
| %L | Outputs the line number from where the logging request was issued. |
| %l | Outputs source code location information. Shortcut for %C.%M(%F:%L). |

Listing 8.7 demonstrates how to build up a PatternLayout. Cross-referencing Table 8.6, this pattern outputs date, thread name, priority, category, ndc, message, and newline.

**Listing 8.7** PatternLayout

```
%d [%t] %-5p %c [%x] - %m%n
```

In addition to the variables defined by Log4Net, there is also formatting of the variables shown in Listing 8.7 as -5. You can use the minus sign (-) to left-justify within a field. The default is to right-justify (pad on left) a field. A positive integer can be used to specify the minimum field width. If the data item requires fewer characters, it is padded with space(s) on either the left or the right until the minimum width is reached. If the item is larger than the minimum field width, the field is expanded to accommodate the data returned from the variable. You can also specify the maximum field width by using a period followed by a positive integer. If the data item is longer than the maximum field, then the extra characters are removed from the beginning of the item rather than the end.

You can also create your own pattern variables in your code for use by the PatternLayout's ConfigurationString.

These Layouts are useful for logging string messages, but if you want to log the state of an Object, then you need to use an ObjectRenderer.

# ObjectRenderer

When using a Logger in your application, you will notice that all Logger functions accept an Object for their message parameters. This takes advantage of the fact that all classes inherit from System.Object in .NET. Another reason for using an Object is for Log4Net to allow you to pass more than just a string to be logged. Log4Net gains a little code reuse by creating a class called ObjectRenderer. ObjectRenderer is used by the Layout class to transform the LoggingEvent into a string message to be logged. By implementing a custom ObjectRenderer, you can pass a custom Object to Log4Net, and the Layout will call your specified custom ObjectRenderer to get a String representation of the state of the Object. This is demonstrated using a DataSet in the "Examples" section of this chapter.

# Configuration

Obviously, one of the keys to Log4Net's success is that it is so configurable. Log4Net's configurations tie together the Loggers, Appenders, Layouts, Levels, and Filters. This configurability can at first glace look very complex, but once you understand the basic classes in Log4Net, the configuration is intuitive and incredibly powerful.

## Programmatic Configuration

Everything in Log4Net can be configured and built up programmatically. The minimal steps to get Log4Net working in a program are:

1. Create a Hierarchy
2. Create a Logger with an associated Level in that Hierarchy
3. Attach an Appender

4. Set an Optional Filter on the Appender
5. Set an Optional Layout for the Appender

Listing 8.8 shows this in C# code. If you are not specifying a Filter or a Layout, this makes the already simple code almost trivial.

**Listing 8.8**  Configuring Log4Net Programmatically

```
using log4net;
using log4net.Appender;
using log4net.spi;
using log4net.Repository.Hierarchy;
// Get the Hierarchy object that organizes the Loggers
Hierarchy h = LogManager.GetLoggerRepository() as Hierarchy;
// Get the specific Logger that you want to configure
// either by name or select the root Logger
Logger l = h.GetLogger("foo"); // or Logger l = h.Root;
// Update the properties on the Logger
l.Level = Level.DEBUG;
l.AddAppender(new appender);
// Get a named Appender from the Logger
ConsoleAppender c = l.GetAppender("ConsoleAppender") as
ConsoleAppender;
// Change the console Appender to use the error stream
c.Target = "Console.Error";
// Tell the Appender to update
c.ActivateOptions();
```

Although this is not really complicated, it is certainly the wrong way to configure Log4Net in most scenarios. The problem in the code in Listing 8.8 is that everything is hard-coded. The Level will always be DEBUG and would need to be recompiled to be anything other than DEBUG. The same applies for the Appender, which would always be ConsoleAppender, which is not very useful in persisting information!

## Runtime Configuration

A better way of configuring a Logger is to use a runtime configuration. This is supported in Log4Net by using a .NET configuration file. The CLI specification allows .NET applications to have an XML application configuration file. By default, this file is named the same as the application, with a

.config added to the end of the filename. These configuration files are used in the runtime engine itself (a machine.config) and in ASP.NET (web.config). These configuration files are Hierarchical so that a value defined in machine.config will automatically be available to all other configuration files because machine.config is the root configuration file.

There are several built-in config file sections that are useable in your code. The most familiar one is the appSettings section where you can store specific information for your applications. Config files are also extendable by using the IConfigurationSectionHandler interface, and you can define your own config file sections. This is what Log4Net has done, as you can see in Listing 8.9.

**Listing 8.9** Log4Net's Custom Configuration File Section

```xml
<?xml version="1.0" encoding="utf-8" ?>
<configuration>
   <!-- Register the section handler for the log4net section -->
   <configSections>
      <section name="log4net"
type="System.Configuration.IgnoreSectionHandler" />
   </configSections>

<!-- This section contains the log4net configuration settings -->
   <log4net>
      <appender name="EventLogAppender"
type="log4net.Appender.EventLogAppender" >
         <layout type="log4net.Layout.PatternLayout">
            <param name="ConversionPattern" value="%d [%t] %-5p %c [%x]
- %m%n" />
         </layout>
      </appender>

<!-- Setup the root category, add the appenders and set the default
priority -->
      <root>
         <level value="INFO" />
         <appender-ref ref="EventLogAppender" />
      </root>
   </log4net>
</configuration>
```

Now the advantages of runtime configuration are a little clearer. The Appender is configured in Listing 8.9 with a PatternLayout. There could be multiple Appenders used. Hierarchy is used in this example because the root Logger is configured with an INFO Level and an Appender (EventLog Appender) that was configured earlier in the config file. This information will be inherited by all Loggers by default. The important thing here is that none of this is hard-coded. It is easily changed in the config file without having to touch the code. As was mentioned at the beginning of this chapter, this allows a developer to not worry about where the log message is going to be stored or how the message will be formatted.

**TIP:** Example Appender Configurations can be found in Appendix D.

When using a .NET config file, the configuration information is read in when the application is started. Any change to the configuration file would not be reflected until the program is restarted. Log4Net has gone a step further and allows configuration changes to be applied on-the-fly by adding this custom attribute to your AssemblyInfo.cs file:

```
[assembly:log4net.Config.DOMConfigurator(ConfigFile="filename", Config-
FileExtension="ext", Watch="true")]
```

This shows the true power and flexibility of Log4Net. A server application does not even have to be restarted to change the logging Level to log more detailed information.

## Configurations in a Smart Client

In .NET, there is a new way to distribute Windows Forms applications from a centralized location, called Smart Clients, and have your application automatically update all clients when the assemblies at the centralized location are updated. In this scenario, you have to be aware that you are running with limited privileges and will not be able to use many of the Log4Net Appenders. In extending Log4Net, I will introduce a new Appender to log to the IsolatedFileStorage that can be used in this semi-trusted environment. Also be careful that when automatically downloading a client, .NET only downloads the config file once unless the .NET GAC cache is cleared. This means that the configuration information is not easily updatable. Even if you manually distribute the client code to all the client machines, the problem still remains of updating all the clients to log at a different Level. Normally you may not desire to do this and flood the system with messages, but if such a need arises, you could possibly fetch the configuration information from a database instead of a config file with a little custom work in the log4net.Configuration class.

# Logging with Context Information

Once you start using logging prevalently in your code, eventually you will want to add custom information into your log messages. This is especially helpful in a large distributed system that has centralized logging to a database or a Web service. You are going to want to know the IP address of the computer, possibly the user logged on at the time of the error, and other specific context information. Log4Net allows for adding context information in your log message with two different classes. Both classes are thread-safe and have their advantages and disadvantages.

## MDC

The Mapped Diagnostic Context (MDC) is implemented as a Dictionary value-key pair lookup. One of the nice features of the MDC is that you have a greater control over the message output than you do with the NDC. Later in this chapter, Listing 8.12 on p. 215 shows using MDC with WMI. You can see in the config file that you can put mapped information anywhere in the conversion pattern string. However, this does come with a price, which is that the Dictionary key used in the code (i.e., clock) has to match exactly in the config file's conversion pattern string (i.e., %X{clock}).

## NDC

The Nested Diagnostic Context (NDC) is similar to the MDC, except that it is Stack-based rather than Dictionary-based. Listing 8.10 shows the use of the NDC.

**Listing 8.10**  Nested Diagnostic Context

```
using(log4net.NDC.Push(System.Environment.UserName.ToString()))
{
    if(_logger.IsDebugEnabled)
```

```
    {
        _logger.Debug("This is just a test of using NDC.");
    }
}
```

The config file Pattern Layout looks like this:

```
<layout type="log4net.Layout.PatternLayout">
    <param name="ConversionPattern" value="%d [%t] %-5p %c [%x] - %m%n" />
</layout>
```

The disadvantage is that in the config file, the %x outputs all the information built up in the NDC. The bright side is that you do not have to worry about matching up strings in your code with strings in your configuration file. Another advantage to the NDC is that you can wrap the code in a C# using statement, which will automatically call the NDC's disposal code and clean up resources for you.

## WMI

There has been some confusion with regard to how the Log4Net project relates to Windows Management Instrumentation (WMI). The short answer is that Log4Net and WMI have very little in common. Log4Net is a .NET application logging framework. WMI is a COM-based view into the internals of the Windows platform. WMI is used to monitor Windows system specifics like network card information, as shown in Listing 8.11.

**Listing 8.11**  A WMI Query

```
SELECT * FROM Win32_NetworkAdapterConfiguration
```

Microsoft even uses WMI in some of its own monitoring utilities. Microsoft married a nice COM interface to a familiar SQL-like query language so that all languages could use WMI. The first thing to note is that WMI is, of course, Windows-specific. You can still get useful logging information from System.NET and System.Environment. Different operating systems have different ways of obtaining this information. As far as I can tell, there is no CLI implementation other than Microsoft's .NET that has a System.Management managed portal into operating system-specific information. The reason this chapter addresses WMI is to clear up some confusion about Log4Net and WMI and also to demonstrate a useful way to use MDC logging.

Listing 8.12 is an example of using System.Management to obtain very specific information about the system that may be used in logging.

**Listing 8.12** Using WMI with MDC

```
manageClass = new ManagementClass("Win32_Processor");
manageCollection = manageClass.GetInstances();
foreach(ManagementObject mo in manageCollection)
{
    foreach(PropertyData s in mo.Properties)
    {
        if(s.Name == "MaxClockSpeed")
        {
            log4net.MDC.Set("clock", mo [s.Name].ToString() + " MHz");
        }
    }
}
```

Next, add the following to your config file to use the custom variable:

```
<layout type="log4net.Layout.PatternLayout,log4net">
        <param name="ConversionPattern" value="%d [%t] %-5p %c
[MaxClock=%X{clock}] [TotalPhysicalMemory=%X{mem}] - %m%n" />
        </layout>
```

This can add very useful information to your log if you happen to be running on a CLI implementation that supports it.

# Performance and Scalability

Log4Net is very performance-driven. While Log4Net has many features and goals, the top priority is performance. The bulk of the added overhead of Log4Net is actually having the Appender write the message to the target. Here are some tips to help Log4Net perform at an optimal Level.

## GAC

Does inserting Log4Net into the Global Assembly Cache (GAC) gain any performance? In .NET, there is some overhead involved with the Just-In-Time (JIT) compiler. Pre-Jitting the assembly into a native image helps speed up the startup process, but it can also prevent the runtime from making some runtime optimizations. Ngen.exe is the tool to pre-jit an assembly that uses the GAC file structure to store the output of ngen but does not require your assembly to be in the GAC. By putting Log4Net into the GAC, you allow for shared memory code pages during execution. If a large number of applications will be using the assembly, you will gain some memory. Microsoft recommends using private deployment unless you really have a good reason to use the GAC. Depending on the number of applications that use Log4Net, you may or may not see performance improvement by putting Log4Net in the GAC. The disadvantage is that you can no longer do XCopy deployment; however, you do gain side-by-side execution to allow multiple versions of Log4Net to be on one system without interference.

### Parameter Construction

Parameter construction, while not extremely costly by itself, can add up when used too often. Listing 8.13 shows how to avoid parameter construction.

**Listing 8.13**  Avoiding Parameter Construction

```
if( _logger.isDebugEnabled)
{
       _logger.Debug("Error: " + exception.ToString());
}
```

While it is not best practice to always log the exception this way, the point of Listing 8.13 is that while the Logger.Debug class will automatically check the Level for you, it will happen after the string has already been constructed, and that could be costly. By checking the Level yourself while adding code, you will improve the performance of your logging.

## Hierarchy

Logger hierarchy walking for every LoggingEvent message is expensive. Every message is passed up through the entire hierarchy and sent to each Logger's Appender. You can gain significant performance by turning off the walking of the hierarchy and logging directly to the root Logger.

## Stack Tracing

The first thing that usually happens with Log4Net is that developers fall in love with it for debugging. Then the developers build their application in Release mode for integration testing and say, "Where did all my line numbers go?"

Table 8.6 on p. 207 showed the different patterns that can be used to capture information like file, method, and line numbers. The following patterns can have significant effect on your application's performance.

%d
%l
%C
%M
%F
%L

Some of these pattern formatters are associated with formatting (like the date pattern), but the big performance problem comes with trying to provide the source file name and line number. In order to achieve this, Log4Net attempts to walk up through the stack and trace the exception. This is done by using the StackTrace and Stackframe classes from the System.Diagnostics namespace, and Log4Net cannot guarantee that the information will be available. This is not the fault of Log4Net because only the Debug builds contain the file information, method name, and line numbers. Even with Debug information, because of security settings, Log4NET may not be able to walk the stack, or because of runtime optimizations, the information may not be deep into the call stack, as you would expect. Thus, turning the Debug flag off for Managed code will not really increase your performance, and leaving them on could be useful. Do keep in mind though that decompilation of the code is much easier if it is shipped with Debug symbols.

# Examples

In the interest of getting Log4Net up and running quickly, this part of the chapter is nothing but examples. To try to mix and match all of the types of .NET applications with all of the Appenders would be a nightmare. These examples are meant to complement the configuration information in Appendix D, "Log4Net Appender Configurations."

## Windows Forms and Console Applications

Console Applications and Windows Forms use Log4Net in the exact same way. A .NET configuration file is needed, and with a few lines of code, Log4Net is up and running. The first example is a Windows Form (Listing 8.14), which is a very common use for Log4Net. This is the code that uses the XML configuration in Listing 8.6 that features a FileAppender.

**Listing 8.14** Windows Form FileAppender

```
private void Form1_Load(object sender, System.EventArgs e)
  {
      try
      {
        manageClass = new ManagementClass("Win32_Processor");
        manageCollection = manageClass.GetInstances();
        foreach(ManagementObject mo in manageCollection)
        {
           foreach(PropertyData s in mo.Properties)
           {
              if(s.Name == "MaxClockSpeed")
              {
                 log4net.MDC.Set("clock", mo[s.Name].ToString() + "
MHz");
              }
           }
        }
        manageClass = new ManagementClass("Win32_ComputerSystem");
        manageCollection = manageClass.GetInstances();
        foreach(ManagementObject mo in manageCollection)
        {
           foreach(PropertyData s in mo.Properties)
           {
```

```
            if(s.Name == "TotalPhysicalMemory")
            {
                log4net.MDC.Set("mem", mo[s.Name].ToString() + "
bytes");
            }
        }
      }
    }
    catch(Exception ex)
    {
        MessageBox.Show(ex.ToString());
    }
  }
```

**NOTE:** File Appenders are not thread-safe, and they acquire a lock on the file. To synchronize the log, you must log to a service process that will synchronize the messages and then write them to a file.

Because the FileAppender takes a write lock on the file to which it is writing, it is not possible to have two FileAppenders configured to use the same file. This is regardless of where the FileAppenders are; they can be in the same AppDomain, different AppDomains, or different processes, but the issue is still the same.

Currently, the only way to have multiple AppDomains/Processes writing to the same file is to configure only one FileAppender in the primary AppDomain and have all the additional AppDomains use the RemotingAppender to deliver the events to the primary AppDomain, which will then log the event using the FileAppender.

This does require different Log4Net configurations for the AppDomains.

The second example (Listing 8.15) is the code that uses Listing 8.10, the NDC example. This is a Console application that uses the EventLogAppender.

**Listing 8.15** Console Application NDC

```
[STAThread]
static void Main(string [] args)
{
        try
        {
```

```
using(log4net.NDC.Push(System.Environment.MachineName.ToString()))
        {

using(log4net.NDC.Push(System.Environment.OSVersion.ToString()))
            {

using(log4net.NDC.Push(System.Environment.Version.ToString()))
                {

using(log4net.NDC.Push(System.Environment.UserName.ToString()))
                    {

                        if(_logger.IsDebugEnabled)
                        {
                            _logger.Debug("This is just a test of using
NDC.");
                        }
                    }
                }
            }
        }
    }
    catch(Exception ex)
    {
        System.Diagnostics.Debug.WriteLine(ex.ToString());
        Console.WriteLine(ex.ToString());
    }
}
```

## ClassLibraries

.NET class libraries are compiled to dll files. Dlls cannot have their own
config file but rather use the config file for the hosting application. Using
.NET reflection, you can allow your class library to have a config file, but this
is not recommended for two reasons. First, if the dll is going to reside in the
GAC, it is very hard (and not recommended) to use a config file. Second, if
several applications use your class library, changing the logging Level in the
class library's config file will affect all applications using your class library,
whereas keeping the Logger Level in the application will allow each application to use the class libraries logging at their own configurable Levels.

## ASP.NET and Web Services

Using Log4Net in an ASP.NET Web site or Web service is a great application of the logging framework. This is an ideal place to use the rolling file Appenders, as you may not have full permissions to the machine if you are using a hosting service.

**NOTE:** For some Appenders like NTEventLog, you may need to perform a one-time elevation of privileges for the ASP.NET user.

Listing 8.16 shows a simple Web service.

**Listing 8.16**  A Simple Web Service Logging Routine

```
[WebMethod]
public void LogAMessage(string message, int level)
{
    _logger = log4net.LogManager.GetLogger(typeof(LoggerService.Log));

    switch(level)
    {
        case 1:
            _logger.Fatal(message);
            break;
        case 2:
            _logger.Error(message);
            break;
        case 3:
            _logger.Debug(message);
            break;
        case 4:
            _logger.Info(message);
            break;
        default:
            _logger.Debug(message);
            break;
    }
}
```

You still need to add the normal configuration information to the web.config file. The problem comes in getting the framework to configure (or reconfigure) each time the web.config file is altered. The normal trick of using [assembly:log4net.Config.DOMConfigurator(ConfigFile = "filename", ConfigFileExtension = "ext", Watch = "true")] will not work. This is because of the way the application is hosted by IIS. However, there is a very easy workaround. Whenever an ASP.NET application is restarted, including when web.config is changed, the application re-reads the Global.asax file. Therefore, you could place the code in Listing 8.17 into the global.asax.cs code file and reload the Log4NET configuration from the web.config file manually. When you change the web.config, this code will be rerun.

**Listing 8.17** Configuring Log4Net for ASP.NET and Web Services

```
namespace SomeNamespace
{
    public class Global : System.Web.HttpApplication
    {
        protected void Application_Start(Object sender, EventArgs e)
            {
            log4net.Config.DOMConfigurator.Configure();
                            log4net.Info("Application Started");
        }
    }
}
```

By using the code in Listing 8.17, you can configure Log4Net whenever the Webform or Web service is initialized.

## Serviced Components

Logging using Log4Net in a Serviced Component (COM+) application is just as easy as logging in a class library dll. The hard part comes when you try to get the configuration information to Log4Net. The recommended way around this is to configure Log4Net programmatically, as in Listing 8.18.

**Listing 8.18** ServicedComponent Programmatic Configuraiton

```
//First configure programatically
//Assume the config file will be named classlibrary1.dll.config
//Could also hardcode this to a specified path.
```

```
StringBuilder configpath = new StringBuilder();
configpath.AppendFormat("{0}.config",
        System.Reflection.Assembly.GetExecutingAssembly().Location);

FileInfo configfile = new FileInfo(configpath.ToString());
log4net.Config.DOMConfigurator.ConfigureAndWatch(configfile);
```

This allows the config file to be named [assemblyname].dll.config, and Log4Net will configure and watch for changes in the file, just like a normal configuration.

## Remoting

Logging from your Remoting application is again similar to logging in any other class library dll. It would probably be best to use a database to log to since Remoting is sometimes distributed. Logging to the EventLog or to a file presupposes certain permissions on the machine. Using the SQL script and configuration from the ADONetAppender in Appendix E in conjunction with the PGAdmin II tool, we can create a PostgreSQL database for logging. This of course requires the use of Npgsql, which we will see in-depth in Chapter 10, "Database Development."

**Listing 8.19**  Logging to PostgreSQL

```
   <appender name="ADONetAppender"
type="log4net.Appender.ADONetAppender">
     <param name="BufferSize" value="100" />
     <param name="ConnectionType" value="Npgsql.NpgsqlConnection,
Npgsql,Version=0.5.0.0, Culture=neutral,
PublicKeyToken=5d8b90d52f46fda7" />
     <param name="ConnectionString" value="data
source=localhost;initial catalog=log4net;User ID=admin;Password=admin"
/>
     <param name="CommandText" value="INSERT INTO Log
([Date],[Thread],[Level],[Logger],[Message],[Exception]) VALUES
(@log_date, @thread, @log_level, @logger, @message, @exception)" />
     <param name="Parameter">
        <param name="ParameterName" value="@log_date" />
        <param name="DbType" value="DateTime" />
        <param name="Layout" type="log4net.Layout.RawTimeStampLayout"
/>
```

```xml
        </param>
        <param name="Parameter">
          <param name="ParameterName" value="@thread" />
          <param name="DbType" value="String" />
          <param name="Size" value="255" />
          <param name="Layout" type="log4net.Layout.PatternLayout">
            <param name="ConversionPattern" value="%t" />
          </param>
        </param>
        <param name="Parameter">
          <param name="ParameterName" value="@log_level" />
          <param name="DbType" value="String" />
          <param name="Size" value="50" />
          <param name="Layout" type="log4net.Layout.PatternLayout">
            <param name="ConversionPattern" value="%p" />
          </param>
        </param>
        <param name="Parameter">
          <param name="ParameterName" value="@logger" />
          <param name="DbType" value="String" />
          <param name="Size" value="255" />
          <param name="Layout" type="log4net.Layout.PatternLayout">
            <param name="ConversionPattern" value="%c" />
          </param>
        </param>
        <param name="Parameter">
          <param name="ParameterName" value="@message" />
          <param name="DbType" value="String" />
          <param name="Size" value="4000" />
          <param name="Layout" type="log4net.Layout.PatternLayout">
            <param name="ConversionPattern" value="%m" />
          </param>
        </param>
        <param name="Parameter">
          <param name="ParameterName" value="@exception" />
          <param name="DbType" value="String" />
          <param name="Size" value="2000" />
          <param name="Layout" type="log4net.Layout.ExceptionLayout" />
        </param>
    </appender>
```

Listing 8.19 is the Log4Net configuration for using Npgsql for appending to a PostgreSQL database table. The script for creating the database table is in Appendix D.

## Windows Services

Windows Services, as far as logging is concerned, are a lot like a Windows Form or Console Application executable. Many times distributed applications, especially when using Remoting, depend on a Windows Service to be running to host them. Many systems depend on services to be running, and there is no simple, nice way to automatically restart or check the health of a Windows Service as there is for a Web service. So, if that service goes down for whatever reason, this would definitely be a FATAL condition. Listing 8.20 shows a configuration that would be ideal for a service. This is a place where multiple Appenders would probably be needed, with this Appender handling the FATAL messages.

**Listing 8.20**  Sending Only Fatal Messages via Immediate Email

```
<appender name="EventLogAppender"
type="log4net.Appender.EventLogAppender" >
          <layout type="log4net.Layout.PatternLayout">
                  <param name="ConversionPattern" value="%d [%t] %-5p
%c [%x] - %m%n" />
          </layout>
</appender>

<appender name="SMTPAppender"
type="log4net.Appender.SMTPAppender">
  <param name="To" value="me@myemail.com" />
  <param name="From" value="MyService" />
  <param name="Subject" value="Fatal Error Occured" />
  <param name="SMTPHost" value="my.mailserver.com" />
  <param name="LocationInfo" value="false" />
  <param name="BufferSize" value="1" />
  <param name="Lossy" value="false" />
  <param name="Threshold" value="FATAL"/>
  <layout type="log4net.Layout.PatternLayout">
      <param name="ConversionPattern" value="%n%d [%t]%-5p %c [%x] -
%m%n%n%n" />
  </layout>
```

```
</appender>
```

Listing 8.20's example shows that Log4Net is more than just a nice way to write out a log message. This example uses the Threshold of an SMTP Appender to send an email out on a FATAL log message. This email could be easily tied to a pager system for remote support.

# Log File Readers

Using a standard Logger, as opposed to creating your own custom logging, has great advantages. The Open Source community has created two Logfile Reading Applications that can be used with Log4Net.

## LogFactor5

LogFactor5 is a Java application that is a part of the Log4J distribution. You can download it at http://jakarta.apache.org/log4j/docs/lf5/overview.html. Figure 8-4 shows what LogFactor5 looks like.

Using the ConversionPattern and FileAppender in Listing 8.21 will format the logfile so that LogFactor5 will work with it.

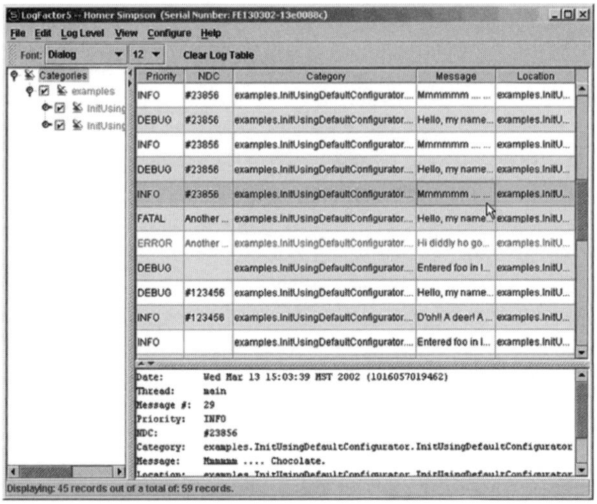

**Figure 8-4** LogFactor5 User Interface.

**Listing 8.21** LogFactor5 using PatternLayout

```
<appender name="FileAppender" type="log4net.Appender.FileAppender">
        <param name="File" value="log-file.txt" />
        <param name="AppendToFile" value="true" />
        <layout type="log4net.Layout.PatternLayout">
        <param name="ConversionPattern"
value="[slf5s.start]%d{DATE}[slf5s.DATE]%n\%p[slf5s.PRIORITY]%n%x[slf5s
.NDC]%n%t[slf5s.THREAD]%n%c[slf5s.CATEGORY]%n\%l[slf5s.LOCATION]%n%m[sl
f5s.MESSAGE]%n%n" />
        </layout>
  </appender>
```

LogFactor5 is not very actively developed compared to Chainsaw.

## Network Log Client

If a C# application suits you better, there is an Open Source project that will listen for input from Log4Net's UdpAppender.

Network Log Client (http://sourceforge.net/projects/netlogclient/) is a simple but effective graphical viewer for logged messages, as shown in Figure 8-5.

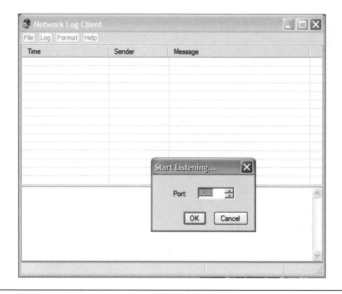

**Figure 8-5** Network Log Client.

## Chainsaw

Chainsaw (Figure 8-6) is another Java application that can be used to read log files. This application can be downloaded from http://sourceforge.net/projects/logui or as part of the Log4J package.

Chainsaw supports the following configurations:

UDPAppender—By default Chainsaw uses port 4445.
XMLLayout Format—As shown in Listing 8.6.

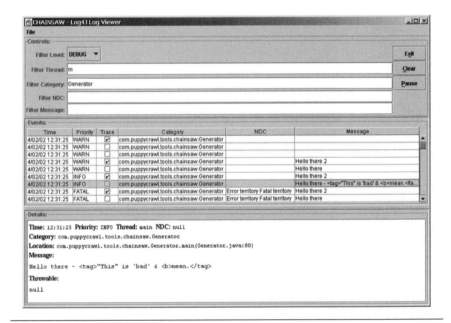

**Figure 8-6**  Chainsaw.

Chainsaw is being actively developed and is a nice cross-platform user interface log reader that gathers information from multiple clients nicely.

# Extending Log4Net

Although Log4Net has a lot of functionality already built in, down the road you may want to extend Log4Net by creating a Custom Filter or Appender. You will find the framework easy and intuitive to work with.

## Error Handling

In a logging framework, great care must be taken so that an error or exception is never passed to the calling assembly. Any errors must be handled internally and must never affect the calling application. In most situations, the calling application is trying to log an error condition of its own and does not expect to have error handling around its error handling logging. Most errors are prone to be in the Appender code when the message is to be written. Figure 8-3 shows that all Appenders inherit from AppenderSkeleton. ApenderSkeleton uses the helper class OnlyOnceErrorHandler to handle its errors, so unless the Appender overrides this functionality, it will get OnlyOnceErrorHandler to handle its errors as well. OnlyOnceErrorHandler implements IErrorHandler and actually writes the errors using another helper class called LogLog. LogLog just writes the message out to the Console.Error or Trace methods. If the fact that you cannot see these messages disturbs you, then you have three options. First, you could implement your own version of IErrorHandler. Second, you could create an application to capture the Debug messages. Third, you could just download DebugView from http://www.sysinternals.com, which is a nice graphical tool that intercepts the system debug messages for Windows. Similar tools are already built into the Linux OS.

## Custom Filters

With the power of Filter Chaining, you rarely would need to create a custom Filter. However, you may want to do so for performance reasons. Chaining too many Filters together does decrease performance. The power of the Level Filtering and string Regex Filtering on the message already provides ample flexibility. The only flexibility not available with LevelRangeFilter and LevelMatchFilter is the ability to specify a list of Levels. While not earth-shattering, it is a good study in creating custom Filters.

The SpecifiedLevelFilter will allow you to specify a comma-separated list of Levels and whether you should accept a match or decline it. Listing 8.22 would be the configuration file syntax.

**Listing 8.22**  SpecifiedLevelFilter's Configuration File Information

```
<filter type="log4net.Filter.SpecifiedLevelFilter">
    <param name="Levels" value="WARN,INFO"/>
    <param name="AcceptOnMatch" value="true"/>
```

```
</filter>
```

Using the LevelRange as a template, first change the code for retrieving the Levels to use the comma-separated Levels (Listing 8.23) for the Filter.

**Listing 8.23**  C# Code for SpecifiedLevelFilter's Levels

```
public string Levels
{
      get
      {
          System.Text.StringBuilder sb = new
System.Text.StringBuilder();
          foreach(Level l in m_levels)
          {
              sb.AppendFormat("{0},", l.Name);
          }
          sb.Remove(sb.Length, 1);
          return sb.ToString();
      }
      set
      {
          string [] sLevels = value.Split(new char[]{','});
          m_levels = new Level[sLevels.Length];
          int i =0;
          LevelMap lm = new LevelMap();
          lm.Add(Level.DEBUG);
          lm.Add(Level.ERROR);
          lm.Add(Level.FATAL);
          lm.Add(Level.WARN);
          foreach(string s in sLevels)
          {
            m_levels[i]= lm[s.ToUpper()];
            i = i +1;
          }
      }
}
```

Listing 8.23 is a little messy, but basically it uses String.Split to retrieve just the Levels, does a look-up on the Level using LevelMap, and creates an array of Levels. Next (Listing 8.24) is the overridden Decide method from FilterSkeleton.

**Listing 8.24**  The Decision logic for SpecifiedLevelFilter

```
override public FilterDecision Decide(LoggingEvent loggingEvent)
{
    if (loggingEvent == null)
    {
        throw new ArgumentNullException("loggingEvent");
    }
     foreach(Level level in m_levels)
     {
         if(loggingEvent.Level == level)
         {
            if (m_acceptOnMatch)
            {
              // this Filter set up to bypass later Filters and always
return
              // accept if level in range
              return FilterDecision.ACCEPT;
            }
            else
            {
              return FilterDecision.NEUTRAL;
            }
         }
     }
      return FilterDecision.DENY;
}
```

This decision defaults to Deny. If any one of the Levels is found in the Level array populated from the config file (Listing 8.22), then if accept on match is set to true, the Filter will return ACCEPT, and the message will be logged.

## Custom Layout

With XML and Pattern Layouts, you can do almost anything. However, just to show how to create a custom Layout, I will create (actually port the Log4j version of) an HTMLLayout. This Layout could be useful to use as an output with a daily RollingFileAppender on a server. The HTML is static, so the pages do not even need to be served.

Following the similar Architecture, the Layout has to inherit from LayoutSkeleton. This means we have to implement a header, footer, and format and decide whether we should ignore exception information. We really should not ignore exception information, as it is very useful. The header is simple; it is just the HTML table in Listing 8.25.

**Listing 8.25** Header Table for HTMLLayout

```
<!DOCTYPE HTML PUBLIC "-//W3C//DTD HTML 4.01 Transitional//EN"
"http://www.w3.org/TR/html4/loose.dtd">
<html>
<head>
<title>Log4Net Log Messages</title>
<style type="text/css">
<!--
body, table {font-family: arial,sans-serif; font-size: x-small;}
th {background: #336699; color: #FFFFFF; text-align: left;}
-->
</style>
</head>
<body bgcolor="#FFFFFF" topmargin="6" leftmargin="6">
<hr size="1" noshade>
Log session start time 2/4/2004 12:18:28 AM<br>
<br>
<table cellspacing="0" cellpadding="4" border="1" bordercolor="#224466"
width="100%">
<tr>
<th>Time</th>
<th>Thread</th>
<th>Level</th>
<th>Category</th>
<th>Message</th>
</tr>
```

The footer just closes the table, as in Listing 8.26.

**Listing 8.26** Footer for HTMLLayout

```
</table>
```

```
<br>
</body>
</html>
```

The overridden Format Method fills in the LoggingEvent information; this C# code is in Listing 8.27.

**Listing 8.27** C# Formating Code for HTMLLayout

```
public override System.String Format(LoggingEvent event_Renamed)
{

        if (sbuf.Capacity > MAX_CAPACITY)
        {
                sbuf = new System.Text.StringBuilder(BUF_SIZE);
        }
        else
        {
                sbuf.Length = 0;
        }

        sbuf.Append(SystemInfo.NewLine + "<tr>" + SystemInfo.NewLine);

        sbuf.Append("<td>");
        sbuf.Append(event_Renamed.TimeStamp);
        sbuf.Append("</td>" + SystemInfo.NewLine);

        sbuf.Append("<td title=\"" + event_Renamed.ThreadName + "
thread\">");
        sbuf.Append(Transform.escapeTags(event_Renamed.ThreadName));
        sbuf.Append("</td>" + SystemInfo.NewLine);

        sbuf.Append("<td title=\"Level\">");
        if (event_Renamed.Level == Level.DEBUG)
        {
                sbuf.Append("<font color=\"#339933\">");
                sbuf.Append(event_Renamed.Level);
                sbuf.Append("</font>");
        }
        else if (event_Renamed.Level >= Level.WARN)
        {
                sbuf.Append("<font color=\"#993300\"><strong>");
```

```
                sbuf.Append(event_Renamed.Level);
                sbuf.Append("</strong></font>");
        }
        else
        {
                sbuf.Append(event_Renamed.Level);
        }
        sbuf.Append("</td>" + SystemInfo.NewLine);

        sbuf.Append("<td title=\"" + event_Renamed.LoggerName + "
category\">");
        sbuf.Append(Transform.escapeTags(event_Renamed.LoggerName));
        sbuf.Append("</td>" + SystemInfo.NewLine);

        if (locationInfo)
        {
                LocationInfo locInfo = event_Renamed.LocationInformation;
                sbuf.Append("<td>");
                sbuf.Append(Transform.escapeTags(locInfo.FileName));
                sbuf.Append(':');
                sbuf.Append(locInfo.LineNumber);
                sbuf.Append("</td>" + SystemInfo.NewLine);
        }

        sbuf.Append("<td title=\"Message\">");
        sbuf.Append(Transform.escapeTags(event_Renamed.Rendered
Message));
        sbuf.Append("</td>" + SystemInfo.NewLine);
        sbuf.Append("</tr>" + SystemInfo.NewLine);

        if (event_Renamed.NestedContext != null)
{
                sbuf.Append("<tr><td bgcolor=\"#EEEEEE\" style=\"font-
size : xx-small;\" colspan=\"6\" title=\"Nested Diagnostic
Context\">");
                sbuf.Append("NDC: " +
Transform.escapeTags(event_Renamed.NestedContext));
                sbuf.Append("</td></tr>" + SystemInfo.NewLine);
        }

        System.String s = event_Renamed.GetExceptionStrRep();
        if (s != null)
        {
```

```
            sbuf.Append("<tr><td bgcolor=\"#993300\"
style=\"color:White; font-size : xx-small;\" colspan=\"6\">");
            appendThrowableAsHTML(s, sbuf);
            sbuf.Append("</td></tr>" + SystemInfo.NewLine);
        }

        return sbuf.ToString();
    }
}
```

The results are seen in Figure 8-7.

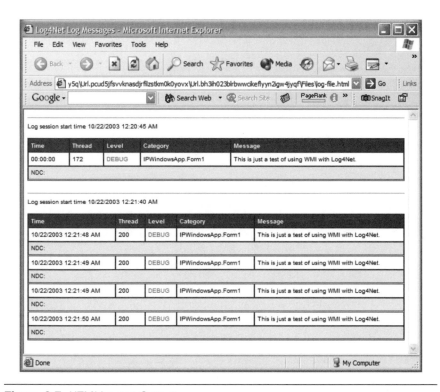

**Figure 8-7** HTMLLayout Output.

## Custom Appender

There are a number of Appenders that would be interesting to implement for Log4Net. I considered a Telnet Appender but thought that would be unnecessarily confusing for just showing how to extend the architecture. As

I mentioned in the Configuration section of this chapter, I settled on an IsolatedFileStorageAppender. IsolatedFileStorage is a temporary cache for files, much like Internet Explorer's Temporary Internet Cache, that allows a .NET application to read and write files even in a semi-trusted environment such as an Internet-deployed Windows Form. IsolatedFileStorage is a stream-based writer similar to a FileStream. So from Figure 8-3, you can see that we should start by inheriting the Appender from TextWriterAppender like the FileAppender. In fact, we can even use the FileAppender as a template and just change a little code.

Listing 8.28 shows the actual code to open the IsolatedFileStorageStream wrapped in a StreamWriter in the already existing Open method.

**Listing 8.28**  Custom Code for IsolatedFileStorageAppender

```
      if(append)
 {
     m_isfs = new IsolatedStorageFileStream(fileName, FileMode.Append,
FileAccess.Write, FileShare.ReadWrite, m_isf);
 }
 else
 {
     m_isfs = new IsolatedStorageFileStream(fileName, FileMode.Create,
FileAccess.Write, FileShare.ReadWrite, m_isf);
 }
 SetQWForFiles(new StreamWriter(m_isfs, m_encoding));
```

Very little code was changed from the FileAppender. The biggest difference from FileAppender is that it does not allow a directory specification but uses Listing 8.29 to get the directory to write to.

**Listing 8.29**  Code Changes to FileAppender to Create IsolatedFileStorageAppender

```
m_isf = IsolatedStorageFile.GetUserStoreForAssembly();
….
protected static string ConvertToJustName(string path)
{
    if (path == null)
```

```
{
     throw new ArgumentNullException("path");
 }
if(path.LastIndexOf("//") > 0)
{
     FileInfo fi = new FileInfo(path);
     path = fi.Name;
}
return path;
}
```

So ConvertToJustName was added to the File property to chop off any directory information. The Layout and Filters are handled for me by the framework. Nice, clean, and easy.

I modified the ProcWindowsApp example from Listing 8.12 in the WMI section to use IsolatedFileStorageAppender and saved it to a new IFSTesterWindowsApp example. After running the IFSTesterWindows-App, you should be able to browse to C:\Documents and Settings\[USER-NAME]\Local Settings\Application Data\IsolatedStorage and see the log-file.txt output.

**NOTE:** This file may be in a series of strangely named folders due to the way the IsolatedStorage works.

### Custom Renderer

Custom Renderers are very useful for logging the state of a Custom Object. To illustrate this, Listing 8.30 shows Log4Net logging a Strongly Typed Dataset.

**Listing 8.30** Logging a Strongly Typed Dataset

```
private void button1_Click(object sender, System.EventArgs e)
{
    _logger.Debug(this.dataset11);
}
```

The config file for the application wanting to render a Dataset is shown in Listing 8.31.

**Listing 8.31** Renderer Configuration Information

```
<log4net>
   <renderer renderingClass="log4net.ObjectRenderer.DataSetRenderer"
renderedClass="DatasetRenderTest.DataSet1, DatasetRenderTest" />

   <appender name="FileAppender"
type="log4net.Appender.FileAppender" >
          <param name="File" value="log-file.txt" />
          <param name="AppendToFile" value="true" />

      <layout type="log4net.Layout.SimpleLayout" />
   </appender>

   <root>
                 <level value="DEBUG" />
                 <appender-ref ref="FileAppender" />
   </root>
</log4net>
```

In order to create a Custom Render, you must implement IObjectRenderer. The class that implements the render can exist either in Log4Net or in your own custom assembly that Log4Net will call. This is done by specifying the assembly and type in the config file in Listing 8.31. Log4Net will call the DoRender method required by the IObjectRenderer. This is where you filter on your type. So if the Object is a System.Data.DataSet, we will operate on it; otherwise, we can only call the ToString method because it is guaranteed to exist since everything inherits from System.Object. Listing 8.32 is the code called if the Object is a Dataset.

**Listing 8.32** C# Dataset Renderer Code

```
virtual protected string RenderDataSet(RendererMap rendererMap, DataSet
dataset)
{
```

```
      StringBuilder buffer = new StringBuilder(dataset.DataSetName +
"{");
      buffer.Append(NewLine);
      foreach(DataTable dt in dataset.Tables)
      {
         buffer.Append("\t" + dt.TableName + "{");
         buffer.Append(NewLine);
         buffer.Append("\t\t");

         foreach(DataColumn column in dt.Columns)
         {
            buffer.Append(column.ColumnName + ",");
         }
         buffer.Remove(buffer.Length-1, 1);

         buffer.Append(NewLine);
         foreach(DataRow row in dt.Rows)
         {
            buffer.Append("\t\t");
            foreach(Object o in row.ItemArray)
            {
               buffer.Append(o.ToString() + ",");
            }

            buffer.Remove(buffer.Length-1, 1);
            buffer.Append(NewLine);
         }
         buffer.Append("\t\t}");
         buffer.Append(NewLine);
      }
      return buffer.Append("}").ToString();
}
```

Very simply, this code loops through a DataSet's tables, rows, and items, printing the values into a comma-separated file. This is a simple example, but it can be a powerful way to persist objects and messages in your distributed application to get an idea of the state of the system.

As you can see, extending Log4Net is easy and somewhat intuitive just by looking at how other already implemented classes in the framework are designed.

# Summary

Log4Net is a great tool for writing better code. This not only helps you but many other developers who may need to support this code down the road. Even though we know that regardless of the amount of testing, software will fail in the field, the failures are sometimes still unbelievably amazing. Log4Net is easy to learn and use and is a great investment in your programming skill set.

# Part III

# Integrating .NET Open Source Projects in Your Development

# CHAPTER 9

# ASpell.NET Case Study

*Nothing you can't spell will ever work.*

—*Will Rogers*

## Introduction

There are three excuses ever present in software development:

1. We don't have time to automate the build.
2. We'll do the documentation later.
3. We don't have time to write tests.

I understand the importance of Time to Market and that the first release of a product is always the hardest to get out the door. However, I believe this "rush-to-market" approach to development is shortsighted and outdated. This philosophy could wind up costing you a lot more time in the end than if you spend a little time up front creating a solid development procedural atmosphere.

Chapters 4 through 7 deal directly with how to solve these problems. Writing documentation along the way is not difficult with NDoc. NAnt allows for an intuitive and solid scriptable build. Testing can actually be enjoyable with NUnit while you try to break your code with the test code you write.

This chapter is a simple but realistic case study of using Open Source tools in everyday development. To illustrate this I chose to create a new Open Source project: ASpell.NET. ASpell.NET (http://aspell-net.sourceforge.net) is a .NET wrapper around the GNU ASpell project (http://aspell.source-forge.net). ASpell is a commercial-caliber spell checking component that supports twenty-some different language dictionaries.

**NOTE:** ASpell.NET is not a good candidate for cross-platform support because PInvoke is not very well supported on CLIs other than Microsoft's .NET.

Thorsten Maerz has created a Win32 port of ASpell, which I will wrap in a C# component. I believe this to be a good example because it includes PInvoke calls into unmanaged code. Realistically, this process of wrapping existing functionality and making it available to managed code will probably be done for quite a while by most corporations.

**TIP:** For a good book on .NET Interop, see:

*.NET and COM: The Complete Interoperability Guide*
by Adam Nathan from Sams Publishing

Adam has also created a wiki (http://www.pinvoke.net) and a Visual Studio.net add in (click the get visual studio add-in link on the Web site).

This example will check the code by using FxCop and NUnit. As we go along, we will utilize NDoc to output a useful help file for redistribution. In the end, an install will be created using MSI, and an iso file will be created using the custom mkisofs task created in Chapter 4. The iso file will then be uploaded to a server for distribution to a testing department or, depending on the extent of your testing, to customers. All this will happen automatically upon checking in code using Continuous Integration if the build succeeds (which also implies that the tests succeed).

I created ASpell.NET as a proof-of-concept to see how easy it would be to get ASpell working for .NET. ASpell.NET would make a great Web service. To eliminate the need to use pointers and the unsafe compiler option, I wrapped the ASpell dll in another C++ dll (AspellDll.dll). This allows ASpell.NET to use methods that have parameters that require pointers. So the base functionality for ASpell.NET is already there, but with no documentation or tests and without support for dictionaries other than the English dictionary. The source is available from the SourceForge project site, and you will be able to see that Log4Net also plays a part in ASpell.NET. We will use .NET's CuturalInfo to automatically detect which language dictionary to use. Finally, we will demonstrate the use in a somewhat real-world application similar to the WordPad app using #develop to create it as Windows form.

# Test First Development

Really, to be fair, I should have developed the tests for ASpell.NET first, but I wanted to see if it was even feasible. Since it seems to be a useful component, now is the time to write the tests while the project is still pretty young. What is nice about developing the tests first is that is forces you to create your API and think about your contract with the outside world in a detailed way. After all, you cannot write the tests for components if you do not know what the signatures of the public methods are or what properties are available. For ASpell.NET, I did not have to spend too much time in the design of the component because it pretty much mimics ASpell's design. This was done for two reasons. First, I wanted ASpell.NET to be familiar to anyone who has used ASpell. Second, I realized the amount of man-hours and development put into ASpell and decided that I probably could not come up with a much better design.

I will start with the following tests:

- What if I pass in a null or empty string to spell check?
- What if I use numerals or punctuation?
- What if the program can't find a dependant dll or dictionary?
- Can it support multiple cultures?
- What if there's nothing to return?

To perform these tests, I will add a reference to NUnit into the build and use it to create the tests. Listing 9.1 shows the simplest test if a null is passed into ASpell.NET.

**Listing 9.1** NUnit Test

```
[TestFixture]
   public class AspellNullTest
   {
     private aspell.net.SpellChecker spellCheck;

     [SetUp]
     public void Init()
     {
       spellCheck = new aspell.net.SpellChecker();
     }
```

```
[Test]
[ExpectedException(typeof(aspell.net.ASpellNullException))]
public void NullCheck()
{
   foreach(CultureInfo ci in spellCheck.CultureInfos)
   {
      spellCheck.CultureInfo = ci;
      spellCheck.checkword(null);
   }
}

[Test]
[ExpectedException(typeof(aspell.net.ASpellNullException))]
public void NullSuggest()
{
   foreach(CultureInfo ci in spellCheck.CultureInfos)
   {
      spellCheck.CultureInfo = ci;
      spellCheck.suggest(null);
   }
}
}
```

**NOTE:** NUnit version 2.1.4 was used for these tests.

This test will take no time at all. The hardest test will be removing the dictionaries and dependant dlls. In designing the tests, we must create them in a way that will not require you to rewrite them for every culture.

# NAnt Build

I will use the NAnt master build, simple dll, simple exe, and winform exe templates all taken from Chapter 4. Listing 9.2 shows the master build file.

**NOTE:** NAnt 0.8.2 was used for this chapter.

**Listing 9.2** ASpell.NET's Build Projects File

```
<projects>
        <!-- ASpell.Net -->
        <project>
                <name>aspell.net\aspell.net</name>
        </project>
        <!-- Tests -->
        <project>
                <name>tests\nunit\nunit</name>
                <dependencies>
                        <dependency>aspell.net</dependency>
                </dependencies>
        </project>
        <project>
                <name>tests\ConsoleAppTester\ConsoleAppTester</name>
                <dependencies>
                        <dependency>aspell.net</dependency>
                </dependencies>
        </project>
        <!-- Examples -->
        <project>
                <name>examples\WindowsApp\WindowsApp</name>
                <dependencies>
                        <dependency>aspell.net</dependency>
                </dependencies>
        </project>
        <project>
                <name>examples\WordPadSpell\WordPadSpell</name>
                <dependencies>
                        <dependency>aspell.net</dependency>
                </dependencies>
        </project>
</projects>
```

Notice that all the example projects are dependent upon the ASpell.NET project. Listing 9.3 shows that after the transform of the project file and building all the subprojects, the setup project is run, and the iso file is created. At this point, the file could be distributed a number of different ways, but Listing 9.3 uses SCP (secure copy) to upload the file to a server.

**Listing 9.3** ASpell.NET's Master Build File

```
<project name="Master Build" basedir="." default="build">
   <sysinfo verbose='true'/>

   <!-- General Build Properties -->
   <property name="debug" value="true" />
   <property name="define" value="DEBUG;TRACE" />
   <property name="build.dir" value="C:\book" />
   <property name="refassemblies" value="${build.dir}\refassemblies "
/>
   <property name="isofile" value="release.iso" />

   <!-- MSI Properties -->
   <property name="product.name" value="ASpell.NET" />
   <property name="company.name" value="OpenSource.NET" />
   <property name="msi.version" value="1.0.2" />
   <property name="msi.guid.product" value="{D9C16B65-BD89-44f5-AEC8-
16775D4A3619}" />
   <property name="msi.guid.upgrade" value="{42D979E5-E2E8-45c6-89D4-
378353848479}" />
   <!-- Location to output the complete msi -->
   <property name="output.dir" value="${build.dir}\output" />

   <target name='build'>

      <exec program=îNantHelper.exeî commandline=îprojects.xmlî
output=îprojects.txtî basedir=î.î />

      <!-- After applying Helper application transform pass the target
to the subprojects -->
      <foreach item='Line' property='filename' in='projects.txt'>
        <nant buildfile='${build.dir}\${filename}.build' target='build'
/>
      </foreach>

      <msi
           sourcedir="${output.dir}"
           license="license.rtf"
           output="${company.name}.${product.name}.msi"
           debug="true"
           verbose="true"
        >
```

```
        <properties>
            <property name="ProductName" value="${product.name}" />
            <property name="ProductVersion" value="${msi.version}"
/>
            <property name="Manufacturer" value="${company.name}" />
            <property name="ProductCode" value="${msi.guid.product}"
/>
            <property name="UpgradeCode" value="${msi.guid.upgrade}"
/>
        </properties>

        <directories>
            <directory name="D__BINDIRECTORY" foldername="bin"
root="TARGETDIR" />
        </directories>
        <components>
            <component name="C__MainFiles" id="{301CC44C-A3A4-4674-
AE04-23D91F156301}" attr="2"
                directory="TARGETDIR" feature="F__DefaultFeature">
                <key file="Test.xml" />
                <fileset basedir="${build.dir}">
                    <includes name="*.*" />
                </fileset>
            </component>
        </components>
        <features>
            <feature name="F__DefaultFeature" title="${product.name}
Main Feature" display="1" typical="true" directory="TARGETDIR">
                <description>${product.name} core
files.</description>
            </feature>
        </features>
    </msi>

    <mkisofs isofilename='${build.dir}\${isofile}'
inputdir='output.dir' />

    <scp file='${build.dir}\${isofile}' server="ReleaseServer"
path="~" />

    </target>
</project>
```

Figure 9-1 is the assurance that the NAnt build, complete with NUnit and NDoc integration, is working.

Before continuing any further, we should set up a Source Code Management (SCM) system.

**Figure 9-1** ASpell.NET's Build Output.

## Subversion

I chose to use Subversion (SVN) with ASpell.NET, even though Source-Forge does not support it, because it is easy to use and has some nice features that CVS does not support.

**NOTE:** TortoiseSVN version 0.21.0 Build 277 and SVN version 0.32.1 were used in this chapter.

First, a repository must be created, which is simple, as Figure 9-2 demonstrates.

Next I will simply import ASpell.NET into the repository. Figure 9-3 shows how to import a Subversion project.

As you can see, using Subversion is very simple and not intrusive in the development cycle. Another great feature of Subversion is that the repository can be easily compressed and moved to a different machine, even if that machine runs a different operating system.

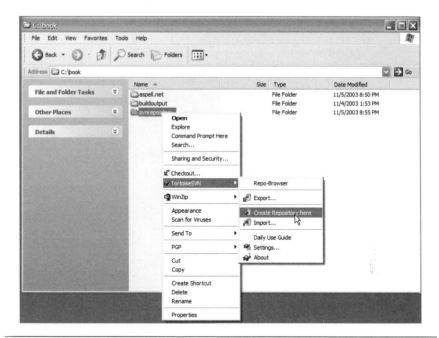

**Figure 9-2** Creating an SVN repository with TortoiseSVN.

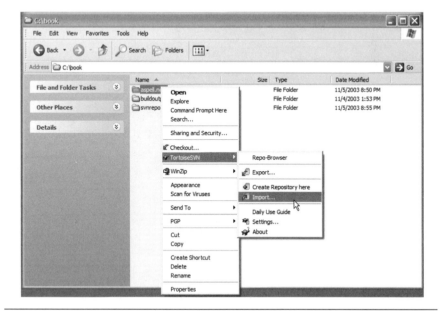

**Figure 9-3** Importing ASpell.NET using TortoiseSVN.

# Draco.NET

I choose Draco.NET because it is so easy to install and simple to use. Although CruiseControl.NET does offer nice features for a large development team, I wanted to eliminate any complexity to emphasize the concepts of a complete case study. Listing 9.4 is the configuration for Draco.NET to build ASpell.NET. Figure 9-4 shows the email notification sent from the initial import's triggering of the build.

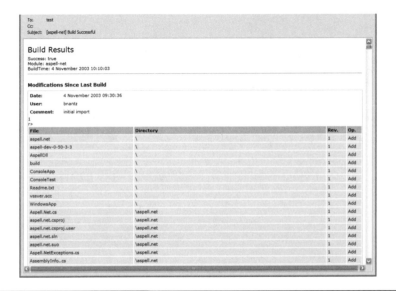

**Figure 9-4**   Draco.NET's Email Notification.

**Listing 9.4**   Draco.NET's Configuration

```xml
<?xml version="1.0" encoding="utf-8"?>
<configuration>
      <configSections>
            <section name="draco"
type="Chive.Draco.Config.ConfigurationSection, Draco"/>
      </configSections>
      <system.diagnostics>
            <switches>
                  <add name="TraceLevelSwitch" value="4"/>
            </switches>
```

```
                <trace autoflush="true" indentsize="4">
                        <listeners>
                                <remove name="Default"/>
                        </listeners>
                </trace>
        </system.diagnostics>
        <system.runtime.remoting>
                <application>
                        <service>
                                <wellknown mode="Singleton"
objectUri="Draco" type="Chive.Draco.DracoRemote, Draco"/>
                        </service>
                        <channels>
                                <channel ref="tcp" port="8086"/>
                        </channels>
                </application>
        </system.runtime.remoting>
        <draco xmlns="http://www.chive.com/draco">
                <pollperiod>60</pollperiod>
                <quietperiod>60</quietperiod>
                <mailserver>mail.securityint.com</mailserver>
                <fromaddress>brian.nantz@somwhere.com</fromaddress>
                <builds>
                        <build>
                                <name>aspell-net</name>
                                <pollperiod>10</pollperiod>
                                <quietperiod>30</quietperiod>
                                <notification>
                                        <email>

<recipient>brian.nantz@somewhere.com</recipient>
                                        </email>
                                        <file>
                                                <dir>C:\book\BuildOutput</dir>
                                        </file>
                                </notification>
                                <nant>
                                        <buildfile>build\master.build</buildfile>
                                </nant>
                                <svn>
                                        <url>file:///C:/book/svnrepository</url>
                                </svn>
                                <ignorechanges>
```

```
                              <ignore comment="autobuild"/>
                        </ignorechanges>
                  </build>
             </builds>
        </draco>
</configuration>
```

Again, in Listing 9.4, all the comments have been removed. These comments more than point you in the right direction with helpful examples. For example, there is a section for each source control that it supports (i.e., Subversion, Visual Source Safe, etc.), and you just have to uncomment it and changed the values (like username, paths, passwords) to fit your environment. By just uncommenting the proper notification XML node, you can now receive build results in multiple formats. All of the supported SCMs are also very configurable and well documented. Notice that you can ignore certain checkins to SCM (if you are triggering builds off of checkins and are not scheduled). You can also potentially monitor multiple source repositories. In Listing 9.4, only the svn XML tag is used to monitor a single Subversion repository.

Next we will add a new example client for greater stressing of the component.

## Adding Functionality

In the original proof-of-concept, I created two example applications. The first example was a C# Console Application to take a word input and if needed return the suggestions for the correct spelling (Figure 9-5).

The second application was a simple VB.NET application (Figure 9-6) that showed checking a single word in a text box and returning the results in a right-click context menu.

While these applications tested the functionality and demonstrated the cross-language capability, they really were not real-world useable applications. There are a few things that Aspell.NET needs to support before even a quality beta cycle. First, I wanted to add Log4Net to the project, even though it is somewhat simple to support good behavior if the system starts to error. This is one example where it may be useful to associate the Logger configuration with a dll. This probably warrants some changes to the code. In the meantime, ASpell.NET should just document the Log4Net requirement in the calling executables configuration file. Second, if I want to check

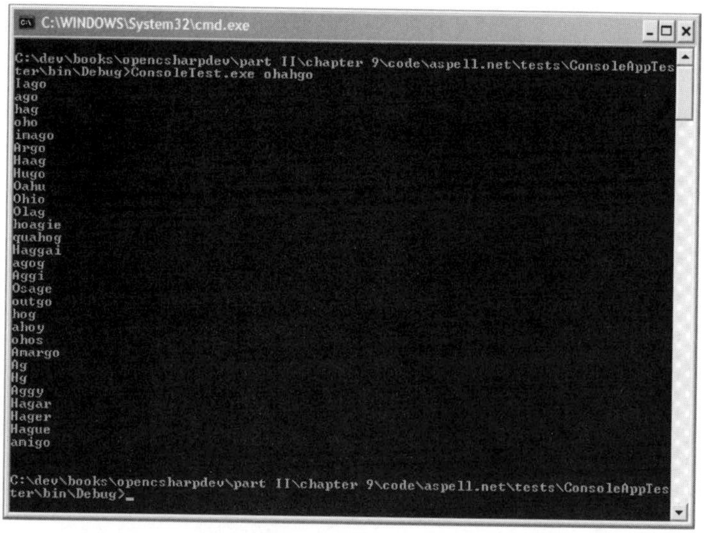

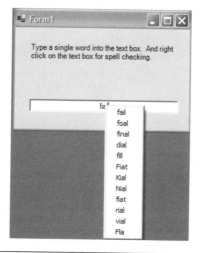

**Figure 9-5** Console Test Application.

**Figure 9-6** VB.NET Windows Form Test Application.

spelling, it usually is not a single textbox field but a whole document like email or a text file, so I decided to create an application much like WordPad that is a Rich Text Format-aware editor application. Figure 9-7 shows using SharpDevelop, which is the only Open Source editor I am aware of that has a Windows Forms designer.

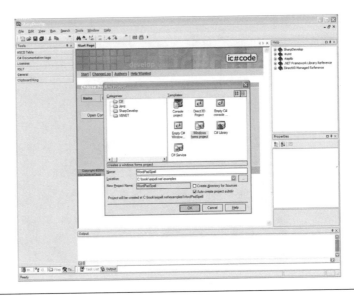

**Figure 9-7** SharpDevelop WordpadSpell Project.

While eventually I would like all the functionality of WordPad, this example application only allows for spell checking and opening a text file for spell checking. Figure 9-8 shows WordpadSpell in action.

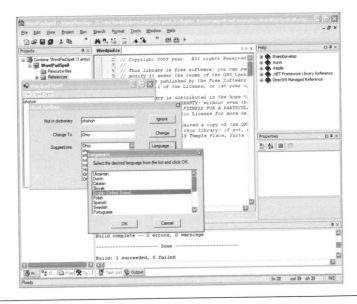

**Figure 9-8** WordpadSpell Example.

Listing 9.5, a sample command-line application from the ASpell.NET distribution, shows that the API for ASpell.NET is fairly simple. The Word-padSpell is responsible for the logic to parse things down to a single word to pass to ASpell.NET for checking.

**Listing 9.5** A Simple Use of ASpell.NET

```
    try
     {
         string word = args[0].ToString();
         aspell.net.SpellChecker spellCheck = new
aspell.net.SpellChecker();
         if(!spellCheck.checkword(word))
         {
             System.Collections.ArrayList suggestions =
spellCheck.suggest(word);
             foreach(string suggestion in suggestions)
             {
                 Console.WriteLine(suggestion);
             }
         }
         else
         {
             Console.WriteLine(word + " is correct");
         }
     }
     catch(Exception ex)
     {
         System.Diagnostics.Debug.WriteLine(ex.ToString());
         Console.Write(ex.ToString());
     }
```

Adding a NAnt build script is a simple copy and paste and a quick edit of the template file. When we add the project to Subversion (Figure 9-9), Draco.NET will be triggered to perform a build. The installation and iso file are created, and the successful result is emailed out.

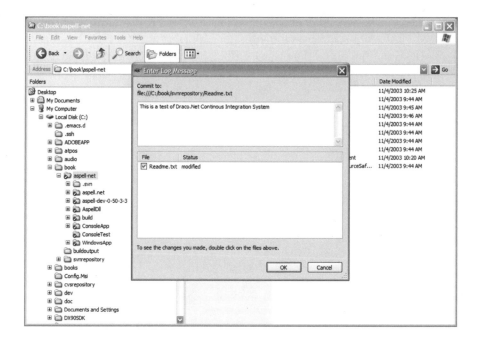

**Figure 9-9** Adding to SVN.

# Summary

While this application is admittedly simple compared to what you develop day in and day out, it is large enough to demonstrate that the process of using these Open Source tools has great benefits. Most real projects can be broken up into smaller projects that are not much more daunting than this one. These tools do not require all that much overhead to the development process. As the project or number of developers increases, the value of these tools increases in more of an exponential rather than linear proportion. These tools could easily be (and actually already are) used in Source-Forge's projects to remotely monitor CVS in a multi-developer project and to automatically build and expose integration issues.

# CHAPTER 10

# Database Development

*Music is Love in Search of a word.*

—Sidney Lanier

## Introduction

Open Source development would not be very useful or even feasible if it did not provide a database in which to store application data. In fact there are many Open Source databases that could be used in .NET development. Unlike previous versions of ADO, ADO.NET is very structured and well defined. Creating an ADO.NET Data Provider for a database, while not a trivial task, is much more viable than with classic ADO.

Developing with disconnected Datasets is a convenience that, once used, is very hard to give up. Having data conveniently packaged in XML allows for a standard, transformable format. Datasets, and especially Strongly-Typed Datasets, give a great object-oriented API to your data. All this is accomplished while keeping track of changes for you and giving you an easy way to only send changes across the wire. There are so many features of ADO.NET that it warrants a great weight when evaluating which Open Source database to use with development.

# Open Source Databases

There are many different Open Source databases like Berkley DB, MySQL, and PostgreSQL, just to name the more popular ones.[1] All of these databases work on multiple operating systems. When narrowing your choices for a database for your project, consider the following features:

- Database Operating System Support
- Open Source Community Support
- Relational vs. Hierarchical Design
- Feature Set
- Scalability
- ADO.NET Provider Support
- Administration and Development Tools
- Open Source License

## Sleepycat Berkeley Database

Although not a relational database, the Berkeley Database engine is used in many products. Sleepycat (http://www.sleepycat.com) is the latest release of the Berkeley Database engine. Unfortunately, Sleepycat does not currently support ADO.NET, but hopefully this will change in the near future. The latest version supports XML natively and is getting rave reviews for embedded systems. This would be a prime candidate for the Compact Framework product that needed structured data storage.

**NOTE:** The Subversion source code repository (see Chapter 3, "General Development") utilizes a Sleepycat database.

Because the API is directly accessing the database files rather than a client-server design, no services need to be running. This makes moving a Berkeley DB from one machine to another very simple, regardless of the operating system. While any of the three databases discussed in this chapter allow a database to be copied to other machines, MySQL and PostgreSQL

---

[1] Also available are mSQL, sapDB, and Firebird.

require a port of the database engine, whereas Sleepycat only needs a port of the API. A .NET API that directly queried the files would make this database available on any CLI that supports ADO.NET (see Chapter 2, "Open Source and the .NET Platform").

For a good book on Sleepycat, see:

*Berkeley DB*
by Sleepycat Software Inc.
SAMS

## MSDE

Microsoft Desktop Engine, as was mentioned in Chapter 3, is a full-featured Microsoft product. MSDE is a scaled down version of Microsoft SQL with the limitations outlined in Chapter 3. Although it is not under an Open Source license, MSDE is freely available for integration into proprietary products. Many freely available IDEs mentioned in Chapter 3, like #Develop and WebMatrix, fully support MSDE as if it were SQL with all the Rapid Development (RAD) features. These features include drag-and-drop creation of a dataset from a database table, direct editing of tables, and data adapter wizards, just to name a few.

## MySQL

MySQL is a very stable and popular relational Open Source database. If you have not yet noticed, the Open Source projects featured in this book tend to be under an Open Source license that can be used in proprietary commercial products as well as in other Open Source projects. MySQL is not under such a license, as was mentioned under the MySQL section of Chapter 3. If your product meets these requirements, there are many administration tools featured in Chapter 3 (Figures 3.13–16). Also, there is an Open Source ADO.NET data provider (http://sourceforge.net/projects/mysqlnet/) and another commercially available provider (http://crlab.com/mysqlnet/). Listing 10.1 is an example from the MySqlNet documentation for comparison with NPgSql (Listing 10.2).

---

**Listing 10.1**  MySqlNet DataAdapter Example

---

```
using ByteFX.Data.MySqlClient;

...

public DataSet SelectRows(DataSet dataset,string connection,string
query)
{
    MySqlConnection conn = new MySqlConnection(connection);
    MySqlDataAdapter adapter = new MySqlDataAdapter();
    adapter.SelectCommand = new MySqlCommand(query, conn);
    adapter.Fill(dataset);
    return dataset;
}
```

---

One great convenience of MySQL is that it does have a native Windows port. This makes it very easy to install MySQL on Windows (it already comes with most Unix distributions) without any dependencies.
For a great book on MySQL, see:

*MySQL*, Second Edition
by Paul DuBois
SAMS

## Which Database to Choose?

This is a very loaded question. To adequately compare these databases would require an entire book. It is a comparison of Speed vs. Features vs. Licensing and Rapid Development (RAD). The goal of this chapter is to give a quick comparison of features and point you to other resources to learn more, with the one requirement of all database engines being Open Source and having ADO.NET support.

**TIP:** To keep up on the latest open source databases and Open Source ADO.NET data providers, see http://www.go-mono.com/ado-net.html.

Carefully read Table 10.1. I will not rehash the available features but rather will add to the table in this discussion.

**Table 10.1** Open Source Database Quick Comparison

|  | Sleepycat | PostgreSQL | MySql | MSDE |
|---|---|---|---|---|
| Relational |  | X | X | X |
| Linux | X | X | X |  |
| Windows | X | Cygwin | X | X |
| PocketPC | X |  |  |  |
| Mono |  | X | X |  |
| .NET CLR |  | X | X | X |
| Compact Framework | X |  |  |  |
| License | BSD | BSD | GPL | N/A |
| ADO.Net |  | X | X | X |
| Transactions |  | X | X | X |
| Stored Procedures |  | X |  | X |
| Triggers |  | X |  | X |
| Rules |  | X |  | X |
| Functions |  | X |  | X |
| SubQueries |  | X |  | X |
| Unions |  | X |  | X |
| Constraints |  | X |  | X |
| Cursors |  | X |  | X |
| Views |  | X |  | X |
| Referential |  | X | X | X |
| Replication |  | X | X | X |

Obviously, for a small footprint, and if management tools and relation support are not important, Sleepycat is an excellent choice.

Comparing RAD functionality of a database is really an ease-of-use issue for the developer. This is more art than science. You have to look at the tools available for the database (see Chapter 3), but more importantly, you have to see how you and your team like the database. I know that sounds simple, but just download the databases, install them and a few tools, and create a very simple application to see which fits you best. But do not forget the licensing issue. You cannot even consider a database that does not fit with your licensing requirements.

For features supported and ease-of-use in an IDE, you probably will not get much better than MSDE and WebMatrix, as was already mentioned. Much of this code is hidden from you in drag-and-drop and wizard functionality.

Now for the hardest and most debated database comparison: PostgreSQL vs. MySQL. First you must look at how the projects started out. MySQL started out for speed and simplicity and PostgreSQL for feature set and ANSI SQL compatibility. Now the race is on to migrate in each other's direction. PostgreSQL has seemed to add speed to their features faster that MySQL can add features and ANSI compatibility to their speed. For instance, MySQL does support transactions but only on InnoDB table types; therefore you must know at design time which type of table you need or, to put it another way, whether you need transactional support (I am assuming that you are not going to want to change your table type after releasing the product because that is painful). However, MySQL is still very simple to use and very appealing to many developers, especially Web developers, and it can be faster than PostgreSQL in specific circumstances. On the flip side, MySQL replication has seen more runtime than PostgreSQL and is therefore more stable and rich. Some nice features unique to PostgreSQL are stored procedures written in a programming language rather than TSQL and the ability to add user-defined data types. I would imagine that stored procedures in C# are already being worked on by the PostgreSQL user group community.

**NOTE:** The next version of Microsoft SQL, codenamed Yukon, does have the ability to write stored procedures or triggers in any .NET language because of the imbedded CLR. This also provides the ability to create user-defined data types. I would hope that the next version of MSDE would also support these features, and I have received some indication from Microsoft that it will. Although a large undertaking, it would be very nice to see Mono embed their runtime within a database like PostgreSQL.

Finally, the issue of licensing. Except for MySQL, all of the databases mentioned can be used in Open Source or proprietary products. If MySQL's license restrictions (see Chapter 3) do not work for you, then you will probably like PostgreSQL or MSDE.

**NOTE:** I have chosen PostgreSQL for the database examples in this book. The main reason is feature set and licensing. My philosophy is that most products, given enough time, grow out way beyond the intent of the original design. Therefore, you do not know at design time what you may need in the future so I usually go with a greater feature set for this reason. I may not use transactions today, but in the future I may need them, and I do not want to change databases sometime in the future. This would be a big waste of time for a development team. With regards to licensing, I always go for Open Source (so that I have the source and can change it if need be) and can use the product in a proprietary fashion to make great profits.

## Cross Database Development

It has long been the dream of many marketing specifications to create an application that can be database vendor-independent. Being able to install a product at a customer's site without requiring a new database engine to be purchased is definitely a big plus. ADO.NET comes the closest of any database API I have seen to allow for standard development using disconnected Datasets, DataViews, and all that great stuff without having to know the database provider and in turn the database engine that you are talking to. The problem with this comes in performance, depending on the performance needs of your application. To get the fastest performance, most databases support stored procedures. These stored procedures are unique to every database engine, preventing the database-agnostic dream. However, the good news is that the .NET code would not have to change if designed properly, only the stored procedures. The better news is that if you do not need stored procedures and can use in-line parameterized queries, then maybe the dream can come true.

On a related note, some development teams use databases to simply store the state of their objects in a non-relational fashion. A new and very popular Open Source project just released call Gentile.NET (http://www.mertner.com/projects/gentle/) supports this out of the box very well! No custom coding is needed. (A similar concept without the relational database is also available from http://www.sourceforge.net/projects/bboopreva-lence.com.) There are a few very impressive aspects of this project. First, it uses other Open Source projects covered in the book: NUnit, NAnt, and Log4NET. Second, Gentile.NET works on both Microsoft .NET and Mono! Third, there is a Visual Studio.NET plug-in for Gentile.NET for rapid development. Finally, the list of databases the framework works with is most impressive: Microsoft SQL, Oracle, PostgreSQL, MySQL, Microsoft Access, Firebird, and SQL Lite! Much can be learned from the experience of these developers in cross-platform development!

# PostgreSQL

PostgreSQL is a multi-user relational database. The community support for PostgreSQL is very strong; in fact, PostgreSQL recently distinguished itself by powering the Internet .org namespace.[2] Getting into PostgreSQL is beyond the scope of this chapter, but for a good book, see:

*PostgreSQL: Introduction and Concepts*
by Bruce Momjian
Addison-Wesley

PostgreSQL does run on both Linux and Microsoft Windows but does not have a native port for the Windows platform (like the MySQL database does). In this chapter, our example will be designed to run on both platforms.

## Installation

Since most mainline Linux distributions install PostgreSQL by default, there is not much to installing the database except maybe for applying the latest upgrade. Thus, this section of the chapter will mainly focus on installing PostgreSQL on Windows. PostgreSQL requires many features of the Unix platform that do not exist on the Windows OS.[3] Therefore, PostgreSQL requires the use of a "Unix-Like" environment running within Windows.

## Cygwin

Cygwin (http://www.cygwin.com) is an Open Source project to bring many of the Unix-based operating system features and tools to the Windows platform. Figure 10-1 shows the installation utility for Cygwin.

In Figure 10-1, the far left of the figure is the Skip column. The way this installation tool works is similar to a normal tree control. At the very top level, you can set this column to Skip, Default, or Install. Each child inherits the setting of the parent. For instance, if you set the top level of the tree to the Install option, the latest version of every child of the tree will be installed. Also, you can go to each child node and change the setting.

---

[2] See http://cw.idg.com.au/idg2.nsf/All/2ADD84E6EBCEADE9CA256CB30075FA01!Open Document.

[3] A native Windows version of PostgreSQL (not requiring cygwin) is due out this summer. See  Interview with the PostgreSQL Team, by Eugenia Loli-Queru - Posted on 2003-04-21 17:26:22 (http://www.osnews.com/story.php?news_id=3341&page=1).

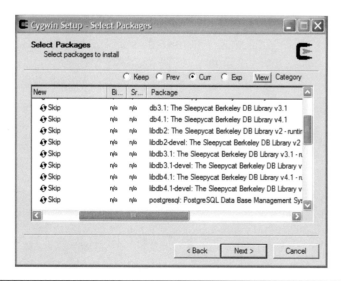

**Figure 10-1** Installing PostgreSQL with Cygwin.

**TIP:** When you click on a child node, the tree node behaves like a multi-state button. This takes a little getting used to; however, it allows the get feature of installing a specific version of the product. For instance, the options change like this with each click: Skip, Install latest version (watch the version column), Install next to latest version, then back to Skip again.

After installing Cygwin, you can run it by using the desktop icon (if you installed it), or you can use the Cygwin icon in the Start Menu. This results in a command window opening with a Unix shell running. For the examples in this book, the Cygwin install was configured at the very top level of the tree as Default. Scroll down to the databases section of the installation tree (shown in Figure 10-1) and click on the PostgreSQL child node of the tree to install the latest version.

Running PostgreSQL using Cygwin requires that ipc-daemon or ipc-daemon2 be running to service the IPC calls from the database. Under Unix, these are daemons that run in the background. In Cygwin, they can be configured to run as a Windows service, but that requires a massive amount of work. So the command Windows in the background of Figure 10-2 shows IPC-Daemon2.

To run the PostgreSQL database engine, just type postmaster –D [path to the database], but first the database must be created by using the initdb utility. Both are shown in Figure 10-2.

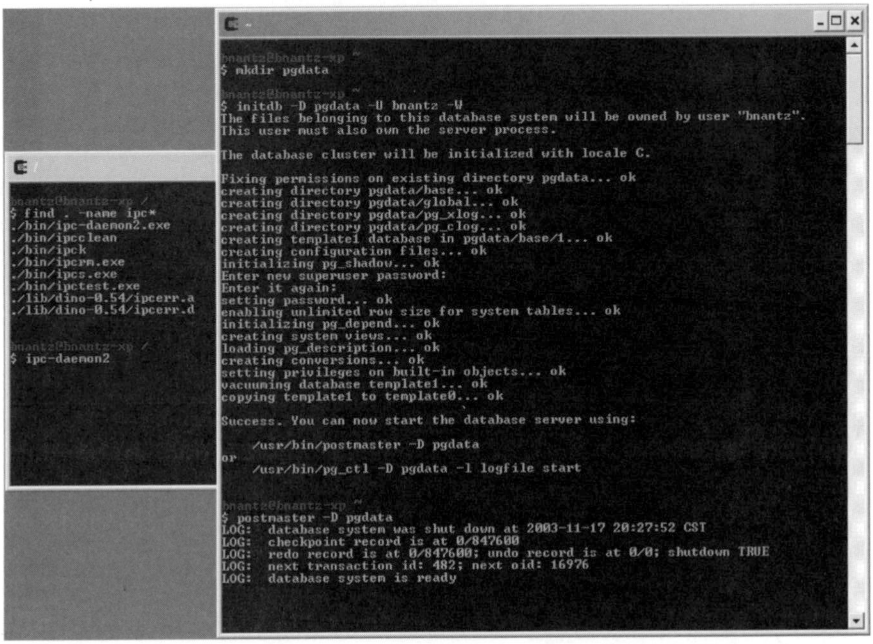

**Figure 10-2**  Running PostgreSQL in Cygwin.

After running ipc-daemon2, run initdb. For more information, see the PostgreSQL online documentation or the man pages for PostgreSQL and initdb. The steps under Linux for creating and running the PostgreSQL database are identical.

## Administration Tools

Like most other Unix-based programs, PostgreSQL has a number of command-line tools. However, to speed up development, there are a number of other Open Source projects that help with the administration and development of PostgreSQL databases.

### Conversion Utilities

PostgreSQL provides conversion tools to convert from other database engines. Some of the supported conversions are:

> MS Access—http://gborg.postgresql.org/project/access2pgconverter/proj
> display.php
> MySQL—http://gborg.postgresql.org/project/mysql2psql/projdisplay.php

These projects can be helpful in converting existing database projects over to PostgreSQL.

### Graphical Tools

PgAdmin III (http://pgadmin.postgresql.org), shown in Figure 10-3, is a very intuitive and time-saving tool. This tool allows you to easily administer and graphically design a database. You can create databases, tables, and stored procedures and perform many other operations. This product will be very familiar to anyone who has used Microsoft SQL Server Enterprise Manager and Query Analyzer.

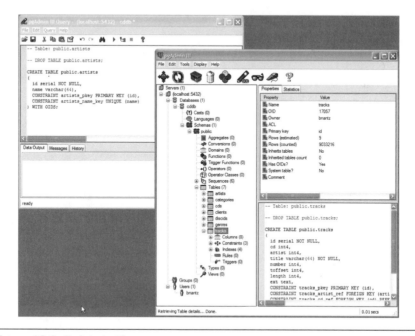

**Figure 10-3** PgAdmin III.

**TIP:** A Web-based application (PHPPgAdmin) similar to PgAdmin III is also available at http://phppgadmin.sourceforge.net.

To get PgAdmin working and to configure PostgreSQL to accept TCP connections, you must edit the PostgreSQL.conf file, as shown in Figure 10-4.

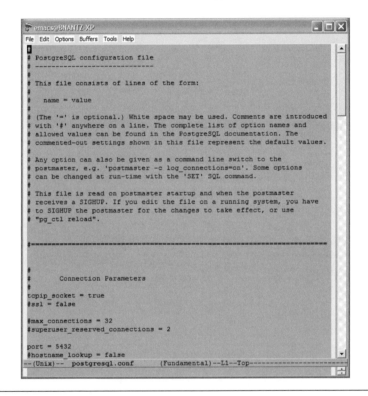

**Figure 10-4**  Editing the PostgreSQL Configuration File.

# PostgreSQL ADO.NET Data Providers

There are a couple of ADO.NET providers for PostgreSQL, most notably PgClient (http://pgsqlclient.sf.net) and NPgSql(http://gborg.postgresql. org/project/NPgSql/projdisplay.php). Of these two, NPgSql is more mature and stable than pgsqlclient.

NPgSql uses the PostgreSQL frontend/backend version 2.0 protocol and many new 3.0 features, such as portals, for communicating with PostgreSQL. This provider is fully implemented in C# and is therefore portable to any of the CLI implementations mentioned in Chapter 2. NPgSql also supports ADO.NET connection pooling, as shown in Figure 10-5.

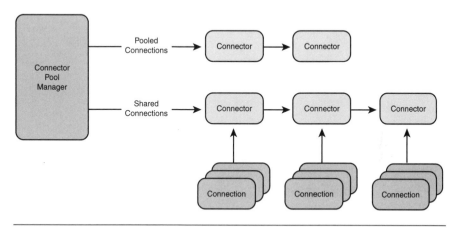

**Figure 10-5**  ADO.NET Connection Pooling.

The NPgSql team chose to use both NAnt and NUnit for their development. The only feature left to evaluate is the useability of the API, which leads to the next section on Examples. Using NPgSql is intuitive and fits very well into ADO.NET. All of the NPgSql commands behave exactly as you would expect with the System.Data classes. Except for the integration with integrated development environments like Visual Studio.Net and #Develop, which let you drag and drop SQLConnections and wizards to configure SqlDataAdapters, using NPgSql classes is exactly the same as using the System.Data.SqlClient or System.Data.OleDb classes. A good example is needed to illustrate the ease of use of NPgSql.

# PostgreSQL, NPgSql, and FreeDB Example

FreeDB has a large, freely available dataset that makes a great sample for using NPgSql and PostgreSQL together. As you may have already noticed in Figure 10-3, FreeDB contains over 9 million records, so this is definitely a real-world test.

## What Is FreeDB?

FreeDB is basically a free (GNU GPL) version of CDDB. CDDB is a database containing information about music CDs such as Artist, Track Titles, etc. that can be queried over the Internet. Originally, CDDB was also free, but as time went on, CDDB became more proprietary and added many restrictions on its users In response, FreeDB was created to be accessed freely and have the data be free as well.

**NOTE:** PostgreSql version 7.3, NPgSql version 0.5, and FreeDB Complete 20020917 were used for the example in this chapter.

## Importing FreeDB to PostgreSQL

Both CDDB and FreeDB support similar APIs. Both projects also use text-based data on the server side. While the text files are formatted in a queryable fashion (much like the ini files used in Windows), there is not much flexibility or optimization of lookups (a.k.a., indexes). So Fabien Coelho, an Open Source developer, contributed a script to import FreeDB into PostgreSQL. This code is available from http://www.coelho.net/cddb_sql.html. The README file in the distribution is very helpful, but here are the steps to get FreeDB into PostgreSQL:

1. Get PostgreSQL running.
2. Import the following PERL modules using CPAN –i: Digest::MD5, DBI, DBD::Pg, DB_File, String::Similarity
3. In the Perl script, copy line 941 and paste between line 369 and 370, add a 2 to the end of the line to make the filename unique.
4. Run createdb -E ISO-8859-1 cddb.
5. Run psql cddb < cddb_base.sql.
6. Run cddb_import.sh -i -b freedb-complete-yyyymmdd.tar.rar.
7. Run psql cddb < cddb_index.sql.

**NOTE:** Perl comes with the default installation of Cygwin. Also, you can download a Windows version of Perl, ActivePerl, at http://www.active state.com.

Now that the FreeDB database is installed, you can run PgAdmin III, and you should see something similar to Figure 10-3. FreeDB is much more powerful now because it is indexed for faster lookups and is relational so that it can be queried in ways never before possible. Go to http://www.freedb.org/modules.php?name=Sections&sop=viewarticle&artid=28 to see the very complex FreeDB protocol. It was not designed as a very intuitive API but as a similar and compatible protocol to CDDB. Figure 10-6 shows the diagram for the PostgreSQL FreeDB.

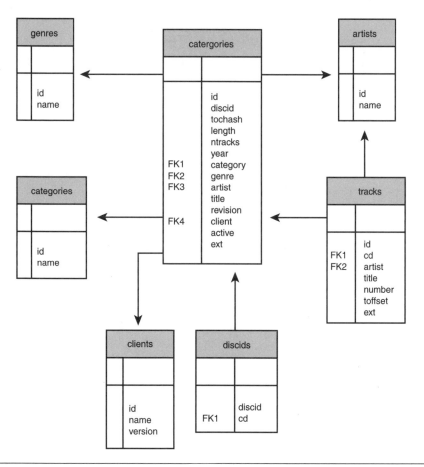

**Figure 10-6** Database Diagram.

The biggest advantage is that this can be queried using standard SQL statements. There is no proprietary protocol to learn, and in fact you can make your own API on top of this database. For example, in the next chapter, a Web service protocol will wrap the class library in the following section and is much more intuitive than the native FreeDB protocol. Most FreeDB queries simply pass in the disc ID and ask for all the tracks. This track information is used by CD player programs to populate the list of CD tracks with meaningful names instead of just track 1, track 2, etc. Some queries this relational model could allow for that the FreeDB protocol does not support is getting all Artists for a given Genre, all Songs for a given Genre, All Songs for a given Artist, and the list could go on and on.

## Creating a .NET Class Library for FreeDB

Creating a C# class library using NPgSql is very simple and straightforward. It is also a good design to create a Class Library Assembly for reuse by ASP.NET pages and Web services (which will be shown in Chapter 12) and also for use from Windows Forms. Listing 10.2 shows that populating a dataset from PostgreSQL using NPgSql works much like any other ADO.NET Data Provider.

**Listing 10.2**  Querying FreeDB for All the Music Genres

```
public DataSet GetGenres()
{
        tsStart = new TimeSpan(System.DateTime.Now.Ticks);

        conn = new NpgsqlConnection("Server=127.0.0.1;Port=5432;User
Id=bnantz;Password=bnantz;Database=cddb;");

   conn.Open();

        ds = new DataSet();
        da = new NpgsqlDataAdapter("select * from genres", conn);

        da.Fill(ds);

        conn.Close();

        if (_logger.IsDebugEnabled)
        {
```

```
            tsEnd = new TimeSpan(System.DateTime.Now.Ticks);
            tsEnd -= tsStart;

            msg = new StringBuilder();
            msg.AppendFormat(@"{0} ms",
               tsEnd.TotalMilliseconds);
            _logger.Debug(msg.ToString());
        }

        return ds;
    }
```

Although it is not good practice to hard-code the connection string for many reasons, this was done in Listing 10.2 for the sake of brevity. For a good discussion about where to centrally store your database connection string in a secure manner, see my book:

*Secure Web Services in the .NET Platform*
APress

Also note the use of Log4Net and the timing code for testing purposes. The support of DataAdapters and Datasets makes programming with Post-greSQL very simple. Listing 10.3 is some simple test code, which could very easily be transformed to NUnit, for the class library (Listing 10.2) demonstrating how to test data access code.

**Listing 10.3** Testing the .NET Class Library

```
using System;
using System.Data;
using System.Diagnostics;

using npgsqlfreedb;
namespace Tester
{
    class Class1
    {
        [STAThread]
        static void Main(string [] args)
        {
    try
```

```
    {
        dataAccess da = new dataAccess(); // <-this is listing 10.2

        Showinfo(da.GetGenres());
    }
    catch(Exception ex)
    {
        Console.WriteLine(ex.ToString());
    }
        }

static private void Showinfo(DataSet ds)
{
    foreach(DataTable dt in ds.Tables)
    {
        Console.WriteLine(dt.TableName);

        foreach(DataColumn column in dt.Columns)
        {
            Console.Write(column.ColumnName + ",");
        }

        Console.WriteLine("");

        foreach(DataRow row in dt.Rows)
        {
            foreach(object o in row.ItemArray)
            {
                Console.Write(o.ToString() + ",");
            }

            Console.WriteLine("");
        }
    }
}
}
}
```

Figure 10-7 is the output from this little application, which, surprisingly, contains close to 4000 musical genres. Because CDDB and FreeDB allow for user updates, many of these Genres are redundant.

```
C:\dev\books\opencsharpdev\part III\Chapter 10\code\Tester\bin\Debug\Tester.exe
3683,Tango Operita,
3684,Musik,
3685,Classical - Opera,
3686,spaans,
3687,Classical, Modern,
3688,Cello,
3689,Symphonic Suites,
3690,Gsopel Instrumental,
3691,Melodien,
3692,noel,
3693,Piano instrumental,
3694,ArtRock,
3695,Classial Piano,
3696,Enigmatic,
3697,Romantique / Symphonique,
3698,Indian flute & tabla,
3699,Coros,
3700,Julesange,
3701,Oratory,
3702,Gregorian,
3703,Classical - Romantic,
3704,Easy Listen,
3705,Pop / Classic,
3706,Klassisch,
```

**Figure 10-7**  Console Output of FreeDB's Genres.

# Summary

Many large-scale projects or products will need to use a relational database. The Open Source community not only provides multiple databases but also provides ADO.NET data providers to enable them to easily integrate into your C# and .NET code. Using the CLI implementations in Chapter 2, the data access code can run on Linux, BSD, Windows, or MAC OS X, and PostgreSQL supports many of these platforms as well, so the different permutations and combinations could have great potential. Currently though, there are only a few CLI implementations that support ADO.NET. Going back to Chapter 2, you can see that the CLIs that currently support ADO.NET are Microsoft's CLR, Microsoft's Compact Framework, and Mono. Therefore, the currently targetable operating systems are Windows, Windows CE and Windows Mac OS X, and Linux, respectively.

# CHAPTER 11

# Web Development

*The Internet is like a vault with a screen door on the back …*

—*Anon.*

## Introduction

.NET and especially ASP.NET development is providing a revolutionary platform for Web development. The ease of debugging an ASP.NET page is truly a killer feature and time-saver for any Web developer. Reusable controls allow for much quicker Web development because they can be used all throughout the site. For example, you can create a navigation user control to navigate through your site and easily include this on every Web page on your site. This not only speeds up development but also isolates the code to one central location. User controls also allow for site redesign like no other Web development platform out there. Validation controls allow for collection of more accurate data on your site. If you are asking for user information such as addresses, zip codes, and the like, you should be using ASP.NET's Validation controls. Through the use of Regular Expressions, many of these informational pages that are so common to Web sites are there out of the box! Not to mention that ASP.NET allows for development in many different languages (C#, VB.NET, MC++, etc.)!

With the next release, ASP.NET 2.0 (see http://www.asp.net/whidbey), the ASP.NET team has reduced the amount of coding required for a normal Web site drastically, in some cases up to 70%! That has got to be the most amazing feature of all. They have added to all the out-of-the-box User controls and Validation controls and created a new concept of Master pages, which is pretty much the equivalent to skinning a Web site!

Of course there is way too much to say about ASP.NET that is beyond the scope of this chapter. For a great book on ASP.NET, see:

*Essential ASP.NET with Examples in C#*
By Fritz Onion
Addison-Wesley

The ASP.NET team has created a great balance of stateless server-side controls. Server-side controls run most of the server-side code, except for validation, which is BOTH server-side and client-side JavaScript for added security, which allows for the greatest multiple browser support. To achieve all the benefits of server-side controls (ease of debugging, rich user interface controls, multiple output targets, and a similar event model to Windows Forms development, just to name a few) did not come without cost. The magic behind the curtain is found mainly in the ASP.NET ViewState tag. This hidden tag, shown in Listing 11.1, holds information for all server-side controls in an ASP.NET page.

**Listing 11.1** ASP.NET ViewState

```
<input type="hidden" name="__VIEWSTATE"
value="dDwtMTkxNTA2MjkwNzt0PDtsPGk8MD47PjtsPHQ8O2w8aTw3PjtpPDE1Pjs+O2
w8dDxwPHA8bDxOYXZpZ2F0ZVVybDs+O2w8V2lraS5hc3B4P3BhZ2U9V2lraUhvbWU7Pj47c
DxsPG9ubW91c2VvdmVyO29ubW91c2VvdXQ7PjtsPHJldHVybiBvdmVyGliKCdSZW
ZyZXNoIGN1cnJlbnQgcGFnZScsQ0FQVElPTiwnV2lraSBHdWlkZScpXDs7cmV0dXJuIG
5kKClcOzs+Pj47Oz47dDxwPHA8bDxUZXh0Oz47bDxaWtpSG9tZTs+Pjs+Ozs+Oz4+Oz
4+Oz7AZtEwI0N/q3zFypouwKCIFvwErw==" />
```

This allows for rich event handlers to be handled on the server side. For instance, if you want to handle a textbox leave event, the server-side process is very similar to the Windows Form's event model. For example, if you wanted a user to enter a zip code into a text box, you could capture the textbox leave event. In this event handler, you could validate the zip code against a database and while you are at it return the city and state to help out the user. This makes the user happy because he or she must enter less data, and it makes your data more reliable and less apt to human error. Notice that in this scenario, I am not really concerned with writing a ton of HTML (this happens automatically); instead I am interacting more with the control on the designer and handling events. This is a much simpler design than most Web development platforms out there today.

You can see the appeal of ASP.NET just based on this one feature of server-side controls. Coupled with the popularity of delivering information and products on the Web, it is no wonder that Open Source (mainly Mono) targeted ASP.NET as such a high priority. Mono estimates to be 98% done implementing System.Web (see http://www.go-mono.com/class-status-System.Web.html). Being able to develop ASP.NET in #Develop for free and deploy it on Linux using Apache (again for free) has immense potential. This means that any Web host can provide ASP.NET at low (or even no) cost because many of them are running Apache already! Coupled with the ease of ASP.NET page development, this low-cost code has propelled ASP.NET to be the most popular Web development platform around.

**TIP:** A few Open Source projects that are very useful in Web development are filezilla (http://filezilla.sourceforge.net/) FTP client and Mozilla (http://www.mozilla.org/products/mozilla1.x/) Web browser. These tools work well on both Linux and Windows and are time-savers.

Just a quick search of the Internet produced the following Open Source or free ASP.NET components in Table 11.1.

**Table 11.1** A Few ASP.NET Controls and Applications

| Component | Description | Web Site |
|---|---|---|
| ASP.NET Forums | A forum-based Web site | http://forums.asp.net/builds/ |
| Sushi Wiki | A WIKI collaboration application | http://egroise.europe.webmatrix-hosting.net/ |
| skmMenu | ASP.NET menu server control | http://www.gotdotnet.com/community/workspaces/workspace.aspx?ID=A8EE64DF-8F2A-483F-8594-10AAA66988CE |
| Rich Text Editor | Rich Text Box Editor control | http://www.exporttechnologies.com/softwareDownloads.asp |
| Email Text Box | Simple control to send text email from an ASP.NET page for users | http://www.codeproject.com/vb/net/tsmailcontrol.asp#xxxx |

**Table 11.1** A Few ASP.NET Controls and Applications (cont.)

| Component | Description | Web Site |
|---|---|---|
| GuestBook | GuestBook control containing name, email, date, and text | http://www.devscripts.com/visit.php?sId=3964 |
| nGallery | A photo album application | http://www.ngallery.org/default.aspx |
| FlexMenu | ASP.NET menu server control | http://www.aitoc.com/en/flex_menu_net.html |
| DatePicker | Advanced DatePicker control | http://www.salimnaim.com/DatePicker.htm |
| Gotdotnet Menu Source | ASP.NET menu server control | http://www.gotdotnet.com/Community/UserSamples/Details.aspx?SampleGuid=513b8f28-a932-4e94-91a8-2cdcf57eb6e9 |

These great components are just a few examples of how quickly you can put together a high-quality ASP.NET Web site.

Finally, after all the ASP.NET build up, we will get to the goal of this chapter, which is to take the FreeDB example from Chapter 10 and expand it into a cross-platform Web service that can run on multiple operating systems. Also an ASP.NET page will be created to run a simple query on the Web service.

## Cross Platform ASP.NET and Web Services

Before diving into developing Web applications and services, it is necessary to choose a Web server. Serving up data and Web page applications is just as important as having a database in which to store the information. As you may have already guessed, there are a number of Open Source Web servers already available. Of course ASP.NET also runs within Microsoft's Internet Information Server (IIS), but IIS is not really free since it is bundled with a Windows Server and therefore incurs Windows Server Licensing pricing.

## Cassini

Cassini (http://www.asp.net/Projects/Cassini/Download/Default.aspx?tabindex =0&tabid=1) is a Microsoft Shared Source Personal Web Server written entirely in C#. Figure 11-1 shows Cassini's startup page.

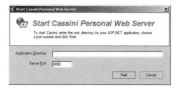

**Figure 11-1** Microsoft's Cassini Web Server.

This managed Web server shows how easy it is to use the BCL of .NET to create a Web server. While this is a useful Web server example, carefully read the Microsoft Shared Source License to ensure it meets the needs of your project, especially considering scalability and performance.

## XSP

If you prefer Open Source to Shared Source, then Mono's XSP (http://www.go-mono.com/asp-net.html) is for you. XSP is also completely managed and written in C# and is under a license that allows for proprietary use or Open Source use. In addition, XSP also runs on all the operating systems that Mono supports!

## Apache

Apache is the most popular Web server in the world, according to Netcraft (http://www.netcraft.com) surveys. Apache (http://httpd.apache.org/) itself is also an Open Source project, which necessitated the Apache Open Source License. Mono also provides an Apache Module (mod_mono) available from http://www.go-mono.com/asp-net.html. Mod_mono works with both 1.3 and 2.0 versions of Apache. This mod_mono Apache module is an extension to support ASP.NET. This requires both the Apache Web server and the Mono runtime. This broadens the operation system support for ASP.NET greatly.

## Which Web Server to Use?

Well, as with many development questions, there is no one right answer. With the Web servers written in C#, there is the obvious advantage of managed environments. Many of the security problems with Web servers spring from memory buffer problems, which are not nearly as prevalent in managed code. Also XSP and Cassini could be run under most operating systems supported by a CLI implementation. XSP is certainly used on multiple platforms, and I have heard of people running Cassini on Mac using the SSCLI.

On the other hand, Apache has much more runtime and is proven to be both stable and scalable, especially the 1.3 version of Apache. Apache and its modules are mostly written in C, which is open to the "security of managed code versus the performance of unmanaged code" debate. But this debate is somewhat old and is becoming more of a moot point as hardware improves.

**NOTE:** For this chapter, the examples will be done using Mono's XSP Server. These examples will feature the PostgreSQL example from Chapter 10 and ASP.NET all running on Mandrake 9 Linux using Mono 0.28.

---

### Web Services Not Just for the Web?

"Web service" is turning out to be a great misnomer. Currently, Web services are used to call methods over the Web in the most general of definitions. This was in use even before standards like SOAP came on the scene. But .NET Web services promised an easy and standardized way of creating and consuming Web services. For the most part, they have succeeded. But many developers like the more structured separation of the Formatters and Channels in .NET remoting. Microsoft quickly realized that Web services should also be channel-independent (not tied to HTTP) and released the Web Service Enhancements (WSE) that allowed Web services over TCP and a host of new APIs for WS-* specifications. Going forward, Indigo (Microsoft's New Messaging System on the next version of Windows) really eliminates the Remoting vs. Web services debate. Both sides are agreeing that Indigo is the way to go! It has been encouraging to see that several Open Source developers and CLI implementers have taken interest in Indigo. Hopefully, Microsoft will continue the current approach of open standardization for Indigo.

# Setting Up the Environment

Many .NET developers are familiar with the Microsoft .NET CLR installation. Just download the SDK (http://www.microsoft.com/downloads/details.aspx? FamilyId=9B3A2CA6-3647-4070-9F41-A333C6B9181D&displaylang=en) and double-click the exe. However, most developers do not realize that installing Mono on Linux is just as easy! This section will discuss setting up Mono on Linux and how that compares to setting up Microsoft's .NET CLR on Windows.

The first thing required here is a Linux operating system distribution. Mandrake 9.2 is a good client-focused distribution of Linux. After visiting http://www.mandrakelinux.com/en/ftp.php3 or any of the mirror servers, downloading the ISO files, and burning the CD-ROMs, just run the rather intuitive installation. You can see in Figure 11-2 the supported operating systems for the version of Mono used in this example.

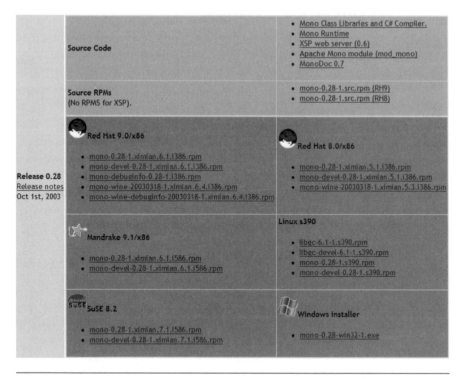

**Figure 11-2** Mono Installs for Various Operating Systems.

So the steps here are just as simple for any of the other supported operating systems (yes, you can install Mono on Windows and even run it side-by-side with Microsoft's .NET CLR). Just install Mono and go. If your target operating system is not supported, then you will have to find a way to compile the Mono sources on that operating system. Always check first with the user group and lists to be sure someone else has not already ported it to your target platform. The steps for compiling Mono's sources are pretty typical for an Open Source project:

1. Download the source for the latest release
2. Open a terminal and run the next 4 steps from the shell
3. tar –xf archive.tar
4. ./configure
5. make
6. make install

## Setting Up Mono and XSP

After downloading Mono and XSP, setting them up (Figure 11-3) on Mandrake is as easy as double-clicking the installation RPM package.

**Figure 11-3**  Setting Up Mono.

Mono automatically installs the BCL as well as many other useful assemblies. Whereas c:\windows\Microsoft.Net\vX.X.XXXX (where the X's are the version numbers) is where Microsoft installs all of its tools (like ngen.exe, csc.exe, and many ASP.NET files), Mono on Linux uses the /usr/lib to store all the BCL dlls and /usr/bin to store all the utility exe files, which makes sense for a Linux application. One thing to keep in mind is that the naming of the dlls on Linux is case-sensitive! Microsoft has the Global Assembly Cache location of c:\windows\assembly\gac, which I don't think Mono has the equivalent of. However, as Chapter 4's discussion on the GAC points out, Microsoft actually recommends private deployment unless you have a really good reason to use the GAC. Side-by-side execution is still achievable on Mono or Microsoft .NET with the correct directory structure naming, strong naming, and the use of the <codeBase> config file element. So Mono on Linux is not all that different if you keep these few things in mind. It really is just as easy to install and run on Linux even if you develop on and are more familiar with Windows!

Downloading and building XSP was very straightforward (much like the steps for building Mono on a non-supported OS). XSP automatically listens on port 8080, which was just fine with Mandrake 9.2. Npgsql and many other useful assemblies were already installed with the Mono 0.28 distribution.

# Web Service Example

Wrapping the FreeDB data access assembly in a Web service is pretty trivial, but it is worth pointing out that the Web service is just a thin wrapper around another assembly. This is currently considered a best practice for remotely exposing functionality. This allows for easily exchanging the Web service with a remoted object or serviced component with very little code change. This also allows for platform interoperability because the data access component does not do anything operating system-specific. However, it is fairly database-specific because the ADO.NET interfaces (i.e., IDataTable, etc.) were not used in the interest of showing the npgsql classes and functionality. But for even greater separation from database-specific code, these interfaces can be used, minimizing the code changes needed to change ADO.NET database providers and database engines. However, in most real-world applications, ADO.NET should use data adapters and stored procedures rather than embedded SQL statements.

Although this practice will tie you to a database (because most databases have proprietary stored procedures and functions), it is more secure, more scalable, and more flexible when changes are needed.

Listing 11.2 is the code from the dataAccess library created in Chapter 10. This is the function that will be wrapped as a Web service and called by the ASP.NET page with the results shown later in Figure 11-4.

**Listing 11.2** Data Access Library Assembly

```
public DataSet GetTracksForCd(string cdname)
{
    tsStart = new TimeSpan(System.DateTime.Now.Ticks);

    conn = new NpgsqlConnection("Server=127.0.0.1;Port=5432;User
Id=bnantz;Password=bnantz;Database=cddb;");
    conn.Open();

    ds = new DataSet();
    ds.Tables.Add("Tracks for CD: " + cdname);

    da = new NpgsqlDataAdapter("select * from tracks where cd =
(select DISTINCT id from cds where title = '" + cdname + "')", conn);

    da.Fill(ds.Tables [0]);

    conn.Close();

    if (_logger.IsDebugEnabled)
    {
        tsEnd = new TimeSpan(System.DateTime.Now.Ticks);
        tsEnd -= tsStart;

        msg = new StringBuilder();
        msg.AppendFormat(@"{0} ms",
          tsEnd.TotalMilliseconds);
        _logger.Debug(msg.ToString());
    }

    return ds;
}
```

Listing 11.3 is simply how to use a C# custom attribute to wrap the functionality of Listing 11.2 in a Web service.

**Listing 11.3** Web Service Wrapper around the Data Access Library

```
[WebMethod]
public DataSet GetTracksForCd(string cdname)
{
        try
        {
          if(cdname.Length>0)
          {
            dataAccess da = new dataAccess();
            return da.GetTracksForCd(cdname);
          }
          else
            throw new ArgumentException("Input can not be empty
string.");
        }
        catch(Exception ex)
        {
          if(_logger.IsErrorEnabled)
            _logger.Error(ex.ToString());
        }
        return new DataSet();
}
```

The custom attribute does all the magic to make sure that the method is now exposed as a Web service. ASP.NET basically takes care of the SOAP messages, which you would otherwise have to do in a custom ASP.NET handler (basically like an ISAPI extension), which is easier than it used to be but still is no small task. In addition, this little tag automatically creates the WSDL needed for the Web service client to consume the Web service. It also maps all the CLI types to SOAP types (like exceptions, strings, ints, etc.). That is a lot of functionality for one line of additional code. The real power is that you can take Listing 11.2 and turn it into Listing 11.3 so easily and get a Web service that anyone (Java, Perl, or anyone talking SOAP) can use!

# ASP.NET Example

As was mentioned in Chapter 10, having FreeDB in a relational format allows for as many queries as you can dream up. Just for a fun example, the ASP.NET page shown in Listing 11.4, allows you to enter a CD Title into a TextBox. Once the button is pushed, all of the track names are returned into a DataGrid on the page.

Listing 11.4 shows the ASP.NET page, and Listing 11.5 shows the code behind C# file.

**Listing 11.4** ASP.NET Page

```
<%@ Page language="c#" Codebehind="WebForm1.aspx.cs"
AutoEventWireup="false" Inherits="FreeDBWP.WebForm1" %>
<!DOCTYPE HTML PUBLIC "-//W3C//DTD HTML 4.0 Transitional//EN" >
<HTML>
   <HEAD>
     <title>WebForm1</title>
content="http://schemas.microsoft.com/intellisense/ie5">
     <meta name="GENERATOR" Content="Microsoft Visual Studio .NET 7.1">
     <meta name="CODE_LANGUAGE" Content="C#">
     <meta name="vs_defaultClientScript" content="JavaScript">
     <meta name="vs_targetSchema"
content="http://schemas.microsoft.com/intellisense/ie5">
   </HEAD>
   <body>
     <form id="Form1" method="post" runat="server">
       <P>
         <asp:Label id="Label1" runat="server">Enter CD
Title:</asp:Label></P>
       <P>
         <asp:TextBox id="TextBox1" runat="server"></asp:TextBox></P>
       <P>
         <asp:Button id="Button1" runat="server" Text="Get Tracks for
CD"></asp:Button></P>
       <asp:DataGrid id="DataGrid1" runat="server"></asp:DataGrid>
     </form>
   </body>
</HTML>
```

This HTML is created automatically by the IDE designer. By double-clicking the button, the IDE creates the event handler and attaches it to the button on the ASP.NET page in Listing 11.4. The designer has written almost all the code. After adding a Web reference to the Web service from Listing 11.2 and a private variable for the Web service, the button click handler code is very simplistic.

**Listing 11.5** Corresponding C# Code Behind File

```csharp
using System;
using System.Collections;
using System.ComponentModel;
using System.Data;
using System.Diagnostics;
using System.Drawing;
using System.Web;
using System.Web.SessionState;
using System.Web.UI;
using System.Web.UI.WebControls;
using System.Web.UI.HtmlControls;

namespace FreeDBWP
{
    /// <summary>
    /// Summary description for WebForm1.
    /// </summary>
    public class WebForm1 : System.Web.UI.Page
    {
    protected System.Web.UI.WebControls.Label Label1;
    protected System.Web.UI.WebControls.TextBox TextBox1;
    protected System.Web.UI.WebControls.Button Button1;
    protected System.Web.UI.WebControls.DataGrid DataGrid1;

    private webservice.Service1 ws;

        private void Page_Load(object sender, System.EventArgs e)
        {
            // Put user code to initialize the page here
        }

        #region Web Form Designer generated code
```

```
          override protected void OnInit(EventArgs e)
          {
               //
               // CODEGEN: This call is required by the ASP.NET Web
Form Designer.
               //
               InitializeComponent();
               base.OnInit(e);
          }

          /// <summary>
          /// Required method for Designer support - do not modify
          /// the contents of this method with the code editor.
          /// </summary>
          private void InitializeComponent()
          {
     this.Button1.Click += new
System.EventHandler(this.Button1_Click);
     this.Load += new System.EventHandler(this.Page_Load);

     }
          #endregion

     private void Button1_Click(object sender, System.EventArgs e)
     {
        try
        {
          if(this.TextBox1.Text.Length>0)
          {
            ws = new webservice.Service1();
            this.DataGrid1.DataSource =
ws.GetTracksForCd(this.TextBox1.Text);
            this.DataGrid1.DataBind();
          }
        }
        catch(Exception ex)
        {
          Debug.WriteLine(ex.ToString());
        }
     }
}
```

The result is shown in Figure 11-4. This also ties back to the beginning of the chapter as a great illustration of a server-side button click event handler populating a Datagrid for display to the user.

Note the two X terminal windows running postmaster/postgresql and XSP. While this is not the most useful query, it does serve as a good proof of concept for operating system-independent ASP.NET and Web service development.

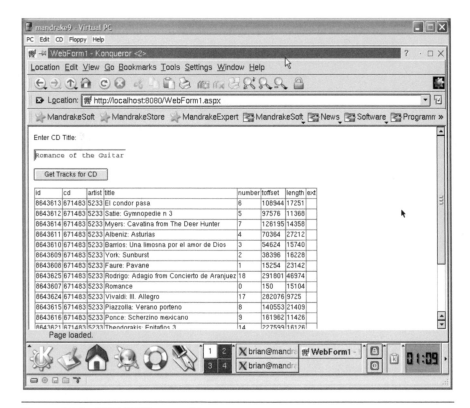

**Figure 11-4**  ASP.NET Page on Linux.

# Summary

This chapter demonstrates one of the strongest aspects of Web development, which is inherent distributed development and operating system-independent availability for the end users. Sometime desktop development can become tightly coupled quite naturally. ASP.NET development, by contrast, is by design a great balance of stateful and stateless development and is now open to many operating systems for developers. Web development is popular because it reaches so many people with a relatively small amount of investment. Everyone needs a Web page, and ASP.NET makes this concept easily achievable. The combination of ASP.NET and Web services is ideal for creating a disconnected distributed system that is very scalable and feature-rich in a short amount of time.

# Simple Project Integration

*It is through cooperation, rather than conflict, that your greatest successes will be derived …*

*—Ralph Charell*

## Introduction

.NET Open Source code is not just some ideal; it is real and useable today. Open Source is useful on many levels. Even if your team or company is not receptive to Open Source, you can still learn from others. Usually, you are not the first one to think of a particular product or idea. Do not misinterpret this; you may have a genuinely unique concept, but often you will find that someone has already thought of it and tried implementing it. If someone has tried out a particular idea, often times they are more than willing to share their knowledge and experience. They can tell you what to watch out for, why they chose a specific implementation, and most importantly, what not to do and what will not work. Learning from others, particularly their mistakes, is probably the one of the strongest arguments for Open Source. Even if you decide not to use an Open Source project, it is still useful to learn by looking at the design and the code. This chapter will demonstrate that integrating several Open Source components can produce a workable product.

## Popular Projects

There are a number of very popular projects already available and stably usable today. For a more complete list, please visit my WIKI site at http://www.nantz.org/SushiWiki/wiki.aspx. Also I have created an Open

Source Downloader Tool, using NAnt of course, which is available from my Web log at http://www.nantz.org/dasBlog/default.aspx?date=2004-02-18. This tool uses the <get> and <cvs> tasks from NAnt to get the latest source from dozens of Open Source projects! Many of the projects come from the following Web sites:

- www.sourceforge.net
- forge.novell.com
- http://go-mono.com/ports

These sites require that the projects be Open Source (as defined by the Open Source Initiative approved licenses). The Novell site has a very interesting LDAP project that works with ActiveDirectory and OpenLDAP. The Mono ports site is maintained by Jackson Harper and contains key projects that are not cross-platform yet but that are strategically targeted by the Mono project. A number of other sites can be useful, but they are not always Open Source, and therefore specific permission must be granted by the authors:

- www.gotdotnet.com workspaces and examples
- www.codeproject.com
- staff.develop.com/woodring and other Developmentor guys

These sites provide a majority of the projects out there. Some additional projects of interest are listed in Table 12.1.

**Table 12.1** Key Open Source Projects

| Project | Web Site | Description |
|---------|----------|-------------|
| SSL | http://www.mentalis.org/soft/projects/seclib/ | A great security library with good SSL support. |
| Genghis | http://www.sellsbrothers.com/tools/genghis/ | A wonderful set of UI components including a wizard engine. |
| MAGIC | http://www.dotnetmagic.com/ | A good mapping to WIN32 cool menus and fancy UI stuff. |

**Table 12.1** Key Open Source projects (cont.)

| Project | Web Site | Description |
|---------|----------|-------------|
| Command Bar | http://www.aisto.com/roeder/dotnet/ | A great C# implementation of cool menus. |
| Remoting | http://www.dotnetremoting.cc/ | A whole set of Remoting channels many from Ingo Rammer himself! |
| XML-RPC | http://www.cookcomputing.com/xmlrpc/xmlrpc.shtml | A strategic project since Microsoft will probably never support XML-RPC since they view it as a competing standard to Web services. |
| Open GL | http://sourceforge.net/projects/csgl/ | Good mapping to OpenGL. |
| CVS Client/ Zip Library | http://www.icsharpcode.net | Great tool for streaming to and from a zip (or compressed) file. |
| PDF.NET | http://sourceforge.net/projects/pdflibrary/ | Good for creating PDFs. |
| nXSLT | http://www.tkachenko.com/dotnet/nxslt.html | A port of the Java XSLT tool. |
| Report.NET | http://report.sourceforge.net/ | Pretty good database reporting tool. |
| Jabber.NET | http://sourceforge.net/projects/jabber-net | Jabber is just a cool idea! |

These projects are very useful because they either address a hole in the .NET framework that Microsoft has not been able to fill yet or an area that Microsoft may never go to in its implementation.

# An Example of Integration

As an example of using .NET Open Source projects together, this example will demonstrate the creation of a very simplistic SVG to GDI+ converter. This will allow a user to draw shapes on the screen and save them as an SVG XML file. First, some terms need to be defined.

## SVG

Scalable Vector Graphics (SVG) is a W3C (http://www.w3.org) standard for representing vector drawings in XML. Vector-based drawing applications are very popular because they are easy to use and can be much more scalable than raster-based graphics. Raster graphics are fixed size graphics that contains many pixel dots. Vector graphics, on the other had, contain vector coordinates that are used to create the graphic via Vector Mathematics. Because of this, scaling a vector graphic to a custom resolution is much simpler than scaling a similar raster graphic. Vector graphics are also smaller than rastor graphics because they store much less data. Adobe (http://www.adobe.com/svg) has probably the most popular SVG viewer that is a plug-in to Microsoft Internet Explorer.

**Listing 12.1**  Simple SVG Document

```
<svg xmlns:xlink="http://www.w3.org/1999/xlink"
xmlns="http://www.w3.org/2000/svg" width="8.5in" height="11in">
<rect x="52" y="176" width="102" height="226"
style="fill:rgb(51,153,51);stroke:rgb(0,0,0);stroke-width:1" />
<ellipse cx="106" cy="118" rx="86" ry="58"
style="fill:rgb(51,0,204);stroke:rgb(0,0,0);stroke-width:1" />
<line x1="204" y1="86" x2="437" y2="151"
style="fill:rgb(0,0,0);stroke:rgb(0,0,0);stroke-width:1" />
</svg>
```

Even if you are unfamiliar with SVG or vector graphics in general, it is clear from the XML element names in Listing 12.1 that this graphical drawing contains a rectangle (rect), an ellipse, and a line. The coordinates are given in a standard x/y Cartesian plane. Also included are fill colors, line weights, and colors in the style attribute. You can see that SVG is complex enough to produce the most amazing graphics. The output in Adobe's SVG Viewer is shown in Figure 12-1.

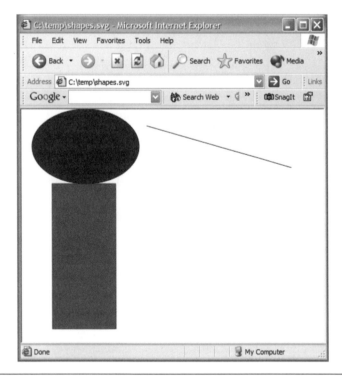

**Figure 12-1** SVG Viewed in Internet Explorer.

There is a fair amount of industry support for SVG. The following vector-based graphic programs support SVG:

■ Adobe Illustrator 10.0
■ Corel Draw!
■ Visio VDX to SVG (http://sourceforge.net/projects/vdxtosvg/)
■ CAD DXF converters (http://sourceforge.net/projects/dxf2svg)

Therefore, in theory the SVG output of this example should be able to be imported from or exported to any of these programs. In the interest of making SVG cover all the bases of a complex vector-based drawing application, SVG can get very complicated. It would be great to have a simple, graphical drawing program something like the paint application shipped with Windows to create an SVG file. Unfortunately, many of these products and programs out there will display SVG code, but most of these programs do not support modifying the SVG. Apache's Batik (http:// http://xml. apache.org/batik) is a notable Open Source SVG project written in Java. Probably the best SVG editor was the JASC Webdraw product that is now discontinued. So this example is a proof of concept to illustrate the speed of integration of Open Source and create a simple program that could be expanded into a very useful application.

### System.Drawing and GDI+

System.Drawing is a part of every CLI implementation discussed in Chapter 2, "Open Source and the .NET Platform." It is a nice standard for basic graphical functionality such as drawing two-dimensional shapes, printing, and imaging. More advanced functionality is found in the System.Drawing.Drawing2D namespace. This namespace is fully implemented in fewer of the CLI implementations. For instance, Mono (http://www.go-mono.com/class-status-System.Drawing.html) reports the namespace as 76% done. It seems to be in the SSCLI, but it's unclear in the DOTGNU documentation. For Microsoft's CLR implementation, System.Drawing is mostly mapped to GDI+ functions.

GDI+ is Microsoft's successor to the GDI (Graphics Device Interface) for drawing on the screen. GDI+ is inherent in Windows XP and 2003 Server. This provides printing and basic drawing for any graphical Windows device.

## SharpVectorGraphics Project

SharpVectorGraphics (http://sourceforge.net/projects/svgdomcsharp) is one of the most popular .NET Open Source projects. SVG# is a .NET XML DOM-based SVG implementation and is well supported, very compliant with SVG standards, (http://www.w3.org/Graphics/SVG/Test/20021115/matrix.html) and easy to use. It is implemented entirely in C#. One of the project's administrators is Niklas Gustavsson, co-author of *SVG Unleashed*, the best SVG book out there. The biggest feature of SVG# is the SVG-to-GDI+ renderer. Based on this renderer, the project offers an SVGPictureBox control that is featured on their SVGViewer. Figure 12-2 shows the SVGViewer application, which happens to be an example application included with SVG# distribution.

**Figure 12-2** SVG# Viewer Application.

Under the Test drop-down menu, you can use this application to test SVG# against the W3C compatibility tests. As you can see, the SVG Picture box is very easy to use. SVG# uses many other Open Source projects within their project. They use NAnt to build the project, NUnit to test the code, NDoc for their documentation, and SharpZipLib (http://www.icsharp-code.net/OpenSource/SharpZipLib/Default.aspx) for compressing and decompressing SVG files.

The goal of this example is to allow users to go both ways: to create a program that allows an SVG file to be displayed onscreen. SVG# already has this functionality. The trick is that this example wants to allow the user to modify the onscreen drawing and save it back as SVG. Thus, System.Drawing.Drawing2D graphics are not enough. The classes in this namespace allow for drawing things onscreen, such as a rectangle, but do not allow the user to change the drawing. This example should let the user change the fill, line width, colors, etc. of the onscreen drawing.

## Didgets Project

Didgets is another Open Source project from http:/sourceforge.net/projects/didgets. Figure 12-3 shows the GDI+ application for drawing and modifying shapes using GDI+.

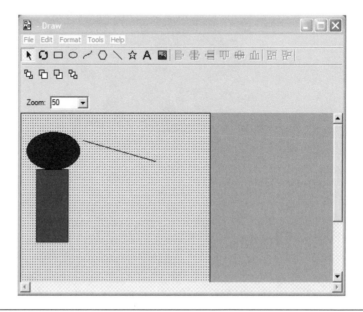

**Figure 12-3**  Didgets UI.

Didgets provides much more functionality than System.Drawing.Drawing2D. The project has a fairly sophisticated architecture, with Workspaces, Widgets, Tools, Properties, Connections, and Commands. This allows Didgets to have its own Shapes and Commands in addition to the ones provided by GDI+. For instance, the Primitive Widgets (rectangles, circles, etc.) know how to size and draw themselves, and the Primitive Tools allow rotation and stretching of the Primitive Widgets using a rubber-band style interface. The Properties allows a Widget to change the Lineweight and color, as well as many other properties like background and foreground colors. Didgets also allows for plug-ins so that additional assemblies can create their own custom Shapes and Widgets that can even be added to the toolbar. There are extension examples included with the Didgets distributions for Parallelogram Shapes. These assemblies inherit from a normal Didget's Widget class and extend the properties like Brushstyles and Lineweights. Didgets also uses the [Tool("Parallelogram","base.101","graphics.ToolParallelogram.ico")] custom attribute to mark the class (in this case, the ParallelogramTool class) that contains the code to put up on a toolbar. The custom attribute contains the icon to be displayed on the toolbar, thus creating a very extendable toolbar. By putting these custom assemblies into a specified directory, Didgets creates a very extendable Shape plug-in architecture using System.Reflection and custom attribute tags.

## Other Open Source Projects

Integrating Log4Net with the SVG# and Didgets projects was pretty trivial. Just inserting the logging code into the exception handling was so quick that it was not even worth creating a Perl script to do it; a simple search within the IDE was adequate. NDoc and NUnit were already being used to some extent in both projects. Since both SVG# and Didgets are fairly large projects, more of a NAnt master build approach (as described in Listings 4.27-4.29) was necessary.

## The Integration

So Didgets provides the ability for a user to intuitively create a drawing on the screen and print it out. SVG# is very good at reading and writing SVG files. The two together make for a primitive SVG editor. Utilizing the SVG# project as the SVG engine for the Didgets project required some code to transform SVG types into Didget types and back again. After exploring the possibility of using inheritance or interfaces, the simplest approach seemed to be putting a thin layer in between the two projects. This would allow for both projects to progress with minimal effect on either project. SVGDidgets in Listing 12.2 is part of the simple class to convert the SVG Objects.

**Listing 12.2** SVGDidgets C# Code

```
foreach(XmlNode node in svgnodes)
{
    if(node.NamespaceURI == SvgDocument.SvgNamespace)
    {
        SvgElement svgnode =
(SvgElement)svgdocument.RootElement.ChildNodes[nodes];
        switch(svgnode.ToString())
        {
            case "SharpVectors.Dom.Svg.SvgEllipseElement":
                EllipseShape ellipse = new EllipseShape();

                ellipse.Size = new
Size((int)((SvgEllipseElement)svgnode).Rx.AnimVal.Value*2,
(int)((SvgEllipseElement)svgnode).Ry.AnimVal.Value*2);
                ellipse.Location = new
Point((int)((SvgEllipseElement)svgnode).Cx.AnimVal.Value -
(int)((SvgEllipseElement)svgnode).Rx.AnimVal.Value,
(int)((SvgEllipseElement)svgnode).Cy.AnimVal.Value -
(int)((SvgEllipseElement)svgnode).Ry.AnimVal.Value);
                d.Widgets.Add(ellipse);
                rotate((SvgElement)svgnode, ellipse);
                break;
.......

            case "SharpVectors.Dom.Svg.SvgTextElement":
                Text text = new Text();
                text.TextProperties.Text =
((SvgTextElement)svgnode).InnerText;
                text.Location = new
Point((int)((SvgTextElement)svgnode).X.AnimVal.GetItem(0).Value,
(int)((SvgTextElement)svgnode).Y.AnimVal.GetItem(0).Value);
                d.Widgets.Add(text);
                rotate((SvgElement)svgnode, text);
                break;
.......

            case "SharpVectors.Dom.Svg.SvgLineElement":
                PlazaConsulting.Didgets.Primitives.Line line = new
PlazaConsulting.Didgets.Primitives.Line();
                line.StartPoint = new
Point((int)((SvgLineElement)svgnode).X1.AnimVal.Value,
(int)((SvgLineElement)svgnode).Y1.AnimVal.Value);
```

```
                line.EndPoint = new
Point((int)((SvgLineElement)svgnode).X2.AnimVal.Value,
(int)((SvgLineElement)svgnode).Y2.AnimVal.Value);
                d.Widgets.Add(line);
                rotate((SvgElement)svgnode, line);
                break;
        }
    }
    nodes++;
}
```

The foreach statement in Listing 12.2 loops through every XMLElement in the list of SVG nodes. The switch statement determines which kind of SVG type it is (Text, Rect, Ellipse), creates a corresponding Didgets type, and adds the widget to the workspace. This allows for the SVG image in Figure 12.3 to be saved into a file output that is Listing 12.1 and be viewed in Internet Explorer as in Figure 12.1.

Reading in the SVG Document into a Didgets workspace is a little harder. This is because many SVG editors punt and just save everything as an SVG path type, which is not as clean as most SVG developers like. This means that everything (even a rectangle) is saved as a group of polylines instead of using the native SVG Rect. This path element will have to map to a polyline for now until Didgets is expanded and can support a better type or until the intelligence is added to detect a built-in shape from the path type, which will require some fairly good artificial intelligence.

## Where to Go from Here

There are obvious shortcomings in this example, but the point is that it took very little work to create a useful application, and we finished relatively quickly. Some improvements for the project could be:

- Compressed SVG output.
- Using Lutz Roeder's CommandBar for .NET to improve the User Interface toolbars and buttons.
- Textual edit mode for direct editing of the SVG XML text that is XML- and SVG-aware.

In the "Popular Projects" section of this chapter, I mentioned both Command Bar and the SharpZipLib. Command Bar empowers you to create dazzling toolbars, menus with icons, and context menus with icons, which users really like. The current implantation of Didgets only uses the System.Windows forms versions, which do not allow for icons currently. You could also use the MAGIC UI library to achieve the same thing, but MAGIC is Win32-specific, and Command Bar is entirely C#. Using the SVG# and SharpZipLib, you could extend this example to support saving in Compressed SVG format (basically a zip file containing the .svg file). This is a big feature because XML, while intuitive, has a lot of whitespace; as the graphics get more complex, the file will get large. Also because SVG is XML, it is entirely text, and text is highly compressible, so this would be a nice addition. Finally, as was shown in Chapter 4's example of using Visual Studio.NET to edit a NAnt file with intellisense (Figure 4-7), it would be nice to let an advanced user switch from graphical drawing mode and rubber-band style stretching to pure text mode where he could easily create Listing 12.1's simple drawing with full intellisense. Then the user could switch back to the graphical view. This concept is also used in Visual Studio.NET for ASP.NET pages. You can use the design mode or the HTML view mode and theoretically switch back and forth. But that is not so easy to support, as Visual Studio.NET illustrates, because sometimes the graphical mode changes everything you did by hand in the HTML view mode. The good news is that Visual Studio.NET 2005 does not do this anymore, but this leads me to believe it is harder to support for Didgets than it appears on the surface.

## Licensing Considerations

Integrating Open Source projects can be powerful, but you must be careful about licensing. Legal advice and exploration would be required when creating a project or product that includes multiple Open Source projects under different licenses. For instance, if one of the products is LGL and the other is BSD or Apache, the licensing issue can get a little messy. But normally this is easily worked out with the Open Source project's leadership.

# Summary

Although the example in this chapter is admittedly simplistic, it illustrates the advantage of combining several unrelated projects in a useful fashion.

Imagine the possibilities of all the combinations of projects listed in this chapter as well as on the WIKI site and OpenSource downloader tool! Many complex systems and even commercial products can benefit from the existing Open Source available today. I hope that you will find Open Source development as useful and exciting as many other developers have. Each time you commit a small contribution to an Open Source project, a sense of accomplishment is felt as you help others at the same time as helping yourself.

# Part IV

# References

# NAnt Tasks

**<al>—Wraps al, the assembly linker for the .NET Framework.**

| Attribute | Description | Required | Type |
|---|---|---|---|
| output | The name of the output file for the assembly manifest. This attribute corresponds to the /out flag. | True | String |
| target | The target type (one of "lib," "exe," or "winexe"). This attribute corresponds to the /t[arget]: flag. | True | String |
| culture | The culture string associated with the output assembly. The string must be in RFC 1766 format, such as "en-US." This attribute corresponds to the /c[ulture]: flag. | False | String |
| template | Specifies an assembly from which to get all options except the culture field. The given filename must have a strong name. This attribute corresponds to the /template: flag. | False | File |
| failonerror | Determines whether task failure stops the build or is just reported. Default is "true." | False | Boolean |
| verbose | Task reports detailed build log messages. Default is "false." | False | Boolean |
| if | If true then the task will be executed; otherwise skipped. Default is "true." | False | Conditional |
| unless | Opposite of if. If false then the task will be executed; otherwise skipped. Default is "false." | False | Conditional |

Example

```
<al output="MyIcons.dll" target="lib">
    <sources>
        <includes name="*.ico"/>
    </sources>
</al>
```

### *<attrib>—Changes the file attributes of a file or set of files.*

The `attrib` task does not have the concept of turning file attributes off. Instead you specify all the attributes that you want turned on, and the rest are turned off by default.

| Attribute | Description | Required |
|-----------|-------------|----------|
| file | The name of the file that will have its attributes set. This is provided as an alternative to using the task's fileset. | False |
| archive | Set the archive attribute. Default is "false." | False |
| hidden | Set the hidden attribute. Default is "false." | False |
| normal | Set the normal file attributes. This attribute is valid only if used alone. Default is "false." | False |
| readonly | Set the read only attribute. Default is "false." | False |
| system | Set the system attribute. Default is "false." | False |
| failonerror | Determines whether task failure stops the build or is just reported. Default is "true." | False |
| verbose | Task reports detailed build log messages. Default is "false." | False |
| if | If true then the task will be executed; otherwise skipped. Default is "true." | False |
| unless | Opposite of if. If false then the task will be executed; otherwise skipped. Default is "false." | False |

Example

```
<attrib normal="true">
    <fileset>
        <includes name="**/*.exe"/>
        <includes name="**/*.dll"/>
    </fileset>
</attrib>
```

### <call>—Calls a NAnt target in the current project.

| Attribute | Description | Required |
|-----------|-------------|----------|
| target | NAnt target to call. | True |
| force | Force an Execute even if the target has already been executed. | False |
| failonerror | Determines whether task failure stops the build or is just reported. Default is "true." | False |
| verbose | Task reports detailed build log messages. Default is "false." | False |
| if | If true then the task will be executed; otherwise skipped. Default is "true." | False |
| unless | Opposite of if. If false then the task will be executed; otherwise skipped. Default is "false." | False |

Example

```
<call target="build"/>
```

### *<cl>—Compiles C/C++ programs using cl, Microsoft's C/C++ compiler.*

| Attribute | Description | Required |
|-----------|-------------|----------|
| options | Options to pass to the compiler. | False |
| outputdir | Directory where all output files are placed. | True |
| pchfile | The name of the precompiled header file. | False |
| failonerror | Determines whether task failure stops the build or is just reported. Default is "true." | False |
| verbose | Task reports detailed build log messages. Default is "false." | False |
| if | If true then the task will be executed; otherwise skipped. Default is "true." | False |
| unless | Opposite of if. If false then the task will be executed; otherwise skipped. Default is "false." | False |

### Example

```
<cl outputdir="build" options="/clr">
    <sources>
        <includes name="helloworld.cpp"/>
    </sources>
</cl>
```

### *<copy>—Copies a file or fileset to a new file or directory.*

Files are only copied if the source file is newer than the destination file or if the destination file does not exist. However, you can explicitly overwrite files with the overwrite attribute.

Filesets are used to select files to copy. To use a fileset, the todir attribute must be set.

| Attribute | Description | Required |
|-----------|-------------|----------|
| file | The file to copy. | False |
| tofile | The file to copy to. | False |
| todir | The directory to copy to. | False |

*(continued)*

| Attribute | Description | Required |
|-----------|-------------|----------|
| overwrite | Overwrite existing files even if the destination files are newer. Defaults to "false." | False |
| failonerror | Determines whether task failure stops the build or is just reported. Default is "true." | False |
| verbose | Task reports detailed build log messages. Default is "false." | False |
| if | If true then the task will be executed; otherwise skipped. Default is "true." | False |
| unless | Opposite of if. If false then the task will be executed; otherwise skipped. Default is "false." | False |

### Example

```
<copy todir="${build.dir}">
    <fileset basedir="bin">
        <includes name="*.dll"/>
    </fileset>
</copy>
```

## &lt;csc&gt;—Copies a file or fileset to a new file or directory.

| Attribute | Description | Required |
|-----------|-------------|----------|
| doc | The name of the XML documentation file to generate. This attribute corresponds to the /doc: flag. | False |
| nostdlib | Instructs the compiler not to import mscorlib.dll (true/false). Default is "false." | False |
| noconfig | Instructs the compiler not to use implicit references to assemblies (true/false). Default is "false." | False |
| output | Output directory for the compilation target. | True |
| target | Output type (library or exe). | True |
| debug | Generate debug output (true/false). | False |
| define | Define conditional compilation symbol(s). Corresponds to /d[efine]: flag. | False |

*(continued)*

| Attribute | Description | Required |
|-----------|-------------|----------|
| win32icon | Icon to associate with the application. Corresponds to /win32icon: flag. | False |
| warnaserror | Instructs the compiler to treat all warnings as errors (true/false). Default is "false." | False |
| main | Specifies which type contains the Main method that you want to use as the entry point into the program. | False |
| failonerror | Determines whether task failure stops the build or is just reported. Default is "true." | False |
| verbose | Task reports detailed build log messages. Default is "false." | False |
| if | If true then the task will be executed; otherwise skipped. Default is "true." | False |
| unless | Opposite of if. If false then the task will be executed; otherwise skipped. Default is "false." | False |

## Example

```
<csc target="exe" output="helloworld.exe" debug="true">
    <sources>
        <includes name="helloworld.cs"/>
    </sources>
    <references>
    </references>
    <resources>
    </resources>
</csc>
```

## <cvscheckout>—Checks out a CVS Module.

| Attribute | Type | Description | Required |
|-----------|------|-------------|----------|
| cvsroot | string | Cvsroot Variable. | True |
| destination | string | Destination directory for the checked out/updated files. | True |
| module | string | The module to perform an operation on. | True |
| failonerror | bool | Determines whether task failure stops the build or is just reported. The default is true. | False |

*(continued)*

| Attribute | Type | Description | Required |
|-----------|------|-------------|----------|
| if | bool | If true then the task will be executed; otherwise, skipped. The default is true. | False |
| password | string | The password for logging in to the CVS repository. | False |
| unless | bool | Opposite of if. If false then the task will be executed; otherwise, skipped. The default is false. | False |
| verbose | bool | Determines whether the task should report detailed build log messages. The default is false. | False |

## Example

```
<cvs-checkout
            destination="c:\src\nant\"

cvsroot=":pserver:anonymous@cvs.sourceforge.net:/cvsroot/nant"
            password=""
            module="nant" />
```

## <cvsupdate>—Updates a CVS Module.

| Attribute | Type | Description | Required |
|-----------|------|-------------|----------|
| cvsroot | string | Cvsroot Variable. | True |
| destination | string | Destination directory for the checked out/updated files. | True |
| module | string | The module to perform an operation on. | True |
| failonerror | bool | Determines whether task failure stops the build or is just reported. The default is true. | False |
| if | bool | If true then the task will be executed; otherwise, skipped. The default is true. | False |
| password | string | The password for logging in to the CVS repository. | False |
| unless | bool | Opposite of if. If false then the task will be executed; otherwise, skipped. The default is false. | False |
| verbose | bool | Determines whether the task should report detailed build log messages. The default is false. | False |

Example

```
<cvs-update
            destination="c:\src\nant\"

cvsroot=":pserver:anonymous@cvs.sourceforge.net:/cvsroot/nant"
            password=""
            module="nant" />
```

## *<delay-sign>—Signs delayed signed .NET assemblies.*

| Attribute | Type | Description | Required |
|---|---|---|---|
| keycontainer | string | Specifies the key container. | False |
| keyfile | string | Specifies the filesystem path to the signing key. | False |
| failonerror | bool | Determines whether task failure stops the build or is just reported. The default is **true**. | False |
| if | bool | If **true** then the task will be executed; otherwise, skipped. The default is **true**. | False |
| timeout | int | The maximum amount of time the application is allowed to execute, expressed in milliseconds. Defaults to no time-out. | False |
| unless | bool | Opposite of if. If **false** then the task will be executed; otherwise, skipped. The default is **false**. | False |
| verbose | bool | Determines whether the task should report detailed build log messages. The default is **false**. | False |

Example

```
<delay-sign keyfile="bar.snk" verbose="false">
          <targets>
              <includes name="foo.dll" />
          </targets>
        </delay-sign>
```

## *<delete>—Deletes a file, fileset, or directory.*

Deletes either a single file, all files in a specified directory and its subdirectories, or a set of files specified by one or more filesets.

**NOTE:** If the file attribute is set, then the fileset contents will be ignored. To delete the files in the fileset, omit the file attribute in the delete element.

| Attribute | Description | Required |
|---|---|---|
| file | The file to delete. | False |
| dir | The directory to delete. | False |
| failonerror | Determines whether task failure stops the build or is just reported. Default is "true." | False |
| verbose | Task reports detailed build log messages. Default is "false." | False |
| if | If true then the task will be executed; otherwise skipped. Default is "true." | False |
| unless | Opposite of if. If false then the task will be executed; otherwise skipped. Default is "false." | False |

### Example

```
<delete dir="${build.dir}" failonerror="false"/>
<delete>
    <fileset>
        <includes name="${basename}-??.exe"/>
        <includes name="${basename}-??.pdb"/>
    </fileset>
</delete>
```

### *<description>—An empty task that allows a build file to contain a description.*

| Attribute | Description | Required |
|-----------|-------------|----------|
| failonerror | Determines whether task failure stops the build or is just reported. Default is "true." | False |
| verbose | Task reports detailed build log messages. Default is "false." | False |
| If | If true then the task will be executed; otherwise skipped. Default is "true." | False |
| unless | Opposite of if. If false then the task will be executed; otherwise skipped. Default is "false." | False |

Example

```
<description>This is a description.</description>
```

### *<echo>—Writes a message to the build log.*

| Attribute | Description | Required |
|-----------|-------------|----------|
| message | The message to display. | False |
| failonerror | Determines whether task failure stops the build or is just reported. Default is "true." | False |
| verbose | Task reports detailed build log messages. Default is "false." | False |
| if | If true then the task will be executed; otherwise skipped. Default is "true." | False |
| unless | Opposite of if. If false then the task will be executed; otherwise skipped. Default is "false." | False |

Example

```
<echo>Base build directory = ${nant.project.basedir}</echo>
```

### &lt;exec&gt;—Executes a system command.

| Attribute | Description | Required |
|---|---|---|
| program | The program to execute without command arguments. | True |
| commandline | The command-line arguments for the program. | False |
| output | The file to which the standard output will be redirected. | False |
| append | True if the output file is to be appended to. | False |
| basedir | The directory the program is in. | False |
| workingdir | The directory in which the command will be executed. | False |
| timeout | Stop the build if the command does not finish within the specified time. Specified in milliseconds. Default is no time out. | False |
| failonerror | Determines whether task failure stops the build or is just reported. Default is "true." | False |
| verbose | Task reports detailed build log messages. Default is "false." | False |
| if | If true then the task will be executed; otherwise skipped. Default is "true." | False |
| unless | Opposite of if. If false then the task will be executed; otherwise skipped. Default is "false." | False |

### &lt;fail&gt;—Exit the current build.

| Attribute | Description | Required |
|---|---|---|
| message | A message giving further information on why the build exited. | False |
| failonerror | Determines whether task failure stops the build or is just reported. Default is "true." | False |
| verbose | Task reports detailed build log messages. Default is "false." | False |
| if | If true then the task will be executed; otherwise skipped. Default is "true." | False |
| unless | Opposite of if. If false then the task will be executed; otherwise skipped. Default is "false." | False |

### Example

```
<fail message="Something wrong here."/>
```

### *<foreach>—Loops over a set of Items.*

Can loop over files in directory, lines in a file, etc.

The Property value is stored before the loop is done and restored when the loop is finished. The Property is returned to its normal value once it is used.

| Attribute | Description | Required |
|-----------|-------------|----------|
| property | The NAnt property name that should be used for the current iterated item. | True |
| item | The type of iteration that should be done. | True |
| in | The source of the iteration. | True |
| delim | The deliminator char. | False |
| failonerror | Determines whether task failure stops the build or is just reported. Default is "true." | False |
| verbose | Task reports detailed build log messages. Default is "false." | False |
| if | If true then the task will be executed; otherwise skipped. Default is "true." | False |
| unless | Opposite of if. If false then the task will be executed; otherwise skipped. Default is "false." | False |

Loops over the files in C:\

Example

```
<foreach item="File" in="c:\" property="filename">
    <echo message="${filename}"/>
</foreach>
```

Loops over the folders in C:\

Example

```
<foreach item="Folder" in="c:\" property="foldername">
    <echo message="${foldername}"/>
</foreach>
```

Loops over a list

Example

```
<foreach item="String" in="1 2 3" delim=" " property="count">
    <echo message="${count}"/>
</foreach>
```

## &lt;get&gt;—Get a particular file from a URL source.

Options include verbose reporting, timestamp-based fetches, and controlling actions on failures.

Currently, only HTTP and UNC protocols are supported. FTP support may be added when more pluggable protocols are added to the System.Net assembly.

The `useTimeStamp` option enables you to control downloads so that the remote file is only fetched if it's newer than the local copy. If there is no local copy, the download always takes place. When a file is downloaded, the timestamp of the downloaded file is set to the remote timestamp.

**NOTE:** This timestamp facility only works on downloads using the HTTP protocol.

| Attribute | Description | Required |
|---|---|---|
| src | The URL from which to retrieve a file. | True |
| dest | Where to store the retrieved file. | True |
| httpproxy | If inside a firewall, proxy server/port information Format: {proxy server name}:{port number} Example: proxy.mycompany.com:8080 | False |
| ignoreerrors | Log errors but don't treat as fatal. ("true"/"false"). Default is "false." | False |
| usetimestamp | Conditionally download a file based on the timestamp of the local copy. HTTP only. ("true"/"false"). Default is "false." | False |

*(continued)*

| Attribute | Description | Required |
|---|---|---|
| failonerror | Determines whether task failure stops the build or is just reported. Default is "true." | False |
| verbose | Task reports detailed build log messages. Default is "false." | False |
| if | If true then the task will be executed; otherwise skipped. Default is "true." | False |
| unless | Opposite of if. If false then the task will be executed; otherwise skipped. Default is "false." | False |

### Example

```
<get src="http://nant.sourceforge.org/" dest="help/index.html"/>
```

### *<if>—Checks the conditional attributes and executes the children if true.*

If no conditions are checked, all child tasks are executed. True is the default condition result.

If more than one attribute is used, they are And'd together. The first to fail stops the check.

| Attribute | Description | Required |
|---|---|---|
| uptodateFile | The file to compare if uptodate. | False |
| compareFile | The file to check against for the uptodate file. | False |
| propertytrue | Used to test whether a property is true. | False |
| propertyexists | Used to test whether a property exists. | False |
| targetexists | Used to test whether a target exists. | False |
| failonerror | Determines whether task failure stops the build or is just reported. Default is "true." | False |
| verbose | Task reports detailed build log messages. Default is "false." | False |
| if | If true then the task will be executed; otherwise skipped. Default is "true." | False |
| unless | Opposite of if. If false then the task will be executed; otherwise skipped. Default is "false." | False |

## Check existence of a property

Example

```
<if propertyexists="myProp">
    <echo message="myProp Exists. Value='${myProp}'"/>
</if>
```

## Check that a property value is true

Example

```
<if propertytrue="myProp">
    <echo message="myProp is true. Value='${myProp}'"/>
</if>
```

## Check that a target exists

Example

```
<target name="myTarget"/>
<if targetexists="myTarget">
    <echo message="myTarget exists."/>
</if>
```

## Checks file dates

Example

```
<if uptodatefile="myfile.dll" comparefile="myfile.cs">
    <echo message="myfile.dll is newer/same-date as myfile.cs"/>
</if>
```

### <ifnot>—The opposite of the if task.

### <include>—Include an external build file.

This task is used to break your build file into smaller chunks. You can load a partial build file and have it included in the build file.

**NOTE:** Any global (project-level) tasks in the included build file are executed when this task is executed. Tasks in target elements are only executed if that target is executed.

**NOTE:** The project element attributes are ignored.

**NOTE:** This task can only be in the global (project-level) section of the build file.

| Attribute | Description | Required |
|---|---|---|
| buildfile | Build file to include. | True |
| failonerror | Determines whether task failure stops the build, or is just reported. Default is "true." | False |
| verbose | Task reports detailed build log messages. Default is "false." | False |
| if | If true then the task will be executed; otherwise skipped. Default is "true." | False |
| unless | Opposite of if. If false then the task will be executed; otherwise skipped. Default is "false." | False |

Example

```
<include buildfile="GetProjectVersion.include"/>
```

### <jsc>—Compiles Microsoft JScript.NET programs using jsc.

| Attribute | Description | Required |
|---|---|---|
| output | Output directory for the compilation target. | True |
| target | Output type (library or exe). | True |
| debug | Generate debug output (true/false). | False |
| define | Define conditional compilation symbol(s). Corresponds to /d[efine]: flag. | False |
| win32icon | Icon to associate with the application. Corresponds to /win32icon: flag. | False |
| warnaserror | Instructs the compiler to treat all warnings as errors (true/false). Default is "false." | False |
| main | Specifies which type contains the Main method that you want to use as the entry point into the program. | False |

*(continued)*

| Attribute | Description | Required |
|-----------|-------------|----------|
| failonerror | Determines whether task failure stops the build or is just reported. Default is "true." | False |
| verbose | Task reports detailed build log messages. Default is "false." | False |
| if | If true then the task will be executed; otherwise skipped. Default is "true." | False |
| unless | Opposite of if. If false then the task will be executed; otherwise skipped. Default is "false." | False |

## Example

```
<jsc target="exe" output="helloworld.exe" debug="true">
    <sources>
        <includes name="helloworld.js"/>
    </sources>
</jsc>
```

## *&lt;lib&gt;—Run lib.exe, Microsoft's Library Manager.*

| Attribute | Description | Required |
|-----------|-------------|----------|
| options | Options to pass to the compiler. | False |
| output | The output filename. | True |
| failonerror | Determines whether task failure stops the build or is just reported. Default is "true." | False |
| verbose | Task reports detailed build log messages. Default is "false." | False |
| if | If true then the task will be executed; otherwise skipped. Default is "true." | False |
| unless | Opposite of if. If false then the task will be executed; otherwise skipped. Default is "false." | False |

## Example

```
<lib output="library.lib">
    <sources>
        <includes name="library.obj"/>
    </sources>
</lib>
```

### *<license>—Task to generate a .license file from a .licx file.*

If no output file is specified, the default filename is the name of the target file with the extension ".licenses" appended.

| Attribute | Description | Required |
|-----------|-------------|----------|
| input | Input file to process. | True |
| output | Name of the resource file to output. | False |
| licensetarget | The output executable file for which the license will be generated. | True |
| failonerror | Determines whether task failure stops the build or is just reported. Default is "true." | False |
| verbose | Task reports detailed build log messages. Default is "false." | False |
| if | If true then the task will be executed; otherwise skipped. Default is "true." | False |
| unless | Opposite of if. If false then the task will be executed; otherwise skipped. Default is "false." | False |

Example

```
<license input="component.licx" target="component.exe" />
```

### *<link>—Links files using link, Microsoft's Incremental Linker.*

| Attribute | Description | Required |
|-----------|-------------|----------|
| options | Options to pass to the compiler. | False |
| output | The output filename. | True |
| failonerror | Determines whether task failure stops the build or is just reported. Default is "true." | False |
| verbose | Task reports detailed build log messages. Default is "false." | False |
| if | If true then the task will be executed; otherwise skipped. Default is "true." | False |
| unless | Opposite of if. If false then the task will be executed; otherwise skipped. Default is "false." | False |

Example

```
<link output="helloworld.exe">
    <sources>
        <includes name="*.obj"/>
    </sources>
</link>
```

### &lt;loadtasks&gt;—Loads tasks from a given assembly or directory.

| Attribute | Type | Description | Required |
|-----------|------|-------------|----------|
| assembly | string | An assembly to load tasks from. | False |
| path | string | A directory to scan for task assemblies. | False |
| failonerror | bool | Determines whether task failure stops the build or is just reported. The default is **true**. | False |
| if | bool | If **true** then the task will be executed; otherwise, skipped. The default is **true**. | False |
| unless | bool | Opposite of if. If **false** then the task will be executed; otherwise, skipped. The default is **false**. | False |
| verbose | bool | Determines whether the task should report detailed build log messages. The default is **false**. | False |

Example

```
<loadtasks assembly="c:foo\NAnt.Contrib.Tasks.dll" />
```

### &lt;mc&gt;—Compiles messages using mc.exe, Microsoft's Win32 message compiler.

| Attribute | Type | Description | Required |
|-----------|------|-------------|----------|
| mcfile | string | Input filename. | True |
| headerpath | string | Path to store Header file. | False |
| options | string | Options to pass to the compiler. | False |

*(continued)*

| Attribute | Type | Description | Required |
|---|---|---|---|
| rcpath | string | Path to store RC file. | False |
| failonerror | bool | Determines whether task failure stops the build or is just reported. The default is true. | False |
| if | bool | If true then the task will be executed; otherwise, skipped. The default is true. | False |
| timeout | int | The maximum amount of time the application is allowed to execute, expressed in milliseconds. Defaults to no time-out. | False |
| unless | bool | Opposite of if. If false then the task will be executed; otherwise, skipped. The default is false. | False |
| verbose | bool | Determines whether the task should report detailed build log messages. The default is false. | False |

### Example

```
<mc mcfile="text.mc" headerpath=".\build" rcpath=".\build" options="-v
-c -u"/>
```

### *<mail>—A task to send SMTP email.*

Text and text files to include in the message body may be specified as well as binary attachments.

| Attribute | Description | Required |
|---|---|---|
| from | Email address of sender. | True |
| tolist | Comma- or semicolon-separated list of recipient email addresses. | True |
| cclist | Comma- or semicolon-separated list of CC: recipient email addresses. | False |
| bcclist | Comma- or semicolon-separated list of BCC: recipient email addresses. | False |
| mailhost | Host name of mail server. Defaults to "localhost." | False |
| message | Text to send in body of email message. | False |

*(continued)*

| Attribute | Description | Required |
|-----------|-------------|----------|
| subject | Text to send in subject line of email message. | False |
| format | Format of the message body. Valid values are "Html" or "Text." Defaults to "Text." | False |
| files | Name(s) of text files to send as part of body of the email message. Multiple filenames are comma- or semicolon-separated. | False |
| attachments | Name(s) of files to send as attachments to email message. Multiple filenames are comma- or semicolon-separated. | False |
| failonerror | Determines whether task failure stops the build or is just reported. Default is "true." | False |
| verbose | Task reports detailed build log messages. Default is "false." | False |
| if | If true then the task will be executed; otherwise skipped. Default is "true." | False |
| unless | Opposite of if. If false then the task will be executed; otherwise skipped. Default is "false." | False |

## Example

```
<mail
  from="nAnt@sourceforge.net"
  tolist="recipient1@sourceforge.net"
  cclist="recipient2@sourceforge.net"
  bcclist="recipient3@sourceforge.net"
  subject="Msg 7: With attachments"
  files="body1.txt,body2.txt;body3.txt,body4.txt"
  attachments="body1.txt,body2.txt;,body3.txt"
  mailhost="smtpserver.anywhere.com"/>
```

## *&lt;mcs&gt;—Compiles C# programs using the Mono mcs compiler.*

| Attribute | Description | Required |
|-----------|-------------|----------|
| nostdlib | Instructs the compiler not to import core assemblies (true/false). Default is "false." | False |
| noconfig | Instructs the compiler not to use implicit references to assemblies (true/false). Default is "false." | False |

*(continued)*

| Attribute | Description | Required |
|-----------|-------------|----------|
| output | Output directory for the compilation target. | True |
| target | Output type (library or exe). | True |
| debug | Generate debug output (true/false). | False |
| define | Define conditional compilation symbol(s). Corresponds to /d[efine]: flag. | False |
| win32icon | Icon to associate with the application. Corresponds to /win32icon: flag. | False |
| warnaserror | Instructs the compiler to treat all warnings as errors (true/false). Default is "false" | False |
| main | Specifies which type contains the Main method that you want to use as the entry point into the program. | False |
| failonerror | Determines whether task failure stops the build or is just reported. Default is "true." | False |
| verbose | Task reports detailed build log messages. Default is "false." | False |
| if | If true then the task will be executed; otherwise skipped. Default is "true." | False |
| unless | Opposite of if. If false then the task will be executed; otherwise skipped. Default is "false." | False |

### Example

```
<mcs target="exe" output="helloworld.exe" debug="true">
    <sources>
        <includes name="helloworld.cs"/>
    </sources>
</mcs>
```

### *<mkdir>— Creates a directory and any non-existent parent directories if necessary.*

| Attribute | Description | Required |
|-----------|-------------|----------|
| dir | The directory to create. | True |
| failonerror | Determines whether task failure stops the build or is just reported. Default is "true." | False |
| verbose | | |
| if | Task reports detailed build log messages. Default is "false." | False |

*(continued)*

| Attribute | Description | Required |
|-----------|-------------|----------|
| unless | If true then the task will be executed; otherwise skipped. Default is "true." | False |
| | Opposite of if. If false then the task will be executed; otherwise skipped. Default is "false." | False |

Example

```
<mkdir dir="build"/>
```

### <move>—Moves a file or fileset to a new file or directory.

Files are only moved if the source file is newer than the destination file, or if the destination file does not exist.

**NOTE:** You can explicitly overwrite files with the overwrite attribute.

Filesets are used to select files to move. To use a fileset, the todir attribute must be set.

| Attribute | Description | Required |
|-----------|-------------|----------|
| file | The file to copy. | False |
| tofile | The file to copy to. | False |
| todir | The directory to copy to. | False |
| overwrite | Overwrite existing files even if the destination files are newer. Defaults to "false." | False |
| failonerror | Determines whether task failure stops the build or is just reported. Default is "true." | False |
| verbose | Task reports detailed build log messages. Default is "false." | False |
| if | If true then the task will be executed; otherwise skipped. Default is "true." | False |
| unless | Opposite of if. If false then the task will be executed; otherwise skipped. Default is "false." | False |

### *<nant>— Runs NAnt on a supplied build file. This can be used to build subprojects.*

| Attribute | Description | Required |
|---|---|---|
| buildfile | The build file to build. If not specified, use the current build file. | False |
| target | The target to execute. To specify more than one target, separate targets with a space. Targets are executed in order if possible. Default to use target specified in the project's default attribute. | False |
| inheritall | Specifies whether current property values should be inherited by the executed project. Default is false. | False |
| failonerror | Determines whether task failure stops the build or is just reported. Default is "true." | False |
| verbose | Task reports detailed build log messages. Default is "false." | False |
| if | If true then the task will be executed; otherwise skipped. Default is "true." | False |
| unless | Opposite of if. If false then the task will be executed; otherwise skipped. Default is "false." | False |

### Example

```
<nant unless="${debug}"
buildfile="${src.dir}/Extras/BuildServer/BuildServer.build"/>
```

### *<nantschema>—Creates a schema file for all available tasks.*

| Attribute | Type | Description | Required |
|---|---|---|---|
| output | string | The name of the output file to which the XSD should be written. | True |
| class | string | The Type for which an XSD should be created. If not specified, an XSD will be created for all available tasks. | False |
| target-ns | string | The target namespace for the output. Defaults to "http://tempuri.org/nant-donotuse.xsd." | False |

*(continued)*

| Attribute | Type | Description | Required |
|-----------|------|-------------|----------|
| failonerror | bool | Determines whether task failure stops the build or is just reported. The default is true. | False |
| if | bool | If true then the task will be executed; otherwise, skipped. The default is true. | False |
| unless | bool | Opposite of if. If false then the task will be executed; otherwise, skipped. The default is false. | False |
| verbose | bool | Determines whether the task should report detailed build log messages. The default is false. | False |

### Example

```
<nantschema output="NAnt.xsd" />
```

### &lt;ndoc&gt;—Runs NDoc to create documentation.

| Attribute | Description | Required |
|-----------|-------------|----------|
| failonerror | Determines whether task failure stops the build or is just reported. Default is "true." | False |
| verbose | Task reports detailed build log messages. Default is "false." | False |
| if | If true then the task will be executed; otherwise skipped. Default is "true." | False |
| unless | Opposite of if. If false then the task will be executed; otherwise skipped. Default is "false." | False |

### Example

```
<ndoc>
    <assemblies basedir="${build.dir}">
        <includes name="NAnt.exe"/>
        <includes name="NAnt.Core.dll"/>
    </assemblies>
    <summaries basedir="${build.dir}">
        <includes name="NamespaceSummary.xml"/>
    </summaries>
    <documenters>
```

```
            <documenter name="MSDN">
                <property name="OutputDirectory" value="doc\MSDN" />
                <property name="HtmlHelpName" value="NAnt" />
                <property name="HtmlHelpCompilerFilename" value="hhc.exe"
/>
                <property name="IncludeFavorites" value="False" />
                <property name="Title" value="An NDoc Documented Class
Library" />
                <property name="SplitTOCs" value="False" />
                <property name="DefaulTOC" value="" />
                <property name="ShowVisualBasic" value="True" />
                <property name="ShowMissingSummaries" value="True" />
                <property name="ShowMissingRemarks" value="True" />
                <property name="ShowMissingParams" value="True" />
                <property name="ShowMissingReturns" value="True" />
                <property name="ShowMissingValues" value="True" />
                <property name="DocumentInternals" value="False" />
                <property name="DocumentProtected" value="True" />
                <property name="DocumentPrivates" value="False" />
                <property name="DocumentEmptyNamespaces" value="False" />
                <property name="IncludeAssemblyVersion" value="False" />
                <property name="CopyrightText" value="" />
                <property name="CopyrightHref" value="" />
            </documenter>
        </documenters>
</ndoc>
```

---

`NamespaceSummary.xml contents`

---

```
<namespaces>
    <namespace name="Foo.Bar">
        The <b>Foo.Bar</b> namespace reinvents the wheel.
    </namespace>
    <namespace name="Foo.Bar.Tests">
        The <b>Foo.Bar.Tests</b> namespace ensures that the Foo.Bar
namespace reinvents the wheel correctly.
    </namespace>
</namespaces>
```

---

## *&lt;nunit&gt;—Runs tests using the NUnit framework.*

The `haltonfailure` or `haltonerror` are only used to stop more than one test suite from running. If any test suite fails, a build error will be thrown. Use `failonerror="false"` to ignore test errors and continue build.

| Attribute | Description | Required |
|-----------|-------------|----------|
| haltonerror | Stops running tests when a test causes an error. Default is "false." | False |
| haltonfailure | Stops running tests if a test fails (errors are considered failures as well). Default is "false." | False |
| timeout | Cancel the individual tests if they do not finish in the specified time (measured in milliseconds). Ignored if fork is disabled. | False |
| failonerror | Determines whether task failure stops the build or is just reported. Default is "true." | False |
| verbose | Task reports detailed build log messages. Default is "false." | False |
| if | If true then the task will be executed; otherwise skipped. Default is "true." | False |
| unless | Opposite of if. If false then the task will be executed; otherwise skipped. Default is "false." | False |

## Example

```
<nunit basedir="build" verbose="false" haltonerror="true"
haltonfailure="true">
    <formatter type="Xml"/>
    <formatter type="Plain"/>
        <test name="MyProject.Tests.AllTests"
assembly="MyProject.Tests.dll" outfile="results"/>
</nunit>
```

## *<nunit2>—Runs tests using the NUnit V2.0 framework.*

| Attribute | Description | Required |
|---|---|---|
| haltonfailure | Stop the build process if a test fails. | False |
| failonerror | Determines whether task failure stops the build or is just reported. Default is "true." | False |
| verbose | Task reports detailed build log messages. Default is "false." | False |
| if | If true then the task will be executed; otherwise skipped. Default is "true." | False |
| unless | Opposite of if. If false then the task will be executed; otherwise skipped. Default is "false." | False |

### Example

```
<nunit2>
    <test assemblyname="MyProject.Tests.dll" outfile="results.xml"/>
</nunit2>
```

## *<property> Sets a property in the current project.*

| Attribute | Description | Required |
|---|---|---|
| name | The name of the property to set. | True |
| value | The value of the property. | True |
| readonly | Determines if the property is read-only or if it is changeable by a target. | False |
| failonerror | Determines whether task failure stops the build or is just reported. Default is "true." | False |
| verbose | Task reports detailed build log messages. Default is "false." | False |
| if | If true then the task will be executed; otherwise skipped. Default is "true." | False |
| unless | Opposite of if. If false then the task will be executed; otherwise skipped. Default is "false." | False |

## Example

```
<property name="debug" value="true"/>
```

### *&lt;readregistry&gt;—A task that reads a value or set of values from the Windows registry into one or more NAnt properties.*

| Attribute | Description | Required |
|-----------|-------------|----------|
| property | The property to set to the specified registry key value. | False |
| prefix | The prefix to use for the specified registry key values. | False |
| key | The registry key to read. | True |
| hive | The registry hive to use. | False |
| failonerror | Determines whether task failure stops the build or is just reported. Default is "true." | False |
| verbose | Task reports detailed build log messages. Default is "false." | False |
| if | If true then the task will be executed; otherwise skipped. Default is "true." | False |
| unless | Opposite of if. If false then the task will be executed; otherwise skipped. Default is "false." | False |

## Example

```
<readregistry property="sdkRoot"
key="\SOFTWARE\Microsoft\.NETFramework\sdkInstallRoot"
hive="LocalMachine" />
```

### *&lt;regex&gt;—Sets properties based on a regular expression.*

| Attribute | Type | Description | Required |
|-----------|------|-------------|----------|
| input | string | Represents the input for the regular expression. | True |
| pattern | string | Represents the regular expression to be evaluated. | True |
| failonerror | bool | Determines whether task failure stops the build or is just reported. The default is true. | False |
| if | bool | If true then the task will be executed; otherwise, skipped. The default is true. | False |

*(continued)*

| Attribute | Type | Description | Required |
|-----------|------|-------------|----------|
| unless | bool | Opposite of if. If false then the task will be executed; otherwise, skipped. The default is false. | False |
| verbose | bool | Determines whether the task should report detailed build log messages. The default is false. | False |

**Example**

```
<regex pattern="(?'lastword'\w+)$" input="This is a test sentence" />
```

### <regsvc>—Installs .NET Windows Services.

| Attribute | Type | Description | Required |
|-----------|------|-------------|----------|
| assembly | string | The source assembly file. | True |
| action | enum | Defines the action to take with the assembly. Supported actions are: FindOrCreate (the default), Create, or Uninstall. | False |
| application | string | Specifies the name of the COM+ application to either find or create. | False |
| componentsonly | bool | Configures components only; ignores methods and interfaces. The default is false. | False |
| existingapp | bool | Expect an existing application. The default is false. | False |
| existingtlb | bool | Uses an existing type library. The default is false. | False |
| noreconfig | bool | Do not reconfigure an existing target application. The default is false. | False |
| partition | string | Specifies the name or ID of the COM+ application to either find or create. | False |
| tlb | string | Specifies the type library file to install. | False |
| failonerror | bool | Determines whether task failure stops the build or is just reported. The default is true. | False |

*(continued)*

| Attribute | Type | Description | Required |
|-----------|------|-------------|----------|
| if | bool | If true then the task will be executed; otherwise, skipped. The default is true. | False |
| timeout | int | The maximum amount of time the application is allowed to execute, expressed in milliseconds. Defaults to no time-out. | False |
| unless | bool | Opposite of if. If false then the task will be executed; otherwise, skipped. The default is false. | False |
| verbose | bool | Determines whether the task should report detailed build log messages. The default is false. | False |

### Example

```
<regsvcs action="FindOrCreate" assembly="myTest.dll" />
```

## &lt;resgen&gt;—Converts files from one resource format to another (wraps Microsoft's resgen.exe).

| Attribute | Description | Required |
|-----------|-------------|----------|
| input | Input file to process. | False |
| output | Name of the resource file to output. | False |
| target | The target type (usually resources). | False |
| todir | The directory to which outputs will be stored. | False |
| failonerror | Determines whether task failure stops the build or is just reported. Default is "true." | False |
| verbose | Task reports detailed build log messages. Default is "false." | False |
| if | If true then the task will be executed; otherwise skipped. Default is "true." | False |
| unless | Opposite of if. If false then the task will be executed; otherwise | False |

Example

```
<resgen input="translations.resx" output="translations.resources" />
```

### <resx>—Task to generate a .resources file from a .resx file.

| Attribute | Description | Required |
|---|---|---|
| input | Input file to process. | True |
| output | Name of the license resource file to output. | False |
| failonerror | Determines whether task failure stops the build or is just reported. Default is "true." | False |
| verbose | Task reports detailed build log messages. Default is "false." | False |
| if | If true then the task will be executed; otherwise skipped. Default is "true." | False |
| unless | Opposite of if. If false then the task will be executed; otherwise skipped. Default is "false." | False |

Example

```
<resx input="translations.resx" />
```

### <script> Executes the code contained within the task.

| Attribute | Description | Required |
|---|---|---|
| language | The language of the script block (VB, C#, JS). | True |
| mainclass | Name of the main class containing the static ScriptMain entry point. | False |
| failonerror | Determines whether task failure stops the build or is just reported. Default is "true." | False |
| verbose | Task reports detailed build log messages. Default is "false." | False |
| if | If true then the task will be executed; otherwise skipped. Default is "true." | False |
| unless | Opposite of if. If false then the task will be executed; otherwise skipped. Default is "false." | False |

## Example

```
<script language="C#">
    <code>
        <![CDATA [
         public static void ScriptMain(Project project)
         {
               System.Console.WriteLine("Hello World from a script task
using C#");
         }
        ]]>
    </code>
</script>
```

## *&lt;servicecontroller&gt;— Starts and stops a Windows service.*

| Attribute | Type | Description | Required |
|-----------|------|-------------|----------|
| action | enum | The action that should be performed on the service—either Start, Stop, Restart, Pause, or Continue. | True |
| service | string | The name of the service that should be controlled. | True |
| machine | string | The name of the computer on which the service resides. The default is the local computer. | False |
| timeout | double | The time, in milliseconds, the task will wait for the service to reach the desired status. The default is 5000 milliseconds. | False |
| failonerror | bool | Determines whether task failure stops the build or is just reported. The default is true. | False |
| if | bool | If true then the task will be executed; otherwise, skipped. The default is true. | False |
| unless | bool | Opposite of if. If false then the task will be executed; otherwise, skipped. The default is false. | False |
| verbose | bool | Determines whether the task should report detailed build log messages. The default is false. | False |

## Example

```
<servicecontroller action="Start" service="w3svc" />
```

### <sleep>— A task for sleeping a specified period of time, useful when a build or deployment process requires an interval between tasks.

| Attribute | Description | Required |
|---|---|---|
| hours | Hours to add to the sleep time. | False |
| minutes | Minutes to add to the sleep time. | False |
| seconds | Seconds to add to the sleep time. | False |
| milliseconds | Milliseconds to add to the sleep time. | False |
| failonerror | Determines whether task failure stops the build or is just reported. Default is "true." | False |
| verbose | Task reports detailed build log messages. Default is "false." | False |
| if | If true then the task will be executed; otherwise skipped. Default is "true." | False |
| unless | Opposite of if. If false then the task will be executed; otherwise skipped. Default is "false." | False |

Example

```
<sleep hours="1" minutes="2" seconds="3" milliseconds="4" />
```

### <solution>—Builds a Visual Studio .NET solution file.

| Attribute | Type | Description | Required |
|---|---|---|---|
| configuration | string | The name of the solution configuration to build. | True |
| includevsfolders | bool | Includes Visual Studio search folders in reference search path. The default is true. | False |
| outputdir | string | The directory where compiled targets will be placed. This overrides path settings contained in the solution/project. | False |
| solutionfile | string | The name of the VS.NET solution file to build. | False |
| failonerror | bool | Determines whether task failure stops the build or is just reported. The default is true. | False |
| if | bool | If true then the task will be executed; otherwise, skipped. The default is true. | False |

*(continued)*

| Attribute | Type | Description | Required |
|---|---|---|---|
| unless | bool | Opposite of if. If false then the task will be executed; otherwise, skipped. The default is false. | False |
| verbose | bool | Determines whether the task should report detailed build log messages. The default is false. | False |

Example

```
<solution configuration="release" solutionfile="test.sln" />
```

## *<style>—Process a document via XSLT.*

| Attribute | Description | Required |
|---|---|---|
| basedir | Where to find the source XML file; default is the project's basedir. | False |
| destdir | Directory in which to store the results. | False |
| extension | Desired file extension to be used for the targets. The default is "html." | False |
| style | Name of the stylesheet to use—given either relative to the project's basedir or as an absolute path. | True |
| in | Specifies a single XML document to be styled. Should be used with the out attribute. | True |
| out | Specifies the output name for the styled result from the in attribute. | False |
| failonerror | Determines whether task failure stops the build or is just reported. Default is "true." | False |
| verbose | Task reports detailed build log messages. Default is "false." | False |
| if | If true then the task will be executed; otherwise skipped. Default is "true." | False |
| unless | Opposite of if. If false then the task will be executed; otherwise skipped. Default is "false." | False |

Example

```
<style style="report.xsl" in="data.xml" out="report.html">
    <param name="reportType" expression="${report.type}"/>
</style>
```

### *<sysinfo>—Sets a number of properties with information about the system environment.*

The intent of this task is for nightly build logs to have a record of system information that the build was performed on.

| Property | Value |
|----------|-------|
| sys.clr.version | Common Language Runtime version number. |
| sys.env.° | Environment variables (e.g., sys.env.PATH). |
| sys.os.folder.system | The System directory. |
| sys.os.folder.temp | The temporary directory. |
| sys.os.platform | Operating system platform ID. |
| sys.os.version | Operating system version. |
| sys.os | Operating system version string. |

| Attribute | Description | Required |
|-----------|-------------|----------|
| prefix | The string to prefix the property names with. Default is "sys." | False |
| failonerror | Determines whether task failure stops the build or is just reported. Default is "true." | False |
| verbose | Task reports detailed build log messages. Default is "false." | False |
| if | If true then the task will be executed; otherwise skipped. Default is "true." | False |
| unless | Opposite of if. If false then the task will be executed; otherwise skipped. Default is "false." | False |

Example

```
<sysinfo verbose="true"/>
```

### *&lt;touch&gt;— Touch a file and/or fileset(s) – corresponds to the Unix touch command.*

| Attribute | Description | Required |
|-----------|-------------|----------|
| file | Assembly Filename (required unless a fileset is specified). | False |
| millis | Specifies the new modification time of the file in milliseconds since midnight Jan. 1, 1970. | False |
| datetime | Specifies the new modification time of the file in the format MM/DD/YYYY HH:MM AM_or_PM. | False |
| failonerror | Determines whether task failure stops the build or is just reported. Default is "true." | False |
| verbose | Task reports detailed build log messages. Default is "false." | False |
| if | If true then the task will be executed; otherwise skipped. Default is "true." | False |
| unless | Opposite of if. If false then the task will be executed; otherwise skipped. Default is "false." | False |

Example

```
<touch>
    <fileset>
        <includes name="**/*.exe"/>
        <includes name="**/*.dll"/>
    </fileset>
</touch>
```

### *&lt;tstamp&gt;—Sets properties with the current date and time.*

By default, tstamp displays the current date and time and sets the following properties:

- tstamp.date to yyyyMMdd
- tstamp.time to HHmm
- tstamp.now using the default DateTime.ToString() method

To set an additional property with a custom date/time, use the property and pattern attributes. To set a number of additional properties, all with the exact same date and time, use the formatter nested element (see example).

The date and time string displayed by the tstamp task uses the computer's default long date and time string format. You might consider setting these to the ISO 8601 standard for date and time notation.

| Attribute | Description | Required |
|---|---|---|
| property | The property to receive the date/time string in the given pattern. | False |
| pattern | The date/time pattern to be used. | False |
| failonerror | Determines whether task failure stops the build or is just reported. Default is "true." | False |
| verbose | Task reports detailed build log messages. Default is "false." | False |
| if | If true then the task will be executed; otherwise skipped. Default is "true." | False |
| unless | Opposite of if. If false then the task will be executed; otherwise skipped. Default is "false." | False |

Example

```
<tstamp property="build.date" pattern="yyyyMMdd" verbose="true"/>
```

### <unzip>—Unzips a zip file.

| Attribute | Type | Description | Required |
|---|---|---|---|
| zipfile | string | The zip file to use. | True |
| todir | string | The directory where the expanded files should be stored. | False |
| failonerror | bool | Determines whether task failure stops the build or is just reported. The default is true. | False |
| if | bool | If true then the task will be executed; otherwise, skipped. The default is true. | False |
| unless | bool | Opposite of if. If false then the task will be executed; otherwise, skipped. The default is false. | False |
| verbose | bool | Determines whether the task should report detailed build log messages. The default is false. | False |

Example

```
<unzip zipfile="backup.zip"/>
```

## *&lt;vbc&gt;—Compiles Microsoft Visual Basic.NET programs using vbc.exe.*

| Attribute | Description | Required |
|---|---|---|
| baseaddress | Specifies whether the /baseaddress option gets passed to the compiler. | False |
| imports | Specifies whether the /imports option gets passed to the compiler. | False |
| optioncompare | Specifies whether the /optioncompare option gets passed to the compiler. | False |
| optionexplicit | Specifies whether the /optionexplicit option gets passed to the compiler. | False |
| optionoptimize | Specifies whether the /optimize option gets passed to the compiler. | False |
| optionstrict | Specifies whether the /optionstrict option gets passed to the compiler. | False |
| removeintchecks | Specifies whether the /removeintchecks option gets passed to the compiler. | False |
| rootnamespace | Specifies whether the /rootnamespace option gets passed to the compiler. | False |
| output | Output directory for the compilation target. | True |
| target | Output type (library or exe). | True |
| debug | Generate debug output (true/false). | False |
| define | Define conditional compilation symbol(s). Corresponds to /d[efine]: flag. | False |
| win32icon | Icon to associate with the application. Corresponds to /win32icon: flag. | False |
| warnaserror | Instructs the compiler to treat all warnings as errors (true/false). Default is "false." | False |

*(continued)*

| Attribute | Description | Required |
|---|---|---|
| main | Specifies which type contains the Main method that you want to use as the entry point into the program. | False |
| failonerror | Determines whether task failure stops the build or is just reported. Default is "true." | False |
| verbose | Task reports detailed build log messages. Default is "false." | False |
| if | If true then the task will be executed; otherwise skipped. Default is "true." | False |
| unless | Opposite of if. If false then the task will be executed; otherwise skipped. Default is "false." | False |

## Example

```xml
<project name="Hello World" default="build" basedir=".">
    <property name="basename" value="HelloWorld"/>
    <property name="debug" value="true"/>
        <target name="clean">
            <delete file="${basename}-vb.exe" failonerror="false"/>
            <delete file="${basename}-vb.pdb" failonerror="false"/>
        </target>
        <target name="build">
            <vbc target="exe" output="${basename}-vb.exe">
                <sources>
                    <includes name="${basename}.vb"/>
                </sources>
            </vbc>
        </target>
        <target name="debug" depends="clean">
            <vbc target="exe" output="${basename}-vb.exe"
debug="${debug}">
                <sources>
                    <includes name="${basename}.vb"/>
                </sources>
            </vbc>
        </target>
</project>
```

## &lt;vjc&gt;— *Compiles Visual J# programs using VJC, Microsoft's J# compiler.*

| Attribute | Description | Required |
|---|---|---|
| securescoping | Specifies whether package-scoped members are accessible outside of the assembly. In other words, package scope is treated as assembly scope when emitting metadata. By default, secure scoping is off. Corresponds to the /securescoping flag. | False |
| X | Specifies whether to disable language extensions. Corresponds to the /x flag. | False |
| libpath | Specifies the location of assemblies referenced by way of the /reference flag. Corresponds to the /libpath:dir[;dir2] flag. | False |
| jcpa | Associate Java-language/COM package names. Corresponds to the /jcpa:package=namespace and /jcpa:@filename flags. | False |
| codepage | Specifies the code page to use for all source code files in the compilation. Corresponds to the /codepage flag. | False |
| output | Output directory for the compilation target. | True |
| target | Output type (library or exe). | True |
| debug | Generate debug output (true/false). | False |
| define | Define conditional compilation symbol(s). Corresponds to /d[efine]: flag. | False |
| win32icon | Icon to associate with the application. Corresponds to /win32icon: flag. | False |
| warnaserror | Instructs the compiler to treat all warnings as errors (true/false). Default is "false." | False |
| main | Specifies which type contains the Main method that you want to use as the entry point into the program. | False |
| failonerror | Determines whether task failure stops the build or is just reported. Default is "true." | False |
| verbose | Task reports detailed build log messages. Default is "false." | False |
| if | If true then the task will be executed; otherwise skipped. Default is "true." | False |
| unless | Opposite of if. If false then the task will be executed; otherwise skipped. Default is "false." | False |

Example

```
<vjc target="exe" output="helloworld.exe" debug="true">
    <sources>
        <includes name="helloworld.jsl"/>
    </sources>
</vjc>
```

## *<xmlpeek>—Extracts text from a given XPath Query.*

| Attribute | Type | Description | Required |
|---|---|---|---|
| file | string | The name of the file that contains the XML document that is going to be peeked at. | True |
| property | string | The property that receives the text representation of the XML inside the node returned from the XPath expression. | True |
| xpath | string | The XPath expression used to select which node to read. | True |
| nodeindex | int | The index of the node that gets its text returned when the query returns multiple nodes. | False |
| failonerror | bool | Determines whether task failure stops the build or is just reported. The default is true. | False |
| if | bool | If true then the task will be executed; otherwise, skipped. The default is true. | False |
| unless | bool | Opposite of if. If false then the task will be executed; otherwise, skipped. The default is false. | False |
| verbose | bool | Determines whether the task should report detailed build log messages. The default is false. | False |

Example

```
<xmlpeek
            file="App.config"
            xpath="/configuration/appSettings/add[@key =
'server']/@value"
            property="configuration.server" />
```

### *<xmlpoke>—Replaces text from a given XPath Query.*

| Attribute | Type | Description | Required |
|---|---|---|---|
| file | string | The filename of the file that contains the XML document that is going to be poked. | True |
| value | string | The value that replaces the contents of the selected nodes. | True |
| xpath | string | The XPath expression used to select which nodes are to be modified. | True |
| failonerror | bool | Determines whether task failure stops the build or is just reported. The default is true. | False |
| if | bool | If true then the task will be executed; otherwise, skipped. The default is true. | False |
| unless | bool | Opposite of if. If false then the task will be executed; otherwise, skipped. The default is false. | False |
| verbose | bool | Determines whether the task should report detailed build log messages. The default is false. | False |

### Example

```
<xmlpoke
            file="App.config"
            xpath="/configuration/appSettings/add[@key =
'server']/@value"
            value="productionhost.somecompany.com" />
```

### *<zip>—A task to create a zip file from a specified fileset.*

| Attribute | Description | Required |
|---|---|---|
| zipfile | The zip file to create. | True |
| ziplevel | Desired level of compression (default is 6). | False |
| failonerror | Determines whether task failure stops the build or is just reported. Default is "true." | False |

*(continued)*

| Attribute | Description | Required |
|-----------|-------------|----------|
| verbose | Task reports detailed build log messages. Default is "false." | False |
| if | If true then the task will be executed; otherwise skipped. Default is "true." | False |
| unless | Opposite of if. If false then the task will be executed; otherwise skipped. Default is "false." | False |

## Example

```
<zip zipfile="backup.zip">
    <fileset basedir="build">
        <includes name="*.*"/>
    </fileset>
</zip>
```

# NAntContrib Tasks

**<adsigetprop>** Used to get the value of a property from an ADSI object.

| Attribute | Description | Required |
|-----------|-------------|----------|
| propname | The name of the property to get. | True |
| storein | The system property to store the value in. | True |
| path | The ADSI path of the location that we want to work with. | True |
| failonerror | Determines whether task failure stops the build or is just reported. Default is "true." | False |
| verbose | Task reports detailed build log messages. Default is "false." | False |
| if | If true then the task will be executed; otherwise skipped. Default is "true." | False |
| unless | Opposite of if. If false then the task will be executed; otherwise skipped. Default is "false." | False |

**<adsisetprop>** Used to set the value of a property from an ADSI object.

| Attribute | Description | Required |
|-----------|-------------|----------|
| propname | The name of the property to set. | True |
| propvalue | The new value of the property. | True |
| path | The ADSI path of the location that we want to work with. | True |
| failonerror | Determines whether task failure stops the build or is just reported. Default is "true." | False |
| verbose | Task reports detailed build log messages. Default is "false." | False |
| if | If true then the task will be executed; otherwise skipped. Default is "true." | False |
| unless | Opposite of if. If false then the task will be executed; otherwise skipped. Default is "false." | False |

Example

```
<adsisetprop path="${iis.path}/Root" propname="AuthAnonymous"
propvalue="true" />
```

**<aximp>** Generates a Windows Forms control that wraps ActiveX controls defined in an OCX.

| Attribute | Description | Required |
|---|---|---|
| ocx | Filename of the ocx. | True |
| out | Filename of the output assembly. | False |
| publickeyfile | Contains the strong name public key. | False |
| keyfile | Contains the strong name pair. | False |
| keycontainer | Container holding string name pair. | False |
| delaysign | Force delay signing. | False |
| generatesource | Should wrapper C# code be generated? | False |
| nologo | Suppresses the banner. | False |
| silent | Suppresses any messages. | False |
| failonerror | Determines whether task failure stops the build or is just reported. Default is "true." | False |
| verbose | Task reports detailed build log messages. Default is "false." | False |
| if | If true then the task will be executed; otherwise skipped. Default is "true." | False |
| unless | Opposite of if. If false then the task will be executed; otherwise skipped. Default is "false." | False |

Example

```
<aximp ocx="MyControl.ocx" out="MyFormsControl.dll" />
```

**<comregister>** COM register task will try to register any type of COM-related file that needs registering. .exe files will be registered as exe servers and .tlb files will be registered with RegisterTypeLib, and it will attempt to register all other file types as dll servers.

| Attribute | Description | Required |
|-----------|-------------|----------|
| file | Name of COM component. | True |
| unregister | Should unregister? Default is false. | False |
| failonerror | Determines whether task failure stops the build or is just reported. Default is "true." | False |
| verbose | Task reports detailed build log messages. Default is "false." | False |
| if | If true then the task will be executed; otherwise skipped. Default is "true." | False |
| unless | Opposite of if. If false then the task will be executed; otherwise skipped. Default is "false." | False |

Example

```
<comregister file="myComServer.exe"/>
```

```
<comregister unregister="false">
    <fileset>
        <includes name="an_ExeServer.exe"/>
        <includes name="a_TypeLibrary.tlb"/>
        <includes name="a_DllServer.dll"/>
        <includes name="an_OcxServer.ocx"/>
    </fileset>
</comregister>
```

**<checksum>** This task takes a set of input files in a fileset and calculates a checksum for each of them. You can specify the algorithm to use when calculating the checksum value (MD5 or SHA1, for example). The calculated value is saved to a file with the same name as the input file and an added extension either based on the algorithm name (e.g., .MD5) or whatever is specified through the fileext attribute.

| Attribute | Description | Required |
|---|---|---|
| algorithm | Can be MD5 or SHA1. | True |
| fileext | File extentions when not using filesets. | False |
| failonerror | Determines whether task failure stops the build or is just reported. Default is "true." | False |
| verbose | Task reports detailed build log messages. Default is "false." | False |
| if | If true then the task will be executed; otherwise skipped. Default is "true." | False |
| unless | Opposite of if. If false then the task will be executed; otherwise skipped. Default is "false." | False |

### Example

```
<checksum algorithm="MD5" fileext="MD5">
    <fileset>
        <includes name="${outputdir}\*.dll"/>
    </fileset>
</checksum>
```

**<concat>** This task takes a set of input files in a fileset and concatenates them into a single file. You can either replace the output file or append to it by using the append attribute.

| Attribute | Description | Required |
|---|---|---|
| destfile | Name of the destination file. | True |
| append | Whether to append to destination file or not. Default is false. | False |
| failonerror | Determines whether task failure stops the build or is just reported. Default is "true." | False |
| verbose | Task reports detailed build log messages. Default is "false." | False |
| if | If true then the task will be executed; otherwise skipped. Default is "true." | False |
| unless | Opposite of if. If false then the task will be executed; otherwise skipped. Default is "false." | False |

## Example

```
<concat destfile="${outputdir}\Full.txt" append="true">
    <fileset>
        <includes name="${outputdir}\Test-*.txt" />
    </fileset>
</concat>
```

**<disco>** Discovers the URLs of XML Web services on a Web server and saves documents related to them to the local disk. The resulting .discomap, .wsdl, and .xsd files can be used with the <WsdlTask> to produce Web service clients and abstract Web service servers using ASP.NET.

| Attribute | Description | Required |
|---|---|---|
| path | URL to discover. | False |
| nologo | Supress Banner. | False |
| nosave | Save the discovery to disk. | False |
| outputdir | Output directory to save discovered documents in. | False |
| username | If Web service requires authentication. | False |
| password | If Web service requires authentication. | False |
| domain | If Web service requires authentication. | False |
| proxy | URL of proxy server to use for HTTP request. | False |
| proxyusername | If proxy requires authentication. | False |
| proxypassword | If proxy requires authentication. | False |
| proxydomain | If proxy requires authentication | False |
| failonerror | Determines whether task failure stops the build or is just reported. Default is "true." | False |
| verbose | Task reports detailed build log messages. Default is "false." | False |
| if | If true then the task will be executed; otherwise skipped. Default is "true." | False |
| unless | Opposite of if. If false then the task will be executed; otherwise skipped. Default is "false." | False |

```
<disco path="http://www.somewhere.com/myservice.wsdl" language="CS"
namespace="MyCompany.MyService" outfile="MyService.cs" />
```

**\<gac>** This task provides some of the same functionality as the gacutil tool provided in the .NET SDK.

| Attribute | Description | Required |
|---|---|---|
| assembly | The name of a file that contains an assembly manifest. | True |
| uninstall | Removes the assembly from the global assembly cache and the native image cache. Default is "false." | False |
| timeout | Stop the build if the command does not finish within the specified time. Specified in milliseconds. Default is no time out. | False |
| failonerror | Determines whether task failure stops the build or is just reported. Default is "true." | False |
| verbose | Task reports detailed build log messages. Default is "false." | False |
| if | If true then the task will be executed; otherwise skipped. Default is "true." | False |
| unless | Opposite of if. If false then the task will be executed; otherwise skipped. Default is "false." | False |

Example

```
<gac
assembly='hello,Version=1.0.0.1,Culture="de",PublicKeyToken=45e343aae32
233ca' uninstall="true"/>
```

**\<hxcomp>** Compiles a Microsoft HTML Help 2.0 Project.

| Attribute | Description | Required |
|---|---|---|
| contents | The name of the contents (.HxC) file. | False |
| logfile | ANSI/DBCS log filename. | False |
| unicodelogfile | Unicode log filename. | False |
| projectroot | Root directory containing Help 2.0 project files. | False |
| output | Output (.HxS) filename. | False |
| noinformation | Generate no informational messages. | False |
| noerrors | Generate no error messages. | False |
| nowarnings | Generate no warning messages. | False |

*(continued)*

| Attribute | Description | Required |
|-----------|-------------|----------|
| quiet | Quiet mode. | False |
| uncompilefile | File to be decompiled. | False |
| uncompileoutputdir | Directory to place decompiled files into. | False |
| failonerror | Determines whether task failure stops the build or is just reported. Default is "true." | False |
| verbose | Task reports detailed build log messages. Default is "false." | False |
| if | If true then the task will be executed; otherwise skipped. Default is "true." | False |
| unless | Opposite of if. If false then the task will be executed; otherwise skipped. Default is "false." | False |

### Example

```
<hxcomp contents="MyContents.HxC" output="MyHelpFile.HxS"
projectroot="HelpSourceFolder"/>
```

**_&lt;hxreg&gt;_** Registers a Microsoft HTML Help 2.0 Collection.

| Attribute | Description | Required |
|-----------|-------------|----------|
| namespace | Help collection namespace. | False |
| title | Title identifier. | False |
| collection | Collection (.HxC) filename. | False |
| description | Description of the namespace. | False |
| helpfile | Help (.HxS) filename. | False |
| index | Index (.HxI) filename. | False |
| searchfile | Combined full-text search (.HxQ) filename. | False |
| attrindex | Combined attribute index (.HxR) filename. | False |
| language | Language ID. | False |
| alias | Alias. | False |
| commandfile | Filename of a file containing HxReg commands. | False |
| unregister | Unregister a namespace, title, or alias. | False |

*(continued)*

| Attribute | Description | Required |
|-----------|-------------|----------|
| failonerror | Determines whether task failure stops the build or is just reported. Default is "true." | False |
| verbose | Task reports detailed build log messages. Default is "false." | False |
| if | If true then the task will be executed; otherwise skipped. Default is "true." | False |
| unless | Opposite of if. If false then the task will be executed; otherwise skipped. Default is "false." | False |

## Example

```
<hxreg namespace="MyProduct.MyHelp" title="MyProductHelp"
collection="MyHelp.HxC" helpfile="MyHelp.HxS"/>
```

**<mkiisdir>** Makes an IIS Virtual Directory if one does not exist. If the directory exists, the properties of the directory will be changed.

| Attribute | Description | Required |
|-----------|-------------|----------|
| vdirname | The name of the Virtual Directory. | True |
| dirpath | The actual path on the file system. | True |
| accessexecute | | False |
| accessnoremoteexecute | | False |
| accessnoremoteread | | False |
| accessnoremotescript | | False |
| accessnoremotewrite | | False |
| accessread | | False |
| accesssource | | False |
| accessscript | | False |
| accessssl | | False |
| accessssl128 | | False |
| accesssslmapcert | | False |
| accesssslnegotiatecert | | False |
| accesssslrequirecert | | False |

*(continued)*

| Attribute | Description | Required |
|---|---|---|
| accesswrite | | False |
| anonymouspasswordsync | | False |
| appallowclientdebug | | False |
| appallowdebugging | | False |
| aspallowsessionstate | | False |
| aspbufferingon | | False |
| aspenableapplicationrestart | | False |
| aspenableasphtmlfallback | | False |
| aspenablechunkedencoding | | False |
| asperrorstontlog | | False |
| aspenableparentpaths | | False |
| aspenabletypelibcache | | False |
| aspexceptioncatchenable | | False |
| asplogerrorrequests | | False |
| aspscripterrorsenttobrowser | | False |
| aspthreadgateenabled | | False |
| asptrackthreadingmodel | | False |
| authanonymous | | False |
| authbasic | | False |
| authntlm | | False |
| authpersistsinglerequest | | False |
| authpersistsinglerequestifproxy | | False |
| authpersistsinglerequestalwaysifproxy | | False |
| cachecontrolnocache | | False |
| cacheisapi | | False |
| cpucgienabled | | False |
| createcgiwithnewconsole | | False |
| createprocessasuser | | False |
| dirbrowseshowdate | | False |
| dirbrowseshowextension | | False |
| dirbrowseshowlongdate | | False |

*(continued)*

| Attribute | Description | Required |
|-----------|-------------|----------|
| dirbrowseshowsize | | False |
| dirbrowseshowtime | | False |
| dontlog | | False |
| enabledefaultdoc | | False |
| enabledirbrowsing | | False |
| enabledocfooter | | False |
| enablereversedns | | False |
| ssiexecdisable | | False |
| uncauthenticationpassthrough | | False |
| aspscripterrormessage | | False |
| defaultdoc | | False |
| failonerror | Determines whether task failure stops the build or is just reported. Default is "true." | False |
| verbose | Task reports detailed build log messages. Default is "false." | False |
| if | If true then the task will be executed; otherwise skipped. Default is "true." | False |
| unless | Opposite of if. If false then the task will be executed; otherwise skipped. Default is "false." | False |

**<iisdirinfo>** Outputs all the settings for an IIS Virtual Directory to the log.

| Attribute | Description | Required |
|-----------|-------------|----------|
| vdirname | The name of the Virtual Directory. | True |
| failonerror | Determines whether task failure stops the build or is just reported. Default is "true." | False |
| verbose | Task reports detailed build log messages. Default is "false." | False |
| if | If true then the task will be executed; otherwise skipped. Default is "true." | False |
| unless | Opposite of if. If false then the task will be executed; otherwise skipped. Default is "false." | False |

Example

```
A<iisdirinfo vdirname="TEMP" />
```

**&lt;deliisdir&gt;** Deletes an IIS Virtual Directory.

| Attribute | Description | Required |
|-----------|-------------|----------|
| vdirname | The name of the Virtual Directory. | True |
| failonerror | Determines whether task failure stops the build or is just reported. Default is "true." | False |
| verbose | Task reports detailed build log messages. Default is "false." | False |
| if | If true then the task will be executed; otherwise skipped. Default is "true." | False |
| unless | Opposite of if. If false then the task will be executed; otherwise skipped. Default is "false." | False |

Example

```
<deliisdir vdirname="TEMP" />
```

**&lt;msi&gt;** Builds a Windows Installer (MSI) file. Requires cabarc.exe in the path. This tool is included in the Microsoft Cabinet SDK.

| Attribute | Description | Required |
|-----------|-------------|----------|
| failonerror | Determines whether task failure stops the build or is just reported. Default is "true." | False |
| verbose | Task reports detailed build log messages. Default is "false." | False |
| if | If true then the task will be executed; otherwise skipped. Default is "true." | False |
| unless | Opposite of if. If false then the task will be executed; otherwise skipped. Default is "false." | False |

**<msm>** Builds a Windows Installer Merge Module (MSM) file. Requires cabarc.exe in the path. This tool is included in the Microsoft Cabinet SDK.

| Attribute | Description | Required |
|---|---|---|
| failonerror | Determines whether task failure stops the build or is just reported. Default is "true." | False |
| verbose | Task reports detailed build log messages. Default is "false." | False |
| if | If true then the task will be executed; otherwise skipped. Default is "true." | False |
| unless | Opposite of if. If false then the task will be executed; otherwise skipped. Default is "false." | False |

**<mgmtclassgen>** A task that generates strongly typed WMI classes using mgmtclass-gen.exe.

The Management Strongly Typed Class Generator enables you to quickly generate an early-bound managed class for a specified Windows Management Instrumentation (WMI) class. The generated class simplifies the code that you must write to access an instance of the WMI class.

| Attribute | Description | Required |
|---|---|---|
| wmiclass | Specifies the name of the WMI class to generate the strongly typed class. | True |
| language | Specifies the language in which to generate the class. Possible values are: CS, VB, JS. | False |
| machine | Specifies the machine to connect to. | False |
| path | Specifies the path to the WMI namespace that contains the class. | False |
| namespace | Namespace of the generated .NET class | False |
| out | Path of the file to generate. | False |
| username | User name to use when connecting to the specified machine. | False |
| password | Password to use when connecting to the specified machine. | False |
| failonerror | Determines whether task failure stops the build or is just reported. Default is "true." | False |

*(continued)*

| Attribute | Description | Required |
|---|---|---|
| verbose | Task reports detailed build log messages. Default is "false." | False |
| if | If true then the task will be executed; otherwise skipped. Default is "true." | False |
| unless | Opposite of if. If false then the task will be executed; otherwise skipped. Default is "false." | False |

## Example

```
<mgmtclassgen
    wmiclass="Win32_LogicalDisk"
    language="CS"
    machine="SomeMachine"
    path="Root\cimv2"
    namespace="Winterdom.WMI"
    out="${outputdir}\LogicalDisk.cs"
    username="Administrator"
    password="password"/>
```

**&lt;ngen&gt;**  Pre-translates native code for an assembly containing IL (Intermediary Language bytecode) on the Windows platform.

| Attribute | Description | Required |
|---|---|---|
| assembly | Assembly path or display name. | True |
| show | If existing images should be shown. | False |
| delete | If existing images should be deleted. | False |
| debug | If an image should be generated that can be used under a debugger. | False |
| debugoptimized | If an image should be generated that can be used under a debugger in optimized debugging mode. | False |
| profiled | If an image should be generated that can be used under a profiler. | False |
| nologo | Suppresses the banner. | False |
| failonerror | Determines whether task failure stops the build or is just reported. Default is "true." | False |

*(continued)*

| Attribute | Description | Required |
|---|---|---|
| verbose | Task reports detailed build log messages. Default is "false." | False |
| if | If true then the task will be executed; otherwise skipped. Default is "true." | False |
| unless | Opposite of if. If false then the task will be executed; otherwise skipped. Default is "false." | False |

### Example

```
<ngen assembly="MyAssembly.dll" />
```

**&lt;nunitreport&gt;** A task that generates a summary HTML from a set of NUnit XML report files. Loosely based on Erik Hatcher JUnitReport for Ant.

This task can generate a combined HTML report out of a set of NUnit result files generated using the XML Result formatter.

By default, NUnitReport will generate the combined report using the NUnitSummary.xsl file located at the assembly's location, but you can specify a different XSLT template to use with the xslfile attribute.

Also, all the properties defined in the current project will be passed down to the XSLT file as template parameters, so you can access properties such as nant.project.name, nant.version, etc.

| Attribute | Description | Required |
|---|---|---|
| out | Name of output HTML file. | True |
| xslfile | XSLT file used to generate the report. | True |
| failonerror | Determines whether task failure stops the build or is just reported. Default is "true." | False |
| verbose | Task reports detailed build log messages. Default is "false." | False |
| if | If true then the task will be executed; otherwise skipped. Default is "true." | False |
| unless | Opposite of if. If false then the task will be executed; otherwise skipped. Default is "false." | False |

## Example

```
<nunitreport out="${outputdir}\TestSummary.html">
    <fileset>
        <includes name="${outputdir}\Test-*.xml" />
    </fileset>
</nunitreport>
```

**\<record\>** A task that records the build's output to a file. Loosely based on Ant's Record task.

| Attribute | Description | Required |
|-----------|-------------|----------|
| name | Name of destination file. | True |
| action | Action to apply to this log instance. It can take one of the following values: start, stop, close. | True |
| failonerror | Determines whether task failure stops the build or is just reported. Default is "true." | False |
| verbose | Task reports detailed build log messages. Default is "false." | False |
| if | If true then the task will be executed; otherwise skipped. Default is "true." | False |
| unless | Opposite of if. If false then the task will be executed; otherwise skipped. Default is "false." | False |

## Example

```
<record name="${outputdir}\Buildlog.txt" action="Start"/>
```

**\<regasm\>** Register an assembly for use from COM clients.

| Attribute | Description | Required |
|-----------|-------------|----------|
| regfile | Registry file to export to instead of entering the types directly into the registry. If a fileset is used. then the entries are all collated into this file. | False |
| codebase | Set the code base registry setting. | False |
| silent | Silent mode. Prevents displaying of success messages. Default is "false." | False |

*(continued)*

| Attribute | Description | Required |
|---|---|---|
| exporttypelib | Export a typelib and register it. The typelib will have the same name as the source assembly unless the "typelib" attribute is used. | False |
| registered | Only refer to already registered type libraries. | False |
| typelib | Export the assembly to the specified type library and register it (ignored when a fileset is specified). | False |
| unregister | Unregistering this time. ( /u parameter )Default is "false." | False |
| failonerror | Determines whether task failure stops the build or is just reported. Default is "true." | False |
| verbose | Task reports detailed build log messages. Default is "false." | False |
| if | If true then the task will be executed; otherwise skipped. Default is "true." | False |
| unless | Opposite of if. If false then the task will be executed; otherwise skipped. Default is "false." | False |

## Example

```
<regasm unregister="false" codebase="true" >
    <fileset>
        <includes name="**/*.dll"/>
        <excludes name="notanassembly.dll"/>
    </fileset>
</regasm>
```

**<scp>** Copies a file using scp to a remote server.

| Attribute | Description | Required |
|---|---|---|
| failonerror | Determines whether task failure stops the build or is just reported. Default is "true." | False |
| verbose | Task reports detailed build log messages. Default is "false." | False |
| if | If true then the task will be executed; otherwise skipped. Default is "true." | False |
| unless | Opposite of if. If false then the task will be executed; otherwise skipped. Default is "false." | False |

## Example

```
<scp file="myfile.zip" server="myServer" path="~">
```

**&lt;*slingshot*&gt;** Converts a Visual Studio.NET Solution to a NAnt build file or nmake file. Convert the Solution MySolution.sln to the NAnt build file MySolution.build and call the new build file.

| Attribute | Description | Required |
|-----------|-------------|----------|
| solution | The Visual Studio.NET Solution file to convert. | True |
| format | The output file format, NAnt or nmake. | True |
| output | The output file name. | True |
| maps | Mappings from URI to directories. These are required for Web projects. | False |
| parameters | Parameters to pass to SLiNgshoT. The parameter build.basedir is required. | False |
| failonerror | Determines whether task failure stops the build or is just reported. Default is "true." | False |
| verbose | Task reports detailed build log messages. Default is "false." | False |
| if | If true then the task will be executed; otherwise skipped. Default is "true." | False |
| unless | Opposite of if. If false then the task will be executed; otherwise skipped. Default is "false." | False |

## Example

```
<slingshot solution="MySolution.sln" format="nant"
output="MySolution.build">
    <parameters>
        <option name="build.basedir" value="..\bin"/>
    </parameters>
    <maps>
        <option name="http://localhost" value="C:\Inetpub\wwwroot"/>
    </maps>
</slingshot>
```

**<stautolabel>** Task for supporting labeling of repositories with incremented version numbers. The version number calculated will be concatenated to the label.

| Attribute | Type | Description | Required |
|---|---|---|---|
| buildversion | int | Build version number used for label. If this value is set, incrementbuild is ignored. | False |
| incrementbuild | bool | Increment build version number. The default is true. If buildversion is set, this property is ignored. | False |
| incrementmajor | bool | Increment major version number. The default is false. If majorversion is set, this property is ignored. | False |
| incrementminor | bool | Increment minor version number. The default is false. If minorversion is set, this property is ignored. | False |
| majorversion | int | Major version number used for label. If this value is set, incrementmajor is ignored. | False |
| minorversion | int | Minor version number used for label. If this value is set, incrementminor is ignored. | False |
| versionfile | string | Allows user to specify the filename where the version XML is stored. The default is version-number.xml. | False |
| label | string | The name to be given to the label; required. | True |
| buildlabel | bool | Should label be marked build? Default is true. | False |
| description | string | Optional description of the label to be stored in the StarTeam project. | False |
| failonerror | bool | | False |
| if | bool | | False |
| password | string | The password used for login. | False |
| projectname | string | The name of the StarTeam project to be acted on. | False |
| revisionlabel | bool | Should label created be a revision label? Default is false. | False |
| servername | string | Name of StarTeamServer. | False |

*(continued)*

| Attribute | Type | Description | Required |
|---|---|---|---|
| serverport | string | Port number of the StarTeam connection. | False |
| timestamp | string | Optional: If this property is set, the label will be created as of the datetime specified. Please provide a datetime format that can be parsed via Parse. | False |
| unless | bool | | False |
| url | string | One stop to set all parameters needed to connect to a StarTeam server. | False |
| username | string | The StarTeam user name used for login. | False |
| verbose | bool | | False |
| viewname | string | The name of the StarTeam view to be acted on. | False |

## Example

```
<stautolabel incrementminor="true" url="${ST.url}" />
```

**&lt;stcheckin&gt;** Task to check in files to StarTeam repositories.

| Attribute | Type | Description | Required |
|---|---|---|---|
| adduncontrolled | bool | If true, any files or folders NOT in StarTeam will be added to the repository. Defaults to "false." | False |
| comment | string | | False |
| unlocked | bool | Set to do an unlocked checkout; optional, default is false. If true, file will be unlocked so that other users may change it. If false, lock status will not change. | False |
| rootstarteamfolder | string | Root StarTeam folder to begin operations on. Defaults to the root of the view. | True |
| excludes | string | Accepts comma-delimited list of expressions to exclude from tree operations. If nothing is specified, NO filespecs are excluded. | False |

*(continued)*

| Attribute | Type | Description | Required |
|-----------|------|-------------|----------|
| failonerror | bool | | False |
| forced | bool | Default: false - force check in/out actions regardless of the status that StarTeam is maintaining for the file. | False |
| if | bool | | False |
| includes | string | Accepts comma-delimited list of expressions to include in tree operations. If nothing is set, ALL filespecs are included. | False |
| label | string | Label used for checkout. If no label is set, latest state of repository is checked out. | False |
| password | string | The password used for login. | False |
| projectname | string | The name of the StarTeam project to be acted on. | False |
| recursive | bool | Default: true - should tasks recurse through tree? | False |
| servername | string | Name of StarTeamServer. | False |
| serverport | string | Port number of the StarTeam connection. | False |
| unless | bool | | False |
| url | string | One stop to set all parameters needed to connect to a StarTeam server. | False |
| username | string | The StarTeam user name used for login. | False |
| verbose | bool | | False |
| viewname | string | The name of the StarTeam view to be acted on. | False |

**<stcheckout>** Task to check out files from StarTeam repositories.

| Attribute | Type | Description | Required |
|-----------|------|-------------|----------|
| createworkingdirs | bool | Default: true - Create directories that are in the StarTeam repository even if they are empty. | False |
| deleteuncontrolled | bool | Not fully tested. CAREFUL. Default false - Should all local files NOT in StarTeam be deleted? | False |

*(continued)*

| Attribute | Type | Description | Required |
|---|---|---|---|
| locktype | string | The type of lock to apply to files checked out. | False |
| | | Unchanged - default: do not make any changes to the lock state of items. | |
| | | Exclusive - Exclusively lock items. No other users can update the object while it is exclusively locked. | |
| | | Nonexclusive - Put a non-exclusive lock on the item. | |
| | | Unlocked - Remove locks from all items checked out. This accompanied by force would effectively override a lock and replace local contents with the current version. | |
| rootstarteamfolder | string | Root StarTeam folder to begin operations on. Defaults to the root of the view. | True |
| excludes | string | Accepts comma-delimited list of expressions to exclude from tree operations. If nothing is specified, NO filespecs are excluded. | False |
| failonerror | bool | | False |
| forced | bool | Default: false - Force check in/out actions regardless of the status that StarTeam is maintaining for the file. | False |
| if | bool | | False |
| includes | string | Accepts comma-delimited list of expressions to include in tree operations. If nothing is set, ALL filespecs are included. | False |
| label | string | Label used for checkout. If no label is set, latest state of repository is checked out. | False |
| password | string | The password used for login. | False |
| projectname | string | The name of the StarTeam project to be acted on. | False |
| recursive | bool | Default: true - Should tasks recurse through tree? | False |
| servername | string | Name of StarTeamServer. | False |
| serverport | string | Port number of the StarTeam connection. | False |

*(continued)*

| Attribute | Type | Description | Required |
|-----------|------|-------------|----------|
| unless | bool | | False |
| url | string | One stop to set all parameters needed to connect to a StarTeam server. | False |
| username | string | The StarTeam user name used for login. | False |
| verbose | bool | | False |
| viewname | string | The name of the StarTeam view to be acted on. | False |

**<stlabel>** Task to create view labels for StarTeam repositories.

| Attribute | Type | Description | Required |
|-----------|------|-------------|----------|
| label | string | The name to be given to the label; required. | True |
| buildlabel | bool | Should label be marked build? Default is true. | False |
| description | string | Optional description of the label to be stored in the StarTeam project. | False |
| failonerror | bool | | False |
| if | bool | | False |
| password | string | The password used for login. | False |
| projectname | string | The name of the StarTeam project to be acted on. | False |
| revisionlabel | bool | Should label created be a revision label? Default is false. | False |
| servername | string | Name of StarTeamServer. | False |
| serverport | string | Port number of the StarTeam connection. | False |
| timestamp | string | Optional: If this property is set, the label will be created as of the datetime specified. Please provide a datetime format that can be parsed via Parse. | False |
| unless | bool | | False |
| url | string | One stop to set all parameters needed to connect to a StarTeam server. | False |
| username | string | The StarTeam user name used for login. | False |
| verbose | bool | | False |
| viewname | string | The name of the StarTeam view to be acted on. | False |

**&lt;stlist&gt;** Task to list StarTeam repositories.

| Attribute | Type | Description | Required |
|---|---|---|---|
| rootstarteamfolder | string | Root StarTeam folder to begin operations on. Defaults to the root of the view. | True |
| excludes | string | Accepts comma-delimited list of expressions to exclude from tree operations. If nothing is specified, NO filespecs are excluded. | False |
| failonerror | bool | | False |
| forced | bool | Default: false - Force check in/out actions regardless of the status that StarTeam is maintaining for the file. | False |
| if | bool | | False |
| includes | string | Accepts comma-delimited list of expressions to include in tree operations. If nothing is set, ALL filespecs are included. | False |
| label | string | Label used for checkout. If no label is set, latest state of repository is checked out. | False |
| password | string | The password used for login. | False |
| projectname | string | The name of the StarTeam project to be acted on. | False |
| recursive | bool | Default: true - Should tasks recurse through tree? | False |
| servername | string | Name of StarTeamServer. | False |
| serverport | string | Port number of the StarTeam connection. | False |
| unless | bool | | False |
| url | string | One stop to set all parameters needed to connect to a StarTeam server. | False |
| username | string | The StarTeam user name used for login. | False |
| verbose | bool | | False |
| viewname | string | The name of the StarTeam view to be acted on. | False |

**<sql>** A task to execute arbitrary SQL statements against an OLEDB data source. You can specify a set of SQL statements inside the sql element or execute them from a text file that contains them. You can also choose to execute the statements in a single batch or execute them one by one (even inside a transaction, if you want to).

| Attribute | Description | Required |
|---|---|---|
| connstring | Connection string used to access database. This should be an OLEDB connection string. | True |
| source | File where the SQL statements are defined. You cannot specify both a source and an inline set of statements. | False |
| delimiter | String that separates statements from one another. | True |
| batch | If true, the statements will be executed as a single batch. If false, they will be executed one by one. Default is true. | False |
| expandprops | If true, then any NAnt-style properties on the SQL will be expanded before execution. Default is true. | False |
| delimstyle | Delimiters can be of two kinds: Normal delimiters are always specified inline, so they permit having two different statements in the same line. Line delimiters, however, need to be in a line by their own. Default is Normal. | True if using delimiter |
| print | If set to true, results from the statements will be output to the build log. | False |
| output | If set, the results from the statements will be output to the specified file. | False |
| transaction | If set to true, all statements will be executed within a single transaction. Default value is true. | False |
| failonerror | Determines whether task failure stops the build or is just reported. Default is "true." | False |
| verbose | Task reports detailed build log messages. Default is "false." | False |
| if | If true then the task will be executed; otherwise skipped. Default is "true." | False |
| unless | Opposite of if. If false then the task will be executed; otherwise skipped. Default is "false." | False |

Examples

Inline

```
<sql
   connstring="Provider=SQLOLEDB;Data Source=localhost; Initial
Catalog=Pruebas; Integrated Security=SSPI"
   transaction="true"
   delimiter=";">
     INSERT INTO jobs (job_desc, min_lvl, max_lvl) VALUES('My Job', 22,
45);
     INSERT INTO jobs (job_desc, min_lvl, max_lvl) VALUES('Other Job',
09, 43);
     SELECT * FROM jobs;
</sql>
```

Execute a set of statements from a file and write all query results to a file

```
<sql
   connstring="Provider=SQLOLEDB;Data Source=localhost; Initial
Catalog=Pruebas; Integrated Security=SSPI"
   transaction="true"
   delimiter=";"
   print="true"
   source="sql.txt"
   output="${outputdir}/results.txt" />
```

Execute a SQL script generated by SQL Server Enterprise Manager

```
  <sql
    connstring="Provider=SQLOLEDB;Data Source=localhost; Initial
Catalog=Pruebas; Integrated Security=SSPI"
    transaction="true"
    delimiter="GO"
    delimstyle="Line"
    print="true"
    source="pubs.xml"
    batch="false"
    output="${outputdir}/results.txt" />
```

**<typedcollection>** Generates collection classes based on a given XML specification file. Code generation is in the specified language.

| Attribute | Description | Required |
|---|---|---|
| language | The language to generate collection classes for. Valid values are "CSharp" or "VB." | True |
| file | The name of the template file for collection generation. This is provided as an alternative to using the task's fileset. | False |
| failonerror | Determines whether task failure stops the build or is just reported. Default is "true." | False |
| verbose | Task reports detailed build log messages. Default is "false." | False |
| if | If true then the task will be executed; otherwise skipped. Default is "true." | False |
| unless | Opposite of if. If false then the task will be executed; otherwise skipped. Default is "false." | False |

Example

```
<typedcollection language="CSharp">
    <fileset>
        <includes name="collections.xml"/>
    </fileset>
</typedcollection>
```

**<validatexml>** A task that validates a set of XML files based on a set of Schemas (XSD).

| Attribute | Description | Required |
|---|---|---|
| files | Set of XML files to use as input. | True |
| schemas | Schema to use in validation. | True |
| failonerror | Determines whether task failure stops the build or is just reported. Default is "true." | False |
| verbose | Task reports detailed build log messages. Default is "false." | False |
| if | If true then the task will be executed; otherwise skipped. Default is "true." | False |
| unless | Opposite of if. If false then the task will be executed; otherwise skipped. Default is "false." | False |

## Example

```
<validatexml>
    <schemas>
        <schemaref source="rcf-schema.xsd"/>
        <schemaref namespace="urn:schemas-company-com:base"
source="base-schema.xsd"/>
    </schemas>
    <files>
        <includes name="*.xml"/>
    </files>
</validatexml>
```

**<vb6>** Compiles Microsoft Visual Basic 6 programs.

| Attribute | Description | Required |
|---|---|---|
| outdir | Output directory for the compilation target. If the directory does not exist, the task will create it. | False |
| project | Visual Basic project or group file. | True |
| checkreferences | Determines whether project references are checked when deciding whether the project needs to be recompiled (true/false). | False |
| errorfile | Errorfile | True |
| failonerror | Determines whether task failure stops the build or is just reported. Default is "true." | False |
| verbose | Task reports detailed build log messages. Default is "false." | False |
| if | If true then the task will be executed; otherwise skipped. Default is "true." | False |
| unless | Opposite of if. If false then the task will be executed; otherwise skipped. Default is "false." | False |

## Example

```
<vb6 project="HelloWorld.vbp" outdir="build" />
```

**<version>** Increments a version number counter from a text file.

| Attribute | Type | Description | Required |
|---|---|---|---|
| buildtype | string | Algorithm for generating build number. Valid values are "monthday," "increment," and "noincrement." The default is "monthday." | False |
| path | string | Path to the file containing the current version number. The default file is "build.number" in the project base directory. | False |
| prefix | string | The string to prefix the property name with. The default is "sys." | False |
| revisiontype | string | Algorithm for generating revision number. Valid values are "automatic" and "increment." | False |
| startDate | string | Start of project. Date from which to calculate build number. Required if "monthday" is used as buildtype. | False |
| failonerror | bool | | False |
| if | bool | | False |
| unless | bool | | False |
| verbose | bool | | False |

**<vssadd>** Adds a file to a Source Safe Repository

| Attribute | Type | Description | Required |
|---|---|---|---|
| comment | string | Places a comment on all files added into the Source Safe repository. | False |
| dbpath | string | The absolute path to the folder that contains the srcsafe.ini. | True |
| path | string | The Source Safe project or file path, starting with "$/". | True |
| user | string | The user ID to use to log in to the Source Safe database. | True |
| failonerror | bool | | False |

*(continued)*

| Attribute | Type | Description | Required |
|-----------|------|-------------|----------|
| if | bool | | False |
| password | string | The password to use to log in to the Source Safe database. | False |
| unless | bool | | False |
| verbose | bool | | False |
| version | string | A version of the path to reference. Accepts multiple forms, including the label, version number, or date of the version. If omitted, the latest version is used. | False |

### Example

```
        <vssadd dbpath="C:\SourceSafeFolder\srcsafe.ini"
user="user1" password="" path="$/Somefolder">
            <fileset basedir="C:\SourceFolder\">
              <includes name="*.dll"/>
            </fileset>
            </vssadd>
```

**<vsscheckin>**  Check in files to a Source Safe Repository

| Attribute | Type | Description | Required |
|-----------|------|-------------|----------|
| localpath | string | The absolute path to the local working directory. | True |
| comment | string | The comment for the new version. | False |
| recursive | string | Determines whether to perform a recursive checkin. Default value is true when omitted. | False |
| writable | string | Determines whether to leave the file(s) as writable. Default value is false when omitted. | False |
| dbpath | string | The absolute path to the folder that contains the srcsafe.ini. | True |
| path | string | The Source Safe project or file path, starting with "$/". | True |

*(continued)*

| Attribute | Type | Description | Required |
|-----------|------|-------------|----------|
| user | string | The user ID to use to log in to the Source Safe database. | True |
| failonerror | bool | | False |
| if | bool | | False |
| password | string | The password to use to log in to the Source Safe database. | False |
| unless | bool | | False |
| verbose | bool | | False |
| version | string | A version of the path to reference. Accepts multiple forms, including the label, version number, or date of the version. If omitted, the latest version is used. | False |

## Example

```
<vsscheckin
          user="myusername"
          password="mypassword"
          localpath="C:\Dev\Latest"
          recursive="true"
          writable="true"
          dbpath="C:\VSS\srcsafe.ini"
          path="$/MyProduct"
          comment="NAnt checkin"
        />
```

**<vsscheckout>** Checks out files from a Source Safe Repository.

| Attribute | Type | Description | Required |
|-----------|------|-------------|----------|
| localpath | string | The absolute path to the local working directory. | True |
| recursive | string | Determines whether to perform a recursive checkout. Default value is true when omitted. | False |
| writable | string | Determines whether to leave the file(s) as writable. Default value is true when omitted. | False |

*(continued)*

| Attribute | Type | Description | Required |
|-----------|------|-------------|----------|
| dbpath | string | The absolute path to the folder that contains the srcsafe.ini. | True |
| path | string | The Source Safe project or file path, starting with "$/". | True |
| user | string | The user ID to use to log in to the Source Safe database. | True |
| failonerror | bool | | False |
| if | bool | | False |
| password | string | The password to use to log in to the Source Safe database. | False |
| unless | bool | | False |
| verbose | bool | | False |
| version | string | A version of the path to reference. Accepts multiple forms, including the label, version number, or date of the version. If omitted, the latest version is used. | False |

Example:

```
<vsscheckout
            user="myusername"
            password="mypassword"
            localpath="C:\Dev\Latest"
            recursive="true"
            writable="true"
            dbpath="C:\VSS\srcsafe.ini"
            path="$/MyProduct"
        />
```

**&lt;vssdiff&gt;** Shows differences in a Source Safe Repository.

| Attribute | Type | Description | Required |
|-----------|------|-------------|----------|
| label | string | The value of the label to compare to. | True |
| outputfile | string | The output file to generate (XML). | True |
| dbpath | string | The absolute path to the folder that contains the srcsafe.ini. | True |

*(continued)*

| Attribute | Type | Description | Required |
|---|---|---|---|
| path | string | The Source Safe project or file path, starting with "$/". | True |
| user | string | The user ID to use to log in to the Source Safe database. | True |
| failonerror | bool | | False |
| if | bool | | False |
| password | string | The password to use to log in to the Source Safe database. | False |
| unless | bool | | False |
| verbose | bool | | False |
| version | string | A version of the path to reference. Accepts multiple forms, including the label, version number, or date of the version. If omitted, the latest version is used. | False |

## Example

```
<vssdiff
                dbpath='ss.ini'
                path='$/My Project'
                label='My Label'
                user='ssuser'
                outputfile='diff.xml'
            />
```

**<vssget>** Retrieves an item from a Source Safe repository.

| Attribute | Type | Description | Required |
|---|---|---|---|
| localpath | string | The absolute path to the local working directory. | True |
| recursive | string | Determines whether to perform the get recursively. Default value is true when omitted. | False |
| removedeleted | string | Determines whether files marked "deleted" in the repository will be removed from the local copy. Default value is false when omitted. | False |

*(continued)*

| Attribute | Type | Description | Required |
|-----------|------|-------------|----------|
| replace | string | Determines whether to replace writable files. Default value is false when omitted. | False |
| usemodtime | string | Determines whether the timestamp on the local copy will be the modification time (if false or omitted, the checkout time will be used). | False |
| writable | string | Determines whether the files will be read-only. Default value is false when omitted. | False |
| dbpath | string | The absolute path to the folder that contains the srcsafe.ini. | True |
| path | string | The Source Safe project or file path, starting with "$/". | True |
| user | string | The user ID to use to log in to the Source Safe database. | True |
| failonerror | bool | | False |
| if | bool | | False |
| password | string | The password to use to log in to the Source Safe database. | False |
| unless | bool | | False |
| verbose | bool | | False |
| version | string | A version of the path to reference. Accepts multiple forms, including the label, version number, or date of the version. If omitted, the latest version is used. | False |

## Example

```
<vssget
          user="myusername"
          password="mypassword"
          localpath="C:\Dev\Latest"
          recursive="true"
          replace="true"
          writable="true"
          dbpath="C:\VSS\srcsafe.ini"
          path="$/MyProduct"
      />
```

**<vsslabel>** Labels an item in a Source Safe repository.

| Attribute | Type | Description | Required |
|---|---|---|---|
| label | string | The value of the label. | True |
| comment | string | The label comment. | False |
| dbpath | string | The absolute path to the folder that contains the src-safe.ini. | True |
| path | string | The Source Safe project or file path, starting with "$/". | True |
| user | string | The user ID to use to log in to the Source Safe database. | True |
| failonerror | bool | | False |
| if | bool | | False |
| password | string | The password to use to log in to the Source Safe database. | False |
| unless | bool | | False |
| verbose | bool | | False |
| version | string | A version of the path to reference. Accepts multiple forms, including the label, version number, or date of the version. If omitted, the latest version is used. | False |

## Example

```
<vsslabel
            user="myusername"
            password="mypassword"
            dbpath="C:\VSS\srcsafe.ini"
            path="$/MyProduct"
            comment="NAnt label"
            label="myLabel"
        />
```

**<vssundocheckout>** Undoes any checkouts in a Source Safe database.

| Attribute | Type | Description | Required |
|---|---|---|---|
| localpath | string | The absolute path to the local working directory. This is required if you wish to have your local file replaced with the latest version from SourceSafe. | False |
| recursive | string | Determines whether to perform a recursive UndoCheckOut. Default value is true when omitted. | False |
| dbpath | string | The absolute path to the folder that contains the src-safe.ini. | True |
| path | string | The Source Safe project or file path, starting with "$/". | True |
| user | string | The user ID to use to log in to the Source Safe database. | True |
| failonerror | bool | | False |
| if | bool | | False |
| password | string | The password to use to log in to the Source Safe database. | False |
| unless | bool | | False |
| verbose | bool | | False |
| version | string | A version of the path to reference. Accepts multiple forms, including the label, version number, or date of the version. If omitted, the latest version is used. | False |

## Example

```
<vssundocheckout
            user="myusername"
            password="mypassword"
            localpath="C:\Dev\Latest"
            recursive="true"
            dbpath="C:\VSS\srcsafe.ini"
            path="$/MyProduct"
        />
```

**<wsdl>** Generates code for Web service clients and XML Web services using ASP.NET from WSDL contract files, XSD Schemas, and .discomap discovery documents. Can be used in conjunction with .disco files.

| Attribute | Description | Required |
|---|---|---|
| path | URL or Path to a WSDL, XSD, or .discomap document. | False |
| nologo | Suppresses the banner. | False |
| language | Language of generated code. "CS," "VB," "JS," or the fully-qualified name of a class implementing System.CodeDom.Compiler.CodeDomCompiler. | False |
| forserver | Compiles server-side ASP.NET abstract classes based on the Web service contract. The default is to create client-side proxy classes. | False |
| namespace | Microsoft.NET namespace of generated classes. | False |
| outfile | Output filename of the created proxy. Default name is derived from the service name. | False |
| protocol | Override default protocol to implement. Choose from "SOAP," "HttpGet," "HttpPost," or a custom protocol as specified in the configuration file. | False |
| username | Username of an account with credentials to access a server that requires authentication. | False |
| password | Password of an account with credentials to access a server that requires authentication. | False |
| domain | Domain of an account with credentials to access a server that requires authentication. | False |
| proxy | URL of a proxy server to use for HTTP requests. The default is to use the system proxy setting. | False |
| proxyusername | Username of an account with credentials to access a proxy that requires authentication. | False |
| proxypassword | Password of an account with credentials to access a proxy that requires authentication. | False |
| proxydomain | Domain of an account with credentials to access a proxy that requires authentication. | False |
| urlkey | Configuration key to use in the code generation to read the default value for the URL property. The default is not to read from the config file. | False |

*(continued)*

| Attribute | Description | Required |
|-----------|-------------|----------|
| baseurl | Base URL to use when calculating the URL fragment. The UrlKey attribute must also be specified. | False |
| failonerror | Determines whether task failure stops the build or is just reported. Default is "true." | False |
| verbose | Task reports detailed build log messages. Default is "false." | False |
| if | If true then the task will be executed; otherwise skipped. Default is "true." | False |
| unless | Opposite of if. If false then the task will be executed; otherwise skipped. Default is "false." | False |

**&lt;xsd&gt;** Compiles an XML Schema into a Microsoft.NET Assembly containing types that can marshal back and forth from XML elements and the objects that represent them. Also can create a W3C XML schema from an existing Microsoft.NET Assembly, XML document, or an old XDR format schema.

| Attribute | Description | Required |
|-----------|-------------|----------|
| failonerror | Determines whether task failure stops the build or is just reported. Default is "true." | False |
| verbose | Task reports detailed build log messages. Default is "false." | False |
| if | If true then the task will be executed; otherwise skipped. Default is "true." | False |
| unless | Opposite of if. If false then the task will be executed; otherwise skipped. Default is "false." | False |

## Examples

### Compile a schema

```
<xsd schema="MySchema.xsd" element="MyRootElement" language="CS"
namespace="MyCompany.MySchema" outputdir="build\bin"
uri="http://MySchema'sTargetNamespace" />
```

## Generate a schema from an Assembly

```
<xsd assembly="MyAssembly.dll" outputdir="build\Schemas" />
```

## Generate a schema from an XML doc

```
<xsd xmldoc="MyDoc.xml" outputdir="build\Schemas" />
```

## Generate a schema from an XDR schema

```
<xsd xdr="MyOldSchema.xdr" outputdir="build\Schemas" />
```

# mkisofs

## NAME

mkisofs—create a hybrid ISO9660/JOLIET/HFS file system with optional Rock Ridge attributes.

## SYNOPSIS

mkisofs [ -abstract FILE ] [ -allow-lowercase ] [ -allow-multidot ] [ -biblio   FILE ] [ -b eltorito_boot_image ] [-eltorito-alt-boot ]   [ -B sparc_boot_image_list ] [ -G generic_boot_image ] [ -gui ] [ -C #,# ] [ -hard-disk-boot ] [ -no-emul-boot ] [ -no-boot ] [ -boot-load-seg ] [ -boot-load-size ] [ -boot-info-table ] [ -c boot_catalog ] [ -check-oldnames ] [ -copyright FILE ] [ -A application_id ] [ -f ] [ -d ] [ -D ] [ -hide glob ] [ -hide-list file ] [ -hidden glob ] [ -hidden-list file ] [ -hide-joliet glob ] [ -hide-joliet-list  file ] [ -hide-joliet-trans-tbl ] [ -hide-rr-moved ] [ -iso-level level ] [ -J ] [ -jcharset charset ] [ -l ] [ -L ] [ -log-file log_file ] [ -max-iso9660-filenames ] [ -M path | device ] [ -nobak ] [ -no-bak ] [ -no-split-symlink-components ] [ -no-split-symlink-fields ] [ -pad ] [ -path-list file ] [ -p preparer ] [ -print-size ] [ -P publisher ] [ -quiet ] [ -r ] [ -R ] [ -relaxed-filenames ] [ -sort sort file ] [ -sysid ID ] [ -T | -table-name TABLE_NAME ] [ -ucs-level level ] [ -use-fileversion ] [ -U ] [ -no-iso-translate ] [ -v ] [ -V volid ] [ -volset ID ] [ -volset-size # ] [ -volset-seqno # ] [ -x path ] [ -exclude-list file ] [ -z ] [ -m glob ] [ -hfs  |-apple ] [ -map mapping_file ] [ -magic magic_file ] [ -probe ] [ -no-desktop ] [ -mac-name ] [ -boot-hfs-file driver_file [ -part ] [ -auto AutoStart_file ] [ -cluster- size size ] [ -hide-hfs glob ] [ -hide-hfs-list file ] [ -hfs-volid hfs_volid ] [ -icon-position ] [ -root-info FILE [ -prep-boot FILE ] [ -hfs-creator CREATOR ] [ -hfs-type TYPE ] [ --cap ] [ --netatalk ] [ --double ]

[ --ethershare ] [ --ushare ] [ --exchange ] [ --sgi ] [ --xinet ] [ -- macbin ] [ --single ] [ --dave ] [ --sfm ] -o filename path- spec [pathspec]

## DESCRIPTION

mkisofs is effectively a pre-mastering program to generate an ISO9660/JOLIET/HFS hybrid file system.

mkisofs is capable of generating the System Use Sharing Protocol records (SUSP) specified by the Rock Ridge Interchange Protocol. This is used to further describe the files in the ISO9660 file system to a Unix host and provides information such as longer filenames, uid/gid, posix permissions, symbolic links, block and character devices.

If Joliet or HFS hybrid command-line options are specified, mkisofs will create additional file system meta data for Joliet or HFS. The file content in this case refers to the same data blocks on the media. It will generate a pure ISO9660 file system unless the Joliet or HFS hybrid command-line options are given.

mkisofs can generate a true (or shared) HFS hybrid file system. The same files are seen as HFS files when accessed from a Macintosh and as ISO9660 files when accessed from other machines. HFS stands for Hierarchical File System and is the native file system used on Macintosh computers.

As an alternative, mkisofs can generate the Apple Extensions to ISO9660 for each file. These extensions provide each file with CREATOR, TYPE, and certain Finder Flags when accessed from a Macintosh. See the "HFS Macintosh File Formats" section later.

mkisofs takes a snapshot of a given directory tree and generates a binary image, which will correspond to an ISO9660 or HFS file system when written to a block device.

Each file written to the ISO9660 file system must have a filename in the 8.3 format (8 characters, period, 3 characters, all uppercase), even if Rock Ridge is in use. This filename is used on systems that are not able to make use of the Rock Ridge extensions (such as MS-DOS), and each filename in each directory must be different from the other filenames in the same directory. mkisofs generally tries to form correct names by forcing the Unix filename to uppercase and truncating as required, but often times this yields unsatisfactory results when the truncated names are not all unique. mkisofs assigns weightings to each filename, and if two names that are otherwise the same are found, the name with the lower priority is renamed to have a 3 digit number as an extension (where the number is guaranteed to be unique). An example of this would be the files foo.bar and foo.bar.~1~ -

the file foo.bar.~1~ would be written as FOO000.BAR;1 and the file foo.bar would be written as FOO.BAR;1.

When used with various HFS options, mkisofs will attempt to recognize files stored in a number of Apple/Unix file formats and will copy the data and resource forks as well as any relevant finder information. See the "HFS Macintosh File Formats" section below for more about formats mkisofs supports.

Note that mkisofs is not designed to communicate with the writer directly. Most writers have proprietary command sets that vary from one manufacturer to another, and you need a specialized tool to actually burn the disk.

The cdrecord utility is a utility capable of burning an actual disk. The latest version of cdrecord is available from ftp://ftp.berlios.de/pub/cdrecord.

Also you should know that most CD writers are very particular about timing. Once you start to burn a disk, you cannot let the buffer empty before you are done, or you will end up with a corrupt disk. Thus it is critical that you be able to maintain an uninterrupted data stream to the writer for the entire time that the disc is being written.

Pathspec is the path of the directory tree to be copied into the ISO9660 file system. Multiple paths can be specified, and mkisofs will merge the files found in all of the specified path components to form the CD-ROM image.

If the option -graft-points has been specified, it is possible to graft the paths at points other than the root directory, and it is possible to graft files or directories onto the CD-ROM image with names different than what they have in the source file system. This is easiest to illustrate with a couple of examples. Let's start by assuming that a local file ../old.lis exists, and you wish to include it in the CD-ROM image.

```
foo/bar/=../old.lis
```

will include the file old.lis in the CD-ROM image at

```
/foo/bar/old.lis
```

while

```
foo/bar/xxx=../old.lis
```

will include the file old.lis in the CD-ROM image at /foo/bar/xxx. The same sort of syntax can be used with directories as well. mkisofs will create any directories required such that the graft points exist on the CD-ROM image

- the directories do not need to appear in one of the paths. Any directories that are created on-the-fly like this will have permissions 0555 and appear to be owned by the person running mkisofs. If you wish other permissions or owners of the intermediate directories, the easiest solution is to create real directories in the path such that mkisofs doesn't have to invent them.

mkisofs will also run on Win9X/NT4 machines when compiled with Cygnus' Cygwin (available from http://sourceware.cygnus.com/cygwin/). Therefore most references in this man page to Unix can be replaced with Win32.

## OPTIONS

### abstract FILE

Specifies the abstract file name. This parameter can also be set in the file .mkisofsrc with ABST=filename. If specified in both places, the command line version is used.

### A application_id

Specifies a text string that will be written into the volume header. This should describe the application that will be on the disk. There is space on the disk for 128 characters of information. This parameter can also be set in the file .mkisofsrc with APPI=id. If specified in both places, the command-line version is used.

### allow-lowercase

This options allows lowercase characters to appear in ISO9660 filenames. This violates the ISO9660 standard, but it happens to work on some systems. Use with caution.

### allow-multidot

This option s allows more than one dot to appear in ISO9660 filenames. A leading dot is not affected by this option; it may be allowed separately using the -L option. This violates the ISO9660 standard, but it happens to work on many systems. Use with caution.

### biblio FILE

Specifies the bibliographic file name. This parameter can also be set in the file .mkisofsrc with BIBLO=filename. If specified in both places, the command-line version is used.

### b eltorito_boot_image

Specifies the path and filename of the boot image to be used when making an "El Torito" bootable CD. The pathname must be relative to the source path specified to mkisofs. This option is required to make an "El Torito" bootable CD. The boot image must be exactly the size of either a 1.2, 1.44, or 2.88 meg floppy, and mkisofs will use this size when creating the output ISO9660 file system. It is assumed that the first 512-byte sector should be read from the boot image (it is essentially emulating a normal floppy drive). This will work, for example, if the boot image is a LILO-based boot floppy.

### eltorito-alt-boot

Start with a new set of "El Torito" boot parameters. This allows you to have more than one El Torito boot on a CD. A maximum of 63 El Torito boot entries may be put on a single CD.

### B img_sun4,img_sun4c,img_sun4m,img_sun4d,img_sun4e

Specifies a comma-separated list of boot images that are needed to make a bootable CD for sparc systems. There may be empty fields in the comma-separated list. This option is required to make a bootable CD for Sun sparc systems. If the -B or -sparc-boot option has been specified, the first sector of the resulting image will contain a Sun disk label. This disk label specifies slice 0 for the ISO9660 image and slice 1 ... slice 7 for the boot images that have been specified with this option. Byte offset 512 ... 8191 within each of the additional boot images must contain a primary boot that works for the appropriate sparc architecture. The rest of each of the images usually contains a UFS file system that is used in the primary kernel boot stage.

    The implemented boot method is the boot method found with SunOS 4.x and SunOS 5.x. However, it does not depend on SunOS internals but only on properties of the Open Boot prom. For this reason, it should be useable for any OS that boots off a sparc system.

If the special filename ... is used, this and all following boot partitions are mapped to the previous partition. If mkisofs is called with -G image -B ... all boot partitions are mapped to the partition that contains the ISO9660 file system image, and the generic boot image that is located in the first 16 sectors of the disk is used for all architectures.

### G generic_boot_image

Specifies the path and filename of the generic boot image to be used when making a generic bootable CD. The generic_boot_image will be placed on the first 16 sectors of the CD. The first 16 sectors are the sectors that are located before the ISO9660 primary volume descriptor. If this option is used together with the -sparc-boot option, the Sun disk label will overlay the first 512 bytes of the generic boot image.

### hard-disk-boot

Specifies that the boot image used to create "El Torito" bootable CDs is a hard disk image. The hard disk image must begin with a master boot record that contains a single partition.

### no-emul-boot

Specifies that the boot image used to create "El Torito" bootable CDs is a "no emulation" image. The system will load and execute this image without performing any disk emulation.

### no-boot

Specifies that the created "El Torito" CD should be marked as not bootable. The system will provide an emulated drive for the image but will boot off a standard boot device.

### boot-load-seg segment_address

Specifies the load segment address of the boot image for no-emulation "El Torito" CDs.

### boot-load-size load_sectors

Specifies the number of "virtual" (512-byte) sectors to load in no-emulation mode. The default is to load the entire boot file. Some BIOSes may have problems if this is not a multiple of 4.

### boot-info-table

Specifies that a 56-byte table with information of the CD-ROM layout will be patched in at offset 8 in the boot file. If this option is given, the boot file is modified in the source file system, so make sure to make a copy of this file cannot be easily regenerated! See the "El Torito Boot Information Table" section for a description of this table.

### C last_sess_start,next_sess_start

This option is needed when mkisofs is used to create the image of a second session or a higher level session for a multisession disk. The option -C takes a pair of numbers separated by a comma. The first number is the sector number of the first sector in the last session of the disk that should be appended to. The second number is the starting sector number of the new session. The expected pair of numbers may be retrieved by calling cdrecord -msinfo ... The -C option may only be used in conjunction with the -M option.

### c boot_catalog

Specifies the path- and filename of the boot catalog to be used when making an "El Torito" bootable CD. The pathname must be relative to the source path specified to  mkisofs. This option is required to make a bootable CD. This file will be inserted into the output tree and will not be created in the source file system, so be sure the specified filename does not conflict with an existing file, as it will be excluded. Usually a name like "boot.catalog" is chosen.

### check-oldnames

Check all filenames imported from old sessions for compliance with actual mkisofs ISO9660 file naming rules. If this option is not present, only names with a length > 31 are checked, as these files are a hard violation of the ISO9660 standard.

### copyright FILE

Specifies the Copyright file name. This parameter can also be set in the file .mkisofsrc with COPY=filename. If specified in both places, the command-line version is used.

### d

Omit trailing period from files that do not have a period. This violates the ISO9660 standard, but it happens to work on many systems. Use with caution.

### D

Do not use deep directory relocation, and instead just pack them in the way we see them. This violates the ISO9660 standard, but it happens to work on many systems. Use with caution.

### f

Follow symbolic links when generating the file system. When this option is not in use, symbolic links will be entered using Rock Ridge if enabled; otherwise the file will be ignored.

### gui

Switch the behavior for a GUI. This currently makes the output more verbose but may have other effects in future.

### graft-points

Allow graft points for filenames. If this option is used, all filenames are checked for graft points. The filename is divided at the first unescaped equal sign. All occurrences of "\\" and "=" characters must be escaped with "\\" if -graft-points has been specified.

### hide glob

Hide glob from being seen on the ISO9660 or Rock Ridge directory. glob is a shell wild-card-style pattern that must match any part of the filename or path. Multiple globs may be hidden. If glob matches a directory, then the contents of that directory will be hidden. All the hidden files will still be written to the output CD image file. Should be used with the -hide-joliet option.

### hide-list file

A file containing a list of globs to be hidden as above.

### hidden glob

Add the hidden (existence) ISO9660 directory attribute for glob. This attribute will prevent glob from being listed on DOS-based systems if the /A flag is not used for the listing. glob is a shell wild-card-style pattern that must match any part of the filename or path. Multiple globs may be hidden.

### hidden-list file

A file containing a list of globs to get the hidden attribute as previously.

### hide-joliet glob

Hide glob from being seen on the Joliet directory. glob is a shell wild-card-style pattern that must match any part of the filename or path. Multiple globs may be hidden. If glob matches a directory, then the contents of that directory will be hidden. All the hidden files will still be written to the output CD image file. Should be used with the -hide option.

### hide-joliet-list file

A file containing a list of globs to be hidden as previously.

### hide-joliet-trans-tbl

Hide the TRANS.TBL files from the Joliet tree. These files usually don't make sense in the Joliet World, as they list the real name and the ISO9660 name, which may both be different from the Joliet name.

### hide-rr-moved

Rename the directory RR_MOVED to .rr_moved in the Rock Ridge tree. It seems to be impossible to completely hide the RR_MOVED directory from the Rock Ridge tree. This option only makes the visible tree easier to understand for people who don't know what this directory is for. If you need to have no RR_MOVED directory at all, you should use the -D option. Note that if the -D option has been specified, the resulting file system is not ISO9660 level-1 compliant and will not be readable on MS-DOS.

### l

Allow full 31 character filenames. Normally the ISO9660 filename will be in an 8.3 format, which is compatible with MS-DOS, even though the ISO9660 standard allows filenames of up to 31 characters. If you use this option, the disc may be difficult to use on an MS-DOS system, but this comes in handy on some other systems (such as the Amiga). Use with caution.

### iso-level level

Set the ISO9660 conformance level. Valid numbers are 1...3. With level 1, files may only consist of one section, and filenames are restricted to 8.3 characters.

With level 2, files may only consist of one section.

With level 3, no restrictions apply.

With all ISO9660 levels all filenames are restricted to uppercase letters, numbers, and the underscore (_). The maximum filename length is restricted to 31 characters, the directory nesting level is restricted to 8, and the maximum path length is limited to 255 characters.

### J

Generate Joliet directory records in addition to regular ISO9660 filenames. This is primarily useful when the discs are to be used on Windows-NT or Windows-95 machines. The Joliet filenames are specified in Unicode, and each path component can be up to 64 Unicode characters long.

### jcharset charset

Local charset that should be used for translating local filenames into Joliet Unicode directory records. To get a list of valid charset names, call mkisofs -jchar-set help. To get a 1:1 mapping, you may use default as charset name. The default initial values are cp437 on DOS-based systems and ISO8859-1 on all other systems. If the -jcharset option is specified, the -J option is implied.

## L

Allow ISO9660 filenames to begin with a period. Usually, a leading dot is replaced with an underscore in order to maintain MS-DOS compatibility. This violates the ISO9660 standard, but it happens to work on many systems. Use with caution.

### log-file log_file

Redirect all error, warning, and informational messages to log_file instead of the standard error.

### m glob

Exclude glob from being written to CD-ROM. glob is a shell wild-card-style pattern that must match part of the filename (not the path as with option -x). Technically glob is matched against the d->d_name part of the directory entry. Multiple globs may be excluded. Example:

```
mkisofs -o rom -m '*.o' -m core -m foobar
```

would exclude all files ending in ".o," called "core" or "foobar," to be copied to CD-ROM. Note that if you had a directory called "foobar," it too (and of course all its descendants) would be excluded.

**NOTE:** The -m and -x option description should both be updated; they are wrong. Both now work identically and use filename globbing. A file is excluded if either the last component matches or the whole path matches.

### exclude-list file

A file containing a list of globs to be excluded as previously.

### max-iso9660-filenames

Allow 37 chars in ISO9660 filenames. This option forces the -N option as the extra name space is taken from the space reserved for ISO9660 version numbers. This violates the ISO9660 standard, but it happens to work on many systems. Although a conforming application needs to provide a buffer space of at least 37 characters, disks created with this option may cause a buffer overflow in the reading operating system. Use with extreme care.

### M path or M device

Specifies path to existing ISO9660 image to be merged. The alternate form takes a SCSI device specifier that uses the same syntax as the dev= parameter of cdrecord. The output of mkisofs will be a new session, which should get written to the end of the image specified in -M. Typically this requires multi-session capability for the recorder and CD-ROM drive that you are attempting to write this image to. This option may only be used in conjunction with the -C option.

### N

Omit version numbers from ISO9660 file names. This violates the ISO9660 standard, but no one really uses the version numbers anyway. Use with caution.

### nobak

### no-bak

Do not include backup files files on the ISO9660 file system. If the -no-bak option is specified, files that contain the characters "~" or "#" or end in ".bak" will not be included (these are typically backup files for editors under Unix).

### no-rr

Do not use the Rock Ridge attributes from previous sessions. This may help avoid getting into trouble when mkisofs finds illegal Rock Ridge signatures on an old session.

### no-split-symlink-components

Don't split the SL components, but begin a new Continuation Area (CE) instead. This may waste some space, but the SunOS 4.1.4 CD-ROM driver has a bug in reading split SL components (link_size = component_size instead of link_size += component_size).

### no-split-symlink-fields

Don't split the SL fields, but begin a new Continuation Area (CE) instead. This may waste some space, but the SunOS 4.1.4 and Solaris 2.5.1 CD-ROM drivers have a bug in reading split SL fields (a "/" can be dropped).

### o filename

This is the name of the file to which the ISO9660 file system image should be written. This can be a disk file or a tape drive, or it can correspond directly to the device name of the optical disc writer. If not specified, stdout is used. Note that the output can also be a block special device for a regular disk drive, in which case the disk partition can be mounted and examined to ensure that the premastering was done correctly.

### pad

Pad the end of the ISO9660 by 16 sectors (32kB). If the total size then is not a multiple of 16 sectors, the needed number of sectors is added. If the option -B is used, then there is a second padding at the end of the boot partitions.

The padding is needed, as many operating systems (e.g., Linux) implement read ahead bugs in their file system I/O. These bugs result in read errors on one or more files that are located at the end of a track. They are usually present when the CD is written in Track at Once mode or when the disk is written as mixed mode CD where an audio track follows the data track.

### path-list file

A file containing a list of pathspec directories and filenames to be added to the ISO9660 file system. This list of pathspecs is processed after any that appear on the command line. If the argument is -, then the list is read from the standard input. There must be at least one pathspec given on the command line as well.

### P publisher_id

Specifies a text string that will be written into the volume header. This should describe the publisher of the CD-ROM, usually with a mailing address and phone number. There is space on the disk for 128 characters of

information. This parameter can also be set in the file .mkisofsrc with
PUBL=. If specified in both places, the command-line version is used.

### p preparer_id

Specifies a text string that will be written into the volume header. This
should describe the preparer of the CD-ROM, usually with a mailing
address and phone number. There is space on the disc for 128 characters of
information. This parameter can also be set in the file .mkisofsrc with
PREP=. If specified in both places, the command-line version is used.

### print-size

Print estimated file system size and exit. This option is needed for Disk At
Once mode and with some CD-R drives when piping directly into
cdrecord. In this case it is needed to know the size of the file system before
the actual CD-creation is done. The option -print-size allows you to get this
size from a "dry-run" before the CD is actually written.

### quiet

This makes mkisofs even less verbose. No progress output will be provided.

### R

Generate SUSP and RR records using the Rock Ridge protocol to further
describe the files on the ISO9660 file system.

### r

This is like the -R option, but file ownership and modes are set to more useful values. The uid and gid are set to zero because they are usually only useful on the author's system and are not useful to the client. All the file read
bits are set true so that files and directories are globally readable on the
client. If any execute bit is set for a file, set all of the execute bits so that
executables are globally executable on the client. If any search bit is set for
a directory, set all of the search bits so that directories are globally search-
able on the client. All write bits are cleared because the CD-ROM will be
mounted read-only in any case. If any of the special mode bits are set, clear
them because file locks are not useful on a read-only file system, and set-id
bits are not desirable for uid 0 or gid 0. When used on Win32, the execute

bit is set on all files. This is a result of the lack of file permissions on Win32 and the Cygwin POSIX emulation layer.

### relaxed-filenames

The option -relaxed-filenames allows ISO9660 filenames to include digits, uppercase characters, and all other 7 bit ASCII characters (resp. anything except lowercase characters). This violates the ISO9660 standard, but it happens to work on many systems. Use with caution.

### sort sort file

Sort file locations on the media. Sorting is controlled by a file that contains pairs of filenames and sorting offset weighting. If the weighting is higher, the file will be located closer to the beginning of the media; if the weighting is lower, the file will be located closer to the end of the media. There must be only one space or tabs character between the filename and the weight, and the weight must be the last characters on a line. The filename is taken to include all the characters up to, but not including, the last space or tab character on a line. This is to allow space characters to be in or at the end of a filename. See README.sort for more details.

### sysid ID

Specifies the system ID. This parameter can also be set in the file .mkisofsrc with SYSI=system_id. If specified in both places, the command-line version is used.

### T

Generate a file TRANS.TBL in each directory on the CD-ROM, which can be used on non-Rock Ridge capable systems to help establish the correct file names. There is also information present in the file that indicates the major and minor numbers for block and character devices, and each symlink has the name of the link file given.

### table-name TABLE_NAME

Alternative translation table file name (see previously). Implies the -T option. If you are creating a multi-session image, you must use the same name as in the previous session.

### ucs-level level

Set Unicode conformance level in the Joliet SVD. The default level is 3. It may be set to 1..3 using this option.

### use-fileversion

The option -use-fileversion allows mkisofs to use file version numbers from the file system. If the option is not specified, mkisofs creates a version of 1 for all files. File versions are strings in the range ;1 to ;32767 This option is the default on VMS.

### U

Allows "Untranslated" filenames, completely violating the ISO9660 standards described previously. Forces on the -d, -l, -L, -N, -relaxed-filenames, -allow-lowercase, -allow-multidot and -no-iso-translate flags. It allows more than one "." character in the filename, as well as mixed case filenames. This is useful on HP-UX system, where the built-in CDFS file system does not recognize ANY extensions. Use with extreme caution.

### no-iso-translate

Do not translate the characters "#" and "~," which are invalid for ISO9660 filenames. These characters, though invalid, are often used by Microsoft systems. This violates the ISO9660 standard, but it happens to work on many systems. Use with caution.

### V volid

Specifies the volume ID (volume name or label) to be written into the master block. This parameter can also be set in the file .mkisofsrc with VOLI=id. If specified in both places, the command-line version is used. Note that if you assign a volume ID, this is the name that will be used as the mount point used by the Solaris volume management system and the name that is assigned to the disc on a Windows or Mac platform.

### volset ID

Specifies the volset ID. This parameter can also be set in the file .mkisofsrc with VOLS=volset_id. If specified in both places, the command-line version is used.

### volset-size #

Sets the volume set size to #. The volume set size is the number of CDs that are in a CD set. The -volset- size option may be used to create CDs that are part of, for example, an operation system installation set of CDs. The option -volset-size must be specified before -volset- seqno on each command line.

### volset-seqno #

Sets the volume set sequence number to #. The volume set sequence number is the index number of the current CD in a CD set. The option -volset-size must be specified before -volset-seqno on each command line.

### v

Verbose execution. If given twice on the command line, extra debug information will be printed.

### x path

Exclude path from being written to CD-ROM. Path must be the complete pathname that results from concatenating the pathname given as command-line argument and the path relative to this directory. Multiple paths may be excluded. Example:

```
mkisofs -o cd -x /local/dir1 -x /local/dir2 /local
```

**NOTE:** The -m and -x option description should both be updated; they are wrong. Both now work identically and use filename globbing. A file is excluded if either the last component matches or the whole path matches.

### z

Generate special SUSP records for transparently compressed files. This is only of use and interest for hosts that support transparent decompression. This is an experimental feature, and no hosts yet support this, but there are ALPHA patches for Linux that can make use of this feature.

## HFS OPTIONS

### hfs

Create an ISO9660/HFS hybrid CD. This option should be used in conjunction with the -map, (Reg.) and/or the various double dash options given hereafter.

### apple

Create an ISO9660 CD with Apple's extensions. Similar to the -hfs option, except that the Apple Extensions to ISO9660 are added instead of creating an HFS hybrid volume.

### map mapping_file

Use the mapping_file to set the CREATOR and TYPE information for a file based on the filename's extension. A filename is mapped only if it is not one of the known Apple/Unix file formats. See the "HFS CREATOR/TYPE" section later.

### magic magic_file

The CREATOR and TYPE information is set by using a file's magic number (usually the first few bytes of a file). The magic_file is only used if a file is not one of the known Apple/Unix file formats, or the filename extension has not been mapped using the -map option. See   the "HFS CREATOR/TYPE" section later for more details.

### hfs-creator CREATOR

Set the default CREATOR for all files. Must be exactly 4 characters. See the "HFS CREATOR/TYPE" section later for more details.

### hfs-type TYPE

Set the default TYPE for all files. Must be exactly 4 characters. See the "HFS CREATOR/TYPE" section later for more details.

### probe

Search the contents of files for all the known Apple/Unix file formats. See the "HFS Macintosh File Formats" section later for more about these formats. However, the only way to check for MacBinary and AppleSingle files is to open and read them. Therefore this option may increase processing time. It is better to use one or more double dash options given later if the Apple/Unix formats in use are known.

### no-desktop

Do not create (empty) Desktop files. New HFS Desktop files will be created when the CD is used on a Macintosh (and stored in the System Folder). By default, empty Desktop files are added to the HFS volume.

### mac-name

Use the HFS filename as the starting point for the ISO9660, Joliet, and Rock Ridge file names. See the "HFS Macintosh File Names" section later for more information.

### boot-hfs-file driver_file

Installs the driver_file that may make the CD bootable on a Macintosh. See the "HFS Boot Driver" section later (Alpha).

### part

Generate an HFS partition table. By default, no partition table is generated, but some older Macintosh CD-ROM drivers need an HFS partition table on the CD-ROM to be able to recognize a hybrid CD-ROM.

### auto AutoStart_file

Make the HFS CD use the QuickTime 2.0 Autostart feature to launch an application or document. The given filename must be the name of a document or application located at the top level of the CD. The filename must be less than 12 characters (Alpha).

### cluster-size size

Set the size in bytes of the cluster or allocation units of PC Exchange files. Implies the --exchange option. See the "HFS Macintosh File Formats" section later.

### hide-hfs glob

Hide glob from the HFS volume. The file or directory will still exist in the ISO9660 and/or Joliet directory. glob is a shell wild-card-style pattern that must match any part of the filename. Multiple globs may be excluded. Example:

```
mkisofs -o rom -hfs -hide-hfs '*.o' -hide-hfs foobar
```

would exclude all files ending in ".o" or called "foobar" from the HFS volume. Note that if you had a directory called "foobar," it too (and of course all its descendants) would be excluded. The glob can also be a path name relative to the source directories given on the command line. Example:

```
mkisofs -o rom -hfs -hide-hfs src/html src
```

would exclude just the file or directory called "html" from the "src" directory. Any other file or directory called "html" in the tree will not be excluded. Should be used with the -hide and/or -hide-joliet options.

### hide-hfs-list file

A file containing a list of globs to be hidden as previously.

### hfs-volid hfs_volid

Volume name for the HFS partition. This is the name that is assigned to the disc on a Macintosh and replaces the volid used with the -V option.

### -icon-position

Use the icon position information, if it exists, from the Apple/Unix file. The icons will appear in the same position as they would on a Macintosh desktop. Folder location and size on screen, its scroll positions, folder View (view as Icons, Small Icons, etc.) are also preserved. This option may become set by default in the future (Alpha).

### root-info file

Set the location, size on screen, scroll positions, folder View, etc. for the root folder of an HFS volume. See README.rootinfo for more information. (Alpha)

### -prep-boot FILE

Prep boot image file. Up to 4 are allowed. See README.prep_boot (Alpha).

### -cap

Look for AUFS CAP Macintosh files. Search for CAP Apple/Unix file formats only. Searching for the other possible Apple/Unix file formats is disabled, unless other double dash options are given.

### -netatalk

Look for NETATALK Macintosh files.

### -double

Look for AppleDouble Macintosh files.

### -ethershare

Look for Helios EtherShare Macintosh files.

### -ushare

Look for IPT UShare Macintosh files.

### -exchange

Look for PC Exchange Macintosh files.

### -sgi

Look for SGI Macintosh files.

### -xinet

Look for XINET Macintosh files.

### -macbin

Look for MacBinary Macintosh files.

### -single

Look for AppleSingle Macintosh files.

### -dave

Look for Thursby Software Systems DAVE Macintosh files.

### -sfm

Look for Microsoft's Services for Macintosh files (NT only). (Alpha.)

## HFS CREATOR/TYPE

A Macintosh file has two properties associated with it that define which application created the file, the CREATOR, and what data the file contains, the TYPE. Both are (exactly) 4-letter strings. Usually this allows a Macintosh user to double-click on a file and launch the correct application, etc. The CREATOR and TYPE of a particular file can be found by using something like ResEdit (or similar) on a Macintosh.

The CREATOR and TYPE information is stored in all the various Apple/Unix encoded files. For other files, it is possible to base the CREATOR and TYPE on the filename's extension using a mapping file (the -map option) and/or using the magic number (usually a signature in the first few bytes) of a file (the -magic option). If both these options are given, then their order on the command line is important. If the -map option is given first, then a filename extension match is attempted before a magic number match. However, if the -magic option is given first, then a magic number match is attempted before a filename extension match.

If a mapping or magic file is not used, or no match is found, then the default CREATOR and TYPE for all regular files can be set by using entries in the .mkisofsrc file or by using the -hfs-creator and/or -hfs-type options; otherwise the default CREATOR and TYPE are "unix" and "TEXT."

The format of the mapping file is the same afpfile format as used by aufs. This file has five columns for the extension, file translation, CRE-ATOR, TYPE, and Comment. Lines starting with the "#" character are comment lines and are ignored. An example file would be like:

```
# Example filename mapping file
#
# EXTN   XLate    CREATOR   TYPE      Comment
.tif     Raw      '8BIM'    'TIFF'    "Photoshop TIFF image"
.hqx     Ascii    'BnHq'    'TEXT'    "BinHex file"
.doc     Raw      'MSWD'    'WDBN'    "Word file"
.mov     Raw      'TVOD'    'MooV'    "QuickTime Movie"
*        Ascii    'ttxt'    'TEXT'    "Text file"
```

Where:

- The first column EXTN defines the Unix filename extension to be mapped. The default mapping for any filename extension that doesn't match is defined with the "*" character.
- The Xlate column defines the type of text translation between the Unix and Macintosh file. It is ignored by mkisofs but is kept to be compatible with aufs(1). Although mkisofs does not alter the contents of a file, if a binary file has its TYPE set as 'TEXT,' it may be read incorrectly on a Macintosh. Therefore, a better choice for the default TYPE may be '????'.
- The CREATOR and TYPE keywords must be 4 characters long and enclosed in single quotes.
- The comment field is enclosed in double quotes - it is ignored by mkisofs but is kept to be compatible with aufs.

The format of the magic file is almost identical to the magic(4) file used by the Linux file(1) command - the routines for reading and decoding the magic file are based on the Linux file(1) command.

This file has four tab-separated columns for the byte offset, type, test, and message. Lines starting with the "#" character are comment lines and are ignored. An example file would be like:

```
# Example magic file
#
# off    type    test        message
0        string  GIF8        8BIM GIFf  GIF image
```

```
        0        beshort    0xffd8      8BIM JPEG   image data
        0        string     SIT!        SIT! SIT!   StuffIt Archive
        0        string     37235       LZIV ZIVU   standard unix compress
        0        string     37213       GNUz ZIVU   gzip compressed data
        0        string     %!ASPS TEXT  Postscript
        0        string     04%!        ASPS TEXT   PC Postscript with a ^D to
start
        4        string     moov        txtt MooV   QuickTime movie file (moov)
        4        string     mdat        txtt MooV   QuickTime movie file (mdat)
```

The format of the file is described in the magic(4) man page. The only difference here is that for each entry in the magic file, the message for the initial offset must be 4 characters for the CREATOR, followed by 4 characters for the TYPE - white space is optional between them. Any other characters on this line are ignored. Continuation lines (starting with a '>') are also ignored, i.e., only the initial offset lines are used.

Using the -magic option may significantly increase processing time, as each file has to opened and read to find its magic number.

In summary, for all files, the default CREATOR is 'unix,' and the default TYPE is 'TEXT.' These can be changed by using entries in the .mkisofsrc file or by using the -hfs-creator and/or -hfs-type options.

If the file is in one of the known Apple/Unix formats (and the format has been selected), then the CREATOR and TYPE are taken from the values stored in the Apple/Unix file.

Other files can have their CREATOR and TYPE set from their file name extension (the -map option) or their magic number (the -magic option). If the default match is used in the mapping file, then these values override the default CREATOR and TYPE.

A full CREATOR/TYPE database can be found at http://www.angelfire.com/il/szekely/index.html.

## HFS MACINTOSH FILE FORMATS

Macintosh files have two parts called the Data and Resource fork. Either may be empty. Unix (and many other OSs) can only cope with files having one part (or fork). To add to this, Macintosh files have a number of attributes associated with them - probably the most important are the TYPE and CREATOR. Again Unix has no concept of these types of attributes.

For example, a Macintosh file may be a JPEG image, where the image is stored in the data fork and a desktop thumbnail stored in the Resource fork. It is usually the information in the data fork that is useful across platforms.

Therefore to store a Macintosh file on a Unix file system, a way has to be found to cope with the two forks and the extra attributes (which are referred to as the finder info). Unfortunately, it seems that every software package that stores Macintosh files on Unix has chosen a completely different storage method.

The Apple/Unix formats that mkisofs (partially) supports are:

### CAP AUFS format

Data fork stored in a file. Resource fork in subdirectory .resource with same filename as data fork. Finder info in .finderinfo subdirectory with same filename.

### AppleDouble/Netatalk

Data fork stored in a file. Resource fork stored in a file with same name prefixed with "%". Finder info also stored in same "%" file. Netatalk uses the same format, but the resource fork/finderinfo is stored in subdirectory .AppleDouble with same name as data fork.

### AppleSingle

Data structures similar to above, except both forks and finder info are stored in one file.

### Helios EtherShare

Data fork stored in a file. Resource fork and finder info together in subdirectory .rsrc with same filename as data fork.

### IPT UShare

Very similar to the EtherShare format, but the finder info is stored slightly differently.

### MacBinary

Both forks and finder info stored in one file.

### Apple PC Exchange

Used by Macintoshes to store Apple files on DOS (FAT) disks. Data fork stored in a file. Resource fork in subdirectory resource.frk (or RESOURCE.FRK). Finder info as one record in file finder.dat (or FINDER.DAT). Separate finder.dat for each data fork directory.

**NOTE:** mkisofs needs to know the native FAT cluster size of the disk that the PC Exchange files are on (or have been copied from). This size is given by the -cluster- size option.  The cluster or allocation size can be found by using the DOS utility CHKDSK.

May not work with PC Exchange v2.2 or higher files (available with MacOS 8.1). DOS media containing PC Exchange files should be mounted as type msdos (not vfat) when using Linux.

### SGI/XINET

Used by SGI machines when they mount HFS disks. Data fork stored in a file. Resource fork in subdirectory .HSResource with same name. Finder info as one record in file .HSancillary. Separate .HSancillary for each data fork directory.

### Thursby Software Systems DAVE

Allows Macintoshes to store Apple files on SMB servers. Data fork stored in a file. Resource fork in subdirectory resource.frk. Uses the AppleDouble format to store resource fork.

### Services for Macintosh

Format of files stored by NT Servers on NTFS file systems. Data fork is stored as "filename." Resource fork stored as a NTFS stream called "filename:AFP_Resource." The finder info is stored as a NTFS stream called "filename:Afp_AfpInfo". These streams are normally invisible to the user.

**WARNING:** mkisofs only partially supports the SFM format. If an HFS file or folder stored on the NT server contains an illegal NT character in its name, then NT converts these characters to Private Use Unicode characters. The characters are: " * / < > ? | also a space or period if it is the last character of the file name, character codes 0x01 to 0x1f (control characters), and Apple' apple logo.

Unfortunately, these private Unicode characters are not readable by the mkisofs NT executable. Therefore any file or directory name containing these characters will be ignored - including the contents of any such directory.

mkisofs will attempt to set the CREATOR, TYPE, date, and possibly other flags from the finder info. Additionally, if it exists, the Macintosh file-name is set from the finder info; otherwise, the Macintosh name is based on the Unix filename—see the "HFS Macinstosh File Names" section later.

When using the -apple option, the TYPE and CREATOR are stored in the optional System Use or SUSP field in the ISO9660 Directory Record in much the same way as the Rock Ridge attributes are. In fact, to make life easy, the Apple extensions are added at the beginning of the existing Rock Ridge attributes (i.e., to get the Apple extensions, you get the Rock Ridge extensions as well).

The Apple extensions require the resource fork to be stored as an ISO9660 associated file. This is just like any normal file stored in the ISO9660 file system except that the associated file flag is set in the Directory Record (bit 2). This file has the same name as the data fork (the file seen by non-Apple machines). Associated files are normally ignored by other OSs.

When using the -hfs option, the TYPE and CREATOR, plus other finder info, are stored in a separate HFS directory, not visible on the ISO9660 volume. The HFS directory references the same data and resource fork files described.

In most cases, it is better to use the -hfs option instead of the -apple option, as the latter imposes the limited ISO9660 characters allowed in file-names. However, the Apple extensions do give the advantage that the files are packed on the disk more efficiently, and it may be possible to fit more files on a CD, which is important when the total size of the source files is approaching 650MB.

## HFS MACINTOSH FILENAMES

Where possible, the HFS filename that is stored with an Apple/Unix file is used for the HFS part of the CD. However, not all the Apple/Unix encodings store the HFS filename with the finder info. In these cases, the Unix filename is used with escaped special characters. Special characters include "/" and characters with codes over 127.

Aufs escapes these characters by using ":" followed by the character code as two hex digits. Netatalk and EtherShare have a similar scheme but use "%" instead of a ":". If mkisofs can't find an HFS filename, then it uses the Unix name, with any %xx or :xx characters (xx == two hex digits) converted to a single character code. If "xx" are not hex digits ([0-9a-fA-F]), then they are left alone, although any remaining ":" is converted to "%", as colon is the HFS directory separator. Care must be taken, as an ordinary Unix file with %xx or :xx will also be converted. For example:

> This:2fFile converted to This/File
> This:File converted to This%File
> This:t7File converted to This%t7File

Although HFS filenames appear to support upper- and lowercase letters, the file system is case-insensitive, i.e., the filenames "aBc" and "AbC" are the same. If a file is found in a directory with the same HFS name, then mkisofs will attempt, where possible, to make a unique name by adding '_' characters to one of the filenames.

If an HFS filename exists for a file, then mkisofs can use this name as the starting point for the ISO9660, Joliet, and Rock Ridge filenames using the -mac-name option. Normal Unix files without an HFS name will still use their Unix name.

For example, if a MacBinary (or PC Exchange) file is stored as someimage.gif.bin on the Unix file system but contains an HFS file called someimage.gif, then this is the name that would appear on the HFS part of the CD. However, as mkisofs uses the Unix name as the starting point for the other names, then the ISO9660 name generated will probably be SOMEIMAG. BIN,, and the Joliet/Rock Ridge would be someimage.gif.bin, although the actual data (in this case) is a GIF image. This option will use the HFS filename as the starting point, and the ISO9660 name will probably be SOMEIMAG.GIF, and the Joliet/Rock Ridge would be someimage.gif.

Using the -mac-name option will not currently work with the -T option - the Unix name will be used in the TRANS.TBL file, not the Macintosh name.

The existing mkisofs code will filter out any illegal characters for the ISO9660 and Joliet filenames, but as mkisofs expects to be dealing directly with Unix names, it leaves the Rock Ridge names as is. But as "/" is a legal HFS filename character, the -mac-name option converts "/" to a "_" in Rock Ridge filenames.

If the Apple extensions are used, then only the ISO9660 filenames will appear on the Macintosh. However, as the Macintosh ISO9660 drivers can use Level 2 filenames, then you can use options like -allow-multidot without problems on a Macintosh. Still take care over the names, though; for example, this.file.name will be converted to THIS.FILE, i.e., only having one ".". Also, the filename abcdefgh will be seen as ABCDEFGH, but abcdefghi will be seen as ABCDEFGHI (i.e., with a "." at the end). I don't know if this is a Macintosh problem or mkisofs/mkhybrid problem. All filenames will be in uppercase when viewed on a Macintosh. Of course, DOS/Win3.X machines will not be able to see Level 2 filenames.

## HFS CUSTOM VOLUME/FOLDER ICONS

To give an HFS CD a custom icon, make sure the root (top level) folder includes a standard Macintosh volume icon file. To give a volume a custom icon on a Macintosh, an icon has to be pasted over the volume's icon in the "Get Info" box of the volume. This creates an invisible file called 'Icon\r' ('\r' is the "carriage return" character) in the root folder.

A custom folder icon is very similar - an invisible file called 'Icon\r' exits in the folder itself.

Probably the easiest way to create a custom icon that mkisofs can use is to format a blank HFS floppy disk on a Mac and paste an icon to its "Get Info" box. If using Linux with the HFS module installed, mount the floppy using something like:

```
mount -t hfs /dev/fd0 /mnt/floppy
```

The floppy will be mounted as a CAP file system by default. Then run mkisofs using something like:

```
mkisofs --cap -o output source_dir /mnt/floppy
```

If you are not using Linux, then you can use the hfsutils to copy the icon file from the floppy. However, care has to be taken, as the icon file contains a control character, e.g.,

```
hmount /dev/fd0
hdir -a
hcopy -m Icon^V^M icon_dir/icon
```

where '^V^M' is control-V followed by control-M. Then run mkisofs by using something like:

```
mkisofs --macbin -o output source_dir icon_dir
```

The procedure for creating/using custom folder icons is very similar - paste an icon to folder's "Get Info" box and transfer the resulting 'Icon\r' file to the relevant directory in the mkisofs source tree.

You may want to hide the icon files from the ISO9660 and Joliet trees.

To give a custom icon to a Joliet CD, follow the instructions found at http://www.fadden.com/cdrfaq/faq03.html#[3-21]

## HFS BOOT DRIVER

It may be possible to make the hybrid CD bootable on a Macintosh.

A bootable HFS CD requires an Apple CD-ROM (or compatible) driver, a bootable HFS partition, and the necessary System, Finder, etc. files.

A driver can be obtained from any other Macintosh bootable CD-ROM using the apple_driver utility. This file can then be used with the -boot-hfs-file option.

The HFS partition (i.e., the hybrid disk in our case) must contain a suitable System Folder, again from another CD-ROM or disk.

For a partition to be bootable, it must have its boot block set. The boot block is in the first two blocks of a partition. For a non-bootable partition, the boot block is full of zeros. Normally, when a System file is copied to a partition on a Macintosh disk, the boot block is filled with a number of required settings - unfortunately I don't know the full spec for the boot block, so I'm guessing that the following will work OK.

Therefore, the utility apple_driver also extracts the boot block from the first HFS partition it finds on the given CD-ROM, and this is used for the HFS partition created by mkisofs.

## PLEASE NOTE

By using a driver from an Apple CD and copying Apple software to your CD, you become liable to obey Apple Computer, Inc. Software License Agreements.

## EL TORITO BOOT INFORMATION TABLE

When the -boot-info-table option is given, mkisofs will modify the boot file specified by the -b option by inserting a 56-byte "boot information table" at offset 8 in the file. This modification is done in the source file system, so make sure you use a copy if this file is not easily re-created! This file contains pointers, which may not be easily or reliably obtained at boot time.

The format of this table is as follows; all integers are in section 7.3.1 ("little endian") format.

| Offset | Name | Size | Meaning |
| --- | --- | --- | --- |
| 8 | bi_pvd | 4 bytes | LBA of primary volume descriptor |
| 12 | bi_file | 4 bytes | LBA of boot file |
| 16 | bi_length | 4 bytes | Boot file length in bytes |
| 20 | bi_csum | 4 bytes | 32-bit checksum |
| 24 | bi_reserved | 40 bytes | Reserved |

The 32-bit checksum is the sum of all the 32-bit words in the boot file starting at byte offset 64. All linear block addresses (LBAs) are given in CD sectors (normally 2048 bytes).

## CONFIGURATION

mkisofs looks for the .mkisofsrc file, first in the current working directory, then in the user's home directory, and then in the directory in which the mkisofs binary is stored. This file is assumed to contain a series of lines of the form TAG=value, and in this way you can specify certain options. The case of the tag is not significant. Some fields in the volume header are not settable on the command line but can be altered through this facility. Comments may be placed in this file, using lines that start with a hash (#) character.

### APPI

The application identifier should describe the application that will be on the disk. There is space on the disk for 128 characters of information. May be overridden using the -A command-line option.

### COPY

The copyright information, often the name of a file on the disk containing the copyright notice. There is space in the disk for 37 characters of information. May be overridden using the -copyright command-line option.

### ABST

The abstract information, often the name of a file on the disk containing an abstract. There is space in the disk for 37 characters of information. May be overridden using the -abstract command-line option.

### BIBL

The bibliographic information, often the name of a file on the disk containing a bibliography. There is space in the disk for 37 characters of information. May be overridden using the -bilio command-line option.

### PREP

This should describe the preparer of the CD-ROM, usually with a mailing address and phone number. There is space on the disk for 128 characters of information. May be overridden using the -p command-line option.

### PUBL

This should describe the publisher of the CD-ROM, usually with a mailing address and phone number. There is space on the disk for 128 characters of information. May be overridden using the -P command-line option.

### SYSI

The System Identifier. There is space on the disk for 32 characters of information. May be overridden using the -sysid command-line option.

### VOLI

The Volume Identifier. There is space on the disk for 32 characters of information. May be overridden using the -V command-line option.

### VOLS

The Volume Set Name. There is space on the disk for 128 characters of information. May be overridden using the -volset command-line option.

### HFS_TYPE

The default TYPE for Macintosh files. Must be exactly 4 characters. May be overridden using the -hfs-type command-line option.

### HFS_CREATOR

The default CREATOR for Macintosh files. Must be exactly 4 characters. May be overridden using the -hfs-creator command-line option.

mkisofs can also be configured at compile time with defaults for many of these fields. See the file defaults.h.

## EXAMPLES

To create a vanilla ISO9660 file system image in the file cd.iso, where the directory cd_dir will become the root directory of the CD, call:

```
% mkisofs -o cd.iso cd_dir
```

To create an HFS hybrid CD with Rock Ridge extensions of the source directory cd_dir:

```
% mkisofs -o cd.iso -R cd_dir
```

To create an HFS hybrid CD with Rock Ridge extensions of the source directory cd_dir where all files have at least read permission and all files are owned by root, call:

```
% mkisofs -o cd.iso -r cd_dir
```

To create an HFS hybrid CD with the Joliet and Rock Ridge extensions of the source directory cd_dir:

```
% mkisofs -o cd.iso -R -J -hfs cd_dir
```

To create an HFS hybrid CD from the source directory cd_dir that contains Netatalk Apple/Unix files:

```
% mkisofs -o cd.iso --netatalk cd_dir
```

To create a HFS hybrid CD from the source directory cd_dir, giving all files CREATOR and TYPES based on just their filename extensions listed in the file "mapping":

```
% mkisofs -o cd.iso -map mapping cd_dir
```

To create a CD with the "Apple Extensions to ISO9660" from the source directories cd_dir and another_dir. Files in all the known Apple/Unix format are decoded, and any other files are given CREATOR and TYPE based on their magic number given in the file "magic":

```
% mkisofs -o cd.iso -apple -magic magic -probe \
     cd_dir another_dir
```

The following example puts different files on the CD that all have the name README but have different contents when seen as an ISO9660/RockRidge, Joliet, or HFS CD.
Current directory contains:

```
% ls -F
README.hfs    README.joliet README.unix    cd_dir/
```

The following command puts the contents of the directory cd_dir on the CD along with the three README files, but only one will be seen from each of the three file systems:

```
% mkisofs -o cd.iso -hfs -J -r \
     -hide README.hfs -hide README.joliet \
     -hide-joliet README.hfs -hide-joliet README.unix \
     -hide-hfs README.joliet -hide-hfs README.unix \
     README=README.hfs README=README.joliet \
     README=README.unix cd_dir
```

In effect, the file README.hfs will be seen as README on the HFS CD, and the other two README files will be hidden, similarly for the Joliet and ISO9660/RockRidge CD.

There are probably all sorts of strange results possible with combinations of the hide options.

## AUTHOR

mkisofs is not based on the standard mk*fs tools for Unix because we must generate a complete copy of an existing file system on a disk in the ISO9660 file system. The name mkisofs is probably a bit of a misnomer, since it not only creates the file system, but it also populates it as well. However, the appropriate tool name for a UNIX tool that creates populated file systems - mkproto - is not well known.

Eric Youngdale <ericy@gnu.ai.mit.edu> or <eric@andante.org> wrote the first versions (1993 ... 1998) of the mkisofs utility. The copyright for old versions of the mkisofs utility is held by Yggdrasil Computing, Incorporated. Joerg Schilling wrote the SCSI transport library and its adaptation layer to mkisofs and newer parts (starting from 1999) of the utility. This makes mkisofs Copyright (C) 1999, 2000 Joerg Schilling.

HFS hybrid code Copyright (C) James Pearson 1997, 1998, 1999, 2000
libhfs code Copyright (C) 1996, 1997 Robert Leslie
libfile code Copyright (C) Ian F. Darwin 1986, 1987, 1989, 1990, 1991, 1992, 1994, 1995.

## NOTES

Mkisofs may safely be installed using suid root. This may be needed to allow mkisofs to read the previous session when creating a multi-session image.

## BUGS

- Any files that have hard links to files not in the tree being copied to the ISO9660 file system will have an incorrect file reference count.
- Does not check for SUSP record(s) in "." entry of the root directory to verify the existence of Rock Ridge enhancements.

This problem is present when reading old sessions while adding data in multi-session mode.

- Does not properly read relocated directories in multi-session mode when adding data.

Any relocated deep directory is lost if the new session does not include the deep directory.

Repeat by: create first session with deep directory relocation, then add new session with a single dir that differs from the old deep path.

- Does not reuse RR_MOVED when doing multi-session from TRANS.TBL
- Does not create whole_name entry for RR_MOVED in multi-session mode.

There may be some other ones. Please report them to the author.

## HFS PROBLEMS/LIMITATIONS

I have had to make several assumptions on how I expect the modified libhfs routines to work; however, there may be situations that I haven't thought of or that happen when these assumptions fail. Therefore I can't guarantee that mkisofs will work as expected (although I haven't had a major problem yet). Most of the HFS features work fine; however, some are not fully tested. These have been marked as Alpha.

Although HFS filenames appear to support upper and lowercase letters, the file system is case-insensitive; i.e., the filenames "aBc" and "AbC" are the same. If a file is found in a directory with the same HFS name, then mkisofs will attempt, where possible, to make a unique name by adding "_" characters to one of the filenames.

HFS file/directory names that share the first 31 characters have _N' (N == decimal number) substituted for the last few characters to generate unique names.

Care must be taken when "grafting" Apple/Unix files or directories (see previous sections for the method and syntax involved). It is not possible to use a new name for an Apple/Unix encoded file/directory. For example, if an Apple/Unix encoded file called "oldname" is added to the CD, then you cannot use the command line:

```
mkisofs -o output.raw -hfs newname=oldname cd_dir
```

mkisofs will be unable to decode "oldname." However, you can graft Apple/Unix encoded files or directories as long as you do not attempt to give them new names as previously.

When creating an HFS volume with the multisession options -M and -C, only files in the last session will be in the HFS volume; i.e., mkisofs cannot add existing files from previous sessions to the HFS volume.

Symbolic links (as with all other non-regular files) are not added to the HFS directory.

Hybrid volumes may be larger than pure ISO9660 volumes containing the same data.

The resulting hybrid volume can be accessed on a Unix machine by using the hfsutils routines. However, no changes should be made to the contents of the volume as, it's not a "real" HFS volume.

Using the -mac-name option will not currently work with the -T option. The Unix name will be used in the TRANS.TBL file, not the Macintosh name.

Although mkisofs does not alter the contents of a file, if a binary file has its TYPE set as 'TEXT,' it may be read incorrectly on a Macintosh. Therefore, a better choice for the default TYPE may be '????'.

The -mac-boot-file option may not work at all.

It may not work with PC Exchange v2.2 or higher files (available with MacOS 8.1). DOS media containing PC Exchange files should be mounted as type msdos (not vfat) when using Linux.

The SFM format is only partially supported—see the "HFS Macintosh File Formats" section.

It is not possible to use the the -sparc-boot or -generic-boot options with the -boot-hfs-file or -prep-boot options.

## SEE ALSO

cdrecord(1) magic(5), apple_driver(8)

## FUTURE IMPROVEMENTS

Some sort of GUI interface.

## AVAILABILITY

mkisofs is available as part of the cdrecord package from ftp://ftp.berlios.de/pub/cdrecord/hfsutils from ftp://ftp.mars.org/pub/hfs.

## MAILING LISTS

If you want to actively take part on the development of mkisofs and/or mkhybrid, you may join the cdwriting mailing list by sending mail to:

other-cdwrite-request@lists.debian.org

and include the word subscribe in the body. The mail address of the list is:

cdwrite@lists.debian.org

## MAINTAINER

Joerg Schilling
Seestr. 110
D-13353 Berlin
Germany

## HFS MKHYBRID MAINTAINER

James Pearson
j.pearson@ge.ucl.ac.uk

Mail bugs and suggestions to:

schilling@fokus.gmd.de or js@cs.tu-berlin.de *or*
joerg@schily.isdn.cs.tu-berlin.de

# Log4NET Appender Configurations

## ADONetAppender

The configuration of the ADONetAppender depends on the provider selected for the target database. Here are some examples.

### MS SQL Server

The following example shows how to configure the ADONetAppender to log messages to a SQL Server database. The events are written in batches of 100 (BufferSize). The ConnectionType specifies the fully qualified type name for the System.Data.IDbConnection to use to connect to the database. The ConnectionString is database provider-specific. The Command-Text is either a prepared statement or a stored procedure; in this case it is a prepared statement. Each parameter to the prepared statement or stored procedure is specified, with its name, database type, and a layout that renders the value for the parameter.

The database table definition is:

```
CREATE TABLE [dbo].[Log] (
    [Id] [int] IDENTITY (1, 1) NOT NULL,
    [Date] [datetime] NOT NULL,
    [Thread] [varchar] (255) NOT NULL,
    [Level] [varchar] (50) NOT NULL,
    [Logger] [varchar] (255) NOT NULL,
    [Message] [varchar] (4000) NOT NULL,
```

```
      [Exception] [varchar] (2000) NULL
)
```

The appender configuration is:

```
<appender name="ADONetAppender" type="log4net.Appender.ADONetAppender">
      <param name="BufferSize" value="100" />
      <param name="ConnectionType"
value="System.Data.SqlClient.SqlConnection, System.Data,
Version=1.0.3300.0, Culture=neutral, PublicKeyToken=b77a5c561934e089"
/>
      <param name="ConnectionString" value="data source=[database
server];initial catalog=[database name];integrated
security=false;persist security info=True;User
ID=[user];Password=[password]" />
      <param name="CommandText" value="INSERT INTO Log
([Date],[Thread],[Level],[Logger],[Message],[Exception]) VALUES
(@log_date, @thread, @log_level, @logger, @message, @exception)" />
      <param name="Parameter">
            <param name="ParameterName" value="@log_date" />
            <param name="DbType" value="DateTime" />
            <param name="Layout"
type="log4net.Layout.RawTimeStampLayout" />
      </param>
      <param name="Parameter">
            <param name="ParameterName" value="@thread" />
            <param name="DbType" value="String" />
            <param name="Size" value="255" />
            <param name="Layout" type="log4net.Layout.PatternLayout">
                  <param name="ConversionPattern" value="%t" />
            </param>
      </param>
      <param name="Parameter">
            <param name="ParameterName" value="@log_level" />
            <param name="DbType" value="String" />
            <param name="Size" value="50" />
            <param name="Layout" type="log4net.Layout.PatternLayout">
                  <param name="ConversionPattern" value="%p" />
            </param>
      </param>
      <param name="Parameter">
            <param name="ParameterName" value="@logger" />
```

```
            <param name="DbType" value="String" />
            <param name="Size" value="255" />
            <param name="Layout" type="log4net.Layout.PatternLayout">
                    <param name="ConversionPattern" value="%c" />
            </param>
      </param>
      <param name="Parameter">
            <param name="ParameterName" value="@message" />
            <param name="DbType" value="String" />
            <param name="Size" value="4000" />
            <param name="Layout" type="log4net.Layout.PatternLayout">
                    <param name="ConversionPattern" value="%m" />
            </param>
      </param>
      <param name="Parameter">
            <param name="ParameterName" value="@exception" />
            <param name="DbType" value="String" />
            <param name="Size" value="2000" />
            <param name="Layout"
type="log4net.Layout.ExceptionLayout" />
      </param>
</appender>
```

## MS Access

This example shows how to write events to an Access Database.

```
<appender name="ADONetAppender_Access"
type="log4net.Appender.ADONetAppender">
      <param name="ConnectionString"
value="Provider=Microsoft.Jet.OLEDB.4.0;Data
Source=C:\\log\\access.mdb;User Id=;Password=;" />
      <param name="CommandText" value="INSERT INTO Log
([Date],[Thread],[Level],[Logger],[Message]) VALUES (@log_date,
@thread, @log_level, @logger, @message)" />
      <param name="Parameter">
            <param name="ParameterName" value="@log_date" />
            <param name="DbType" value="String" />
            <param name="Size" value="255" />
            <param name="Layout" type="log4net.Layout.PatternLayout">
                    <param name="ConversionPattern" value="%d" />
```

```xml
                        </param>
                </param>
                <param name="Parameter">
                        <param name="ParameterName" value="@thread" />
                        <param name="DbType" value="String" />
                        <param name="Size" value="255" />
                        <param name="Layout" type="log4net.Layout.PatternLayout">
                                <param name="ConversionPattern" value="%t" />
                        </param>
                </param>
                <param name="Parameter">
                        <param name="ParameterName" value="@log_level" />
                        <param name="DbType" value="String" />
                        <param name="Size" value="50" />
                        <param name="Layout" type="log4net.Layout.PatternLayout">
                                <param name="ConversionPattern" value="%p" />
                        </param>
                </param>
                <param name="Parameter">
                        <param name="ParameterName" value="@logger" />
                        <param name="DbType" value="String" />
                        <param name="Size" value="255" />
                        <param name="Layout" type="log4net.Layout.PatternLayout">
                                <param name="ConversionPattern" value="%c" />
                        </param>
                </param>
                <param name="Parameter">
                        <param name="ParameterName" value="@message" />
                        <param name="DbType" value="String" />
                        <param name="Size" value="1024" />
                        <param name="Layout" type="log4net.Layout.PatternLayout">
                                <param name="ConversionPattern" value="%m" />
                        </param>
                </param>
</appender>
```

## Oracle9i

This example shows how to write events to an Oracle9i Database. The database table definition is:

```sql
create table log (
   Datetime timestamp(3),
```

```
Thread varchar2(255),
Log_Level varchar2(255),
Logger varchar2(255),
Message varchar2(4000)
);
```

The appender configuration is:

```
<appender name="ADONetAppender_Oracle"
type="log4net.Appender.ADONetAppender" >
    <param name="ConnectionType"
value="System.Data.OracleClient.OracleConnection,
System.Data.OracleClient, Version=1.0.3300.0, Culture=neutral,
PublicKeyToken=b77a5c561934e089" />
    <param name="ConnectionString" value="data source=[mydatabase];User
ID=[user];Password=[password]" />
    <param name="CommandText" value="INSERT INTO Log
(Datetime,Thread,Log_Level,Logger,Message) VALUES (:log_date, :thread,
:log_level, :logger, :message)" />
    <param name="BufferSize" value="128" />
    <param name="Parameter">
            <param name="ParameterName" value=":log_date" />
            <param name="DbType" value="DateTime" />
            <param name="Layout"
type="log4net.Layout.RawTimeStampLayout" />
    </param>
    <param name="Parameter">
            <param name="ParameterName" value=":thread" />
            <param name="DbType" value="String" />
            <param name="Size" value="255" />
            <param name="Layout" type="log4net.Layout.PatternLayout">
                <param name="ConversionPattern" value="%t" />
            </param>
    </param>
    <param name="Parameter">
            <param name="ParameterName" value=":log_level" />
            <param name="DbType" value="String" />
            <param name="Size" value="50" />
            <param name="Layout" type="log4net.Layout.PatternLayout">
                <param name="ConversionPattern" value="%p" />
            </param>
    </param>
```

```
<param name="Parameter">
        <param name="ParameterName" value=":logger" />
        <param name="DbType" value="String" />
        <param name="Size" value="255" />
        <param name="Layout" type="log4net.Layout.PatternLayout">
                <param name="ConversionPattern" value="%c" />
        </param>
</param>
<param name="Parameter">
        <param name="ParameterName" value=":message" />
        <param name="DbType" value="String" />
        <param name="Size" value="4000" />
        <param name="Layout" type="log4net.Layout.PatternLayout">
                <param name="ConversionPattern" value="%m" />
        </param>
</param>
</appender>
```

## ASPNetTraceAppender

The following example shows how to configure the ASPNetTraceAppender to log messages to the ASP.NET TraceContext. The messages are written to the System.Web.TraceContext.Write method if they are below level WARN. If they are WARN or above, they are written to the System.Web.TraceContext.Warn method.

```
<appender name="ASPNetTraceAppender"
type="log4net.Appender.ASPNetTraceAppender" >
        <layout type="log4net.Layout.PatternLayout">
                <param name="ConversionPattern" value="%d [%t] %-5p %c
[%x] - %m%n" />
        </layout>
</appender>
```

## BufferingForwardingAppender

The following example shows how to configure the BufferingForwardingAppender to buffer 100 messages before delivering them to the ConsoleAppender.

```
<appender name="BufferingForwardingAppender"
type="log4net.Appender.BufferingForwardingAppender" >
        <param name="BufferSize" value="100"/>
        <appender-ref ref="ConsoleAppender" />
</appender>
```

This example shows how to deliver only significant events. A LevelEvaluator is specified with a threshold of WARN. This means that the events will only be delivered when a message with level of WARN or higher level is logged. Up to 512 (BufferSize) previous messages of any level will also be delivered to provide context information. Messages not sent will be discarded.

```
<appender name="BufferingForwardingAppender"
type="log4net.Appender.BufferingForwardingAppender" >
        <param name="BufferSize" value="512" />
        <param name="Lossy" value="true" />
        <evaluator type="log4net.spi.LevelEvaluator">
                <param name="Threshold" value="WARN"/>
        </evaluator>
        <appender-ref ref="ConsoleAppender" />
</appender>
```

## ConsoleAppender

The following example shows how to configure the ConsoleAppender to log messages to the console. By default, the messages are sent to the console standard output stream.

```
<appender name="ConsoleAppender"
type="log4net.Appender.ConsoleAppender">
        <layout type="log4net.Layout.PatternLayout">
                <param name="ConversionPattern" value="%d [%t] %-5p %c
[%x] - %m%n" />
        </layout>
</appender>
```

This example shows how to direct the log messages to the console error stream.

```
<appender name="ConsoleAppender"
type="log4net.Appender.ConsoleAppender">
      <param name="Target" value="Console.Error" />
      <layout type="log4net.Layout.PatternLayout">
            <param name="ConversionPattern" value="%d [%t] %-5p %c
[%x] - %m%n" />
      </layout>
</appender>
```

## EventLogAppender

The following example shows how to configure the EventLogAppender to log to the Application event log on the local machine using the event Source of the AppDomain.FriendlyName.

```
<appender name="EventLogAppender"
type="log4net.Appender.EventLogAppender" >
      <layout type="log4net.Layout.PatternLayout">
            <param name="ConversionPattern" value="%d [%t] %-5p %c
[%x] - %m%n" />
      </layout>
</appender>
```

This example shows how to configure the EventLogAppender to use a specific event Source.

```
<appender name="EventLogAppender"
type="log4net.Appender.EventLogAppender" >
      <param name="ApplicationName" value="MyApp" />
      <layout type="log4net.Layout.PatternLayout">
            <param name="ConversionPattern" value="%d [%t] %-5p %c
[%x] - %m%n" />
      </layout>
</appender>
```

### FileAppender

The following example shows how to configure the FileAppender to write messages to a file. The file specified is log-file.txt. The file will be appended to rather than overwritten each time the logging process starts.

```
<appender name="FileAppender" type="log4net.Appender.FileAppender">
     <param name="File" value="log-file.txt" />
     <param name="AppendToFile" value="true" />
     <layout type="log4net.Layout.PatternLayout">
          <param name="ConversionPattern" value="%d [%t] %-5p %c
[%x] - %m%n" />
     </layout>
</appender>
```

This example shows how to configure the file name to write to using an environment variable TMP. The encoding to use to write to the file is also specified.

```
<appender name="FileAppender" type="log4net.Appender.FileAppender">
     <param name="File" value="${TMP}\\log-file.txt" />
     <param name="AppendToFile" value="true" />
     <param name="Encoding" value="unicodeFFFE" />
     <layout type="log4net.Layout.PatternLayout">
          <param name="ConversionPattern" value="%d [%t] %-5p %c
[%x] - %m%n" />
     </layout>
</appender>
```

### ForwardingAppender

The following example shows how to configure the ForwardingAppender. The forwarding appender allows a set of constraints to be used to decorate an appender. In this example the ConsoleAppender is decorated with a Threshold of level WARN. This means that an event directed to the ConsoleAppender directly will be logged regardless of its level, but an event directed to the ForwardingAppender will only be passed on to the ConsoleAppender if its level is WARN or higher. This appender is used only in special circumstances.

```
<appender name="ForwardingAppender"
type="log4net.Appender.ForwardingAppender" >
        <param name="Threshold" value="WARN"/>
        <appender-ref ref="ConsoleAppender" />
</appender>
```

## MemoryAppender

It is unlikely that the MemoryAppender will be configured using a config file, but if you want to do it, here's how.

```
<appender name="MemoryAppender" type="log4net.Appender.MemoryAppender">
        <param name="OnlyFixPartialEventData" value="true" />
</appender>
```

## NetSendAppender

The following example shows how to configure the NetSendAppender to deliver messages to a specific user's screen. As this appender is typically only used for important notifications, a Threshold of level Error is specified. This example delivers the messages to the user nicko on the machine SQUARE. However, things are not always straightforward using the Windows Messenger Service; one possible outcome using this configuration is that the Server will broadcast looking for a WINS server, which it will then ask to deliver the message to the Recipient, and the WINS server will deliver it to the first terminal that the user logged in from.

```
<appender name="NetSendAppender"
type="log4net.Appender.NetSendAppender">
        <param name="Threshold" value="ERROR" />
        <param name="Server" value="SQUARE" />
        <param name="Recipient" value="nicko" />
        <layout type="log4net.Layout.PatternLayout">
                <param name="ConversionPattern" value="%d [%t] %-5p %c
[%x] - %m%n" />
        </layout>
</appender>
```

## OutputDebugStringAppender

The following example shows how to configure the OutputDebugStringAppender to write logging messages to the OutputDebugString API.

```
<appender name="OutputDebugStringAppender"
type="log4net.Appender.OutputDebugStringAppender" >
      <layout type="log4net.Layout.PatternLayout">
            <param name="ConversionPattern" value="%d [%t] %-5p %c
[%x] - %m%n" />
      </layout>
</appender>
```

## RemotingAppender

The following example shows how to configure the RemotingAppender to deliver logging events to a specified Sink (in this example the sink is tcp://localhost:8085/LoggingSink). In this example the events are delivered in blocks of 95 events because of the BufferSize. No events are discarded. The OnlyFixPartialEventData option allows the appender to ignore certain logging event properties that can be very slow to generate (e.g., the calling location information).

```
<appender name="RemotingAppender"
type="log4net.Appender.RemotingAppender" >
      <param name="Sink" value="tcp://localhost:8085/LoggingSink" />
      <param name="Lossy" value="false" />
      <param name="BufferSize" value="95" />
      <param name="OnlyFixPartialEventData" value="true" />
</appender>
```

This example configures the RemotingAppender to deliver the events only when an event with level ERROR or above is logged. When the events are delivered, up to 200 (BufferSize) previous events (regardless of level) will be delivered to provide context. Events not delivered will be discarded.

```
<appender name="RemotingAppender"
type="log4net.Appender.RemotingAppender" >
      <param name="Sink" value="tcp://localhost:8085/LoggingSink" />
      <param name="Lossy" value="true" />
      <param name="BufferSize" value="200" />
      <param name="OnlyFixPartialEventData" value="true" />
      <evaluator type="log4net.spi.LevelEvaluator">
            <param name="Threshold" value="ERROR"/>
      </evaluator>
</appender>
```

## RollingFileAppender

The RollingFileAppender builds on the FileAppender and has the same options as that appender.

The following example shows how to configure the RollingFileAppender to write to the file log.txt. The file written to will always be called log.txt because the StaticLogFileName param is specified. The file will be rolled based on a size constraint (RollingStyle). Up to 10 (MaxSizeRollBackups) old files of 100 KB each (MaximumFileSize) will be kept. These rolled files will be named: log.txt.1, log.txt.2, log.txt.3, etc.

```
<appender name="RollingFileAppender"
type="log4net.Appender.RollingFileAppender">
      <param name="File" value="log.txt" />
      <param name="AppendToFile" value="true" />
      <param name="RollingStyle" value="Size" />
      <param name="MaxSizeRollBackups" value="10" />
      <param name="MaximumFileSize" value="100KB" />
      <param name="StaticLogFileName" value="true" />
      <layout type="log4net.Layout.PatternLayout">
            <param name="ConversionPattern" value="%d [%t] %-5p %c
[%x] - %m%n" />
      </layout>
</appender>
```

## SMTPAppender

The following example shows how to configure the SMTPAppender to deliver log events via SMTP email. The To, From, Subject, and SMTPHost are required parameters. This example shows how to deliver only significant events. A LevelEvaluator is specified with a threshold of WARN. This means that an email will be sent for each WARN or higher level message that is logged. Each email will also contain up to 512 (BufferSize) previous messages of any level to provide context. Messages not sent will be discarded.

```
<appender name="SMTPAppender" type="log4net.Appender.SMTPAppender">
        <param name="To" value="to@domain.com" />
        <param name="From" value="from@domain.com" />
        <param name="Subject" value="test logging message" />
        <param name="SMTPHost" value="SMTPServer.domain.com" />
        <param name="LocationInfo" value="false" />
        <param name="BufferSize" value="512" />
        <param name="Lossy" value="true" />
        <evaluator type="log4net.spi.LevelEvaluator">
              <param name="Threshold" value="WARN"/>
        </evaluator>
        <layout type="log4net.Layout.PatternLayout">
              <param name="ConversionPattern" value="%n%d [%t] %-5p %c
[%x] - %m%n%n%n" />
        </layout>
</appender>
```

This example shows how to configure the SMTPAppender to deliver all messages in emails with 512 (BufferSize) messages per email.

```
<appender name="SMTPAppender" type="log4net.Appender.SMTPAppender">
        <param name="To" value="to@domain.com" />
        <param name="From" value="from@domain.com" />
        <param name="Subject" value="test logging message" />
        <param name="SMTPHost" value="SMTPServer.domain.com" />
        <param name="LocationInfo" value="false" />
        <param name="BufferSize" value="512" />
        <param name="Lossy" value="false" />
```

```
    <layout type="log4net.Layout.PatternLayout">
        <param name="ConversionPattern" value="%n%d [%t] %-5p %c
[%x] - %m%n%n%n" />
    </layout>
</appender>
```

## TraceAppender

The following example shows how to configure the TraceAppender to log messages to the System.Diagnostics.Trace system. These messages will be logged to any System.Diagnostics.TraceListener that is registered in the config file.

```
<appender name="TraceAppender" type="log4net.Appender.TraceAppender">
    <layout type="log4net.Layout.PatternLayout">
        <param name="ConversionPattern" value="%d [%t] %-5p %c
[%x] - %m%n" />
    </layout>
</appender>
```

## UdpAppender

The following example shows how to configure the UdpAppender to send events to a RemoteAddress on the specified RemotePort.

```
<appender name="UdpAppender" type="log4net.Appender.UdpAppender">
    <param name="LocalPort" value="8080" />
    <param name="RemoteAddress" value="224.0.0.1" />
    <param name="RemotePort" value="8080" />
    <layout type="log4net.Layout.PatternLayout, log4net">
        <param name="ConversionPattern" value="%-5p %c [%x] -
%m%n" />
    </layout>
</appender>
```

# APPENDIX E

# Open Source Security Observations

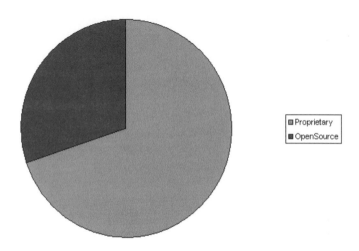

| 2000 | Proprietary | Open Source |
|---|---|---|
| CERT Incident Note IN-2000-01 Windows Based DDOS Agents | 1 | |
| CERT Advisory CA-2000-01 Denial-of-Service Developments | 1 | 1 |
| CERT Vulnerability Note VN-2000-01 Multiple Vulnerabilities in Vixie Cron | 1 | |
| CERT Advisory CA-2000-02 Malicious HTML Tags Embedded in Client Web Requests | 1 | |
| CERT Advisory CA-2000-03 Continuing Compromises of DNS servers | 1 | 1 |

*(continued)*

| 2000 | Proprietary | Open Source |
|------|-------------|-------------|
| CERT Advisory CA-2000-06 Multiple Buffer Overflows in Kerberos Authenticated Services | 1 | |
| CERT Advisory CA-2000-05 Netscape Navigator Improperly Validates SSL Sessions | 1 | |
| CERT Advisory CA-2000-04 Love Letter Worm | 1 | |
| CERT Incident Note IN-2000-04 Denial of Service Attacks Using Nameservers | 1 | 1 |
| CERT Incident Note IN-2000-03 911 Worm | | |
| CERT Incident Note IN-2000-02 Exploitation of Unprotected Windows Shares | 1 | |
| CERT Incident Note IN-2000-01 Windows Based DDoS Agents | 1 | |
| Input Validation Problem in rpc.statd | 1 | 1 |
| Two Input Validation Problems In FTPD | 1 | 1 |
| Exploitation of "Scriptlet.Typelib" ActiveX Control | 1 | |
| HHCtrl ActiveX Control Allows Local Files to be Executed | 1 | |
| Exploitation of Hidden File Extensions | 1 | |
| Microsoft Outlook and Outlook Express Cache Bypass Vulnerability | 1 | |
| Chat Clients and Network Security | 1 | 1 |
| Compromises Via a Vulnerability in the IRIX Telnet Daemon | 1 | |
| VBS/Loveletter.AS Worm | 1 | |
| QAZ Worm | 1 | |
| Multiple Denial of Service Problems in ISC BIND | 1 | 1 |

| 2001 | Proprietary | Open Source |
|------|-------------|-------------|
| CERT Advisory CA-2001-01 Multiple Vulnerabilities in BIND | 1 | 1 |
| CERT Incident Note IN-2001-01, Widespread Compromises via "ramen" Toolkit | 1 | |
| CERT Advisory CA-2000-22 Input Validation Problems in LPRng | 1 | 1 |
| CERT Advisory CA-2001-03 VBS/OnTheFly (Anna Kournikova) Malicious Code | 1 | |
| CERT Advisory CA-2001-11: sadmind/IIS Worm | 1 | |

*(continued)*

| 2001 | Proprietary | Open Source |
|---|---|---|
| CERT Advisory CA-2001-12: Superfluous Decoding Vulnerability in IIS | 1 | |
| CERT Advisory CA-2001-10: Buffer Overflow Vulnerability in Microsoft IIS 5.0 | 1 | |
| CERT Advisory CA-2001-05: Exploitation of snmpXdmid | 1 | 1 |
| CERT Incident Note IN-2001-03: Exploitation of BIND Vulnerabilities | 1 | 1 |
| CERT Advisory CA-2001-02: Multiple Vulnerabilities in BIND | 1 | 1 |
| CERT Incident Note IN-2001-05: The "cheese" Worm | 1 | 1 |
| CERT Advisory CA-2001-09: Statistical Weaknesses in TCP/IP Initial Sequence Numbers | 1 | 1 |
| CERT Advisory CA-2001-13: Buffer Overflow In IIS Indexing Service DLL | 1 | |
| CERT Advisory CA-2001-19: "Code Red" Worm Exploiting Buffer Overflow in IIS Indexing Service DLL | 1 | |
| CERT Advisory CA-2001-23: Continuing Threat of the "Code Red" Worm | 1 | |
| CERT Advisory CA-2001-22: W32/Sircam Malicious Code | 1 | |
| CERT Advisory CA-2001-21: Buffer Overflow in telnetd | 1 | 1 |
| CERT Advisory CA-2001-15: Buffer Overflow in Sun Solaris in.lpd Print Daemon | 1 | |
| CERT Advisory CA-2001-20: Continuing Threats to Home Users | 1 | 1 |
| CERT Incident Note IN-2001-07: W32/Leaves: Exploitation of previously installed SubSeven Trojan Horses | 1 | |
| CERT Advisory CA-2001-26: Nimda Worm | 1 | |
| Vulnerability Note #945216: SSH CRC32 attack detection code contains remote integer overflow | 1 | 1 |
| Incident Note IN-2001-11: Cache Corruption on Microsoft DNS Servers | 1 | |
| Vulnerability Note #109475: Microsoft Windows NT and 2000 Domain Name Servers allow non-authoritative RRs to be cached by default | 1 | |

| 2002 | Proprietary | Open Source |
|---|:---:|:---:|
| CERT Advisory CA-2002-03: Multiple Vulnerabilities In Many Implementations of the Simple Network Management Protocol (SNMP) | 1 | 1 |
| CERT Advisory CA-2002-01: Exploitation of Vulnerability in CDE Subprocess Control Service | 1 | |
| CERT Advisory CA-2001-31: Buffer Overflow in CDE Subprocess Control Service | 1 | |
| CERT Advisory CA-2001-37: Buffer Overflow in UPnP Service On Microsoft Windows | 1 | |
| CERT Advisory CA-2001-35: Recent Activity Against Secure Shell Daemons | 1 | 1 |
| CERT Advisory CA-2001-33: Multiple Vulnerabilities in WU-FTPD | 1 | 1 |
| CERT Incident Note IN-2001-14: W32/BadTrans Worm | 1 | |
| CERT Incident Note IN-2001-13: "Kaiten" Malicious Code Installed by Exploiting Null Default Passwords in MS-SQL | 1 | |
| CERT Incident Note IN-2002-04: Exploitation of Vulnerabilities in Microsoft SQL Server | 1 | |
| CERT Advisory CA-2002-13: Buffer Overflow in Microsoft's MSN Chat ActiveX Control | 1 | |
| CERT Advisory CA-2002-12: Format String Vulnerability in ISC DHCPD | 1 | |
| CERT Advisory CA-2002-11: Heap Overflow in Cachefs Daemon (cachefsd) | 1 | |
| CERT Advisory CA-2002-09: Multiple Vulnerabilities in Microsoft IIS | 1 | |
| CERT Advisory CA-2002-08: Multiple Vulnerabilities in Oracle Servers | 1 | |
| CERT Incident Note IN-2002-03: Social Engineering Attacks via IRC and Instant Messaging | 1 | 1 |
| CERT Advisory CA-2002-26: Buffer Overflow in CDE ToolTalk | 1 | |
| CERT Advisory CA-2002-20: Multiple Vulnerabilities in CDE ToolTalk | 1 | |
| CERT Advisory CA-2002-25: Integer Overflow in XDR Library | 1 | |
| CERT Advisory CA-2002-23: Multiple Vulnerabilities in OpenSSL | | 1 |

| 2002 | Proprietary | Open Source |
|---|---|---|
| CERT Advisory CA-2002-22: Multiple Vulnerabilities in Microsoft SQL Server | 1 | |
| CERT Advisory CA-2002-19: Buffer Overflows in Multiple DNS Resolver Libraries | 1 | 1 |
| CERT Advisory CA-2002-18: OpenSSH Vulnerabilities in Challenge Response Handling | | 1 |
| CERT Advisory CA-2002-17: Apache Web Server Chunk Handling Vulnerability | | 1 |
| CERT Advisory CA-2002-15: Denial-of-Service Vulnerability in ISC BIND 9 | 1 | 1 |
| CERT Advisory CA-2002-27: Apache/mod_ssl Worm | | 1 |
| CERT Advisory CA-2002-23: Multiple Vulnerabilities in OpenSSL | | 1 |
| CERT Advisory CA-2002-28: Trojan Horse Sendmail Distribution | 1 | 1 |
| CERT Advisory CA-2002-30: Trojan Horse tcpdump and libpcap Distributions | 1 | 1 |
| CERT Advisory CA-2002-31: Multiple Vulnerabilities in BIND | 1 | 1 |
| CERT Advisory CA-2002-33: Heap Overflow Vulnerability in Microsoft Data Access Components (MDAC) | 1 | |
| | 71 | 31 |

Cert Incidents Reports (http://www.cert.org/stats/)

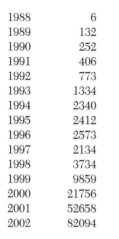

| | |
|---|---|
| 1988 | 6 |
| 1989 | 132 |
| 1990 | 252 |
| 1991 | 406 |
| 1992 | 773 |
| 1993 | 1334 |
| 1994 | 2340 |
| 1995 | 2412 |
| 1996 | 2573 |
| 1997 | 2134 |
| 1998 | 3734 |
| 1999 | 9859 |
| 2000 | 21756 |
| 2001 | 52658 |
| 2002 | 82094 |

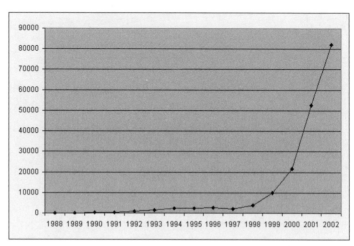

**ADO.NET**   A new disconnected data programming model from Microsoft that relies heavily on XML to easily pass around data and keep track of the changes. The new data provider model incorporated with ADO.NET allows many different databases to easily plug into this nice API.

**ASP.NET**   Microsoft's new programming platform for Web development. The key concepts are server-side controls, being able to program in any CLS-compliant language, and rapid development from Visual Studio.NET's IDE.

**BCL**   Base Class Libraries are the standard set of libraries that are available to all CLS-compliant .NET language. This provides a standard programming model for all languages to access XML or use collections.

**C#**   Microsoft's new programming language that has now become an ISO standard and showcases many of new features of the .NET runtime.

**C# XML Documentation**   The C# standard allows for a specialized commenting scheme to embed documentation within your code. The C# compiler then will extract that into a standardized XML file.

**CERT**   The CERT® Coordination Center (http://www.cert.org/) is the first computer security incident response team. As a federally funded research and development division of Carnegie Mellon University, CERT tracks computer security breaches.

**CHM**   Microsoft's now defunct but still very useful Compiled HTML Help format. For more information, see http://savannah.nongnu.org/projects/chmspec and http://www.armadaonline.co.uk/microsoft-html-help-index.htm. Microsoft has now announced that it is canceling HTML Help 2.0 and has revealed its new Help standard at http://longhorn.msdn.microsoft.com/lhsdk/help/hachelpauthoringguide.aspx and http://www.winwriters.com/mshelp_future.htm.

**CIL**    Common Intermediate Language is a standard language that is the output from each CLS-compliant .NET compiler. This language, which is similar to p-code, is still pretty high level and intuitive compared to assembly language from traditional C++ and other compilers. The CIL is attractive to many .NET developers who create tools for other developers.    They can target this CIL language and have a tool that is effective for all CLS-compliant programming languages. Such tools include FxCop and decompilers.

**CLI**    Common Language Infrastructure is the ISO standard that encompasses the CLS and all other technology allowing for a single type system. Many CLI implementations are discussed in Chapter 2, "Open Source and the .NET Platform." Microsoft's CLI implementation is called the CLR.

**CLR**    The Common Language Runtime is Microsoft's proprietary implementation of the ISO CLI standard that is available for most Windows platforms.

**CLS**    As part of the CLI, the Common Language Specification is the standard that all programming languages must adhere to in order to participate in the CLI common type system and take advantage of the BCL. Many CLS-compliant languages are listed in Chapter 2.

**Continuous Integration**    The agile development term for repeatedly building and running tests on a software product. "Continuous" alludes to the fact that, in theory, it should be done with every change committed to the source control repository, but the integration can also be periodic.

**Copyleft**    The Free Software Foundation coined this term in protest of copyrights. The term refers to software that is free for use and is supported and developed by a community that believes in free software.

**CTS**    The Common Type System is a part of the CLI that ensures that all programming languages that adhere to the CLS have common types. Therefore, a string or integer is exactly the same for VB.NET as C# or any other CLS language.

**Decompile**    The process of taking a compiled file, exe or dll, and re-creating the original source code that produced it.

**Disassemble**   The process of taking a compiled file, exe or dll, and re-creating the intermediate language that created it. For .NET, disassembling would consist of taking a packaged assembly and re-creating the CIL instructions. For C++, this is taking a file and re-creating the assembly language instruction set.

**DOTGNU Portable.NET**   An Open Source CLI implementation committed to implementing a CLI that is very portable and very close to the ISO CLI standard.

**EMCA**   An international standards organization; see http://www.ecma-international.org/.

**Filesets**   A NAnt concept of a set of files. Since files are often operated on during a build process, NAnt has created a way to represent many files together as a common set.

**Free Software**   See http://www.gnu.org/philosophy/free-sw.html. Free software is a matter of the users' freedom to run, copy, distribute, study, change, and improve the software. More precisely, there are four kinds of freedom for the users of the software:

- The freedom to run the program for any purpose (freedom 0).
- The freedom to study how the program works and adapt it to your needs (freedom 1). Access to the source code is a precondition for this.
- The freedom to redistribute copies so you can help your neighbor (freedom 2).
- The freedom to improve the program and release your improvements to the public so that the whole community benefits (freedom 3). Access to the source code is a precondition for this.

A program is free software if users have all of these freedoms.

**Fxcop**   A lint checker of sorts for .NET assemblies. FxCop has many built-in rules and an extendable rule engine. For more on FxCop, see http://www.gotdotnet.com/team/fxcop/.

**GAC**     The Global Assembly Cache makes an assembly available for use by many different programs. In order to insert an assembly into the GAC, you must first version it and sign it. The GAC inherently allows for side-by-side execution of different versions of the same assembly.

**Garbage Collector**     A memory management system where unused memory is freed and made available to other programs on the system.

**GNOME**     The GNOME project provides a Linux desktop environment and a development platform for building LINUX desktop applications. For more information, see http://www.gnome.org/about/.

**GTK#**     A C# binding to the popular GTK user interface widget library. This is useful when designing a Windows Form that targets multiple operating systems.

**IDE**     Integrated Development Environment to integrate development, design, and debugging of software. Chapter 2 exhibits several different IDEs for .NET.

**Interpreter**     Interpreters, unlike compilers, read the program line by line. Because the .NET standard allows for both a just-in-time compiler and an interpreter it becomes confusing as to what the difference is. The JIT compiler takes the CIL pcode outputted from the  compiler and JITs it to native instructions on the first execution. An interpreter interprets each line of CIL and executes a corresponding predefined algorithm upon each and every execution. The Mono project's Mint interpreter is a good example of a CLI Interpreter.

**JavaDoc**     A documentation output created by Sun Microsystems (http://java.sun.com/j2se/javadoc/) that is supported by NDoc.

**JIT Compiler**     Just-In-Time Compiler to compile intermediary languages to native computer instruction sets.

**LATEX**     A type setting system targeted to developing technical documentation; see http://www.latex-project.org/.

**Linear HTML**     A supported output from NDoc where all documentation is contained in one HTML file.

**MAKE**   Make is a tool that controls the generation of executables and other non-source files of a program from the program's source files.(http://www.gnu.org/software/make/).

**Mono**   An Open Source CLI implementation from Ximian. Novell has now acquired Ximian and is still committed to the Mono project. Mono allows .NET programs to run on Linux, Windows, etc. and is committed to implementing as much of .NET to be competitive with Microsoft's CLR.

**MSBuild**   A new build system and XML file format announced by Microsoft to compile .NET applications.

**MSDE**   Microsoft Desktop Engine is a scaled down version of Microsoft SQL Server that is freely available to be integrated into a product. MSDE is available for most versions of Windows and in many foreign languages.

**NAnt**   An Open Source .NET build tool with an XML file format.

**NDoc**   An Open Source tool to create end-user library documentation for .NET assemblies from C# XML Documentation files.

**Obfuscation**   The act of obfuscating, or hiding, the structure of your intermediary code to protect from decompiling.

**Open Source Software**   Open Source doesn't just mean access to the source code. The distribution terms of Open Source software must comply with the following criteria:

1. Free Redistribution
2. Source Code
3. Derived Works
4. Integrity of the Author's Source Code
5. No Discrimination Against Persons or Groups
6. No Discrimination Against Fields of Endeavor
7. Distribution of License
8. License Must Not Be Specific to a Product
9. License Must Not Restrict Other Software
10. License Must Be Technology-Neutral

**Optionsets**    An option set is an alternative way for a NAnt task to receive input. Typically tasks use XML attributes to receive input.

**Patternsets**    Patternsets allow for advanced pattern matching or wildcard-like functionality within NAnt, such as specifying *.cs to indicate all C# source files. This is most often used to specify files or filesets.

**Projects**    NAnt build term for a collection of tasks and targets to create a build file.

**Properties**    NAnt variable-like functionality for storing information used throughout the project. Properties allow for changing the behavior of a build just as properties on a component alter that component's behavior.

**References**    Required or dependent assemblies for the assembly you are trying to build. References in NAnt are handled as filesets.

**RPM**    A system for packaging and redistributing software code and/or applications (http://www.rpm.org/).

**SCM**    Source Control Management consists of the tools and methods used to manage the versioning and maintaining of source code.

**Shared Source Software**    This license allows for a way to share proprietary sources. (http://www.microsoft.com/presspass/exec/craig/05-03sharedsource.asp).

**SSCLI**    The Shared Source CLI is a Microsoft Research project that was created in academia. This was a proof of concept that a CLI could target multiple operating systems.

**Targets**    A collection of NAnt tasks to operate on a piece of software. Common build targets are build, clean, and lint.

**Tasks**    NAnt operations that can be performed on a piece of software. Common tasks are csc compiling, delete, and mkdir.

**UDP**    User Datagram Protocol (http://www.faqs.org/rfcs/rfc768.html) is a standard packet-switching method of data transfer.

**UML**    Universal Modeling Language is a standard way to document software design, functionality, and interaction.

**VES** Virtual Execution System for a hypothetical machine within the CLI that provides an execution system for CIL.

**Windows Forms** The new programming model for Graphical User Interface applications in the .NET platform.

**Windows Help** See CHM.

# INDEX

## A

Addison-Wesley warrants the enclosed disc to be free of defects in materials and faulty workmanship under normal use for a period of ninety days after purchase. If a defect is discovered in the disc during this warranty period, a replacement disc can be obtained at no charge by sending the defective disc, postage prepaid, with proof of purchase to:

Editorial Department
Addison-Wesley Professional
Pearson Technology Group
75 Arlington Street, Suite 300
Boston, MA 02116
Email: AWPro@awl.com

Addison-Wesley makes no warranty or representation, either expressed or implied, with respect to this software, its quality, performance, merchantability, or fitness for a particular purpose. In no event will Addison-Wesley, its distributors, or dealers be liable for direct, indirect, special, incidental, or consequential damages arising out of the use or inability to use the software. The exclusion of implied warranties is not permitted in some states. Therefore, the above exclusion may not apply to you. This warranty provides you with specific legal rights. There may be other rights that you may have that vary from state to state. The contents of this CD-ROM are intended for personal use only.

More information and updates are available at:
http://www.awprofessional.com

About the CD-ROM

The CD-ROM included with Open Source .NET Development contains the following:

All software provided on this CD-ROM is the property of the respective copyright owner as shown within the files. All files and software on this CD-ROM is passed on without warranty either express or implied.

The CD-ROM included with Open Source .NET Development contains the following:

All software provided on this CD-ROM is the property of the respective copyright owner as shown within the files. All files and software on this CD-ROM is passed on without warranty either express or implied.

This CDROM is organized as follows:

```
/
|-- Chap03     (Chapter 3 source code, examples, tools)
|-- Chap04     (Chapter 4 code listings, source code, tools)
|-- Chap05     (Chapter 5 code listings, source code, tools)
|-- Chap06     (Chapter 6 code listings, source code, tools)
|-- Chap07     (Chapter 7 code listings, tools)
|-- Chap08     (Chapter 8 code listings, source code, tools)
|-- Chap09     (Chapter 9 code listings)
|-- Chap10     (Chapter 10 code listings and source code)
|-- Chap11     (Chapter 11 code listings, source code, tools)
|-- Chap12     (Chapter 12 source code, examples, tools)
|-- Other tools     (Additional open source tools for .NET development)
\-- README
```

The CD-ROM can be used on Linux platforms running on Intel x86 architecture hardware. Most Executable files and all MSI (Microsoft Installer Files) are meant for any Windows Platform that supports the .NET Runtime. Many of the tools, as mentioned in the text, work both on Mono and Microsoft .NET. The discussion of these tools in the text most often will tell you which operating systems (Windows or Linux) and which CLI (.NET, Mono, SSCLI, etc) the tool is supported under.

## Limited Warranty

Use of the software accompanying Open Source .NET Development is subject to the terms of the Limited Warranty found on the previous page.

## Technical Support

If the CD-ROM is damaged, you may obtain a replacement copy by writing to:

Editorial Department
Addison-Wesley Professional
Pearson Technology Group
75 Arlington Street, Suite 300
Boston, MA 02116
Email: AWPro@awl.com